BS/189286

GANDHI AND THE GEETA

GANDHI AND THE GEETA

A.D. MISHRA
SAROJ K. JHA
SOHAN RAJ TATER

ABHIJEET PUBLICATIONS
DELHI 110094

ABHIJEET PUBLICATIONS
2/46 Tukhmeerpur Extension
Delhi-110 094
Phone: 011-22960492, 65698474
E-mail: abhijeetpublication@gmail.com

GANDHI AND THE GEETA

First Published 2010
© Reserved
ISBN 978-93-80031-83-5

[All rights reserved. No part of this publication may be reproduced, copied, stored in a retrieval system, transmitted or used in any form or by any means, whether electronic, mechanical, photocopying, recording or otherwise, without the prior permission from the author or publishers, except for a brief quotations in critical articles or reviews.]

PRINTED IN INDIA

Published by J.K. Singh for Abhijeet Publications, Delhi-110 094, Lasertypeset by Gaurav Graphics, New Delhi and Printed at Himanshu Printers, Delhi.

Preface

Mohandas Karamchand Gandhi popularly known as Mahatma Gandhi had become acquainted with the Bhagavad Gita during his student days in London. His study of the Gita grew and deepened alongwith his involvement in public life and freedom struggles. In South Africa where Gandhi spent 21 years of youthful life started living his life according to the tenets of the Gita and had taken to it as his primary source of ethical, moral and spiritual inspiration. He applied teaching of Gita in the political, social and economic fields. In fact, Gandhi used the teaching of Gita to provide leadership to the Indian masses by upholding the ethical values in public and private life. Gandhi called the Gita as 'mother', 'Kamadhenu', 'spiritual dictionary', 'dictionary of references for the solution of all troubles and trials', 'the Book of life', his 'refuge' and so on. He himself said that his "life is based on the teaching of the Gita". Gita became Gandhi's friend, philosopher and guide in practically all matters. Gandhi extensively studied, wrote and spoke on the various facets and teaching of the Gita and applied in day-to-day affairs as well as in freedom struggle. Gandhi had given very comprehensive, contemporary and relevant meanings and interpretation of the Gita's philosophy and teachings.

In 1926 in the Satyagraha Ashram, Sabarmati Gandhi delivered 218 discourses in Gujarati on Gita. These discourses are relevant for contemporary management expert who only believes in Western theories. Recently some professors have done wonderful work by locating management ethos in Indian scriptures. Their efforts bring the fruits and now management experts are working on Indian ethos of management.

The Western concept of management no doubt dominated in 20th Century. The liberalisation, privatisation and globalisation forced the management expert and policy makers to change their mindset. The Great Asian crisis, European meltdown, economic crisis and crash of sensex all over the world compelled the economists, policy makers, and management experts to think beyond production, profit and consumption. Human centric and integrated balance approach is the need of the hour. Gita is one of the finest text on modern management. Gandhiji had made the Gita a people's scripture and guide to all aspects of life. Further 'Mother Gita' has been 'brought down' by Gandhi as a precious treasure within an easy reach of every person, including the 'last' and the 'least' of the human beings. This he has achieved by his relating the understanding and application of its teachings to nearly every activity of human existence. Whether in difficulty, in doubt, in depression, in sorrow, in pain or in failure, he would dip into the inexhaustible ready wisdom of "the living life-giving immortal mother", the Gita, and find the necessary answer, direction, solace and guidance. Gita is a book of primary support in all human life including even in the darkest periods of anyone life. It is a book of tranquillity and wisdom.

The Upanishads, the Brahmasutras and the Bhagavad Gita constitute the 'Prasthantreyi or Jnanatreyi' that is, the three sets of scriptures which contain the quintessence of the Hindu philosophical thought. Of these, the Gita is the most perennial and integrated guide for every possible strand of human conduct in thought, word and deed. Gita has 700 verses and divided into 18 chapters. Every time you read Gita you will gain new insight and wisdom. One life is not enough to understand the simple truth of the Gita. It remains the fountainhead of inexhaustible wisdom.

The Gita had already entered into the contemporary public discourse when learned scholar-leaders of Indian renaissance and freedom struggle, such as Swami Vivekananda, Bal Gangadhar Tilak and Aurobindo Ghosh made its study and application a vital element in their thought and action. Gandhi's approach was unique. He relate every teaching of the Gita to the day-to-day existence. Shankaracharya and Ramanuja enriched the Gita by providing interpretation.

Gandhi's association with Gita started in 1890 with his study of Edwin Arnold's English translation of the Gita, 'The Song Celestial'.

The Gita is a small, self-contained scripture of 700 Sanskrit verses, appearing in the Shantiparva of the *Mahabharata*. It is a comprehensive sysnthesis of the various philosophical doctrines and paths to salvation of a human being, an integrated and holistic presentation of doctrine of knowledge (Jnana), Devotion (Bhakti), and Action (Karma), and of the paths of renunciation of action (sanyasa) and of remaining active in life as duty without attachment to the fruit of action (karmayoga).

It was in 1890 at 21 years of age Gandhi came across two Theosophical brothers who invited him to read the Gita in original with them. He started reading Sir Edwin Arnold's translation of the Gita, The Song Celestial, with them. It was only after some years that it became a book of daily reading. The verses 62 and 63 of Chapter II made a deep impression on Gandhi's mind.

While Gandhi was very keen that the Gita was widely read and recited, he was also particular how it was done and how its Sanskrit text was pronounced. He further insisted that mere reading, recitation and memorising of the verses was of no avail unless these were also understood and put into practice. The Gita was an essential part of the Ashram prayers, and even when he was in Jail he would continue to guide regarding the content and form of the Gita in prayers.

Gandhi wrote in a letter on October 11, 1930: "If you learn by heart some chapters of the Gita, you will find that you feel more peaceful in mind. If not more, learn only one verse at a time. Try to memorize it after you have understood its meaning and learn to pronounce each word in it correctly".

What is the importance of Gita in day to day life.

(a) It gives peace and equanimity to spirit.

(b) It fulfills the need of a scripture to serve as an unfailing guide through the trials and temptation of life.

(c) The conflict about the rightness or otherwise is solved by the Gita.

(d) The Gita taught duty of perseverance in the face of deeming failure.

(e) The Gita gives the food that we need for spiritual and mental sustenance.

(f) The Gita is a key to success by performing duty.

Gita with its unique poetic charm, simple language, effective expression, and deep religious, ethical and philosophical doctrines helps the individual to grow in harmony with nature and circumstances. The limits of time, place and culture and barriers of language do not bind the Gita. Men of all times were likely to seek a solace and sure guidance from Gita. The spirit of the Gita is large and universal and it enfolds humanity at large in its loving embrace.

Gita is a management text. It provides priceless wisdom applicable in all aspects of human behaviour. All problems of human kind in modern times one can get lessons from Gita. Gita provides a code of conduct in human behaviour. Gita provides wisdom to see beauty of humility in every person.

Gita must be regarded not merely in light of a general spiritual philosophy or ethical doctrine, but as bearing upon a practical crisis in the application of ethics and spirituality to human life. The Gita is a book that has worn extraordinarily well and it is almost as fresh and still in its real substance, as when it first appeared in or was written into the frame of the Mahabharata. Gita's influence is not merely philosophic or academic but immediate and living, an influence both for thought and action, and its ideas are actually at work as a powerful shaping factor in the revival and renewal of a nation and a culture.

Geeta is the most influential work in Indian thought. Geeta extends beyond all limitations of time, place, cultures and language. The doctrine of Geeta knows no barriers as both eastern and western scholars accept. Firstly the Bhagavad Gita is the only single work in Hindu Dharma that brings religion, ethics, and philosophy in perfect unity in the way of life of man. Secondly, Geeta is the first work in Hindu dharma that talks directly to man in his own easy, flowing, and straight language, a language that penetrates into the heart itself. Thirdly, the Gita is a shastra that is bent upon doing good to all men. A shastra that propounds a doctrine that will be suitable of attainment by all men. It is the Gita that can become a solace of life and death both, to most of us. Fourthly, the uniqueness of the Gita is that it is a work equally appealing to almost all men and women, whatever their age, understanding, intellect and status in life. Gita teaches us Gyanmarg, Karmamarg, and Bhakti marg. Fifthly, the Gita embraces humanity at large and carves out a way of life, on ethics of life and the ultimate aim of life. Sixthly, Gita approach is that of Samanvaya (harmony) and Samvada (dialogue). Seventhly, the Gita permits a variety of ways of life and accepts varied approaches in perfect equanimity. As the Gita accepts a variety of ways in life, it also permits three main and many more paths of the realization of God. Gita's principle doctrine and way of life is that of detached karma and so, its approach is easier and more appealing to man. Lastly, Gita's supreme effort, first to solve man's problems of this life and the ethics thereof and then to sublimate man and lift him higher and higher till he hears divine music and ultimately wins self-realization.

In a nutshell (a) the Gita is an all time work for humanity at large, it is universal. (b) The Gita lays down an original rule of conduct which is more advance than contemporary management principles. (c) The Gita records the highest aspirations of the human species. The Gita is a book of life and it lays down a religion and ethics that light up man's path when he is deluded by darkness and has lost hope.

In contemporary world everyone wants to reach the top. But in reality it is not possible. We have control over karma (duty) not fruit (result). Gita provides a way out. We are sure and hopeful that the work will be worthwhile contribution to the growing literature on Gandhi.

The book provides a detailed study of Mahatma Gandhi's view on Gita. Part one is "Discourses on the Gita" by Mahatma Gandhi from February 24, 1926 to November 27, 1926. It contain 218 discourses touching all aspects of life. This section also include 21 discourse on Gita by Gandhi is the core of the Gita. In Part II Anasaktiyoga is placed for reader for deeper understanding of Gita. In part three letters on the Gita are placed. Written during Gandhiji's incarceration in Yervada Central Prison in 1930 and 1932, these were sent weekly along with letters to Narandas Gandhi for being read out at the Ashram prayer meetings.

This work is an outcome of collective endeavour of three individuals who belong to different discipline by training and education, working at three different places with one goal to locate and place Gandhi in contemporary debate.

We are grateful to all those who directly or indirectly helped us in the compilation of this work; it has been such as demanding task.

Salkhani, Bihar
21 May 2010

A.D. Mishra
S.K. Jha
Sohan Raj Tater

accepts a variety of ways in life; it also permits three main and many more paths of the realization of God. Gita's principle doctrine and way of life is that of detached karma and so its approach is easier and more appealing to man. Lastly, Gita's supreme effort first to solve man's problems of this life and the ethics thereof and then to sublimate man and lift him higher and higher till he hears divine music and ultimately wins self-realization.

In a nutshell (a) the Gita is an all time work for humanity at large, it is universal. (b) The Gita lays down an original rule of conduct which is more advance than contemporary management principles. (c) The Gita records the highest aspirations of the human species. The Gita is a book of life and it lays down a religion and ethics that light up man's path when he is deluded by darkness and has lost hope.

In contemporary world everyone wants to reach the top. But in reality it is not possible. We have control over karma (duty) not fruit (result). Gita provides a way out. We are sure and hopeful that the work will be worthwhile contribution to the growing literature on Gandhi.

The book provides a detailed study of Mahatma Gandhi's view on Gita. Part one is "Discourses on the Gita" by Mahatma Gandhi from February 24, 1926 to November 27, 1926. It contain 218 discourses touching all aspects of life. This section also include 22 discourse on Gita by Gandhi is the core of the Gita. In Part II Anasaktiyoga is placed for reader for deeper understanding of Gita. in part three letters on the Gita are placed. Written during Gandhiji's incarceration in Yervada Central Prison in 1930 and 1932, these were sent weekly along with letters to Narandas Gandhi for being read out at the Ashram prayer meetings.

This work is an outcome of collective endeavour of three individuals who belong to different discipline by training and education, working at three different places with one goal to locate and place Gandhi in contemporary debate.

We are grateful to all those who directly or indirectly helped us in the compilation of this work; it has been such a demanding task.

Sallhani, Bihar **A.D. Mishra**
21 May, 2010 **S.K. Jha**
Sohan Raj Tater

Contents

Preface *v*

Part One

Discourses on Gita 1

Part Two

Anasaktiyoga 304

Part Three

Letters on Gita 352

PART ONE

DISCOURSES ON THE "GITA"[1]

[1] February 24, 1926

This verse[2] provides the key to the study of the *Gita*. It is both a prayer and a stipulation. It says,"Whatever you may be, whether Vishnu or Siva, if you are free from attachment and aversions, I bow to you."

The *Mahabharata* is not history; it is a *dharma-grantha*[3]. Who can ever describe an actual event? A man cannot exactly describe even a drop of water seen by him. God having created him so weak, how can he describe an actual event perfectly? In this battle, moreover, the warriors were, on the one side, the sons[4] of Dharma, Vayu, Indra and Ashvinikumars and, on the other, a hundred brothers[5] all born at the same instant. Have we ever heard of such a thing actually happening?

Duryodhana[6] rode on the chariot of *adharma*[7], and Arjuna[8] that of dharma. The battle described here is, therefore, a struggle between dharma and *adharma*. Sanjaya[9] is a man of devotion. The battle takes place far away from where he is, and he cannot see it; Vyasa[10], therefore, endows him with divine vision so that he can see what is happening.

And what does this signify? Only this: that the epic describes the battle ever raging between the countless Kauravas and Pandavas dwelling within us. It is a battle between the innumerable forces of good and evil which become personified in us as virtues and vices. We shall leave aside the question of violence and non-violence and say that this *dharma-grantha* was written to explain man's duty in this inner strife.

Notes

1. The talks were given at the Satyagraha Ashram, Ahmedabad, during morning prayers over a period of nine months from February 24 to November 27, 1926. Notes were taken by Mahadev Desai and Punjabhai, an inmate of the Ashram. These were edited by Narahari Parikh and published in book form in 1955 under the title *Gandhijinu Gitashikshan*.
2. The verse in question was recited by Narayan Moreshwar Khare, music teacher at the Ashram.
3. Work treating of religious and ethical questions.
4. Yudhishthira, Bhima, Arjuna, Nakula and Sahadeva whose fatherhood has been attributed to the five gods listed.
5. The Kauravas
6. Eldest of the Kauravas
7. The opposite of dharma
8. Third among the Pandavas, the central figure in the epic
9. Who saw and reported the battle to the blind King Dhritarashtra, father of the Kauravas
10. Author of the *Mahabharata*; he himself figures in some of the episodes described in the epic.

[2][1] Chapter I: February 25, 1926

Quite a few such blind men[2] live within us. This is not a battle which took place so many thousand years ago; it is one which is raging all the time, even today. Duryodhana tells Dronacharya[3] that his own pupil, Dhrishtadyumna[4], has planned the deployment [on the Pandava side].

They are, on both sides, his pupils, to whom he has imparted the same knowledge. But it depends on themselves whether they use that knowledge well or ill.

Notes

1. This talk covers the first three verses of Chapter I.
2. The reference is to Dhritarashtra.
3. The Brahmin preceptor who had taught the Pandavas and the Kauravas the art and science of war.
4. Brother of Draupadi, wife of the Pandavas.

[3] February 26, 1926

I displayed my ignorance, not knowledge, on the first day.[1] But there is much in the *Gita* for anyone who, though ignorant of grammar, aspires after *moksha*. It is stated in the *Gita* itself that everyone, whether a woman, a Vaisya or a Sudra, can acquire spiritual knowledge if they have devotion to God. All the same, learning should not be slighted. To understand any matter, one must have the knowledge which comes from learning. If any one of you had committed the mistake which I did, I would not have overlooked it.

Well, then, the battle-field described here is primarily the one inside the human body. Does the *Gita* then prohibit physical fighting altogether? No; fighting there may well be. But here the physical battle is only an occasion for describing the battle-field of the human body. In this view the names mentioned are not of persons but of qualities which they represent. What is described is the conflict within the human body between opposing moral tendencies imagined as distinct figures. A seer such as Vyasa would never concern himself with a description of mere physical fighting. It is the human body that is described as Kurukshetra, as *dharma-kshetra*[2]. It does become that when used in the service of God. The epithet may also mean that for a Kshatriya a battle-field is always a field of dharma. Surely a field on which the Pandavas too were present could not be altogether a place of sin.

Bankimchandra[3] says that it is doubtful whether Draupadi had five sons. It is, however, difficult to decide. Karna had the Sun-god as father. Every one of the characters had a miraculous birth. Whether out of compassion for Duryodhana, or because he was generoushearted, Karna joined the former's side. Besides Karna, Duryodhana had good men like Bhishma[4] and Drona also on his side. This suggests that *evil cannot by itself flourish in this world*. It can do so only if it is allied with some good. This was the principle underlying non-co-operation, that the evil system which the Government represents, and which has endured only because of the support it receives from good people, cannot survive if that support is withdrawn. Just as the Government needs the support of good men in order to exist, so Duryodhana required men like Bhishma and Drona in order to show that there was justice on his side.

Notes

1. That is, on February 25, 1926. Gandhiji had made a mistake while splitting a vowel combination (*pashya+etam* in I. iii).
2. Field of dharma.
3. Bankimchandra Chatterjee (1838-1894); Bengali poet and novelist; author of *Krishnacharitra*—a book which Gandhiji had read during his imprisonment in Yeravda.
4. Uncle of Pandu and Dhritarashtra; to enable his father Santanu to marry Satyavati, he renounced his claim to kingship and pledged that he would never marry.

[4][1] February 27, 1926

This pair of words can be interpreted in two different ways: *aparyapta* may mean (1) boundless, limitless, or (2) inadequate, insufficient; and *paryapta* may mean (1) limited or (2) adequate, sufficient. The meaning will depend on what we believe to be the feeling in Duryodhana's heart. Of the two meanings of *aparyapta*, I have accepted "inadequate","insufficient". It has appealed to me from my earliest days. What Duryodhana felt was that their army, protected by Bhishma, was not sufficiently strong, whereas the Pandava army, protected by Bhima[2], was; for grandfather Bhishma loved both sides and Duryodhana had, therefore, a secret fear that he might not fight with his whole heart.

Notes

1. This talk covers verses 10 to 16 dwelling chiefly on verse 10.
2. The second of the Pandavas

[5] February 28, 1926

The use of Sanskrit for prayers is a mere form; the real aim is to let the meaning of dharma sink into one's heart. Simple like a villager that I am, why should I insist on reading the *Gita* myself? Why should Mahadev refuse to do that?[1] Why did I take this upon myself? Because I have the necessary humility. I believe that we are all imperfect in one way or another. But I know well enough what dharma means, and have tried to follow it in my life. If I have somewhere deep in me the spirit of dharma and loving devotion to God, I shall be able to kindle it in you.

But one cannot light a piece of stone. Only those of you who have some oil and wick in them will light their lamp with this match-stick of mine; only those who have something in them will profit from this discussion.

Our pronunciation should be such that the recitation of the verses would immediately please the mind. I committed a grammatical error yesterday. In the clause *shankham dadhmau pratapavan*[2], I explained *pratapavan* as being in apposition to *shankham*. It should be applied to Bhishma, the grandfather. But my Sanskrit is no better than a villager's. I am not so proficient in it that, if I commit an error, it would be immediately felt by my ear, would jar on it.

Sanjaya is proceeding with his description of the conches which are being blown in the Pandava camp. *Kairmaya saha yoddhavyam*:[3] Arjuna is asking, not whether it is necessary that he should fight, but against whom he has to fight. If he did not wish to fight, he would have told Krishna so on the previous day itself. He had no aversion to fighting as such. In fact, he had obtained Yudhishthira's[4] permission and secured weapons from Indra that he might fight. Krishna would have, in that case, asked Arjuna to go to Duryodhana and win him over. But that was not the case. Arjuna had fought even during the exile. He had fought when King Virat[5] was attacked by Duryodhana. He was always prepared to fight. His question, therefore, was who they were against whom he would be fighting. We should always bear this in mind.

Notes

1. Gandhiji had remarked that Mahadev Desai knew better how to read the verses and explain the meaning, and the latter had demurred.
2. The valiant one blew his conch; I, 12.
3. Against whom I must fight; I, 22.
4. The eldest of the Pandavas.
5. With whom the Pandavas lived in disguise during the last year of their exile.

[6] March 2, 1926

Arjuna requests Shri Krishna to station his chariot between the two armies, so that he may see the warriors on the field.

He sees that all of them are relatives and friends, whom

one cannot easily bring oneself to kill. Arjuna says: "I do not see any good in killing one's kinsmen."

The stress here is on "kinsmen". He says:

I would not fight against them, even for the kingdom of the three worlds; how could I, then, fight against them for a few clods of earth?[1] Because he has asked for only five villages as the Pandavas' share. He repeatedly asks how he can be happy after killing his kinsmen. All his arguments are summed up in the question: *Kairmaya saha yoddhavyam*?

He is unhappy, not at the thought of killing, but at the thought of whom he was required to kill. By putting the word "kinsmen" repeatedly in his mouth, the author of the *Gita* shows into what darkness and ignorance he has sunk. Arjuna has been arguing from a practical point of view and Shri Krishna, it is hinted here, will try to meet that very argument.

The world will blame a person even for going to a court against his relations. Arjuna is shaken in his whole being, but it is not as if Shri Krishna wanted him to cast off this weakness of his forthwith. If, while seeking to follow the path of good, we do not eschew something which even in practical life we are required to eschew, dharma would cease to be dharma. In our daily life we avoid doing things out of fear of society. In this case, it is not merely a question of avoiding something which even ordinary people would avoid; it is a question of killing hundreds of thousands of men. How could Arjuna bring himself to do that? He had no need to go to Krishna for an answer to the question. If he could have approached us, even we could have told him; "Do not fight." When the dharma laid down for even this *kaliyuga*[2] requires us to refrain from unnecessary fighting, we should ask why Arjuna thought it necessary to put the question to Shri Krishna and why the two had such a long discussion. We can, therefore, understand the teaching of the *Gita* aright only if we give careful thought to the author's aim and the attendant circumstances.

These last verses, however, are of great importance, for the entire argument which follows is based on them; we shall discuss them tomorrow.

Notes

1. *Bhagavad Gita*, I, 35.
2. Age of strife.

[7] March 3, 1926

What people would generally do in their common dealings is regarded as good. If we see anyone here, or elsewhere, who renounces a right in regard to worldly matters and forgives even strangers, not to speak of relations, we would think of him as a good man. If we desist from beating up a thief or any other felon, do nothing to get him punished but, after admonishing him and recovering from him the stolen article, let him go, we would be credited with humanity and our action would be regarded as an instance of non-violence; a contrary course would be looked upon as violence. How is it, then, that Shri Krishna stops Arjuna from advancing such an argument? How can we explain a plainly contrary teaching in *Bhagavad Gita*? Why does Shri Krishna describe Arjuna as cowardly and weak?

The *Bhagavad Gita* is consistent from the first to the last verse. That is why we meditate on its teaching and hope to discover from it the path to *moksha*. We should, therefore, think whether Arjuna's argument is valid or contains some flaw.

As though he were digging up a mountain to discover a mouse, Shri Krishna[1] describes the *Gita*, at the conclusion of each chapter, as an Upanishad, as a *Yogashastra*[2] and as *brahmavidya*[3] and describes this particular one as a chapter on Arjuna's despondency.

It is important to consider what Arjuna's question was and what the circumstances were in which he raised it. Having got his chariot stationed between the two armies, he said he wanted to see who those men were against whom he would be fighting. His reason is, for the time being, clouded. He has lost his nerve. All that has gone before shows that Arjuna is a great warrior and that, when starting out to fight, he does not, like Dharmaraja[4], hesitate and ask all manner of questions. In the past, he never hesitated even when he had to fight against relations. Even during their fourteen years' exile, he gave free expression to his hatred for the Kauravas before Dharmaraja; what is more, victory in the battle depends entirely on him. Bhima is physically strong and daring, but he lacks Arjuna's power. In their preparations for the battle during the fourteen years' exile, the other brothers always placed Arjuna at their head. When there was a battle outside Viratnagar, Arjuna, who had been living there in disguise wanted to be led to the place of fighting. Why does a man, who loves fighting to this extent, want his chariot to be stationed between the two armies and to see who the warriors are on the other side? He knows every one of them well enough. Why does he argue with Shri Krishna and tell him all that he does? He could have left the place immediately.

Arjuna has a smaller army—an army of seven *akshauhini*[5] as against the Kauravas' of eleven. Let us suppose that Arjuna flees the battle field. Though his enemies are wicked people, are sinners, they are his relations and he cannot bring himself to kill them. If he leaves the field, what would happen to those vast numbers on his side? If Arjuna went away, leaving them behind, would the Kauravas have mercy on them? If he left the battle, the Pandava army would be simply annihilated. What, then, would be the plight of their wives and children? I publish in *Navajivan* a narrative of the European War, and there is a reason for this. It reminds us of the battle of the *Mahabharata*.

I give the narrative so that readers may know the ruin which such a war brings on a whole people. If Arjuna had left the battlefield, the very calamities which he feared would have befallen them. Their families would have been ruined, and the traditional dharma of these families and the race would have been destroyed. Arjuna, therefore, had no choice but to fight. This is the meaning of the battle in crude physical terms; I shall discuss later what it would be if the battlefield were taken to be the human being. I will tell you tomorrow what I said when I discussed the *Gita* in Phoenix[6].

Notes

1. Evidently, this is a slip for Vyasa, author of the *Mahabharata*.
2. A treatise on yoga.
3. Knowledge concerning the *Brahman*, the Absolute.
4. Yudhishthira.
5. A division of the army comprising 1,09,350 foot-soldiers, 65,610 horsesoldiers, 21,870 chariot-soldiers and 21,870 elephant-soldiers.
6. Settlement near Durban, which Gandhiji had founded in 1904.

[8] Chapter II: March 4, 1926

Shri Krishna tells Arjuna: Shake off this faintness of heart and arise. His state of mind is imagined to be like that of Christian in the Slough of Despond. Why does Krishna say this to Arjuna, who is in fact ready to forgo everything?

When I was in London, I had talks with many revolutionaries. Shyamji Krishnavarma, Savarkar[1] and others used to tell me that the *Gita* and the *Ramayana* taught quite the opposite of what I said they did. I felt then how much better it would have been if the sage Vyasa had not taken this illustration of fighting for inculcating spiritual knowledge. For when even highly learned and thoughtful men read this meaning in the *Gita*, what can we expect of ordinary people? If what we describe as the very quintessence of all Shastras, as one of the Upanishads, can be interpreted to yield such a wrong meaning, it would have been better for the holy Vyasa to have taken another, more effective, illustration to teach sacred truths.

He has drawn Arjuna and Shri Krishna so vividly that we are inclined to regard them as historical figures. The historian-author, moreover, gives the histories of cities, communities and individual characters and claims that he is describing a battle in which the best men of his age took part. I said how much better it would have been if the revered Vyasa had not adopted the method which he did. This, you may say, was impertinence on my part. But what should one seeking to serve truth do? What must one do if one sees an error? It is not wrong to draw attention, in all humility, to what one feels to be an error. This thought remained in my mind for many years. Then I thought I should read the *Mahabharata*. I decided to do so, that I might understand the atmosphere of the age in which the *Gita* was written and feel the good and the evil influences at work in that age. I read in jail a Gujarati version of the *Mahabharata* which I could get there. I saw that Vyasa did not believe that fighting was wrong. The illustration which he has taken is a very beautiful one. Just as in Aesop's *Fables* and in *Panchtantra*, the authors have created conversations among birds and animals to impart moral teaching, so in the *Mahabharata* virtues and vices are personified and great moral truths conveyed through those figures. The description of the battle serves only as a pretext. The *Mahabharata* itself was not composed with the aim of describing a battle. In the *Gita*, the author has cleverly made use of the event to teach great truths. If the reader is not on his guard, he may be misled. The very nature of dharma is such that one may easily fall into error if one is not vigilant. Anyone rashly imitating Prahlad would do something very wrong. This is the reason for the injunction against the reading of the Shastras by one without qualification.

It is not easy for any person to solve the problems of dharma which may face him. He will not succeed till he has made himself fit by observing the *yama-niyamas*[2] and similar other rules of discipline.

To take up a work like the *Gita* without having equipped oneself in this manner is the surest way of falling into the Slough of Despond. It would be like taking up a study of botany without ever having seen plants.

The author has used the word *Gudakesha* for Arjuna. It means one who has conquered sleep, who is always vigilant. We should, therefore, think carefully about this illustration of the battle. The first thing to bear in mind is that Arjuna falls into the error of making a distinction between kinsmen and outsiders. Outsiders may be killed even if they are not oppressors, and kinsmen may not be killed even if they are. My son, even if a drunkard, would inherit my property. I would write in *Navajivan* about another's son if he was wicked, but would not treat my own son in that manner. The *Gita* says, "No, this is not right. We have no right to point an accusing finger at others. We should point out the lapses of our own people first." Arjuna was Dronacharya's best pupil. Bhishma had actually showered love on him as if he had been his first-born. Arjuna should be ready to kill either of them. It has become his duty to non-co-operate with both, for they have joined the wrong side. Should it become necessary to cut off, with a sword, one's father's head, one must do so if one has a sword and is a Kshatriya, and if one would be ready to cut off anyone else's head in similar circumstances. Shri Krishna, therefore, asks Arjuna to free himself from ignorant attachments in this world. How should I act as editor of *Navajivan*? Would it be right for me to proclaim with beat of drum the theft committed by an outsider's child and say nothing about a boy of my Ashram, who may have misbehaved in the same way? Certainly not. The *Gita* permits no distinction between one's relations and others. If one must kill, one should kill one's own people first. Shri Krishna asks Arjuna: "What is this you are saying about people being your relations?" The *Gita* wants to free him from this ignorant distinction of some people being his relations and others not. He has resolved to kill. It was not right, then, that he should shrink from killing particular individuals. It was not with any selfish motive that he had gone out to kill. Ravana deserved to be killed by Rama. Why did not the latter take cover behind such wise talk? He knew well enough that Ravana could do no harm to Sita. But he did not argue with himself in that manner. We never say that he fought for the sake of Sita; we believe that he fought in order to kill Ravana.

Even if we believe in non-violence, it would not be proper for us to refuse, through cowardice, to protect the weak. If Arjuna had forgotten the difference between kinsmen and others and had been so filled with the spirit of non-violence as to bring about a change of heart in Duryodhana, he would have been another Shri Krishna.

Actually, however, he believed Duryodhana to be wicked. I might be ready to embrace a snake, but, if one comes to bite you, I should kill it and protect you. Arjuna has two courses open to him: he should either kill Duryodhana and others, or else convert them. In the circumstances, Arjuna's laying down arms would mean the annihilation of all those on his side. His refusal to fight would bring on a disaster. Thus, Vyasa has taken the right illustration. A person who believes in fighting and does not regard it as violence, though it is violence, is here being asked to kill.

Note

1. Vinayak Damodar Savarkar.
2. Rules of moral discipline and religious observances

[9] March 5, 1926

The question which Arjuna asks Shri Krishna is not whether it is right for him to kill. His question is whether it would be right to kill his kinsmen. This question arises out of bias. Bhishma and Drona, a kinsman and an honoured person, stand vividly before his eyes. How can he kill them? To a person whose dilemma is not concerning violence and non-violence but is only about whom he may kill, our commonsense can give only one answer. But a godfearing man like Arjuna should pause and reflect before acting. Only a person with deep understanding can solve the rather fine problem whether he should go on with the recitation of *gayatri*[1] or run to the help of someone who is crying out in distress. To a godfearing man, the problem would present no difficulty. The author of the *Mahabharata* has discussed such delicate issues on almost every page of the epic. He has taken instances from the lives of individual characters and drawn lessons from them. Some of the instances may well have been incidents of history, but he has treated them as poets and seers have always treated such incidents. English poets, too, have written plays and poems with historical figures as subjects. The author of the *Mahabharata* raises, for instance, the question whether the sage Vishvamitra had secretly eaten beef[2] and whether one should accept food offered by a chamar. The author has, thus, discussed problems of three kinds.

Notes

1. Vedic prayer to Sun-god for illumination.
2. The story is told in the Shanti Parva of the *Mahabharata*.

[10] March 6, 1926

From today we begin the argument of the *Gita* and shall not, therefore, be able to go as fast with the verses as we have been doing. "Accept innocent happiness, innocent joy, whatever the source," said Raychandbhai. Accordingly, we may derive a variety of meanings from the verses of the *Gita*. The argument addressed to Arjuna begins with the eleventh verse[1], and continues right up to the last chapter. Shri Krishna starts with the distinction between the *atman*[2] and the body, for that is the first step to spiritual knowledge. We must first know certain definitions, then alone can we proceed. Arjuna is represented as a seeker, as a man who believes in the *atman* and observes the disciplines of *yama-niyama*, and so Shri Krishna starts giving him the knowledge of the *atman*. One becomes entitled to ask questions and seek illumination only if one has observed *brahmacharya*[3] and always followed truth, and only then will one's questions deserve to be answered.

Arjuna has this fitness; he has the genuine spirit of submission and humility. We have not yet fully discussed the premise on which the argument of the *Gita* is based. Yesterday we were discussing Arjuna's plea that it is wrong to kill one's kinsmen, not that it is wrong to kill at all. He was asked to forget the distinction of kinsmen and outsiders. The Hindu Shastras say that non-violence is the supreme dharma. The question, therefore, whether or not it is right to kill does not arise. Only an atheist would raise such a question. Arjuna has observed the disciplines of *yama-niyama*, among which ahimsa is placed first. But ahimsa is an ideal which it is impossible to realize to perfection. It may be possible to realize it in thought, but not in action.

Shankaracharya[4] has said that one seeking *moksha* should have far greater patience than one who would try to empty the sea, drop by drop, with a blade of grass. One must have equal patience for realizing the ideal of perfect non-violence. It is impossible in this body to follow ahimsa fully. That is why *moksha* is laid down as the supreme end of life.

Violence is inescapable. While the eyes wink and nails have to be pared, violence in one form or another is unavoidable. Evil is inherent in action, the *Gita* says further on. Arjuna did not, therefore, raise the question of violence and non-violence. He simply raised the question of distinction between kinsmen and others, much in the same way that a fond mother would advance arguments favouring her child.

The *Bhagavad Gita* traces all maladies to their one source. A physician treats different diseases with different remedies. But, on the basis of researches in medical science, physicians are now coming to the conclusion that, though diseases seem different from one another, in the final analysis they are one. The cause is one, and so is the cure.

Similarly, Shri Krishna says that there is only one spiritual evil, with only one cause and one remedy. To explain this oneness, an extreme example is used. If one's kinsmen deserve to be killed, they ought to be killed; and one must not hesitate even if the entire world were likely to be destroyed in consequence. It is not only Arjuna's right but his duty to act in this manner. To his question whether one ought not to make an exception in regard to relations, he gets an unambiguous answer. The principle, thus, admits of no exception, just as there can be no exception in the matter of following truth, for truth is God and, if exceptions were admitted in regard to it, God also would be sometimes truth and sometimes not-truth. Thus the rule in this instance admits of no exception.

Shri Krishna tells Arjuna that he is talking specious wisdom. The *Gita* does not teach the path of action, nor of knowledge, nor of devotion. No matter how well one cultivates *vairagya* or how diligent one is in performing good actions or what measure of *bhakti*[5] one practises, one will not shed the sense of "I" and "mine" till one has attained knowledge. One can attain self-realization only if one sheds this attachment to the ego. It is possible only for a person who has succeeded in doing so. In English, 'i' is a vertical line with a dot[6] above it. Only when this 'I' is done away with can one attain self-realization.

A man's devotion to God is to be judged from the extent to which he gives up his stiffness and bends low in humility. Only then will he be, not an impostor, but a truly illumined man, a man of genuine knowledge. The *Gita* does not advocate any one of the three paths; I have from my experience come to the conclusion that it has been composed to teach this one truth which I have explained. We can follow truth only in the measure that we shed our attachment to the ego.

It is to teach this that Shri Krishna has advanced the beautiful argument of the *Gita*.

Notes

1. Of Chapter II.
2. The self, unidentifiable with any one aspect of human individuality.
3. Celibacy, as an expression of perfect control of all the senses.
4. 780-812; philosopher and teacher of Vedanta. He travelled all over the country and established a number of *mathas*. His works include commentaries on the *Bhagavad Gita* and the Upanishads and many hymns.
5. Devotion.
6. Gandhiji uses the word *'shunya'* for 'dot'. The suggestion is that one progress on the spiritual path in the measure that one travels towards this *shunya* or zero.

[11] March 7, 1926

As every human being passes through childhood, youth and so on to old age, so also does he or she meet death. The phrase *dehantarprapti*[1] used here does not mean a new body or another life, for what is being discussed here is the fear of death, not that of a new life.

Note

1. Passing into another body; II, 13.

[12] March 9, 1926

We feel afraid only so long as we take the rope to be a serpent.

Likewise, if we know the natural stages of growth of the body, we shall not grieve over death. In order to help Arjuna to overcome his agitation, Shri Krishna tries to explain to him the difference between the *atman* and the body.

O Kaunteya, contacts of the senses with their objects bring cold and heat, pleasure and pain; they come and go and are transient. Endure them, O Bharata.

O noblest of men, the wise man who is not disturbed or agitated by these, who is unmoved by pleasure and pain, he alone is fitted for immortality.[1]

Any being who is not subject to the impressions of senses will never experience fear. It is these impressions which are responsible for the feelings of happiness and misery. Someone has said that the muscles of a man who is angry become thirteen times as tense as when he is normal, and of a man who is laughing nine times as tense. That is, one spends more energy when one is angry, and one whose energy is thus wasted cannot attain to immortality. The cultivation of this state requires practice. We can even say of a person who has attained to it that he is God. Once a sannyasi, an impostor, paid a visit to Phoenix. He asked me to recite any verse from the *Gita* which I knew. I recited this one. During the early days of my legal practice, I was on one occasion very much troubled in my mind. I then went out for a walk. I was very much agitated. I then remembered this verse, and the very next moment I was almost dancing with relief. We should identify ourselves with Arjuna and have faith that Shri Krishna is driving our chariot. Thus, the meaning of the *Gita* on the commonsense level is that, once we have plunged into a battle, we should go on fighting.

One ought not to give up the task one has undertaken. In this way, the illustration used should not be pointless or inadequate and a wise man should not read a wrong meaning in it either.

Vyasa's own intention was something different. He wanted to write the *Mahabharata* in such a way that even little boys and girls would study it, remember the virtuous characters in it and learn to keep away from people like the wicked characters in the epic. His aim was to strengthen the finer impulses in us and help us to overcome the evil ones. Before the women, too, he held up the example of Draupadi and thus taught them that they should, when threatened with danger, roar like lionesses and protect their honour. Draupadi could do this and rouse Arjuna, Yudhishthira and Bhima. The author of the *Mahabharata* has raised woman to a great height through his epic. The chief aim of the epic, however, is to represent the most invisible of all invisible wars. It tells of the Arjuna and other Pandavas in our minds who are battling with the Kauravas in it. The moral problems which confront one in this inner war are far more difficult than those of a physical war. An error in the sphere of practical action will at the most result in the destruction of this perishable body, but the result of an error in this inner invisible war will lead to perdition. The most painful punishment is appointed for evil intention. In the course of time, Pandavas and Kauravas are bound to be forgotten. They will most certainly be forgotten when this Age ends. We should not delude ourselves with the belief that they will continue to be remembered for ever. This Age of ours was preceded by many others. Even when all of them are forgotten, this war in our heart will go on. The *Gita* shows how we may emerge safe from it. The Krishna of the *Gita* is not the person who, when the hour of his death arrived, fell to a hunter's arrow, and Arjuna is not that person from whose hand the Gandiva bow slipped. Krishna is the *atman* in us, who is our charioteer. We can win only if we hand over the reins of the chariot to him. God makes us dance, like the master in a puppet show. We are smaller than even puppets. We should, therefore, trust everything to God, as children to parents. Let us not eat uncooked stuff. Let Krishna the cook prepare and give us what food of grace. He wills for our *atman*. The *Gita* does not decide for us. But if, whenever faced with a moral problem, you give up attachment to the ego and then decide what you should do, you will come to no harm. This is the substance of the argument which Shri Krishna has expanded into 18 chapters.

Note

1. II, 14 and 15. The translation of this and other verses from the *Gita* is reproduced from Mahadev Desai's *The Gita According to Gandhi*.

[13] March 10, 1926

The verse[1] beginning with the phrase *matrasparsha* applies to sleeping as much as to waking. We have to make ourselves conscious machines. We should cultivate such perfect concentration that, like a man asleep, we are aware of nothing else. Hazrat Ali told his people to draw out the arrow from his body while he was praying, for at that time he would be totally absorbed in devotion to God. One cannot say that such a thing could be done when one was asleep, for one would not be able to fall asleep at all when the body was pierced with an arrow. A person who can be totally absorbed in every task on hand, as Hazrat Ali could be in prayer, who lives in such a state of self-absorption all the twenty-four hours of the day, will attain to immortality.

Shri Krishna now explains why the impressions of the senses are unreal:

What is non-Being is never known to have been, and what is Being is never known not to have been. Of both these the secret has been seen by the seers of the Truth.[2]

That which never was cannot exist, and that which exists cannot cease to exist. Even the sun is transient, coming into existence and vanishing. The candle both exists and does not exist, for, when it is burnt up, its substance dissolves back into the five elements.

Everything which has a name and a form ceases one day to exist in that particular mode, though it does not cease to be as a creation of God.

Notes

1. II, 14.
2. II, 16.

[14] March 11, 1926

The *jnanis*, the men of knowledge, have discovered what exists and what does not exist. Name and form are brittle as glass. The *jnanis* know what is implied in the difference between existence and non-existence. We only know one simple thing: God is, nothing else is. We shall breathe life into the Ashram by laying down our own lives. Its lands and buildings may disappear, but the spirit we inform it with will never perish.

Know that to be imperishable whereby all this is pervaded. No one can destroy that immutable Being.[1]

Know that his Bodiless One, which can lift many Govardhan mountains on its little finger,[2] is imperishable.

Avyaya means that which cannot be spent.

Notes

1. II, 17.
2. Shri Krishna as a boy is said to have lifted the Govardhan mountain on his little finger.

[15] March 12, 1926

These bodies of the embodied one who is eternal, imperishable and immeasurable are finite. Fight, therefore, O Bharata.[1]

Aprameya means that for which there can be no evidence, that is, no evidence in the sense in which smoke is regarded as evidence of fire. Therefore fight, O Bharata. If we argue that since all bodies are perishable, one may kill, does it follow that I may kill all the women and children in the Ashram? Would I have in doing so acted according to the teaching of the *Bhagavad Gita*, merely because their bodies are perishable? We believe the watchman to have been mad because he had killed a person; if, however, he were to cite this verse of the *Gita* to justify what he did, we would call him wicked. What, then, shall we say of a person who mouths these seemingly learned arguments and then commits wickedness? To know the answer to this, we should go back to the First Chapter. Arjuna had said that he did not want even the kingdom of gods if he had to kill his kith and kin for that. But he is bound, in any case, to kill them, for he has accepted the dharma which requires him to kill. This verse with the word *yudhyasva* applies to him, but it does not apply to others. In this verse, Shri Krishna wants to free Arjuna from his ignorant attachment. When Harishchandra was required to kill a virtuous woman like Taramati[2], his eyes fell on her *mangal-sutra*[3] and [recognizing her], he held back. He would not have done so if it had been some other woman. In this case Shri Krishna would have told him that it was his duty to kill her. He would say to Harishchandra: You have lost your wits; you have killed people in the past and now you shrink from killing the woman because of your attachment for her as your wife. You would thus betray your dharma. He would tell Harishchandra that his body as well as his wife's was perishable. If a person would cut his own throat rather than another's, then Krishna would tell him that he could kill others as a duty.

Shri Krishna advances another argument.

He who thinks of This (*Atman*) as slayer and he who believes This to be slain, are both ignorant. This neither slays nor is ever slain.[4] The *atman* neither kills nor is killed. This argument can be advanced only to a person. . .[5] It is like putting the cart before the horse. As that is impossible, so the body, if it sought to drive the *atman,* would never succeed. If anyone says that it can, he does not know what he is talking about.

Notes

1. II, 18.
2. Harishchandra's wife.
3. Ornament carrying black or purple coral beads worn as a symbol of the married state.
4. II, 19.
5. Some words have been missing here in the source.

[16] March 13, 1926

Suppose that your father was a teacher,[1] that you and . . . misbehaved in the same way and your father punished . . . but not you; would that be right?[2] Arjuna did not understand what even a child like you does. Shri Krishna told him all this long argument of the *Gita* just to explain this.

He who is afraid kills. He for whom there is no death will not kill. Those who come to the prayer meeting but do not follow the readings from the *Gita* should be regarded as not attending the prayers. We shall have truly welcomed the guest who has arrived at our place only if we receive him into the home with love, help him to wash, offer him a clean seat and serve him the best food prepared for ourselves, and ourselves eat only what remains after he has finished.

We shall have welcomed him, shall have acted truthfully, only if we act in this manner. But if one frowns at the guest, does not speak to him with love, places before him a dirty, unwashed plate and serves stale food, fails to ask him if he would have another helping and then claims to have welcomed him and offered him a meal, one would have done nothing of the sort but would in fact have insulted the guest.

Such conduct, therefore, would be a violation of truth. Rotten and foul-smelling food or, food which has been left over ought not to be offered even to a beggar. If at all we wish to offer food to a beggar, we should offer clean grain. If we would rather give him nothing, we should tell him so discreetly. This would be acting truthfully. We can thus, by exercising our discrimination, decide what is truthful and what is not.

This is never born nor ever dies, nor having been will ever not be any more; unborn, eternal, everlasting, ancient. This is not slain when the body is slain.[3]

This *atman* was never born and will never die; it is not as though it ever was not and may not be again. The author has used a separate epithet to indicate each of these several aspects. The *atman* is unborn, eternal and ancient. Everyone knows it. The body perishes, but it does not. One generation knows of it from another. It is a thing that all parents must have explained, or ought to explain, to their children.

He who knows This, O Partha, to be imperishable, eternal, unborn, and immutable—whom and how can that man slay or cause to be slain?[4]

The *Gita* has been composed not in the form of aphorisms, but so as to be carried in the mind from moment to moment. It was written not for the learned, but for all the four castes,—rather, all the eighteen castes—to read and understand. It was written for the Sudras, the Bhangis[5], and for women—in fact, for all classes. If the author has used a variety of epithets for a subject, though all of them mean the same thing, it is simply in order that we may grasp what he wants us to understand—in the same way that a mother explains a point to her children over and over again in different words.

Notes

1. This was addressed to a child in the audience.
2. The child replied to this in the negative.
3. II, 20.
4. II, 21.
5. Community regarded as untouchables attending to scavenging work.

[17] March 14, 1926

As a man casts off worn-out garments and takes others that are new, even so the embodied one casts off worn-out bodies and passes on to others new.[1]

Would I be ready to change this body for another, unless I would give up a worn-out one and have a fresh one? If the eyes cannot see, the ears cannot hear and the palate cannot relish food, would a person wish to live on bed-ridden, or die?

This no weapons wound, This no fire burns, This no waters wet, This no wind doth dry.[2]

Weapons cannot cleave it. If we strike the air with a weapon, can we hurt it? The *atman* is subtler even than air. Fire cannot burn it, nor can water wet it; how can air, then, ever dry it? Having described the *atman* thus, the author gives an appropriate epithet to indicate each of its several aspects:

Beyond all cutting, burning, wetting and drying is This—eternal, allpervading, stable, immovable, everlasting.[3]

More epithets again: eternal, all-pervading, stable, immovable and everlasting. The verse which follows states the same thing.

Perceivable neither by the senses nor by the mind. This is called unchangeable; therefore, knowing This as such, thou shouldst not grieve.[4]

Such is the *atman*, Krishna says and you should not, therefore, grieve over anyone's death. Why should you, then, grieve over the death of your relations?

Notes

1. II, 22.
2. II, 23.
3. II, 24.
4. II, 25.

[18] March 16, 1926

What do you call the thing which protects us against the sun?[1]

Likewise, there is a word, *aja*, to designate that which was never born, and another, *achhedya*, to designate that which cannot be pierced. Shri Krishna takes Arjuna slowly from darkness to light. Have you seen the *atman*?[2]

It is so naughty that it dwells in us and yet we cannot see it. It is the deer that even Ramachandra would not be able to kill. Ramachandra is omnipotent, and so he could kill only that which deserved to be killed.

Having argued thus, Shri Krishna says: "But suppose that the *atman* has none of these attributes. What of it? What even if it is born and dies again and again? All the more reason why you should not grieve over death."

And if thou deemest This to be always coming to birth and always dying, even then, O Mahabahu, thou shouldst not grieve. For certain is the death of the born, and certain is the birth of the dead; therefore, what is unavoidable thou shouldst not regret.[3]

He who dies is certain to be born again. We ought not to grieve over what is inescapable, what cannot be helped.

Notes

1. The question was addressed to a child who replied: *chhatri*, an umbrella.
2. The question was again put to a child who answered in the negative.
3. II, 26 and 27.

[19] March 17, 1926

The state of all beings before birth is unmanifest; their middle state is manifest; their state after death is again unmanifest. What occasion is there for lament, O Bharata?[1] All beings were unmanifest before birth and will again become unmanifest after death. Birth and death are God's concern. He alone, therefore, knows their mystery. Even doctors have failed here, for they cannot create a body. "Who am I, whence do I come? Am I destined to rise to heaven?" The *atman* becomes incarnate in birth. We can see this, the middle stage. Men who have thought over these problems have asserted that, for bestowing and taking away life, God does not require even a fraction of the time that is required for drawing and erasing a circle on the blackboard. No mathematician can ever calculate the measure of that time.

Tatra ka paridevana. Why, then, grieve? This is the great mystery of God. As a magician creates the illusion of a tree and destroys it, so God sports in endless ways and does not let us know the beginning and the end of his play. Why grieve over this?

One looks upon This as a marvel; another speaks of This as such; another hears thereof as a marvel; yet having heard of This none truly knows This.[2]

Some wise men see the *atman* as a thing of wonder and some

describe it so. Others hear it so described but cannot understand what it is. Such is our pathetic state. There can be no end to describing God's greatness, so mysterious is His sport.

Finally, Shri Krishna sums up: This embodied one in the body of every being is ever beyond all harm, O Bharata; thou shouldst not, therefore, grieve for anyone.[3]

"O Arjuna, this *atman* which dwells in everyone's body can never be killed." The body's death is like the breaking of a piece of glass. This cycle of birth and death goes on for ever and ever.

Note

1. II, 28.
2. II, 29.
3. II, 30.

[20] March 18, 1926

The theft which took place today[1] provides a lesson in the application of the *Gita*. Where there is possessiveness, there is violence. We have to guard things which we think are ours; when we give away a thing to someone, this possessiveness disappears since we no longer regard that thing as ours. All things in the world belong to us, but we are indifferent towards them and do not lose any sleep on their account. In the same way, we should think that the things we keep in the Ashram belong to others as much as to us, and so remain indifferent towards them. The other way is the way of violence, of Satan. That is not the way we have chosen. Ours, however, is a mixed way at present. We have adopted the principle of collective possession, and individual possession is restricted to a minimum. Krishna tells Arjuna to give up this possessiveness, and through these two characters Vyasa tells us to do so.

After discussing the problem from the spiritual point of view Shri Krishna considers it from the mundane point of view. He tells Arjuna what his duty in the practical world requires.

Again, seeing thine own duty thou shouldst not shrink from it; for there is no higher good for a Kshatriya than a righteous war.[2]

A Kshatriya has no duty higher than that of fighting in a righteous war. Why is the war described as righteous? Because it is not of Arjuna's seeking. He was happy enough in his home, but he was challenged by Duryodhana. The war came to him without his seeking, and had as it were opened the door of heaven to him.

Proceeding, Shri Krishna talks about one's good name in the world:

The world will for ever recount the story of thy disgrace; and for a man of honour disgrace is worse than death.[3] If a person who has accepted cleaning of latrines as his work wearied of it, saying that it was a Bhangi's work, Shri Krishna would tell him that he was betraying his dharma, that he would lose his good name, that people would for ever talk ill of him. For a man who has a good reputation in society, its loss is worse than death. Arjuna, Shri Krishna said, would give the great warrior a ground for accusing him of having fled from the battlefield in fear. He sums up this part of the argument with the following verse:

Hold alike pleasure and pain, gain and loss, victory and defeat, and gird up thy loins for the fight; so doing thou shalt not incur sin.[4]

The argument in this verse is not practical, but spiritual.

Notes

1. In the Ashram.
2. II, 31.
3. II, 34.
4. II, 38.

[21] March 19, 1926

The verse about "pleasure and pain" is not addressed to Arjuna alone but to all of us. "You will incur no sin by killing your kinsmen."—this is said repeatedly in the *Gita*. If a person remains unconcerned with defeat or victory, knowing that they are a part of life, he commits no sin in fighting. But we should also say that he earns no merit. If we seek merit, we shall also incur sin. Even the best thing has an element of evil in it. Nothing in the world is wholly good or wholly evil. Where there is action there is some evil. If Harishchandra had felt any doubt in his mind, what would a holy sage have told him? "Cut your wife's throat; you will incur no sin." If a person learns to make no distinction between gain and loss, pleasure and pain, he would rarely be tempted to commit a sin.

If we had blamed the thieves and regarded them as very wicked men, we would have been filled with rage and wanted to kill them.

We can do without beating of drums over a birth, but it is difficult not to grieve over a death. If we thus cultivate an attitude of indifference and learn to check anger, we shall one day succeed in freeing ourselves from these pairs of opposites.

The argument in the *Bhagavad Gita* falls into three parts: (1) "Whence this weakness in you?" (2) Arjuna's questioning; (3) Krishna awakening his intellect and explaining to him how the *atman* and the body are separate things. Then follow the practical considerations. What is one to do? How is one to proceed having known that the *atman* is different from the body? This is the fourth stage in the argument.

Thus have I set before thee the attitude of Knowledge; hear now the attitude of Action; resorting to this attitude thou shalt cast off the bondage of action.[1]

The word *sankhya*, it has been said, is somewhat confusing. It may be so for the learned, it is not so for us. All that Shri Krishna means is this: "I explained the matter to you from a theoretical point of view. I pointed out the difference between the *atman* and the body.

Having explained this to you, I will now put the argument with reference to yoga. Yoga means practice. After understanding this, you will have to translate your knowledge into action in the manner I shall explain." The word yoga is used repeatedly in the *Gita*. It explains how to act. "If you understand this," Shri Krishna says, "you will escape from the bondage of action."

Note

1. II, 39.

[22] March 20, 1926

There is much disputation concerning the meaning of the verse which we took up for discussion yesterday, as will be evident to anyone who makes a deep study of the *Gita*. I however feel that you should follow the rule that I have followed. It does not matter if that seems like making a virtue of our weakness. We should not involve ourselves in disputations about the meaning of Shastras. Bishop Butler was a man of great learning, but he took a pledge never to enter in a religious controversy. An atheist happened to be on a visit [to England]. The Bishop could have argued with him. But he wrote to a friend saying that he would not enter into any discussion with the atheist. It was possible, he said, that he might not be able to answer an argument of the latter on the instant. It was also possible, he added, that his reasoning might have no effect on others, in which case he would produce on them a wrong impression. It was therefore better, he said, to remain quiet. The atheist was free to question any belief. Why enter into any argument, about the existence of God, which was self-evident?

Raychandbhai once thought that he could do good to the world through his gift of attending to a hundred things simultaneously. If, he thought, he gave demonstrations of that gift in the Town Hall in Bombay, with a High Court judge presiding over the function, people would be converted and seek the welfare of their soul. After two or three days, he felt doubts about the wisdom of such a demonstration.

It would be, he thought, a display of his own attainments, but would prove nothing about the power of God. Accordingly, he wrote a letter of apology and said that he had decided not to give the demonstration, but did not wish to explain why.

A person may say about Siva: 'He may be naked, He may wear human skulls round his neck, but He is my God, I want no other.' We may say the same thing in regard to this verse. *Sankhya* may mean any number of things. I have explained the idea to the best of my understanding and I have set you thinking. Now I shall demonstrate a practical application. Its many explanations may be of interest to learned men; they are not for us. We wish to study so that we may learn to be servants and devotees of God, may see God. To see God we do not have to enter into disputes. At the moment these children make my world. I wish to awaken their thought, entertain them and explain things to them. I have no aim beyond this. Every day we recite:

What is non-Being is never known to have been,
And what is Being is never known not to have been.

If, despite that, we act as if the unreal was the real, to what purpose do we recite the verse?

At every moment we have to decide whether a particular action will serve the *atman* or the body. We cannot, however, break open the cage of the body, and so we must simultaneously follow *vidya*[1] and *avidya*[2].

And now follows a verse which explains how a person who tries to put this teaching into action is saved. Here no effort undertaken is lost, no disaster befalls. Even a little of this righteous course delivers one from great fear.[3] No sin is incurred by those that follow the path of action. A beginning made is not wasted. Even a little effort along this path saves one from great danger. This is a royal road, easy to follow. It is the sovereign yoga. In following it, there is no fear of stumbling. Once a beginning is made, nothing will stand in our way. Only yesterday I wrote to a friend and told him that he suffered not from fistula but from something else. I advised him to keep repeating Ramanama. What one does in this way never goes in vain.

How would it have helped him if I had advised him to have a *yajna*[4] performed? He would not have got a genuine priest to conduct the *yajna*. There would be many other difficulties. Nor would I advise him to go to Jagannath Puri[5] and make such and such an offering to such and such a deity. What if following my advice, he became an atheist? If, instead, he got smitten with love for Rama, he would be saved from a great fear. He suffers from a mental disease and should become free from attachments. He should constantly think on Rama. Doctors, too, advise us not to think of the disease from which we may be suffering.

This is a very important verse. It contains the profound idea that nothing done is ever lost, that there is no sin there, only safety. This is the royal road, the right angle. All right angles are of 90 degrees. This path is the path of truth. There is no harm, no fear of destruction, in following it. On the other hand, a person who argues whether it is right to tell a lie in order to save a cow or to eat meat to save one's life, can never be sure where he will end up.

Notes

1. Knowledge.
2. Ignorance; for Gandhiji's meaning here, *vide Isopanishad*.
3. II, 40.
4. Sacrifice.
5. A centre of pilgrimage in Orissa.

[23] March 21, 1926

Three points, tests or conditions are mentioned for proving that the *atman* is different from the body. We can act every moment on the assurance: in this path no effort is ever lost. What can we do right now which will never be lost? What can we think of? There is only one reply, that we must follow the prayers, and that too with perfect concentration.

Ramaswamy Aiyar once addressed a meeting in Bombay in the early days of non-co-operation. Khadilkar[1] said then that among all political activities there was only one which satisfied all the three conditions. That activity yields immediate result; there is no obstacle to its progress; and there is the advantage of being saved from the fear of loss of sixty crores of rupees.

Shri Krishna explained the same thing over again in the verse which follows:

The attitude, in this matter, springing, as it does, from fixed resolve but one, O Kurunandana; but for those who have no fixed resolve the attitudes are many-branched and unending.[2]

O Arjuna, the resolute intellect here is one-pointed. Along this path which I shall explain to you, one must hold one's intellect so firm that there is no wavering. The actions of a man whose intellect is not fixed on one aim, who is not single-minded in his devotion, will branch out in many directions. As the mind leaps, monkey-fashion, from branch to branch, so does the intellect. A person who clings to his life will seek help from any *vaid* or saint or witch-doctor whom he meets. Similarly, a monkey will fly from branch to branch and ultimately meet an untimely death, the victim of a sling-shot. The mind of a person of uncertain purpose grows weak day by day and becomes so unsettled that he can think of nothing except what is in his mind at the moment. In present-day politics, there is no good at all and plenty of evil, for it is full of flattery and one is not protected from dangers, but, on the contrary, surrounded by them. It does not help us to realize the *atman;* in fact we lost our soul. We lose our dharma, we lose the capacity for good works, lose both this world and the other. If, on the other hand, we can have faith in this spinningwheel movement, we can serve the world, be happy ourselves, can live safe from a great danger, that is, can live without fear of those who would hold us down. We also secure, simultaneously, a means of ensuring our welfare in the other world. If a person who takes up this work does not seem to be of a fixed mind, you may conclude that he is not following the royal path.

It is only if we have the faith in our hearts that we are all one, though we exist as separate beings, it is only then that we can feel a sense of equality. Otherwise, even two leaves are not equal.

The next three verses describe the man whose intellect is not resolute.

Notes

1. Presumably, Krishnaji Prabhakar Khadilkar, a scholar, journalist, dramatist and public worker of Maharashtra.
2. II, 41.

[24] March 23, 1926

A person who is of fixed mind in a small matter can be so even in a big matter. If he is asked to make an ellipsoid of clay and concentrate on it, he would do so. In trying to concentrate on any object, one is likely to be distracted by all manner of troublesome thoughts.

A person to whom this happens may be described as one whose intellect is not fixed on one aim. One who would succeed in the yoga of works must be of a fixed mind in small matters as well as big.

Now follows the description of an intellect not fixed on one aim. In describing it, Vyasa has run down the Vedas as he has done nowhere else. So many things were interpolated into the Shastras in the course of time, but we have gone on believing that everything in them is divinely inspired. By doing this, we make ourselves mere pedants. *Veda* means to know. That which helps us to acquire the knowledge of the *Brahman*, which provides us the best means of acquiring such knowledge, that is the Veda.

The ignorant, revelling in the letter of the Vedas, declare that there is naught else; carnally-minded, holding heaven to be their goal, they utter swelling words which promise birth as the fruit of action and which dwell on the many and varied rites to be performed for the sake of pleasure and power; intent, as they are, on pleasure and power their swelling words rob them of their wits, and they have no settled attitude which can be centred on the supreme goal.[1]

Ignorant people, that is persons who are learned and yet devoid of knowledge, utter flowery speech, that is speech which is attractive, on which blossom new flowers every day. Men who wrangle over the meaning of the Vedas; men filled with endless desires (men who have many wishes and teach others to be like them); men who are ever thinking of heaven (who are merely for enjoyments, who always talk of enjoying even this world thoroughly and paint glowing and attractive pictures of life in heaven and) who assert that there is nothing beyond heaven; who always say that our actions in life unfailingly bear appropriate fruits and persuade people to perform innumerable rituals to secure enjoyments and win greatness (there are people who say these things even today.); who advise us to propitiate a great many gods and so make us feel helpless; who induce us to offer fanciful prayers to imaginary gods and turn us away from prayer to the God of all gods—such men push us deeper and deeper into quagmire. The fancies and thoughts which often trouble our minds are also evidence of an intellect branching out in many directions. Even in small matters, we can say, our intellect is not resolute. It will be resolute only if we fix our minds on one purpose and cling to it with discrimination, only if we work without looking for immediate results. At present, whether in politics or social reform we leap from one branch to another. I began with the illustration of a ball of earth and told you that, even if we concentrate on that, we can realize the *atman*. I was once asked by someone why I had not succeeded in realizing the *atman*. I told him that for me the means themselves stood for such realization. The fact that such a question was asked is enough to suggest that the person who put it would not understand the humility which inspired my reply and would approach many others with the same question. This same condition prevailed in Vyasa's time. How can we expect that a person who is attached to enjoyments of the senses and possession of power, whose mind has been led away by all manner of attractive words, will have a resolute intellect?

Samadhi means fixing the mind on God. How can one's intellect remain fixed and motionless in such a state? The mind of a person who is not satisfied with a lakh which he has earned and hopes to earn ten lakhs the next day, who, addressed as a *Mahatma* this day, hopes to be so addressed ever afterwards—the mind of such a person is distracted by all manner of thoughts and attractive visions. His mind will not be plain white, like khadi; he is ever wanting to dress his mind, as fashionable women do their bodies in many-coloured saris with borders of various designs. Such a person can never be devoted to God. Only he who has a spirit of extreme humility, who has the faith of Faithful[2], can be said to have a resolute intellect.

Note

1. II, 42, 43 and 44.
2. In *Pilgrim's Progress.*

[25] March 24, 1926

We saw yesterday that those who hanker after enjoyments and power can never fix their intellect on one aim. Only a person like Hazrat Ali who is completely absorbed in God can succeed in doing so. Only a person whose *chitta*[1] has become absolutely purified, whose mind has expanded and awakened to light, has become as clear as a mirror, can have in his stainless mind, a vision of God. If any sound emanates from such a person it can only be that of the name of Rama.

After explaining this, Shri Krishna described the pedantic student of the Vedas. He now sums up the idea of the three verses in one:

The Vedas have as their domain the three *gunas*[2]; eschew them, O Arjuna. Free thyself from the pairs of opposites, abide in eternal truth, scorn to gain or guard anything, remain the master of thy soul.[3]

The Vedas treat of the three *gunas*; you rise above them. (But this is not true. If it is, the Vedas would not be God's word. Shri Krishna is here talking about the Vedas as expounded by the ritualist pedants. The statement, therefore, gives only one side of the truth. The Vedas which utter *neti neti*[4]—there is nothing except truth—those Vedas are ever the objects of reverence for us. We can cite verses from the *Gita* itself and that it tells us to accept the Vedas as thus understood.) Arjuna is asked to be above the pairs of opposites, which means to be indifferent to happiness and suffering. He should act in the fighting between the Kauravas and the Pandavas as if he was not personally involved in it. He should be *nityasattvastha*, which means that his mind should always remain steadfast. He should be *niryogakshema*, that is, give up all thought of acquiring, holding and defending possessions. But one must preserve one's body, at any rate.

Arjuna should, therefore, cultivate detachment in that respect. He should cease to concern himself with yoga and *kshema* and live in the *atman*. He should live always thinking that he is not the body, not an entity with a name and a form, that he transcends these.

To the extent that a well is of use when there is a flood of water on all sides, to the same extent are all the Vedas of use to an enlightened *Brahman*.[5]

What may be found in a tank will also be found in a big lake. He who knows the *Brahman* will know everything else. He possesses occult powers, too, for the knowledge of the *Brahman* is the perfection of these powers. The three *gunas* are dealt with in the Vedas; he who rises above them attains to the knowledge of *Brahman*. The person who has the throne will not covet a position of civil or police authority. He who has reached the Gangotri1 has known the Ganga.

We get from the former all the benefit we would from the latter, and in addition the person taking his abode near the Gangotri is away from the crowd and lives unattached to the pairs of opposites. Near the Hoogli, the Ganga water is turbid, but it is fresh and clear near Rishikesh and Hardwar. The higher one ascends towards the top, the greater the purity and cleanliness.

(Some interpret this verse in a different way, but we shall not go into that.)

After this introduction, Shri Krishna tells Arjuna that the sovereign yoga which he wished to explain to the latter was this:

Action alone is thy province, never the fruits thereof; let not thy motive be the fruit of action, nor shouldst thou desire to avoid action.[7]

Your right is to work, and not to expect the fruit. The slaveowner tells the slave: "Mind your work, but beware lest you pluck a fruit from the garden. Yours is to take what I give." God has put us under restriction in the same manner. He tells us that we may work if we wish, but that the reward of work is entirely for Him to give. Our duty is to pray to Him, and the best way in which we can do this is to work with the pickaxe, to remove scum from the river and to sweep and clean our yards. This, certainly, is a difficult lesson to learn. The relationship between the slave-owner and his slave is an unhealthy one. It is based on [the owner's] self-interest. That between the lion and the goat is of the same character. But man is ever rushing into the mouth of God. A wise man does so consciously and deliberately, and tells God that he wishes to be His slave, and not the world's. The more God seems to reject him, the more he strives to be near Him. This verse is intended to describe this peculiar relationship. The eye-lids certainly protect the eyes, but they do not do so with conscious intention. They protect the eyes by reflex action. The relationship between God and man is similarly spontaneous. Mirabai has sung:

"By a slender thread has Hari tied me to Him, and I turn as He pulls the thread." The relationship between us and God is of the kind described here. The thread is slender, and a single one besides.

Ma karmafala, etc., means: "Do not act so as to be the cause of your suffering fruits of action; do not be attached to action; or be over-eager to do anything. Think that everything is done by Me. What reason do you have to believe that you do things?" So, if it is God's will that we must die, He will destroy us; if such is not His will, He will arrest the hand raised against us.

Notes

1. Mind-stuff.
2. *Sattva, rajas* and *tamas*, modes of being.
3. II, 45.
4. "Not this, not this".
5. II, 46.
6. Source of the Ganga in the Himalayas.
7. II, 47.

[26] March 25, 1926

Ma te sangostvakarmani: In reading this yesterday, I said *karmani* instead of *akarmani*, for that is how I have always read this verse. *Akarma* means all work which falls outside the sphere of one's duty. "You should not," Krishna says to Arjuna,"feel tempted to take up such work, feel drawn to work which is not your duty."

Act thou, O Dhananjaya, without attachment, steadfast in Yoga, evenminded in success and failure. Even-mindedness is Yoga.[1]

Work without attachment, being established firmly in yoga.

Yoga means renouncing the fruit of action. It means not desiring the fruit of work which is *akarma*. We should do no work with attachment.

Attachment to good work, is that too wrong? Yes, it is. If we are attached to our goal of winning swaraj, we shall not hesitate to adopt bad means. If a person is particular that he would give slivers to me personally, one day he might even steal them. Hence, we should not be attached even to a good cause. Only then will our means remain pure and our actions too.

Proceeding, Shri Krishna says: One should be even-minded in success and failure. In other words, one should dedicate to Krishna all that one does, surrender oneself completely to Him. The person who has an equal mind towards all things may be described as one established in yoga. Krishna explains the same idea further:

For action, O Dhananjaya, is far inferior to unattached action; seek refuge in the attitude of detachment. Pitiable are those who make fruit their motive.[2]

Work done without the yoga of intellect is extremely harmful.

One should, therefore, seek refuge in intellect."Intellect" means a resolute intellect. Having once made a decision there is no arguing the matter further. Anyone who works for reward is a *kripan,* that is, a person deserving our pity.

Notes

1. II, 48.
2. II, 49.

[27] March 26, 1926

A person without a fixed purpose has an unsteady mind. Bhartrihari[1] has described many forms of this weakness of mind.

Here in this world a man gifted with that attitude of detachment escapes the fruit of both good and evil deeds. Gird thyself up for yoga, therefore. Yoga is skill in action.[2]

A person who is firmly yoked to his intellect, an intellect which is resolute, who is totally merged in it and who is a yogi, such a one renounces [the fruit of] work both good and bad, that is, is disinterested towards either. Shri Krishna, therefore, asks Arjuna to be a yogi. Yoga means nothing but skill in work.

Anyone who wants to decide whether he should or should not do a particular thing, should seek a yogi's advice. This is why it is said that where there is a prince of yogis like Shri Krishna and a bowman of prowess like Arjuna, prosperity and power follow as a matter of course.

For sages, gifted with the attitude of detachment, who renounce the fruit of action, are released from the bondage of birth and attain to the state which is free from all ills.[3]

Yogis renounce the fruits of work, and are freed from the bonds of birth. How can a person who has awakened to the truth about his body ever die? Such a one attains to immortality.

When thy understanding will have passed through the slough of delusion, then wilt thou be indifferent alike to what thou hast heard and wilt hear.[4]

When your intellect, Shri Krishna tells Arjuna, has crossed the slough of delusion, you will become disinterested towards all that you may have heard in the past or that may seem to you worth hearing in future; that is, you will remain indifferent.

When thy understanding, distracted by much hearing, will rest steadfast and unmoved in concentration, then wilt thou attain Yoga.[5]

When your intellect, once perverted by listening to all manner of arguments, is totally absorbed in the contemplation of God, you will then attain to yoga. When a person is firmly established in *samadhi*[6] he is filled with ecstatic love and, therefore, can be completely indifferent to this world.

Notes

1. A celebrated poet and grammarian of ancient India, who is said to have been the brother of King Vikramaditya.
2. II, 50.
3. II, 51.
4. II, 52.
5. II, 53.
6. The eighth stage in yoga.

[28] March 27, 1926

Arjuna now asks how we may know the man established in *samadhi* from his speech. "Speech" means outward sign. The food which the *Gita* offers is different from what one's mother gives.

Before Mother *Gita,* the earthly mother stands no comparison. He who has the *Gita* always engraved in his heart and keeps it there till the moment of death, will attain to *moksha*. A boy who gives himself to daily worship of the *Gita* will be another Dhruva or Sudhanva. We recite these verses daily so that we may understand their meaning and be guided by them.

[29] March 28, 1926

"You are my arm," Shri Krishna tells Arjuna. "It is I who make it move." We say, likewise, in our morning prayers: "You it is that makes our senses function." One who is ever patient and works with single-minded attention to the task on hand may be described as a yogi skilled in action.

[30] March 30, 1926

When a man puts away, O Partha, all the cravings that arise in the mind and finds comfort for himself only from *atman*, then is he called the man of secure understanding.[1]

He who banishes all bad desires arising in his mind may be described as a *sthitaprajna*[2]. We add the word "bad" because here in the Ashram we engage ourselves in ceaseless work and we cannot ask a cripple to get up and walk. Though, of course, ultimately we arrive at a stage when we should banish all desires, even the desire to see God, for to a person in that stage all action becomes spontaneous.

After one has seen God face to face, how can the desire to see Him still remain? When you have already jumped into the river, the desire to do so will no longer be there. Our desire to see God ceases when we are lost in Him, have become one with Him.

We would be ill if we remained in a river the whole day. Anyone who sleeps all the twenty-four hours will fall ill, and so also anyone who eats all day long. There is not a single thing in the world which we can go on desiring perpetually. It is because of this that we have the problem of happiness and misery. The more often we desire a thing, the stronger our desire becomes every time. The more we satisfy desires, the more urgent they become. That is also true about our daily discussions of the *Gita*.

Though I cannot make them very interesting, those who really wish to follow them will find their desire becoming daily stronger. No one, of course, will fall ill because of that. Or, maybe, we need not consciously desire a thing which we always want. The sun rises and sets every day; we do not consciously wish that it may. He who has overcome his desires completely, should be natural in all his actions, as walking and similar movements of the body are natural.

There is only one desire in life which is good and the desire for the means to realize it is also good.

Who can succeed in banishing desires in this manner? He whose self abides content in itself is known as a *sthitaprajna*.

Whenever we hear anyone speaking about God, we should forget everything else and attend to his words. A person such as described above, if he is attending a reading of the *Ramayana* or the *Gita*, will be completely absorbed in following them. He will never feel it a strain to rise even at four in the morning.

The state in which the self abides in itself in serene content is the same as described by Narasinh Mehta[3] in this line in a poem of his:

"The *Brahman* dancing in sportive play in front of the *Brahman*."

The poet here expresses the very same truth. The *Brahman* has all its joy through the *Brahman* in the company of the *Brahman*. The slave can never conceive of his existence without his master. A person who has the name of another on his lips all the twenty-four hours will forget himself in the latter. The *atman*[4] becomes the *Paramatman*[5] in the same manner. The *atman* may be a ray of the *Paramatman*, but a ray of the sun is the sun itself. Apart from God, we can have no existence at all. He who makes himself God's slave becomes one with God. The state described here is not that of a person who lives selfsatisfied, surrounding himself with possessions of all kinds. We should learn to be content in ourselves. The means and the end should become one. But who can find joy in the self through the self? One can do that by learning to work in a new spirit. One who takes opium before going to bed will not sleep well, but the man who sleeps in the natural course will sleep in peace, his mind abiding in God.

The verses which follow are by way of an explanation of this verse. Self-help does not consist merely in not seeking help from others; it consists in not needing such help.

If children have faith, they can live as a *sthitaprajna* does. They have their parents and teachers to look after their needs. They have, therefore, no need to take thought for themselves. They should always be guided by their elders. A child who lives in this manner is a *brahmachari*, a *muni*, a *sthitaprajna*. He is so in the sense that he does what he is asked to and carries out every instruction. Such a child could even become Prahlad. God, we can have no

Notes

1. II, 55.
2. One who is of steadfast intellect.
3. A 15th-century saint-poet of Gujarat.
4. The individual self.
5. The Universal Self.

[31] March 31, 1926

The verse[1] beginning with *prajahati* can never mean that we may remain as we are. If that were the meaning, the second line would have no place in it. The man who lives contented in the self through the self will give up all desires, but one can live in such a state only if the desire to become better, to grow spiritually awakens in one. Anyone who wants to live in such a state must give up everything which is likely to obstruct his effort. If all that we do is merely to indulge in fancies, like Shaikhchilli[2], it would be better not to think at all, neither good thoughts nor bad. The road to hell is paved with good intentions. That is why it is said that one may cast into a river a ton of thoughts and cling to an ounce of practice.

(I have read in an English book that a boy who eats till he is full cannot preserve celibacy. One should not overload one's stomach.)

Whose mind is untroubled in sorrows and longeth not for joys, who is free from passion, fear and wrath—he is called the ascetic of secure understanding.[3]

The man who does not feel depressed by suffering, is not overcome by suffering (knowing that suffering is always the effect of some cause), who is indifferent amid pleasures and is no more subject to attachments, fear and anger—such a person may be described as *sthitadhi*, that is, one whose intellect remains steadfast and is never caught in a whirlpool.

Who owns attachment nowhere, who feels neither joy nor resentment whether good or bad comes his way—that man's understanding is secure.[4]

The man who has withdrawn interest from all objects, given up desire for them, who is unconcerned, indifferent in good or ill chance, who is neither pleased nor annoyed by anything—such a person's intellect is steadfast. Shri Krishna gives an illustration of this:

And when, like the tortoise drawing in its limbs from every side, this man draws in his senses from their objects, his understanding is secure.[5]

The man who holds in his senses to prevent them from going out to their objects, as the tortoise draws in his limbs and holds them as if under a shield, has an intellect which is steadfast. Only that man who voluntarily holds in his senses may be known as completely absorbed in God. When our senses seem to move out of our control, we should think of the tortoise. The objects of the senses are like pebbles. If we hold in the senses, the pebbles will not hurt, that is, if we hold under control our hands, our feet, our eyes, and so on.

Notes

1. II, 55.
2. Day-dreamer.
3. II, 56.
4. II, 57.
5. II, 58.

[32] April 1, 1926

Shri Krishna now explains how the senses may be held back from their objects. When a man starves his senses, the objects of those senses disappear from him, but not the yearning for them; the yearning too departs when he beholds the Supreme.[1]

Only a person who denies the body the food it craves for will cease to be troubled by his senses. The senses of a well-fed man always keep awake, but they lose all their power when he stops eating.

The Shastras say that, if a man's appetites are not under

his control, it would be best for him to fast. We are enjoined to fast during the Ramadan and the extra lunar month of the Hindus to discipline the senses. Suppose that I have decided to go to the city and see a play; if however, I have been fasting on that day, I would feel disinclined to go. If our senses cannot be controlled we should undertake a fast; if they cannot be controlled fully, we should give up food altogether.

This is what the first half of the verse means.

And now about the second half:

The appetites subside, but our pleasure in the objects of senses remains. If a person who is fasting feels that his life is secure, he will not suffer because of the fast, but ordinarily desire for food persists. During a fast, impure desires will probably subside, but one gets impatient for the fast to end. Unless the desire for food disappears completely, the fast will not endure. The desire for sacrifice will not endure without renunciation. When we have an opportunity to enjoy anything, we find that our physical appetites become strong again.

This, of course, does not mean that we should not occasionally give up things for a temporary period. We should certainly give up anything we can give up.

In the first half, we are told that we should curb impure desires by fasting; but fasting alone does not yield the required result. Something more is needed. If we see God, our instinctive desire for objects of senses will also subside. This last thing confronts us with a problem. Until one's pleasure in objects of the senses has disappeared, one cannot become established in *samadhi*, and until one has become so established one will not succeed in overcoming desires.

How to solve this problem? We should persevere in our effort. We should, slowly and gradually, learn to feel God's presence in the depths of our heart. We should, occasionally, banish the very thought of eating and feel that it would be much better that our body should perish than that we should be enslaved by pleasures. One does not, of course, achieve self-conquest by committing suicide. It is the desires which need to be conquered. Anyone who eats to keep alive his body may certainly eat, but he should stop eating if he finds that eating food rouses his appetites. If he can be patient when fasting, they will subside completely. He may, when they have subsided, ask for milk or water if he wants these for keeping himself alive. It is said about

Lord Buddha that he once fainted because he had been fasting. At that time, a woman came and placed a few drops of milk on his lips. Did the milk rouse his appetites? No; on the contrary, he realized God soon after.

The purport of this verse is that we should fast for self-purification. But the Shastras tell us that, while fasting, we should wish with all our strength for freedom from desire. If, in addition, we also yearn to see God, then only will our fasting bear fruit. If we desire that our appetite should subside, it is in order that we may see God. When we are fasting, our one desire should be to see God. Our appetites stand in the way, and so we must weaken their hold on us. After a person has seen God, it is all one to him whether he eats or does not eat. Vinoba told me a story about Chaitanya[2], that a lump of sugar placed on his tongue remained there undissolved, like a stone. The reason for this was that his pleasure in objects of sense had completely died away. I have said that it is not the palate, but the mind, which feels pleasure. If a man's pleasure in objects of sense has disappeared, if he has become established in *samadhi*, or if he is suffering from a disease 'like jaundice, nothing placed on his tongue will dissolve. Thus, the man who has turned away from pleasures and the man who is stricken with disease ultimately reach the same state, one voluntarily, the other against his will. Chaitanyadeva felt all the time that it was God's grace which sustained him and that if he should eat at all, it must be only that he may see God one day. To see Him one should completely conquer one's appetites, and even the instinctive pleasure one feels in objects of sense must subside. This verse provides the key to such a state. To curb the appetites, we should stop eating, that is, deny our senses their food. When they have no occasion to function, they will be denied their food. If, after this, we take the next step and concentrate our attention on attaining self-realization, our instinctive pleasure in objects of sense will subside completely. The man who attains such a state will be in the same condition as Janaka[3].

Notes

1. II, 59.
2. A 16th-century religious reformer of Bengal.
3. Philosopher-king, famous in the Upanishads as a knower of Reality and master of desireless action.

[33] April 2, 1926

We shall proceed with the verse we took up yesterday. It is a very important verse. I kept thinking on it the whole day. Four or five hundred years ago, in Europe and Arabia they attached great importance to mortification of the flesh. In the time of the Prophet, prayer, fasting and keeping awake at night were considered essential for subduing the *nafas* (this is a very good word denoting the sense-organs collectively; it also means desire). The Prophet was often awake till two or three after midnight, and was never particular when and what he ate. It was not merely that he kept the *roza* fast. That was necessary for everyone to keep, even for people engrossed in worldly affairs. The Prophet, however, undertook a *roza* fast every now and then. While one is keeping this fast, one is not permitted to take water during day-time, but after sunset it is absolutely necessary that one must drink some water. The Prophet, however, did not apply this rule to himself, and so an associate of his told him: "Since you do not eat, we too will not eat." The Prophet's reply was:"No, you should not fast. God sends you no such food as He sends me." Silenced by the reply, the questioner slapped himself on the face and left, thinking:

"We, others, observe the *roza* because he falls into ecstasies and asks us to fast, but in actual practice we only make a fuss." To the Prophet, fasting brought happiness, for it was an occasion when he could live constantly in the presence of God. His food consisted of dates. Just as in countries where people drink every home has a vineyard, so in Arabia there are date-palms near every house, and when the Prophet wished to eat he plucked a few dates from these trees. Some others who lived with the Prophet and served him also ate dates. the little flour that was ground for them was also coarse. He used to keep awake for such long hours that the Bibisaheb would wait impatiently for him to lie down to sleep. Besides keeping awake thus, he would withdraw himself into solitude so that he might subdue the senses and be blessed with a vision of God. Jesus did likewise. He lived in solitude, fasted for forty days and subjected his body to the utmost mortification. At the end of forty days, he felt that he heard a mysterious voice, that God was talking to him and that the veil which hid God from him had lifted. Those who followed him taught the same thing. There has been a tradition of fasting and prayer in Europe right to the present day.

And then came Luther in Germany. He said that the others had misinterpreted the texts, and that their lives were all deception. As the sun moves westward, darkness follows close behind it, reaching almost as far as the sun but not quite; in the same way, hypocrisy follows close behind holiness. Luther saw through all this. He plainly saw the superstitions and hypocrisies which flourished in monasteries. It is a strange law of nature that once men become accustomed to a certain thing they continue to do it through sheer inertia. In those days, they even burnt people alive. Those who believed in mortifying the flesh thought it their duty to curb the senses and to kill others who did not do so. Observing these evils, Luther went to the opposite extreme.

After all, whatever the evils associated with external practices, it is only through self-control that one can see God. The Protestants, however, believed that there was nothing but hypocrisy in the Catholic practices, and so they destroyed a most potent means of realizing God. Because this means harmed some people, it does not follow that it harms all. But they believed that it did.

In India, too, this wind is blowing at present. It is often said that control of the senses is difficult to achieve, but in truth it is not so.

This is not only my present belief; I held it even when I was conducting my experiments. Three things are essential for control of the senses: (1) faith; (2) a conviction of the necessity of subjugating the senses, so strong that we would persist even if we were all alone in this belief; (3) food is body's nourishment, a means of keeping it alive, but it is also the cause of the senses becoming turbulent and, therefore, when it ceases to serve the purpose of nourishing the body, eating should cease. When steam fails to make the engine run, when the pipe through which it flows is rusted, its supply ought to be stopped. A wise engineer would know that, if this supply were not stopped, the engine could burst. The position with regard to food and the body is identical, and, therefore, if feeding the body results in the senses becoming turbulent, we should stop eating. As, however, our instinctive pleasure in food will not disappear when we stop eating, we should also pray for God's grace. We have a poem in which we say that we should pray for God's forgiveness for the thousand sins which we commit. We are drawn to these sins against our will, we slip into them slowly and gradually without consciously wishing to commit them. We should pray for God's mercy so that we may be forgiven the many thousand sins of this kind. Hence, if anyone is convinced that he ought to kill his physical appetites, he does nothing wrong is fasting. If he has faith, it will certainly be rewarded. If it is not rewarded, God's promise to man will be falsified; but our experience is that this never happens. One must not shrink from a fast of ten or twenty or fifty days. Gibbon[1] never made any statement without first verifying its truth. He has mentioned Catholics fasting for as many as fifty days. They had certainly mastered the senses to the degree. In this miserable age, people become impatient if they get no result in five days. Let no one think that our pleasure in objects can be quickly destroyed. If it is not destroyed and the man can control himself no longer, he may eat, but he should not accept defeat. He should start a fast again. This readiness to stake one's all and perish is bound to be rewarded with victory. The man will ultimately win but only if he perseveres after failing ten or even twenty times. There is such great beauty in this effort, and that is why I advise it. What is followed in the Roman Catholic Church is also enjoined in Islam. The people who at present do evil things in the name of Islam have little understanding of it. Those, on the other hand, who go on praying in their obscure homes, certainly realize God. They give up all indulgences. One cannot indulge in pleasures and live a life of renunciation at the same time. If we understand the truth that we eat only to give the body its hire, then we are fit to understand the *Gita*.

One more point (which I will not elaborate today). It is, that the author of the *Gita* has categorically laid down the principles. We shall find no error in them if we examine them in the abstract, but when we try to put them into practice we experience difficulties. But I will take up this point later.

Having told Arjuna this with regard to cravings of the senses, Shri Krishna proceeds as in the next verse:

For, in spite of the wise man's endeavour, O Kaunteya, the unruly senses distract his mind perforce.[2]

However much an intelligent man may strive, the senses are restless, they shake his self-control and forcibly draw his mind towards their objects; they draw even a *jnani*[3] after them. The senses are like uncontrollable horses. If the rider is not vigilant and the reins are not all right, there is no knowing where they will carry him. "A monkey, and drunk besides"[4], that is how it will be.

Holding all these in check, the yogi should sit intent on Me; for he whose senses are under control is secure of understanding.[5]

"The *sthitadhi*, having controlled all his senses, will rest wholly absorbed in Me. Anyone who strives in this manner and succeeds in holding his senses under control, such a one is a *yogi*."

Thus Shri Krishna shows how to become a *sthitaprajna*.

Notes

1. Edward Gibbon (1733-94); author of *The History of the Decline and Fall of the Roman Empire.*
2. II, 60.
3. A man of spiritual knowledge and illumination.
4. A Gujarati saying.
5. II, 61.

[34] April 3, 1926

I explained yesterday that, in order that our pleasure in the objects of senses may subside completely, fasting, *bhakti*,[1] prayer and vigils are necessary. But the pleasure [in objects] will not disappear till we have realized God. The question is, can it disappear completely while the body is there? I have come to the conclusion that no one can be called a *mukta* while he is still alive; one may be said at the most to have become fit for *moksha*. When we speak of Janaka as a *muktatma*, the word *mukta* is used in a general sense and the term means that he was a man who would attain deliverance after his death, that he would not have to be born again. It is doing violence to the meaning of words to say that a man has attained deliverance even while he lives in the body, for the necessity for deliverance remains so long as connection with the body remains. A little reflection will show us that,if our egoistic attachment to ourselves has completely disappeared, the body cannot survive. If we have no wish at all to keep the body alive, it must cease to exist. If we but move our hand the mind is bound to move too. If, now, we would completely withdraw the mind from the body, the latter should become "as the burnt silken thread, only the form surviving". Some attachment is bound to persist while our bodies are capable of motion. Scientists remove air from a bottle, but a little of it remains in it. The air becomes more and more rarefied, and only a scientist would know that there was any inside. Similarly, our pleasure in objects does not disappear completely while the least degree of association with the body persists, as signified by its movements. Moreover, as long as we commit even a little violence, *moksha* is not possible, and the slightest movement of the body involves some violence. Even if the body is lying completely motion-less, its functioning involves some violence, however little it may be. There is violence even in the act of thinking, and so long as that is so man cannot attain a state of perfect self-realization, his mind cannot even comprehend such a state. Thus, the cravings of the senses die away only when we cease to exist in the body. This is a terrible statement to make, but the *Gita* does not shrink from stating terrible truths. Truth does not remain hidden because it is not stated. *Moksha* is the supreme end, and even yogis can experience it only in contemplation. We must, therefore, say that the Dweller in the body cannot be free while He dwells in it. The prisoner is in jail and the king promises him that he will be released; but till he is actually released he cannot be said to have come out of the cage.

He can only imagine his condition after release. In the same way, if there is anyone waiting to receive and greet the *atman* on its release, he cannot do that as long as it remains imprisoned in this cage of the body. And this cannot but be so. How can it be otherwise than that the state after release will be different from the state before it?

Truth is so profound and great a thing that, as we think more and more about it, we realize that to have a direct experience of it, we should completely shed our attachment to the body and yearn every moment for *moksha*. As we think of *moksha* in this light, its value in our eyes should daily increase. If it is the most important thing in life, it should be clear to us that it cannot be attained while we live in this body. Till the gate of the body prison has opened, the fragrance of *moksha* is beyond our experience. Whether terrible or not, this is the truth.

We need not spend much thought or indulge in intellectual exercises over this problem. Once we are decided on the end, we should concentrate our attention on the means; if they are right, the end is as good as attained. If we have trust in our father, we may rest assured that we shall get our share in his property and need not ask him whether he has made a will. Similarly, we need not argue about this matter. The thing is like Euclid's straight line. No one in the world has as yet succeeded in drawing a perfect right angle, but we can construct buildings with the help of instruments which approximate to a right angle. Likewise, we can only conceive the state of *moksha*.

We can conceive a perfect straight line only when we erase the straight line before us; similarly, we can attain deliverance only when we leave the body.

In a man brooding on objects of the senses, attachment to them springs up; attachment begets craving and craving begets wrath.

Wrath breeds stupefaction, stupefaction leads to loss of memory, loss of memory ruins the reason, and the ruin of reason spells utter destruction.[2]

Dwelling constantly on objects of sense-pleasure produces attachment for them. Shri Krishna here explains the order in which withdrawal from sense-objects is to be accomplished. If we constantly think about having a certain object, the mind will become strongly attached to the thought of its possession, and this in turn will grow into a passionate desire to possess it so that the object takes still greater hold of our mind. Attachment produces impatience and passion gives rise to anger. When we fail to get the object of our desire, we become angry. As it recedes from us, we get angry with others. Anger clouds a man's vision, so that he loses his judgment and forgets what he is.

"Who am I, and from whence?"—he forgets to ask. If he could but recollect, would he not realize what was proper and what was not proper for him? The man who forgets what he is loses his power of discrimination. Such a person is as good as dead. Quite a few persons mount the gallows with perhaps a smile on their face. But they depart from this world and have no future in the other. Thus, through constant dwelling on objects of sense the man is ultimately destroyed.

He as good as commits suicide. It is not merely that his body perishes; he will not rise from his fallen state for many lives to come. One should, therefore, crush the craving of sense the moment it arises. The first thing to do is to get over the habit of dwelling on objects of sense-pleasure in our imagination. For that purpose, one should constantly think on God, should live as it were in a state of *samadhi*.

Notes

1. Devotion to God.
2. II, 62 and 63.

[35] April 4, 1926

But the disciplined soul, moving among sense-objects with the senses weaned from likes and dislikes and brought under the control of *atman*, attains peace of mind.[1]

He who lives with his senses no longer subject to attachments and aversions and perfectly under his control becomes fit for God's grace. When a man's ears, nose, eyes, and so on, go on performing their functions naturally without conscious willing on his part—the winking of the eyelids does not need to be willed, there must be some disease if it is otherwise—we say of such a person that his sense-organs, having become free from attachments and aversions, functionspontaneously.

What is the natural work of the ear? We describe a man as established in *samadhi* when his *atman* abides in serene content in itself. His senses must be under his perfect control. The ears of a man whose mind has become one-pointed must have become the servants of his *atman*. Actually, however, we are the slaves of our senses. From this slavery we must win swaraj for the *atman*. The ears should in fact listen only to the divine music of the *atman*. They would not, then, hear even the loud beating of drums. While the *atman* dwells in this body, it should live as the latter's master and god, and use the senses to do only their natural work. Such a person has no charm for Panditji's singing; he attends only to the praise of God.

As Sanjaya had been given the gift of divine vision, so there are divine eyes and ears behind our bodily eyes and ears. The person who is ruled by his *atman* will have the gift of inner senses and will not need the outer ones. These latter are always subject to some degree of attachment and aversion. Our hands may be cut off, but they will not move on their own—such should be the degree of our self-control.

There was once a great bishop[2] in England who held out his hands to be burnt first. Hazarat Ali did not feel the pain of the arrow, for his mind was absorbed in the contemplation of God. The man who has not sold himself to his senses as their slave, but has made himself God's slave has no right to ask for a reward from Him in the form of His grace. He who has become God's slave will, instead of trying to be a master in this world, believe even while he suffers God's lashes that they are for his good. Why do we pray to God to breathe greater life into us? God had His own interest—a divine interest—in creating man and that is that the latter should so live that he would not seek pleasures of the senses, but would devote himself entirely to His contemplation and service. This is the principle. In daily life, one should choose the best that is possible for one. If a man is incapable of hearing the divine song in him, he may listen to good songs sung by others. He should do work which would make him feel in tune with his *atman*. As long as we must use our moral judgment, we should choose what is good and shun what is evil. We shall then succeed in making the senses do their natural work. For one who lives in this way, Peace of mind means the end of all ills, for the understanding of him whose mind is at peace stands secure.[3]

When God's grace descends on us, bringing us peace, all our suffering ends. Who can harm him who is protected by Rama? He on whom God daily showers His grace has all his sufferings destroyed.

The intellect of a man whose *chitta* has become calm and whose only thought is of God, stands secure and is protected against error. Shri Krishna now describes a condition the opposite of this:

The undisciplined man has neither understanding nor devotion; for, for him who has no devotion there is no peace, and for him who has no peace whence happiness?[4]

The meaning is that the man who has not become one in God, who is not a yogi established in *samadhi;* lacks the faculty of intellect altogether. One who is unsteady has an intellect which is manybranched; of what good is such an intellect? It feels no devotion, it does not utter Ramanama. He who lacks devotion and does not meditate on God, how can he attain peace? The man who is filled with devotion sits in single-minded contemplation of God, but the other man who has no peace, how can he be happy?

Notes

1. II, 64.
2. Presumably this refers to Thomas Cranmer (1489-1556), Archbishop of Canterbury, who was burnt at the stake.
3. II, 65.
4. II, 66.

[36] April 6, 1926

Before we resume our reading of the *Gita*, let us apply to our practical situation what we have already learnt. Today is the sixth[1], the day of India's awakening. I look upon it as a day of religious awakening, though ordinarily it would be regarded as a day of political significance. On that day we had kept a fast, bathed in a river and gone to temples; Muslims had offered prayers in mosques and Parsis in their fire-temples. Who can say how many of them were sincere? At that time, of course, everyone seemed to be sincere. That was the day on which we started satyagraha. We commenced civil disobedience in the evening by selling copies of *Hind Swaraj*[2]. All, Hindus, Muslims and Parsis, seemed to have gone crazy on that day.

Today, too, we have kept a twenty-four hours' fast. We should understand the aim behind it. The aim is to bring about spiritual awakening in us. Our aspiration to go from untruth into truth, from darkness into light, is not something for the distant future; it is immediate. For us, non-violence and truth are symbolized in the spinning-wheel. It may be made only of wood, but if we see in it the *chintamani*[3] then it becomes the *chintamani*. It is intelligent to regard the spinning-wheel to be what it is, but it is more intelligent to regard it as the *chintamani*.

If even the dullest can see God in a clod of earth, what may we not see in the spinning-wheel?

What is wrong, if we see swaraj in the spinning-wheel? Our idea, therefore, does not violate dharma. We should understand this when we keep a fast and spin. The Satyagraha Ashram will go on doing its work even when the rest of the country goes to sleep. And we shall, as I have said, get swaraj through the spinning-wheel. The *Bhagavad Gita* says that women, Vaisyas and Sudras, all classes of people, can win freedom. In the same way, all of us can do this. Whether or not we are stout and well-fed, we can do this work if we are strong in mind.

Let us, therefore, cultivate firmness of mind; if we do not let the senses distract the mind, we can become fit for satyagraha.

Let us now take up the verse which we are to discuss today. For when his mind runs after any of the roaming senses, it sweeps away his understanding, as the wind a vessel upon the waters.[4]

A pleasure-loving man wastes his time in aimless wandering; he must have new suits of clothes every day, he eats and drinks what pleases his palate and goes about dressed in finery. If one of his pleasure-loving senses is so undisciplined that it seeks gratification anywhere and anyhow and if his mind is totally enslaved by this one sense, it will drag his intellect behind it as the wind drives a ship before it in the sea and wrecks it on a rock or runs it aground. Thus the man whose senses are completely out of his control and whose mind is totally enslaved by one of them will be ruined through gradual stages explained earlier as the consequences of attachment. If the mind is enslaved by even a single sense, one is lost.

Therefore, O Mahabahu, he, whose senses are reined in on all sides from their objects, is the man of secure understanding.[5]

The man whose senses are under his control and are kept away from their objects is a man established in *samadhi.*

When it is night for all other beings, the disciplined soul is awake; when all other beings are awake, it is night for the seeing ascetic.[6]

In conclusion, Shri Krishna gives the mark of a *sthitaprajna* in one verse. He is awake when it is night for other human beings, and when other human beings and all the creatures seem to be awake, it is night for the ascetic who sees.

This should be the ideal for the Satyagraha Ashram. Let us pray that we may see light when all around us there is darkness. If we are brave, the whole world will be brave; as in our body, so in the universe—this is how we should feel. We should thus be ready to take upon ourselves the burden of the whole world, but we can bear the burden only if we mean by it doing *tapascharya*[7] on behalf of the entire world. We shall then see light where others see nothing but darkness. Let others think that the spinning-wheel is useless, and believe that we cannot win swaraj by keeping fasts. We should tell them that we are sure we shall get it; for, as the *Gita* says, *yavanartha udapane*[8], that is, if through fasts and similar practices we can obtain the position of a liveried servant in God's Kingdom, why cannot we secure such a position in our swaraj? The world will tell us that the senses cannot be controlled. We should reply that they certainly can be. If people tell us that truth does not avail in the world, we should reply that it does. The world and the man established in *samadhi* are like the west and the east. The world's night is our day and the world's day is our night. There is, thus, non-co-operation between the two. This should be our attitude if we understand the *Gita* rightly.

This does not mean that we are superior to others; we are humble men and women, we are a mere drop while the world is the ocean. But we should have the faith that, if we succeed in crossing to the other shore, the world, too, will. Without such faith we cannot claim that the world's night is our day. If we can achieve self-realization through fasting and spinning, then self-realization necessarily implies swaraj.

Notes

1. April 6, 1919 was observed throughout India as a day of protest against the Rowlatt Bills: *vide* "Speech at Chowpatty, Bombay", 6-4-1919.
2. Published in 1909 and proscribed in March 1910 by the Government of Bombay 3.
3. A fabulous gem that fulfils all the desires of its owner.
4. II, 67.
5. II, 68.
6. II, 69.
7. Voluntary suffering as moral discipline.
8. A reference to II, 46.

[37] April 7, 1926

Yesterday, we learnt an important mark of the *sthitaprajna*. What seems light to other people is darkness to the yogi. For instance, we tell a great number of people that they should eat sparingly, but a man who has spent his days in devotion to God will immediately understand that, if he eats full meals every day, it will be a hindrance to his life of devotion. Such a yogi, therefore, will keep himself alive on very little food while other people go on feasting on delicacies. But he will not parade his self-control. Narasinh Mehta ridiculed in his song renunciation, knowledge, meditation, etc., and gave the palm to the *gopi's* love, but this sounds strange to people in the modern age.

The truth is that those whom the world knows as yogis are not really yogis, nor what the world describes as the four modes of liberation[1] or as spiritual enlightenment are such in fact. These phrases are used merely to deceive the world. The man who really lives a life of contemplation will outwardly seem a man of the world. His mind may be absorbed in God all the hours of the day, but he will move in the world like other men. He will not go about trumpeting that he lives a life of contemplation. The *gopis* in their love go on dancing, for, knowing that their love is pure, they are not afraid of the world's censure. Mira said that she paid no heed to what the world said, since she had not left her husband but only wished to discover the true meaning of devotion to one's husband. Gopichand[2] is living in a palace of gold. He is looking admiringly at his body, which is exuding the fragrance of *abir*[3] and *gulal*[4], and his face is lit up with a smile of joy. And then, it happens, tears drop from the eyes of Mainavati[5] who is watching him from the balcony above. Gopichand wonders from where the water-drops can come, seeing that there are no clouds in the sky. Mainavati explains to him that his body which he so admired will one day perish, it will be covered with wrinkles, the teeth in the mouth will loosen and come out and the eyes will see no more. What will his body avail him, she asks, if he were to die just then? She has wasted her whole life, but he has time yet to escape and save himself. Is it likely that a mother would give such advice? What the world prizes highly seemed of little worth to this mother, for she was a woman of spiritual wisdom. As the earth rotates on its axis, once every twenty-four hours we are hanging with our feet up and heads down. We can move about in this position because the earth pulls us towards itself like the ants moving on the surface of a lump of sugar.

We, the ants on the earth, do not know that the latter is round and is in constant motion. The spiritually enlightened man and the yogi know the hidden truth of these things and tell us what is unreal. What the world takes as real is unreal to them. What it describes as darkness, they will describe as light. The yogi has an inner vision which is different from the world's. The body should live as prisoner of the *atman*. It should function entirely under the latter's control. He is whom all longings subside, even as the waters subside in the ocean which, though ever being filled by them, never overflows—that man finds peace; not he who cherishes longing.

The sea, though being ever added to, remains confined within its bounds; it stands where it has always stood despite countless rivers emptying their waters into it. The man in whom evil impulses and desires subside in the same manner is a yogi. The man who is a slave of desires, whose senses are for ever being allured by their objects, such a person is not a yogi. He is a yogi who is like the sea, who is not like a rivulet or a brook which soon overflows and soon dries up.

Christian[6], too, was a yogi and a man of contemplative life. His voice sounded but one refrain. A man, whose mind is constantly absorbed in God, whether he is bathing or eating or drinking, how can he feel evil desires? Like the sea, he is ever full. Rivers and streams fall into it and come to rest, and their waters are cleansed of their dirt. If this dirt spread out in the sea-water, would the latter be as clear as it is? We actually go to a sea-coast to enjoy its fresh air. In like manner, every evil desire subsides and disappears in the sea of a yogi's mind.

The man who sheds all longing and moves without concern, free from the sense of 'I' and 'mine'—he attains peace.[7] Such peace may be experienced by a man who has given up all cravings and lives untroubled by desires. He attains to it by shedding the consciousness of "I" and "mine". He alone is a true yogi who never feels "I am doing this".

This is the state, O Partha, of the man who rests in *Brahman*; having attained to it, he is not deluded. He who abides in this state even at the hour of death passes into oneness with *Brahman*.[8]

The *brahmi* state is that in which we realize the *Brahman*.

Having attained it, we are never overpowered by the darkness of ignorance again. It has already been said that objects of sense lose all attraction for us when we have seen God. Similarly, here again Shri Krishna sums up the argument by saying that, having attained to the *brahmi* state, a man never falls again into delusion. A person who is in this state at the moment of his death attains *brahma-nirvana*[9]. This statement can mean either of two things: one, that he will attain to the *Brahman* if he is in that state at the moment of death, and, two, that he will attain eternal peace if he always lives in such a state, right up to the moment of death. If a man who has lived a wicked life till now takes to a good life from tomorrow, there is nothing he will lack. But it will not avail a man to have been good all his life if in his last days he becomes wicked. That man, then, may be said to be good who remains so till the last day of his life. That is why it is said: "Call no man good till he is dead." However good a man may have been, he may yet weaken in his old age and worry over his children and his social affairs. We may know that a man has attained *moksha* only if he died in the *brahmi* state.

The nirvana of the Buddhists is *shunyata*[10], but the nirvana of the *Gita* means peace and that is why it is described as *brahma-nirvana*.

We need not concern ourselves with this distinction. There is no reason for supposing that there is a difference between the nirvana mentioned by Lord Buddha and the nirvana of the *Gita*. Buddha's description of nirvana and this other description of nirvana refer to the same state. A number of learned men have shown that the Buddha did not teach a doctrine denying the existence of God. But all these are pointless controversies. What can we say about a state which is so different from anything known in our life that we cannot describe it even when we have attained to it? If it is agreed that our bodily existence is not a thing to be cherished, all these other controversies are unmeaning.

This is the end of Chapter II. *Sthitaprajna* means a person who has become completely free from attachments and aversions.

Notes

1. Namely, attaining *salokya* (the world of God), *samipya* (nearness to God), *sarupya* (the form of God), *sayujya* (union with God).
2. A king in Hindu mythology who by his renunciation displayed the purest love for his mother.
3. White powder.
4. Red powder.
5. Gopichand's mother.
6. In *Pilgrim's Progress*.
7. II, 71.
8. II, 72.
9. Absorption in the *Brahman*.
10. Nothingness.

[38] [Chapter III] April 8, 1926

The Chapter which we completed yesterday is known as Sankhyayoga. We saw that, after discussing the distinction between the body and the *atman*, Shri Krishna told Arjuna that he had explained the Sankhya view, that is, analysed logically the distinction between the body and the *atman*. This did not help Arjuna to know it in his own experience, but he grasped it intellectually. Arjuna's duty of fighting was explained to him, but only so far as it could be done with the help of argument. Shri Krishna then explained yoga to him, that is, the method of acting in a disinterested spirit. This led to the discussion concerning the *sthitaprajna*.

From the last verse of Chapter II, it would seem that Shri Krishna had nothing further to add. Indeed, if Arjuna had not again put a question to him, there was really nothing for him to add. The *brahmi* state includes *bhakti* too. But in view of the natural tendency in everyone to let his desires rule his reason, truth has to be repeated often so that it may be made more clear. If an unenlightened man decides for himself, he usually decides in favour of worldliness.

Therefore he has to keep on repeating to himself that he is the *atman*, for it is not a truth experienced by him at all hours of the day. A son who has no doubt in his mind at all need not tell his mother that he is her son. The repetition of Ramanama and *dwadashmantra*[1] are for people who have not had self-realization. After release from the body, the man who explains and the man who listens, the two will be one. So long as the body exists, the problems of the means [of attaining *moksha*] will remain; that is why Vyasa expanded the *Gita* this length.

There is nothing in it which is not contained in the verses which we recite at the time of our evening prayers. Vyasa has placed before readers a divine truth through the *Gita*. Whether Sankhya or yoga, sannyasa or the life of the house-holder, all these paths are essentially one. Action and inaction mean the same thing, this is the substance of the *Gita's* teaching. Since these different paths are so mixed up with one another, we should understand their essential identity if our one aim is to know God and realize the unreality of all else. The way to know Him is not to sit cross-legged, but to work in a disinterested spirit.

A man does not become a yogi because he is known to have performed a thousand *yajnas* or made huge gifts. We have to take into account whether he was free from attachment to the ego, whether he willingly turned [in Mira's words] as God pulled him with a slender thread, whether he worked accordingly, and so on. Vyasa wants to tell us that a yogi should offer up to God everything he does, whether it be good or indifferent, should look upon Him as the sole author of everything. And so he makes Arjuna ask Krishna:

If, O Janardana, thou holdest that the attitude of detachment is superior to action, then why, O Keshava, dost thou urge me to dreadful action?

Thou dost seem to confuse my understanding with perplexing speech; tell me, therefore, in no uncertain voice, that alone whereby I may attain salvation.[2]

First, Shri Krishna put forward the logical argument, and then he described the marks of the *sthitaprajna*. He also explained that yoga meant *karmasu kaushalam*[3]. Arjuna complains that Shri Krishna has confused his judgment by such contradictory advice, and requests him to tell him some one thing clearly and definitely.

I have spoken, before, O sinless one, of two attitudes in this world—the Sankhyas', that of *jnanayoga* and the yogis', that of *Karmayoga*.[4]

Notes

1. Literally, sacred formula of twelve syllables: *Om Namo Bhagavate Vasudevaya*.
2. III, I & 2.
3. Skill in action.
4. III, 3.

[39] April 9, 1926

Arjuna tells Shri Krishna: I cannot judge what is good. At moments I feel that I should fight, and then again I feel that a *sthitaprajna* should have no work to do.

Never does man enjoy freedom from action by not undertaking action, nor does he attain that freedom by mere renunciation of action.[1]

Merely by refusing to work, one can never experience the state of *naishkarmya* (freedom from experiencing results of action), or attain to *moksha*.

We shall meet this word karma again and again in the *Gita*. What can it mean? It must have, of course, a restricted meaning. But it will help us to understand the relevant verses in the *Gita* if we take the word in its broadest meaning. Karma means any action, any bodily activity or motion. In the *Gita's* definition of the word, however, karma includes even thought. Any motion, any sound, even breathing, are forms of karma. Some of them we cannot avoid performing.

Some of them we perform as a matter of necessity, some others are involuntary. The divine in us urges us on to the path of good, and the demoniac to that of evil. Even if the man is good the demoniac element in him drives him to evil courses. Another man may be wicked, but the divine element in him forces him to follow good. Thus action is impelled by nature, or is the result of compulsion or volition. How do you say, Shri Krishna asks Arjuna, that you will not work? You will not stop riding the horses of your fancies. Even sannyasis are helpless, let them say what they will. Even the decision to stop breathing is karma. Even the refraining from karma is karma. It will not, help one, therefore, to attain to the state of *naishkarmya*. Renunciation of action and the state of *naishkarmya* should come spontaneously.

For none ever remains inactive even for a moment; for all are compelled to action by the *gunas* inherent in *prakriti*.[2,3] No one can cease from karma even for a moment. To listen and not to listen, both are forms of karma. *Sattva, rajas* and *tamas,* the three forces or modes of *prakriti,* drive everyone to action, whether he will or no. A *tamasik* man is one who works in a mechanical fashion, a *rajasik* man is one who rides too many horses, who is restless and is always doing something or other, and the *sattvik* man is one who works with peace in his mind. One is always driven to work by one or another of these three modes of *prakriti* or by a combination of them.

He who curbs the organs of action but allows the mind to dwell on the sense-objects—such a one, wholly deluded, is called a hypocrite.[4]

Anyone who curbs the organs of action outwardly but dwells all the time on the objects of sense and gives free rein to his fancies, and then believes that he has attained to *naishkarmya*, such a person is sunk in ignorance and his claim is mere hypocrisy. A person who gets his hands tied up but in his mind strikes the enemy, does in reality strike, though outwardly he does not seem to do so. He does not get the pleasure of actually striking, but certainly experiences the fruit of doing so. Please do not misunderstand what I have said. It does not mean that there is no scope for effort or striving, nor that, in that case, we had better act as we feel inclined to. We are constantly thinking of doing something or other, but reflection also helps us in restraining our hands. There can be no hypocrisy in ceaselessly fighting the enemy who holds us in his grip. The point of the verse is that there should be no contradiction between thought and action. It is hypocrisy to yearn inwardly for an object and outwardly keep away from it. It is not hypocrisy if, despite one's best efforts, one does not succeed in always remaining vigilant, for the evil habit has had a long hold over us. Only, one should not merely try but also wish to remain vigilant. Hence, it is wrong for anyone who mentally dwells on objects of sense and outwardly shuns them to describe himself as a sannyasi or yogi. The psychological effects of our actions in past lives cannot be wiped out all at once. Waves of desire will continue to rise. They will drench us again and again, but one day they will leave us dry. If someone forces me to take up and hold a lamp in my hand, I can say that I did not hold it, for I was not willing to do so. If a person is forced to do anything, his action is not his. For instance, a person who is forced to let off a gun is not a murderer. On the other hand the man who supplied him the powder and planned everything is a murderer.

If the man who actually fires the shot does so of his own free will, he too is a murderer. In this way, there should be concord between thought and action. Where this is absent, it is difficult to judge to whom to attribute intention and to whom action. We kept a fast on the sixth; if, however, we dwelt in our minds the whole day on the pleasure of eating, our fast was no fast. On the other hand, a person is not a hypocrite if, though tempted to eat, he suppresses the desire every time he feels it and so keeps struggling all the time. The man who does evil things has no hope. But he who struggles against evil thoughts will tell himself that he would die rather than let himself do an evil thing; he will go on fighting against his evil thought. The *brahmachari* between whose thoughts and actions reigns perfect harmony and who is always pure in mind deserves the highest reverence.

It is the nature of the mind to be ceaselessly active, thinking of one thing or another. He who strives ceaselessly to restrain it is sure to win the battle. It is not as if he never gratified sex-urge, but he does so with discrimination. He is a true sannyasi and yogi between whose thoughts and actions there is such complete harmony that he is not even aware that he observes *brahmacharya*. He should be a man who has made himself a eunuch. If the person is a woman, she should not be conscious at all of being a woman. The man's impotence should not be the incapacity of disease; he should have voluntarily cultivated it. He should become completely free from desire, should become incapable of doing evil. Even a vigilant man may fall, but ultimately he will win complete freedom from desire. A man who remains nonviolent in action will in time become free even from the desire to strike anyone.

There is no outward difference between a fool and a wise man. The former has no pretensions. The latter wants to be taken as a fool. Outwardly, the behaviour of the two will seem alike. The man whose mind is active with intense energy will appear dull. The earth rotates with such great speed that it seems to be stationary. There is no reference here to the idea of *shunya*. Buddha's nirvana was also not *shunya*. There is only a seeming inertness.

Notes

1. III, 4.
2. Cosmic energy, as distinguished (in the Sankhya philosophy) from *Purusha,* the Cosmic Consciousness, witness of the action of *prakriti*.
3. III, 5.
4. III, 6.

[40] April 10, 1926

We saw yesterday that a man, while himself remaining in the background, may provide the means of killing and get someone else to do it, and thus become guilty of the heinous sin of murder. His guilt is even greater than that of the person who actually kills.

Yudhishthira went to Drona and Bhishma and asked them: 'What is this you have decided to do?'[1] They replied that it was their stomach which had forced them. This means that a slave or servant, being unable to oppose his master's wishes, is less guilty than the latter. The person, on the other hand, who plots a murder and gets someone else to execute the plot is far more wicked than the latter. He is a hypocrite, moreover, as the verse explains.

Proceeding, Shri Krishna explains the opposite manner of acting:

But he, O Arjuna, who keeping all the senses under control of the mind, engages the organs in *karmayoga*, without attachment—that man excels.[2]

The first point is that one should go on doing karma through the respective organs of action, and the second is that one should hold the same organs under one's control. Shri Krishna has thus divided the physical organs into two classes. The ten organs are the sentries. Five of them function as spies and the other five carry out orders.

Hands, feet, etc., belong to the latter class. If the eyes, the nose and other sentries of their class do not remain under our control, we can stop using them. We can curb them every moment. Holding them under control, we make the sentries of the other class carry out orders.

He is the best man who controls the functioning of his organs in this manner and works without attachment. A man who gets angry cannot be described as non-attached, he is, in truth, strongly attached.

Do thou thy allotted task; for action is superior to inaction; with inaction even life's normal course is not possible.[3]

One should do the appointed work, the task which has been assigned to one, for action is superior to inaction. No one can cease completely from action even for a moment. If that is so, it is better that we work of our own free will. Why need we consult anyone for doing *niyata* karma, that is, for doing work specially meant for us?

For, we cannot even keep our bodies alive without working.

This world of men suffers bondage from all action save that which is done for the sake of sacrifice; to this end, O Kaunteya, perform action without attachment.[4]

Yesterday I explained the meaning of the word karma. Similarly, we should discuss the meaning of *yajna* too. Some learned students of the Shastras believe that the *Gita* is not concerned with work like a cobbler's or like spinning, that is, with work which we do in our practical life. By karma they mean such things as ritual offering of food to the manes, and exclude spinning and weaving from its definition. But the *Gita* is very much concerned with practical life. A dharma which does not serve practical needs is no dharma, it is *adharma*[5]. Even cleaning of latrines should be done in a religious spirit. A man of such spirit will ask himself, as he does the work, why there should be so much foul smell. We should realize that we are full of evil desires. The excreta of a person who is suffering from a disease or is full of evil desires are bound to emit foul smell. Another person who does not do this work in a religious spirit but shirks his duty will remove the contents anyhow, and not clean the bucket; such a man does not do the work as a religious duty. He has no compassion in him, nor discrimination. Thus, dharma is certainly connected with practical life. We have, therefore, accepted a broad definition of karma, and will accept an equally broad definition of *yajna*. We will discuss this tomorrow.

Notes

1. They had agreed to fight on the side of the Kauravas though they knew that justice was on the side of the Pandavas.
2. III, 7.
3. III, 8.
4. III, 9.
5. The opposite of dharma.

[41] April 11, 1926

As we have the word *yajna* in our language and the practice is enjoined in our dharma, so the Bible and the holy books of the Jews too have each a corresponding word, and an idea similar to that of *yajna*. We find three things in the Koran: (1) animal sacrifices, on the Bakr-i-Id day; (2) it refers to a practice which also obtained among the Jews, a father sacrificing his son—Ibrahim does this; and (3) Ramadan, which is a form of sacrifice, that is, parting with or giving up something which is dear to us. In the same way, we see in the Bible the meaning of the term sacrifice expanding after Jesus. He told the people that they could not realize their aim by this sacrifice of animals, that for performing a sacrifice in the right sense of the term they would have to do much more than kill animals. He told them that it was not a sacrifice to destroy other lives, that one should give one's own life as sacrifice. With that idea, he sacrificed his own life for the eternal welfare of the world, for its spiritual welfare, for washing away its sins and not merely for feeding the people. Among the Hindus, too, the practice of human sacrifice was prevalent at one time. Then followed animal sacrifice. Even today, thousands of goats are sacrificed to Mother Kali. *Yajnas* are also performed for securing the fulfilment of many worldly desires. The root word in the English term "sacrifice" had a good meaning; it meant "to sanctify". In Sanskrit, *yaj* means "to worship". In the Old Testament, the word for *yajna* means "to renounce". But the underlying idea, that all actions performed for the good or service of others are forms of *yajna*, will be accepted by everyone. Maybe our motive in sacrificing an animal is that of public good, for instance, securing rainfall. The motive in this may be that of public good, but it is not a true sacrifice in which we kill other creatures. We may tell ourselves that we have made a sacrifice in paying for the goat, but the crores of other Hindus are not likely to share that belief.

In Gujarat, too, we find this practice prevails in places. A buffalo is sacrificed on the Dushera Day[1]. Our reason, however, tells us that there is no sacrifice in this, that we do not really worship God by doing this. However, the belief underlying this practice, too, is that we serve public good through it. We should, therefore, include two points in the definition of *yajna*: it is something which is done to serve others' good, but without causing suffering to any creature. We serve the good of the world by refraining from causing suffering to other creatures, because we shall refrain from doing so only if we cherish the lives of other creatures as we do our own, only if we believe that the body is transient. If we interpret correctly the word *yajna* as it is used in the *Gita*, we shall find no difficulty in understanding its teaching and living in accordance with it. We can perform a *yajna* with the mind as much as with the body. Of these two meanings of *yajna*, we should accept that which suits the context every time.

We need not go into why in the past people performed—or even at the present time do perform—animal sacrifice. We shall answer the question in one or two sentences. Man selects for his food what is available in his environment. What objection, moreover, can there be from people's point of view to anything done for public good which is not in itself regarded as sinful?

Where people believe that the rains will not come unless some person or creature is sacrificed, no hesitation is felt in performing such a sacrifice. As man's beliefs become more enlightened, the meanings, which people attach to certain words also become more enlightened. Even if Vyasa had defined the words which he used, we would ask why we should accept the meanings given by him. For instance, non-co-operation has come to mean much more than we at first intended it to mean. There is no harm in our enlarging the meaning of the word *yajna,* even if the new meaning we attach to the term was never in Vyasa's mind. We shall do no injustice to Vyasa by expanding the meaning of his words. Sons should enrich the legacy of their fathers. Why should we object if anyone regarded the spinning-wheel with greater sentiment than what we seek to create in the people about it? It is quite possible that in future people may see harm in the spinning-wheel, may come to think that no one should wear cotton clothes at all, because they do harm. They may, for instance, believe that clothes should be made from fibres extracted from banana leaves. If people should come to feel that way, anyone who still clings to the spinning-wheel would be looked upon as a fool.

A wise man, however, will mean by the spinning-wheel not an article made of wood but any type of work which provides employment to all people. That is also the case with regard to the meaning of the term *yajna*. Thus, we may, and should, attach to it a meaning not intended by Vyasa.

Together with sacrifice did the Lord of beings create, of old, mankind, declaring:

"With this may you cherish the gods and may the gods cherish you; thus cherishing one another may you attain the highest good.[2]

We should think carefully what the term god, too, means. Who are god Indra and other gods? Who are the god of water and the god of woodlands? There was an argument once over one of the verses in our morning prayers, whether it was proper to worship Saraswati conceived as a figure with hands and feet. Just as it was explained at the time that Saraswati was not a goddess living somewhere far away in the clouds, so are Indra and others not gods living in the heavens; they symbolize the forces of nature. If only we take the thirty-three crores of gods in whom we believe to stand for man, we would serve our own good and also that of the whole world, of all the creatures in it. The gods symbolize the different forms of energy, the forces which sustain the universe. Even the belief in terrible gods does not deserve to be dismissed. The power of God in all its three aspects—creative, protective and destructive—is beneficial, but we do not understand the real meaning of these three aspects because of our limited knowledge.

The *Nagapanchami* day is observed to save ourselves from harm by snakes. It is not right to observe any such day to appease snakes. And so also about ghosts and spirits. What are ghosts? They are merely creatures of our imagination. Our aim should be, instead, to worship the sustaining energy of God, to worship it in all its aspects.

Notes

1. The tenth day of *Asvina*, the month in the Hindu Calendar roughly corresponding to October.
2. III, 10 & 11.

[42] April 13, 1926

We cannot give any arbitrary meaning to the term *yajna*. We can adopt only a meaning which is consistent with the use of the word in the *Gita*. We may draw all possible conclusions from the principles of geometry, but they should be such as Euclid would not question or oppose. We do no injustice to the poet in going beyond his meaning.

Any purpose which a well serves will be served by a lake too. If water can be used for a good purpose, it can also be used for an evil purpose. We can destroy a dam and thereby render innumerable fields useless. So the meaning which we have attached to the term *yajna,* namely, any action performed with a view to public good, is not inconsistent with the use of the term in the *Gita*.

"This world suffers bondage from work unless it is work done as *yajna*"; in this verse, the word *yajna* can also be interpreted to mean Vishnu and the worshippers of Siva may take it to mean Siva. In other words, any work dedicated to God helps one to attain *moksha*.

"Along with *yajna* the Lord created men." Which type of *yajna* is meant here? Does the term have any special meaning?

I think it has. The reference here is not to mental or intellectual work.

Brahma[1] did not ask human beings to multiply and prosper merely by working with their minds; what He meant was that they should do so through bodily *yajna*, by working with the body. Scriptures of other religions enjoin the same thing. The Bible says: "With the sweat of thy brow thou shalt earn thy bread."[2] Thus bodily labour is our lot in life; it is best, then, to do it in the spirit of service and dedicate it to Shri Krishna. Anyone who works in that spirit all his life becomes free from evil and is delivered from all bonds. Such a person is like a soldier in the King's army, who is content to carry out orders. He is as worthy as the General. Both have equal value in God's eyes, for He looks only to the attitude. Arjuna's arrows availed him not when Krishna was no longer by his side, and he was robbed by a Kaba[3]. The verse, commencing with *sahayajna* then, talks of bodily *yajna*, of a kind, moreover, through which gods and men would serve each other's needs. By gods we may understand all living beings or God's sustaining energy. Gods are the invisible forces. So long as a person has someone in sight for whom he works, he is not engaged in service; real service consists in working for those whom one does not know personally. The thirty-three crores of gods belong to the world of imagination. Children cannot even conceive this number. We cannot take in with our eyes so many beings assembled at one place, nor count them. We cannot see these gods, as we see our children, and yet we cultivate a living relationship with them. By and by, the sphere of our service will enlarge itself to embrace the whole world. We have thus left aside the word gods and interpreted the verse to mean that we should serve the humblest human beings, even those whom we never see, with respect and honour and looking upon them as gods and not as our servants; we should, in other words, serve the whole world.

This verse tells us that we should undertake bodily labour to do service. Man simply cannot live without such work. If he had not violated this law, he would not suffer as much as he does, the rich would not have become masters of immeasurable stores of wealth and the millions would not be suffering in poverty. God is a great economist. He is omnipotent. We cannot refrain completely from storing things for future use. But God never stores, for he can destroy and create the universe with a mere thought. He wants us, therefore, to provide only for each day. If we want anything the next day, we must labour for it. He has warned that we are doomed if we do not labour, if we do not bend the body and work with it. He has commanded that we should willingly endure every kind of suffering. If we honour this law in our life, there would be no hunger and no sin or immorality in this world. Evil desires will never disturb a man who labours all the twenty-four hours for the good of the world (I say twenty-four hours because one keeps working even in sleep.). If the labourers in the world were filled with evil desires as we are, the world could not last.

The rich seek all kinds of luxuries. If the workers, too, did that, where would the world be? In the West, nowadays the idea has come to prevail that men and women are born to gratify all their desires.

Adharma is being propagated. If people worked with the shovel or pick-axe, would they be disturbed with evil desires? We should submit ourselves, therefore, to this restraining law. If we do our bodily *yajna* properly, all will be well with us, we shall advance the good of our *atman* and of the world, our mind and body will be ruled by our *atman* and we shall be filled with serene peace. It can be said that such a person, even though acting, does nothing.

I cannot understand the idea that one can perform a *yajna* by lighting a few sticks. It does not do to say that doing so purifies the air. There are many other ways of purifying the air. Why should we at all pollute the air? It is always pure. It is we who pollute it. But this is not the aim behind a *yajna*. When the Aryans first came to this country, they tried to civilize the non-Aryan races. Maybe the idea of *yajna* was originally conceived for the uplift of the latter. There were big forests in those days, and it may have been regarded as everyone's duty to help in clearing these forests, for it was a social necessity. And because this work was regarded as a duty, it came to be looked upon as a means of attaining *moksha*. Innumerable ceremonies were devised, all of which required the lighting of fire. If these *rishis*[4] had lived in the desert of Sahara, they would have conceived of *yajna* as refraining from cutting a single twig, as planting of trees or drawing a certain quantity of water. In burning wood in this age, we misuse the capital of our forefathers; or we show ourselves witless pedants by understanding the thing in a literal sense. If we think of the matter now, we shall see that burning sticks is no longer a form of bodily *yajna*. If we would undertake any such *yajna* in this age and in this country, it is spinning, the reason being the same as in the instance I cited of the forests. At that time, the very thought of cutting trees for wood in a forest might have shaken a man with fear; but the man who had faith would have started the work straightway, for the person who had asked him to do it was inspired with absolute conviction. Such a man of faith would simply go on cutting trees (Recall the instance of Stevenson and the ditch near Manchester. He asked people to go on and on filling it with earth.) If the order for cutting down trees had not gone out, snakes and poisonous air would have remained of course. Someone has said that a true idea is born in the mind of one person who acts upon it, and thus, it starts on its career. If you employ the right means, the end is certain to follow. All that is necessary is to make a start. A man of faith will go ahead with his work, undeterred by difficulties. He knows no such thing as failure. Let the world believe in failure, he would say, I do not know what it is. This is what is meant by disinterested work. Such a person hopes for nothing, and works in patience; he resorts to no scheming and is never in too much hurry for the result.

Notes

1. The Creator
2. Gandhiji said this in English.
3. A highway robber.
4. Literally, seers.

[43] April 14, 1926

We discussed yesterday the meaning of the term *yajna*. Using one's limbs, labouring, working for others' good, these ideas follow from this one verse. What is meant by saying that mankind was created along with *yajna*? As we cannot escape the cycle of birth, old age and death, so also bodily labour is our lot in life from which there is no escape. But what actually happens is that man becomes selfcentred and follows his own wishes in every matter, or works in order that he may be able to indulge in pleasures. But the world cannot go on thus, and if the world cannot go on, the individual who behaves in this manner also cannot live. Man is born a helpless creature. The child needs someone—a mother-god or father-god—to look after it.

Man is born dependent, and dies in dependence. Freedom is a state of the mind. A man can describe himself as *swadhin*[1] only to the extent that he feels so, for he can say that he submits himself to a law of his own free will. But there are laws disregard of which would make government impossible; a man cannot, however, commit a crime and escape its consequences. Not only that, the relations of the person committing a crime also suffer with him. A crime ultimately proves as harmful to its author as the swallowing of raw mercury. Man is, thus, dependent on others in all things. He is his own master in only a few matters. It is, therefore, best for him to do everything in the spirit of *yajna*. *Yajna* was created simultaneously with us, so that we may serve the gods and the latter may serve us. If we let ourselves be ruled by them, they, too, will be ruled by us. The right *yajna* for this age is the *yajna* of spinning. We should, however, think of *yajna* only in its primary meaning which we have discussed. All other forms of *yajna* follow from that. Our most important activity is eating and drinking.

Even our body is born as a slave. If we learn to keep it alive exclusively for the good of the *atman*, we should attain *moksha*. The body is meant to be spent for the good of the *atman* and of the world. Different men act in different ways, and if we believe in what the law terms "a legal fiction", that the king does no wrong, then the king also becomes good. If today the Princes are wicked, so are their subjects. In these other matters too, we keep up some legal fictions.

We entertain such a fiction about the spinning-wheel, too, that through it we establish a bond with the world, having abandoned the old fiction that we establish such a bond by burning sticks and pouring ghee into the fire.

It is not recently that I have come to attach this meaning to *yajna*; I have understood it in that sense ever since I first read the *Gita*. What I read about the Russian writer Bondoref's [views on] "bread labour"[2] only confirmed my idea, but the idea was with me from the beginning and has grown stronger with years. The Russian writer has stated one side of the truth. We understand the other side too. We now understand the idea of bread labour better, for by *yajna* we do not mean labour as a means of livelihood. Thanks to the associations which the term calls up, we do not restrict *yajna* to mean this and no more. Labour in this context means bodily labour. He alone should eat who has laboured for twelve hours. Anyone who sincerely wants to observe *brahmacharya*, to preserve purity and to be free from evil desires, must engage himself in bodily labour. People who do physical work are not subject to the sway of such desires as much as we are. Maybe they are dull in mind; but it is better to be dull in mind than to be a prey to evil desires. The world would go on even if there were no intelligent men and women in it, but it would be nowhere if all people refused to do physical work. We have exercised our intelligence in acknowledging the law of bodily labour. The one universal form of such labour is agriculture and it should, therefore, be looked upon as *yajna*. "Cherished with sacrifice, the gods will bestow on you the desired boons." He who enjoys their gifts without rendering aught unto them is verily a thief.[3]

The gods, gratified by *yajna*, that is, by your work for the service of others and your bodily labour, will grant you the means to gratify your desires; that is, the gods in the form of society will grant them to you. Anyone who receives what they give but offers nothing to others is a thief. He is a thief who does not do bodily labour for society.

The righteous men who eat the residue of the sacrifice are freed from all sin, but the wicked who cook for themselves eat sin.[4] Those holy persons who eat only what is left behind after the *yajna* is over become free from all sins. They who first offer to society, to Shri Krishna, what they get to eat, live free from sin. But those who cook food only for themselves, who work only for selfish ends, take in nothing but sin when they eat. That is why one should regularly and daily perform *yajna*, make a sacrifice, of which body labour is the foundation. The greatest *yajna* consists in observing the very first commandment of God, the commandment with which every human being is sent into this world.

From food springs all life, from rain is born food; from sacrifice comes rain and sacrifice is the result of action.[5] If people did nothing, there would be no rains, which means that there would be no rains if people did not perform *yajna*. Work which is necessary must be done. But people are simply not ready to exert themselves and plant trees. Rains are plentiful in forests. But there they are of no benefit to human beings; in fact they do terrible harm. They do not do that after human beings start working in those forests.

Cherapunji has the heaviest rainfall in the world, but what

good does all that rain do? (Of course, the rainfall there serves as a standard of comparison for rainfall in other parts of the world, but that is a different matter.)

In this verse, the *Bhagavad Gita* enunciates the principle explained by scientists that there can be no rain in regions barren of vegetation.

Notes

1. Dependent on oneself.
2. Gandhiji uses the English expression.
3. III, 12.
4. III, 13.
5. III, 14.

[44] April 15, 1926

Know that action springs from *Brahman* and *Brahman* from the Imperishable; hence the all-pervading *Brahman* is ever firm-founded on sacrifice.[1]

This verse is a little difficult to understand. "You should know," Krishna says to Arjuna, "that karma springs from *Brahman*, and the latter from *yajna*." In an annotated *Gita* found in Bihar, karma is explained as *Brahman*, and a little below, the latter is explained as the source of the universe, as that which fills the entire universe, and from which arise Brahma, Vishnu and Siva, or, in other words, as that which we describe as dwelling in the hearts of all creatures, that which is the common element of belief among all faiths and sects.

It is true that *Brahman* springs from *yajna*. Wherever we find anyone filled with the spirit of renunciation, anyone whose *atman* abides in serene content within itself, who suffers when others suffer and who practises the supreme *yajna* of maintaining a sameness of attitude towards all, there we may be sure that *Brahman* is present. But there is one thing, whether about this *yajna* or any other, namely, that it should not be so performed as to cost the body nothing. Dharma is not to be followed with tender regard for one's body. That is dharma in following which one suffers in the body to the limit of one's endurance. There is no *yajna* for him who is not ready to mortify his body. What right does a person have who undertakes bodily labour for the sake of the world—if there are thirty-three crores in India, there must be billions in the whole world, and if to these we add the insects and other forms of life, then each of us is but one hair on the body as compared with the total number of living creatures in the world—what right does such a person have to feel that he works for the world? If all my hairs were to be plucked off, I would die, but one hair lost means nothing. If we look round in the world, we shall see that the whole of it is within us. If we forget which is the hair and which the world, we shall come to feel one with the world. We shall then spend this body in the service of the world all the hours of the day.

All this talk about knowledge is because of the body; otherwise, for an unembodied one, how can there be any question of knowledge? The highest knowledge of all in the world is knowledge of the self. Moreover, the idea of a human being having no body exists only in our imagination. Mortification of the body, therefore, is the only means of self-realization and the only *yajna* for everyone in this world. We are all labourers. If the rich would look upon themselves as labourers as much as the people who work with their bodies are labourers, the latter would get all that they want. They would then feel quite satisfied with their condition and devote themselves wholeheartedly to their work. If the working men, however, deliberately claim that they are the equals of their masters, they are sure to come to grief. If we follow the methods of the British in running our government when we have swaraj, we would be behaving as masters.

But we wish to give up the ways of masters and turn ourselves into workers. If, while working as labourers, we learn to be detached and make ourselves ciphers, we would come out of the darkness of night. This is the idea in the verse containing the phrase eternally founded in yajna.

But, then, who is the Brahma mentioned in the first verse of this group? Who, again, are Vishnu and Siva? I do not look upon them as distinct Beings. We may take them to represent aspects of God or His powers. They are represented in the *puranas* as being different from other gods. All that is partly right and partly wrong. They imagined all these things because they wanted to teach people dharma somehow. In truth, there is no such Being as Brahma or Siva. The only reality is the neuter *Brahman*. But as God is conceived of as doing nothing, it was imagined that this universe comes into existence out of Brahma. If I destroy a man's belief in a Brahma with four faces, in what way do I enlighten him? How will that profit me? If such a person asks me whether I share his belief, I will tell him that I do not.

But others who believe in a personal God should be free to do so. And so Brahma means the active energy of God. In fact in Tilak Maharaj's *Gita*, Brahma is explained as *prakriti*; I will say, then, that *prakriti* is Brahma. Whatever our belief, what we have to understand from all this is that in every *yajna* God's presence may be felt, and that, where there is no *yajna* of body labour, God, too, is absent, though, of course, we believe that God is present everywhere. Human beings go on working with their bodies and that keeps the cycle going. I have no doubt at all that the Imperishable here means God.

He who does not follow the wheel thus set in motion here below, he, living in sin, sating his senses, lives, O Partha, in vain.[2]

Such a person's life is a burden on others. The earth rotates ceaselessly all the twenty-four hours of the day, and anyone who merely rests on it doing nothing lives to no purpose. One who is always engaged in *yajna* is not subject to the binding effects of karma. But he who, disinclined to work, pleads *aham Brahmasmi*[3] in justification of his idleness, is stated by the *Gita* to be living in sin.

This is what Narasinha Mehta meant when he wrote that those who renounce the world will not win deliverance and those who enjoy life will. Here, "those who enjoy life" means all the people in the world who labour with their bodies and "those who renounce the world" means the incorrigible idlers.

I have explained the wheel in this verse to mean the spinningwheel. I look upon it as the means of supreme *yajna* in this age. He who plies it will have lived worthily, will have won the battle of life.

Notes

1. III, 15.
2. III, 16.
3. I am *Brahman*; one of the four "great utterances" in the Upanishads.

[45] April 16, 1926

Yajna means any activity for the good of others.[1] A man works for the good of others when he spends his body in their service. If we look upon our body as the property of the world and use it so, we would retain our control over it but always keep it clean, would not let it be eaten up by white ants. All this, however, should be done in a spirit of dedication to God. It would give us profound happiness if in using it we act as its trustees or guardians. A watchman who serves as one who held his body as a trust may assure us that he would be constantly seen coming to our house, and that this fact by itself was enough to keep off thieves, and if we have trust in such effect of his name we might let this Rama[2], this watchman, go, grant him *moksha*.

Similarly, [we should have faith that] any physical labour undertaken in the spirit of service will produce rain. That is a poet's explanation[3] and it is correct. The word *yajna* comes from the root *yaj*, which means "to worship", and we please God by worshipping Him through physical labour. What should we do if we want rain over a desert? We should plant trees there. We should plant trees in any region over which we want rain, and cut them down in those regions where it rains in excess.

The original intention behind the idea of *yajna* was that people should do physical work. We forgot the root and came to concern ourselves with branches and leaves, believing that by pouring oblations into fire we perform a *yajna*. In the old days, it was necessary to cut down trees and burn up the wood in order to clear the land. What was the idea in the pupils approaching their teachers wood in hand? Cutting down trees and burning wood had become a form of *yajna*. At the present time, spinning has become a *yajna*. If water was scarce and we had to fetch it from a distance of two miles, fetching water would be a *yajna*.

Laborare est orare—Work is worship. We can connect this dictum with the idea in this verse.

Notes

1. A member of the audience had asked Gandhiji how *yajna* could produce rain.
2. A general name for servant, current among Gujaratis in Bombay.
3. A child in the audience had said that their service through physical labour would please God.

[46] April 17, 1926

If we use our intellect for serving others, would that also not be a form of *yajna*? This verse does not say that all forms of *yajna* produce rain. It only says that without *yajna* there can be no rain.

That does not mean that all forms of *yajna* can produce rain, just as it is not true that all edible things can support life.

It may be asked what connection there can be between the facts of physical life and spiritual matters? The laws which hold in the spiritual world hold also in the phenomenal world. All the rules which concern the physical body have the welfare of the *atman* as their aim.

That should be our primary aim in all our physical activities. We must turn away from everything which does not help us to attain selfrealization.

One thing, of course, is true. Just as bodily labour undertaken with a view to service will produce rain, so the employment of our intellect in the service of others will promote the welfare of the world.

How do we explain the fact that sometimes *yajna* fails to produce rain? An effect follows a chain of causes, all of which are not visible to us. Besides *yajna*, many other favourable circumstances have to be present. We have no ground for believing that a given action must always produce a given effect. There may have been a thousand other factors which had contributed to the appearance of that effect on a previous occasion.

No event or action is without its effect. Was the earthquake in Japan at the end of the last war the result of Divine wrath? The explanation given by. . .[1] was that when man becomes cruel, nature too may become so. There is, however, no question of cruelty on the part of nature. How can we regard anything which is pure justice as cruelty? Man does everything through pride. Not so God. To attribute cruelty to Him is to measure Him with a yardstick which we apply to human beings. This is the point of view which produced philosophical atheism. How can we turn God into a human being?

From another point of view, He certainly acts, for he bestows life and consciousness. It is He who is ever active and does everything, hears without ears and sees without eyes. It is not correct to believe that an earthquake may be punishment for sin. Why should we believe, either, that an earthquake is a punishment? If a nation is sunk in sin and God wants to save it, He might send an earthquake with that aim. If I wish to commit an immoral act, a most heinous one, and if God sends a snake to bite me in order to prevent me from doing what I intend, would that be His wrath? He does that in order to save me. Take the story of Nala and Karkotak. Karkotak told Nala that if he did not transform him into an ugly figure, he, Nala, would perish with the advent of *Kaliyuga*. Similarly, we should not believe that possession of a kingdom is necessarily the reward of holy merit earned by our goodness. God's ways are inscrutable. We should be afraid of answering all such questions. We may answer simply that we do not know. Of course, we can know God's laws, we have a right to ask what they are. But a wise man restrains his curiosity and tries to know only as much as is necessary for attaining self-realization. Even in that sphere, there ought to be a limit somewhere. Even scientists have not been able to discover how the soul comes into being. I do not find it impossible to imagine that one day man will be able to prevent earthquakes, just as he is able to change the courses of rivers. But the power to bring about such changes is a trival matter. The laws of physical nature pale into insignificance when compared with those of the *atman*, for the former concern only the world of name and form.

It is wise not to have too much curiosity regarding them. We may know what is necessary for us in order to offer praise to God, and, having acquired enough for that purpose, we should have no more curiosity in such matters.

Notes

1. The name is omitted in the source.

[47] April 18, 1926

But the man who revels in *atman*, who is content in *atman* and who is satisfied only with *atman*, for him no action exists.[1] He has no interest whatever in anything done, nor in anything not done, nor has he need to rely on anything for personal ends.[2]

There is nothing for such a person to do; not that he does nothing, but it makes no difference to him whether he does or does not do it. He is equally unconcerned in either case. He has no end to pursue through other beings.

It may seem to us that both the verses say the same thing. If we do not think carefully, we shall probably feel that they contradict the verses which precede them. It was said in one of them that anyone who refused to work the rotating wheel was a sinful and indolent man.

Here, on the other hand, it is said with reference to the man living contented in the *atman* that there is noting for him to do. It may seem, but it is not, a paradox to say that one who works in the spirit of service will live contented in his self and there will be nothing which he wants to do. If we place an ant on a ball and keep the latter rotating, there will be nothing for the ant to do but to rest where it is, content with itself. It will tell itself that the ball was rotating, and itself with it, and that was enough. If, now, an ant-hill was provided inside the ball and it was necessary for the ant to move and reach it, it would say that it would be moving inside a rotating ball and have to exercise no choice in doing so. What duty can a prisoner have? He merely carries out orders. The man who lives in the self makes himself the slave of the self. He carries out the orders of the self, and, therefore, has his happiness in the self and lives contented in it. (If the prisoner I referred to just now was a satyagrahi, he would say that he would go on listening carefully to this master, the self, and so win it over.) If he is all the time absorbed in listening to the voice of the self and acts so as to conform to the turning wheel, what would be there for him to do? Tolstoy states somewhere this same thing, that man in his foolishness boasts that he will do this and he will do that, that he will relieve the suffering of people in distress and so on. But it will be enough, says Tolstoy, if this person comes down from off the backs of the people he is sitting on. The people on whose backs he is riding, they have nothing to do. We are riding on the backs of the poor. There is nothing we need do, except get off their backs—if, that is, we follow only the voice of the self inside. There is nothing for us to do because we are not even aware of doing anything when we do it spontaneously.

Thus, the man who refused to do *yajna* was described earlier as *indriyarma*,[3] as an incorrigible idler, and another who is ceaselessly employed in work is described as one who is content in the self. He works so much, and that spontaneously, that there is nothing for him to do.

I understand better than Panditji himself the point of the question[4] which he put. How is it that the *Gita* talks about rain? In a discussion about spiritual matters, everything must be about the *atman*. This is probably what he has in mind. The *Gita* leads the reader on to worms and insects, to birds and animals, and so on finally to rain, and tells him that, if people do enough physical work, they will get as much rain as they need. We can infer some such general principle from its teaching.

Can rain have any connection at all with whether we lead sinful or virtuous lives? It may have, but we do not know how. If we understand a part of the whole, then we shall understand the whole. We know something about the world of invisible things if we understand the visible world. For instance, if we make it a practice to walk long distances, the *atman* within us too will be governed by the rhythm. If, thus, we understand how we should act in one matter, we shall also know how to act in other matters. For this purpose, too, there is a rule we can follow, and that is that we should discover a principle or a law which has no exception. For instance, water is water only if it contains one part oxygen and two parts hydrogen. This law has no exception, in the same way that a right angle must have ninety degrees, neither more nor less. If, therefore, we know what the "wheel thus set in motion"[5] is, in accordance with the rule explained above that a principle should have no exception, we shall experience no difficulty. Shri Krishna has explained here a law of physical nature first and then, through it, a spiritual law.

Notes

1. III, 17 & 18.
2. III, 17 & 18.
3. III, 16.
4. How could *yajna* produce rain?
5. *Vide* translation of III, 16.

[48] April 20, 1926

Therefore, do thou ever perform without attachment the work that thou must do; for performing action without attachment man attains the Supreme.[1]

The verses here have different meanings, but it is not that one verse applies to the enlightened man and the other to the man yet striving for enlightenment. One and the same verse can be understood to apply to both, in the same way that the *Gita* as a whole can be interpreted to refer to both the types of war, the outer and the inner.

This verse, therefore, means that we may say of a person whose attachment to the ego has disappeared that there is no karma for him, that he may do something and yet do nothing.

For through action alone Janaka and others achieved perfection; even with a view to the guidance of mankind thou must act.[2]

When Janaka was informed that his city was burning, he merely said: what if it is burning? The man who is directing the operations of a fire brigade can go on giving directions only if he keeps himself where he is. Can he leave his place of duty if he is told that his town or his house is on fire? He has completely given up thinking about himself. The person who follows the maxim, "Honesty is the best policy", exchanges a diamond for a cowrie. If the man who follows truth does so with the hope that he will thereby succeed better in his business, his truthfulness will be a cause of bondage for him, but it will be the cause of his deliverance if he follows it for the sake of *moksha*. Anyone who acts in this manner is a yogi, for yoga means skill or wisdom in action. He who does all these things with a selfish motive is a mere stone; he who does them for the highest end is like Jada Bharata[3], though, in the end, he does attain illumination. The line "Live as you like"[4] applies to him. For that, however, the person should go on working ceaselessly. "He intends nothing to serve other ends".[5] This can be said only of one who has cleansed himself completely of the ego.

Whatever the best man does is also done by other men; what example he sets, the world follows.[6] People will adopt the standards which such a person sets. They will always observe what the eminent do. To what extent does Gandhi follow truth in life? Even the thoughts in which a great man indulges will produce an effect. His is a lame truthfulness who speaks truth as a matter of policy, but he who is truthful in his thoughts will act aright though he be dumb. Every thought of such a person is bound to come true. He is the ideal man whose actions, speech and thought are in harmony with one another. Everyone will follow him. This is the reason why I have placed the spinning-wheel before people; if there are any who devote themselves to it whole-heartedly, all will follow them. If those who worship an image of clay can realize God, why not a person who spins in this spirit?

Notes

1. III, 19.
2. III, 20.
3. His story is told in the *Bhagavat*. An illuminated soul from his birth, outwardly he lived as an imbecile, indifferent to all slights.
4. The first line of a verse from Akha, a 17th-century Gujarati poet, whom Gandhiji often quotes.
5. A line from Rajchandra, who had exercised a profound influence on Gandhiji's thinking in his early years.
6. III, 21.

[49] April 21, 1926

Today is Ramanavami Day[1]. On this day we have a reading from the *Ramayana* for two hours and, in the morning, there is a discourse on the incarnation of Rama. People fast, or take only one meal or eat only fruit. We shall put into practice what we have learnt from the *Gita* by celebrating the Ramanavami today in this manner. I am faced with a conflict of duties. Though I am in the Ashram, I may not be able to join in the celebration. There is another duty I have to discharge.

Pandit Motilal has written to me and asked me to send for a certain person and discuss some matters with him. I shall, therefore, be in the Ashram but engaged in discussions with him; when the *Ramayana* is being read, I shall be busy looking after the preparations for his lunch. All this is wrong. If I had become totally absorbed with all these activities in the Ashram and made it a rule to join in every celebration as I unfailingly attend prayers at four in the morning, I would have told Motilalji that today being Ramanavami I would be able to free myself only for half the day. But I do not yet have such firmness of mind, and therefore, cannot act in that manner. It would not seem natural in me to do so. But I should let the Ashram advance in that direction. So long as we have not become truly civilized, we are half animal and half human. If we could be complete men, our lives would be devoted wholly to the pursuit of goodness. I often feel that, as your leader, I should set an example in every matter. But I cannot do so unless there is complete harmony between my thought, speech and action. You should, of course, go on with the usual programme.

Keep a fast and have a reading from the *Ramayana*. Please bear with my deficiency, and see that you do not follow this weakness of mine after I am dead. My inability today to remain firm is not part of my normal nature. But it is my duty, I owe it to you, to present myself to you as I am.

I shall take no time now, speaking on Rama's life; I shall speak about it when readings from the *Ramayana* begin soon after the rest period is over.

Just now I shall only say that we should make it our aim to spread among the people a realization of the holy power of Ramanama[2].

Which is the Rama of the *Ramadhun*[3] that follows the *bhajan*[4]? Is he the Rama of Tulsidas or Valmiki, or the Rama whose birthanniversary falls today? Are these Ramas different from one another, or are they the same Rama? We shall understand all this if we reflect carefully over the matter. I shall have to leave some of these points. I can only follow my own sentiment in this matter. Let every-one dwell today on the thought that Ramanama will save us. I still feel troubled in my mind sometimes. When I worry over my work, like other people, I start repeating Ramanama. I sometimes keep thinking about the *Gita* and the meaning of particular verses when I retire for the day; I start repeating Ramanama, then fall asleep, for I know that it is my duty at that time to sleep. If we wish to fill the whole world with the power of Ramanama, it is not by constantly repeating the sounds *ra* and *ma* that we can succeed; we must ceaselessly think on God.

If the mind is disturbed by all kinds of evil thoughts or if we get angry, we should start repeating Ramanama. If our aim is to use Ramanama to deceive the country so that it may follow us, it is a very wicked thought. For us Ramanama is a boat for crossing to the other shore. We should, therefore, put it in the proper place, enveloped with sweet fragrance. I was once presented with a copy of the Koran. Haji Habib told me that it could be kept with proper care only at his place, and nowhere else, for they would put it above other books and touch it with their hands only after washing them properly. This, he said, I might not do. In this way man envelops in fragrance the thing which is dear to his heart. God will certainly be displeased with the man who keeps the Koran in the holiest place but his mind in an unholy place.

We should thus give a wide meaning to Ramanama. We should extract the utmost benefit from anything to which our heart is drawn.

Notes

1. The birth-anniversary of Rama on the ninth day of the bright half of *Chaitra,* a month corresponding to April-May.
2. Repeating the name Rama as a sacred formula.
3. A song for group singing, with frequent repetition of the name 'Rama'.
4. Devotional song.

[50] April 22, 1926

Whatever the best man does is also done by other men; what example he sets, the world follows.[1]

We should learn from this verse that if young people follow the bad example of their elders, it is the elders who should be blamed. For me, O Partha, there is naught to do in the three worlds, nothing worth gaining that I have not gained; yet I am ever in action.[2]

For whom should one cook, for one already full or for one fasting? For others, of course. To Shri Krishna, the whole world is a guest, and he loves all the creatures in it (and he must, for the world is his creation!). People look upon me as Purushottam, says Krishna, so I must observe proper measure in everything, otherwise the universe would perish.

Indeed, for were I not, unslumbering ever to remain in action, O Partha, men would follow my example in every way.[3]

I have to be busy every moment to see that the world goes on, for I am its ruler, I am the master of the ceremonies. Since I make the world dance as I will, I am also called Natavar[4]. This ruler of the world cannot afford to sleep by day or by night, nor can he rest from work.

If I were not to perform my task, these worlds would be ruined; I should be the cause of chaos and of the end of all mankind.[5]

I must, says Krishna, keep the fire burning the whole day, otherwise there would be confusion in the social order, and, I would be responsible for the destruction of society. We work so that we may please God, and if we give up doing that the people will observe no discipline, will refuse to work and feel completely lost.

Just as, with attachment, the unenlightened perform all actions, O Bharata, even so, but unattached, should the enlightened man act, with a desire for the welfare of humanity.[6]

One must work just as ignorant people do, except that they work with attachment. We, too, must take up a pick-axe and work like them. A wise man should be as industrious and work as hard as others; only, he should work for the good of the world, disinterestedly and without attachment. (If you spin for the poor without attachment to your work, you will serve your own good and theirs). If you work in this spirit, you are a man of spiritual knowledge and, though working, are doing nothing. Does a person who has kept the *ekadashi*[7] fast commit a sin by attending to cooking? He or she cooks, in a disinterested spirit, for children and guests.

Notes

1. III, 21.
2. III, 22.
3. III, 23.
4. The Supreme Player.
5. III, 24.
6. III, 25.
7. The eleventh day in either half of the lunar month.

[51] April 23, 1926

The enlightened may not confuse the mind of the unenlightened, who are attached to action; rather must he perform all actions unattached, and thus encourage them to do likewise.[1]

A wise man should not confuse the judgment of ignorant people who are attached to the work which they do, should not, for instance, ask them to go without a thing because we can do so. Shri Krishna has said a little earlier that if he did not work for the people, there would be confusion of *varnas* in society. He says the same thing in this verse in different words. If Arjuna took any unexpected step, people would not understand his intention and might do something which he had never wanted them to do. He had asked those hundreds of thousands of men to assemble there ready for battle. How could he, now, cause confusion in their minds? He should, therefore, go on doing his duty in the spirit of yoga, unattached to the fruits of his work, and inspire others to work likewise.

All action is entirely done by *gunas* of *prakriti*. Man, deluded by the sense of 'I', thinks 'I am the doer'.[2]

The man who is sunk in ignorance believes in his pride that his actions are his, whereas they are prompted by his nature, by *sattva, rajas* and *tamas*. (Anyone who says that he bats his eyelids is either a fool or suffering from a disease of the eye. He does not wink his eyes really, he harms them.) But he who acts as if he were a mere witness of his actions will win admiration for everything he does. The work done by a person without much ability but also without attachment to his ego will produce better results than that done by another who is attached to his ego. Take the example of a state ruled by a king and his minister. The latter works within the framework of the administrative setup. In just the same way, we are pilgrims in this world and obey the laws of the world. If we lay claim to what we are prompted by our nature to do, we sow confusion in the minds of the ignorant.

We should realize that we are no more than servants bound to carry out another's orders, and should voluntarily act as if we were slaves.

Mira described herself as being a slender thread, because she submitted to her nature. She used the phrase "slender thread" because she had submitted herself to God's will so completely that there was no question of her resisting. He who eats simply to give the body its hire will not think of pleasing his palate. Anyone who lives in accordance with this law will forget his ego completely, surrender to Krishna everything he does.

Notes

1. III, 26.
2. III, 27.

[52] April 24, 1926

The verse which we shall discuss today presents a problem, for its meaning has been completely perverted. It is interpreted without any reference to the context. There was a libertine in

Rajkot. He used this verse to justify his dissolute life. He was a student of the shastras and could cite appropriate Sanskrit verses, on occasion, and so enjoyed a good status in society. He used to say that nature followed its own urges and that, therefore, he was not to blame, that he was untouched by either sin or virtue.

But he, O Mahabahu, who understands the truth of the various *gunas* and their various activities, knows that it is the *gunas* that operate on the *gunas*; he does not claim to be the doer.[1]

He who classifies *gunas* and karma into their sub-divisions, divides them into their different types and then analyses each, and so arrives at the truth about them will know that everything is the result *gunas* acting upon one another and will not get involved in their activities through attachment to them. The impostor I mentioned used to say that *prakriti* was God's *maya*[2], and he was not responsible for her actions. If, however, we understand the meaning which the term *prakriti* bears in the preceding verse, we shall see that there was nothing we need do of our own choice. Only that person who has ceased to be attached to any work can say, like King Janaka, that he is not responsible for the actions of his *prakriti*. But the man who is full of ignorant attachment and thinks little cannot take cover behind this verse. The point of this verse is, in the extremely difficult business of running this world, in the running of this intricate machine (the very thought of which is sufficient to make one's head spin), what is there that I can do? What strength have I? I dare not touch a single part of it. Anyone who considers carefully how this world is kept going will see that the different *gunas* are ceaselessly active and doing their work. Let us take the small example of the spinning-wheel. Suppose for a moment that the spindle became conceited. Its part in the working of the wheel is quite small. It has no motion of its own, and if it believed itself or the string to be the source of the motion, it would commit a grievous error. If it decides to become bent, it would produce a discordant note while rotating. It might feel that, instead of rotating monotonously, it was now moving in a novel manner, but it would soon lose its place. When dying, it might perhaps realize that it had made a terrible mistake, that its pride had cost it its very life. Let us suppose now that the spindle has no such pride. It will then think that its motion was not its own, that it contributed nothing to the spinning, the string did its work and the wheel did its. It might then say that the *gunas* operate on the *gunas* and that it was of no interest to itself how they worked. I must work, the spindle would tell itself, as a mere slave, otherwise I and my relations would be ruined. It would then feel no pride and would no longer be carried away by foolish notions. We could say of such a spindle that it had learnt wisdom. The same argument applies to human beings. No one can go on indulging himself and then argue that his conduct was the result of the *gunas* doing their work according to their nature. We would come to grief if we made wrong comparisons. If, pointing to the example of an animal, we, too, act as it does, we would become animals. A man, on the contrary, must bear in mind that he is a human being, and that he resembles animals up to a point and no more; that is, he resembles them in respect of the physical needs of sleeping, eating, breeding, etc.

The man who decides that he need not eat and sleep as animals do, that he need not, like a dog fight for a piece of bread, such a person will reflect deeply and, having discovered the truth, always live as a mere witness. The animal instincts will not have completely disappeared, but he will realize, if he has understood the law which rules human life, that he must not be a slave to sleep, food and sex, that, in other words, the laws of animal life do not apply to him. As soon as he has understood the laws of *prakriti*, he will see that they are the basis of the laws governing human life. In regard to the machine of his body his only right, he now sees, is to maintain a disinterested attitude towards it. He will not, then, touch anything unclean with his hand or see it with his eyes. Such a person will become free from bondage to the body and be able to say that in all his actions it is the *gunas* which act according to their nature, that the ears do their work of hearing, the eyes of seeing, and so on. He will act like the spindle in our example as if he were inert matter with no will of his own. His body will function mechanically. It will then indulge in immorality no more than a log of wood does. By its nature, the human body is but a corpse and, by itself, is as sinless as a log. The senses will not do evil of themselves, so long as the mind which controls them does not wish to do evil. He who has discovered the law of human life will study the working of the *gunas* and act accordingly like the man who prints after setting the types carefully. The types which have become worn out have to be melted back into metal and cast again, and then reset; in like manner, the man who is guided by the truth that in all matters it is the *gunas* which do their work will make himself completely inert, doing nothing on his own.

Notes

1. III, 28.
2. A term in Vedanta; it means the illusory world of phenomena and also the creative energy which projects that world.

[53] April 25, 1926

The senses are not just 16,000[1], their number is infinite. If we make them dance as we wish, instead of ourselves dancing as they wish, we would be the directors of the drama of life. In the first Chapter, even the evil-minded Duryodhana asks his warriors to remain in their positions and protect the patriarch Bhishma. If, likewise, we protect the director of the drama, who dwells within us, play our part in accordance with his instructions, the director would not become weak.

Deluded by the *gunas* of *prakriti* men become attached to the activities of the *gunas;* he who knows the truth of things should not unhinge the slowwitted who have not the knowledge.[2]

This world is *maya,* it is a rotating wheel, and, therefore, those who are sunk in darkness remain attached to *guna* and karma. Those who are under the spell of the *gunas* of *prakriti* are swayed by all kinds of desires, yield to grief and ignorant attachments. The man of knowledge should not unsettle the ignorant, he should not lift him from one place and put him in another. For instance, says Shri Krishna to Arjuna, you are on a battle-field, ready for fighting, and so are these others; you have now chanced to learn some wisdom, but you should not, because of that, shake others from their beliefs. If anyone of us should suddenly become enlightened with profound knowledge, it does not mean that he would be able to change all others immediately. He is a fool who seeks to change overnight other people who are following their own ways in life. This, of course, does not mean that, where the system itself is bad, we should not try to reform it. That would be a complete perversion of this idea.

Notes

1. Lord Krishna is believed to have ruled over 16,000 senses, which are represented as His queens.
2. III, 29.

[54] April 27, 1926

Cast all thy acts on Me, with thy mind fixed on the indwelling *atman*, and without any thought of fruit or sense of 'mine' shake off thy fever and fight![1]

After explaining all this—after explaining what karma is and why one should do it—Shri Krishna tells Arjuna that, dedicating every action to Him, having purified his mind, fixed it on his *atman* and emptied it of all desires, and without entertaining any thought of gain, he should go on doing karma (not that, Shri Krishna explains, he should win a kingdom and enjoy it but) as a matter of duty and irrespective of whether or not he was likely to benefit. (We should, for instance, get up at four in the morning as a matter of duty without thinking whether it will do us any good). You should, Shri Krishna says, shed your attachment to the ego and work—that is, work with the thought that you are not the doer of the karma and its fruit is not meant for you to enjoy, acting as if you were a piece of inert matter like the spindle of the spinning-wheel and like the wick of a lamp which goes on burning by itself. If I did not bring into existence all the factors necessary for the burning of the lamp, how would the wick burn? The wick was shut up within the cotton pad. How did that cotton know that it would one day be made into a wick? It was spun and twisted and then made into a wick. If Arjuna wanted to be like the wick, to think of himself as the *atman* within and not his body, he must learn to shed his attachment to the ego and empty himself of all desires. By first choosing good against evil and then becoming unattached to either, one can transcend both. So long as we dwell in the body, it functions according to its nature. We should live in accordance with this truth, otherwise we shall invite moral ruin. We should, therefore, aim at the highest. The same is true about our aspiration for *moksha*. One who is already in water no longer desires to jump into it. If it were true that in water we melt away, we would not at all want to jump into it. Just then, however, *moksha* was not Arjuna's goal, nor did he aspire after it or hope for it. We should have as our ideal a state unaffected by hope or desire though, of course, our present state is that of human beings full of desires. Being in a state unaffected by desire is the same as having the absolute conviction that we shall attain *moksha*. This idea of a state unaffected by desire is to be understood both in regard to our spiritual aspiration and the needs of the body, that is, both in regard to the ultimate goal and practical concerns. In regard to the former, there is no question of being affected by desire. The man who is incapable of doing evil, what interest can he have in good and evil? It is not true that, after the evil in one is completely destroyed, one is able to do good. We only imagine that it is so. When a person never feels the urge to use a sword, how can we attribute non-violence to him? This is a scientific truth, and not poetry; it states a principle concerning the *atman*. Be in such a state, Shri Krishna tells Arjuna, that is, be perfectly still in your mind, and fight. This idea that one should learn to act like inert matter occurs at many places in the *Mahabharata*. Why did Shri Krishna ask them to place an iron image of Bhima before Dhritarashtra?[2] He made everyone his instrument, and then asked them to place an iron image of Bhima—what does all this mean? He asked Arjuna to become passion-free and fight, that is, to banish all impatience and anxiety from his mind and then fight. I would kill a snake or flea or bug only if I am angry or annoyed.

We shall discuss tomorrow what Krishna meant when he asked Arjuna to "fight".

Notes

1. III, 30.
2. At the end of the fighting, the blind Dhritarashtra wanted to embrace Bhima, but Shri Kṛishna saw that he wished to crush Bhima in his arms and so advised an iron image of Bhima to be placed before the king.

[55] April 28,1926

Shri Krishna asked Arjuna to banish all impatience and anxiety and then fight. When he said "fight", he meant that Arjuna should do what he regarded as his duty. If we could know every time what we should do, if everyone's duty, in a given situation was evident to him, all of us would have the same ideas of duty. But that is not so. On the contrary, we have to reflect to discover what our duty is. We have to apply numerous tests and then only do we see what our duty is. That is why Shri Krishna asks Arjuna to be passion-free and do his duty.

One can do one's duty only if one banishes all impatience and anxiety in regard to it. Anyone who has lost control over his speechorgans will seem to talk in a disconnected fashion. The fact is that all of us talk in that manner. An Italian has described all human beings as mad. If we were not mad, we would not indulge in all this vain prattle; though, even when prattling, we prefer to prattle in one way rather than another. Since, therefore, we must make a choice at every step, Arjuna is asked to do his duty without being over-excited about it, that is, without attachments and aversions. We need not doubt the intentions behind the actions of a mother who has ceased to make any distinction between her own child and another's. Freedom from attachment and aversion is the first step towards understanding one's duty. Following this line of thinking to its logical conclusion, we would see that a non-violent man is one who is free from attachments and aversions. For instance, Harishchandra saw the auspicious necklace round Taramati's neck and recognized it. He saw that he had to cut off the dear head of her whom he adored. You will ask me how this is an illustration of non-violence. Violence does not consist in the act of cutting off someone's head; it consists in the motive behind the act. How if we knew that Harishchandra would have preferred to kill himself rather than kill Taramati? Suppose it had been the King's order that, if the *Chandal* could not bring himself to kill the person before him, he could kill himself, Harishchandra would have certainly preferred to put the knife to his own throat. But he was given no such choice. He had actually brought down the knife and it was then that the gods held back his hand.

Take another instance, that of a doctor who has to carry out an operation. The doctor who operated upon me was all kindness. Even if he was not, he did not in any case wish to harm me. If the doctor was called upon to amputate someone's leg, he would certainly not derive pleasure from the operation. His only motive would be to help the patient. Not only the doctor, but the patient too knows that the amputation is for his benefit. Thus operations involve the use of all kinds of knives and lancets, but they involve no violence.

A third instance. Let us suppose that a man has had his head half cut and it is hanging loose from the neck. He signs to passers-by and requests them to kill him so that he might be spared the suffering.

Most passers-by, let us suppose, take no notice and go on. One, however, stops and looks at the man, sees his suffering and realizes that his death is certain. This person, then, may surely sever the head completely and end his suffering. This, too, is non-violence. It is so because the passer-by was not prompted by any selfish motive in what he did.

We hear in our country many persons advance such arguments to justify killing, but they are insincere; those, for example, who kill snakes are cowards. They are afraid of dying themselves, and their only thought in killing a snake is to save themselves from being bitten by it. The violence involved in killing a snake may be pardonable, but violence there certainly is. There is violence (may be pardonable violence) in killing even a person who is the most wicked of men in the eyes of the world, for killing him will not make the world a happier place, and those who kill him do not do so because they are really concerned about his welfare. If one person is out to destroy the entire world, and all the people in the world prefer to be destroyed rather than kill him, it is possible that that person will be terrified by the violence he would have perpetrated, and after that there would be no more violence[1] in the world.

Thus, to be *vigatajvara* means to be without aversions and attachments. One may even commit violence then. If anyone, deceiving himself, commits violence in the name of non-violence, of course he would not attain *moksha*. There is a possibility of *moksha* for one who commits violence but knows that he does so, but there is none for the hypocrite.

And so Shri Krishna said, "Cast all thy acts on Me."[2] He thus asked Arjuna to fulfil a number of conditions and then to fight.

Those who always act according to the rule I have here laid down, in faith and without cavilling,—they too are released from the bondage of their actions.[3]

To do one's duty means to fight and struggle. Since every karma involves a choice, there is necessarily a struggle. Even though caught in this way between opposites, you will have transcended them if you dedicate every action to Krishna, do everything without attachment or aversion, have faith in God and present every karma as a gift to Him. If you believe God to be the author of all you do, you will be touched neither by sin nor by virtue. God comes down in the form of Vaman[4], with an appealing face like a mother's, and begs us to trust everything to Him. He who accepts my teaching, says Shri Krishna, and acts accordingly, without attachments and aversions and without partiality to anyone, is not bound by the effects of any karma.

Notes

1. The source has 'non-violence', evidently, a slip.
2. III, 30.
3. III, 31.
4. One of the incarnations of Vishnu. He begged from the demon King Bali as much ground as he could cover in three steps and, on the request being granted, covered Heaven and Earth in two steps and claimed the King's head for the third.

[56] April 29, 1926

But those who cavil at the rule and refuse to conform to it are fools, dead to all knowledge; know that they are lost.[1]

Even a man of knowledge acts according to his nature; all creatures follow their nature; what then will constraint avail?[2]

This verse has been taken to mean that a wicked person can never reform himself. An instance of this is provided here by. . .[3]; she lies there away from us, and how can we persuade her to change her ways? But, then, the aspiration to realize God is also part of human nature. The beast's nature is merely to feed and sleep. It cannot meditate on Rama every morning, but man is different. Ramdas Swami[4] exhorted people never to depart from the path of virtue, the path of the highest virtue. But this verse says something altogether different; (all creatures follow their nature). If a person has the nature of an animal, how far will another succeed, try as long as he might, in reforming that person? How long can we keep such a person suppressed? What can we do to a person who refuses to behave better than an animal? I could have hit that girl with my sandals, but it would have made her more obstinate still. One day, however, she may feel Rama's grace and, remembering this incident, reform herself. This verse is not intended to discourage a man from struggling against his nature. One must of course struggle to improve oneself. But should some other person tell us day in and day out that we remain as beasts and do not improve, there is bound to be a quarrel every time. Take the example of a teacher and a pupil. If the pupil himself tells the teacher that the latter should cane him or box his ears whenever he did anything wrong, the teacher should certainly do that.

Yesterday, we mentioned three illustrations of non-violence. This is one more instance of it. Pupils such as the one in this illustration control themselves and are also controlled by others. Our minds may be disturbed by innumerable evil desires, but we do not welcome them, as we do not welcome a disease which may attack us. Our natural desire is to get well, and the doctor, therefore, is free to put any restrictions on us; the patient will thank him for doing so. But what good will it do to punish a person who does not himself wish to change? Anyone who has ceased to be a human being and behaves like a beast cannot be reformed by others, true though it is that Rama dwells in his heart too. Of course, one should never despair of being able to improve oneself. But how can outward self-control help a man to whom wickedness has become second nature? His release can come only with death. Ravana told Mandodari[5] that he was an enemy of Rama, that he wished to die. And die he did, through his own sins.

Nigraha means trying to control oneself or others. One may try to control a friend, or one's wife or sister or pupil, if they wish to reform themselves. But what can we do if they oppose us? What can even an emperor do to a person who has abandoned all shame? No one will succeed in his efforts to reform such a person. We can offer satyagraha only against a person who has some love in his heart. We can control another only if there is mutual love between us; where there is no such love, the only course for us is non co-operation with the other party. Tulsidas advised non-co-operation with the wicked.

Notes

1. III, 32.
2. III, 33.
3. The name is omitted in the source.
4. A 17th-century religious reformer of Maharashtra.
5. His wife.

[57] April 30, 1926

Men believe in their pride that they can imprison others and beat them into submission. But we know that thefts and murders have not stopped. What, then, should one do? Everyone should look after himself. This verse certainly does not mean that one should not try even to control oneself, for we have already read: holding all these in check, the yogi should sit intent on Me.[1] The senses are so powerful that trying to control them taxes our energy to the utmost and involves us in violent struggle against ourselves. Shri Krishna tells Arjuna there that he who controls them—passionately beats them down into submission and reins them in, as we do a horse—we do no violence in using the whip thus—and sits meditating on Him, selfcontrolled, is a man established in *samadhi*. A little later, he says: therefore Mahabahu, he whose senses are reined in on all sides from their objects. . . .[2]

Nigraha means another person trying to impose discipline on us. Addressed to Arjuna, the verse means: "If you believe that you can control your army, you should understand that it will not obey you, for it does not think as you do, its heart is set on fighting. By running away from battle, you will be instrumental in the warriors forsaking the traditional duty of their caste and being guilty of conduct unworthy of themselves."

Each sense has its settled likes and dislikes towards its objects; man should not come under the sway of these, for they are his besetters.[3]

Attachment and aversion are an inseparable pair. The senses feel either the one or the other towards their objects. We should not be swayed by them, for they are the thieves trying to rob the *purusha*[4] within us. They are ever after us, go where we will, and rob us of all our earnings. There is thus the fullest scope for human striving; in fact, it is one's duty to strive. Having done that duty, one may console oneself with the preceding verse; struggling tirelessly, we may tell ourselves that we can go no further than our nature permits. But taking up such an attitude does not help us. We must continue to struggle ceaselessly. We should continue till we reach the breaking point and that with the conviction that we are bound to succeed. Any man or woman or child who takes cover behind the preceding verse and stops struggling will be a thief in God's eyes. The line, "seeking pearls, men plunge into the sea, reckless of their lives,"[5] describes the spirit of desperate earnestness in striving. Better one's own duty, bereft of merit, than another's well-performed; better is death in the discharge of one's duty; another's duty is fraught with danger.[6]

We should strive to the best of our ability in our own sphere of work, but waste no effort on anything which lies outside it. It would be dangerous for us to go and live in a mansion in Bombay, but it would be a sign of our being happy if we are content to live here in the Ashram.

Notes

1. II, 61.
2. II, 68.
3. III, 34.
4. In Sankhya philosophy, the inner witness watching the play of *prakriti*.
5. From a poem by Pritam, a Gujarati poet, (1720-98).
6. III, 35.

[58] May 1, 1926

To speak the truth is a dharma common to all. But there are special duties, that is, duties which pertain to individuals. Suppose that one's job is to clean lavatories. Such a person should not envy another whose job is to keep accounts, The man who cleans lavatories as carefully as he does the utensils in his home observes his dharma in the truest manner. It would not be right for Arjuna to think of retiring to a forest and spending his days telling beads on the rosary. His duty was to fight and kill. Retiring to a forest may be the right course for a *rishi*, it was not so for Arjuna. Even if the dharma meant for Arjuna seemed less worthy, for him it was the best. Why should he, Shri Krishna asks him, talk egotistically, acting like the proverbial dog who believed that he was drawing the heavily-laden cart? He assures Arjuna that, if there was any sin in the latter following his dharma, the responsibility for that would be His, Krishna's. During the years which Ramachandra spent in the forest, Bharat did not himself rule the kingdom as king but acted as the former's representative. Ramachandra's sandals were placed on the throne and Bharat carried on the administration in Ramachandra's name. There was not a moment when he was not absorbed in thinking on

Rama. Similarly, Shri Krishna asks Arjuna why he thought that, if he won the battle, the kingdom would be his. If he had no wish to enjoy the fruits of his effort, it was actually his dharma to fight and win the kingdom. He should act only as an instrument.

Then what impels man to sin, O Varshneya, even against his will, as though by force compelled?[1]

We shall discuss Shri Krishna's reply tomorrow.

Note

1. III, 36.

[59] May 2, 1926

How is it that a person is often driven to a wrong path against his or her will?

It is Lust, it is Wrath, born of the *guna—rajas*. It is the archdevourer, the arch-sinner. Know this to be man's enemy here.[1]

The reply, according to Shri Krishna, was simple. When the child refuses to go to school, is simply unwilling to go, what is the reason? He refuses to go because he wants to run away with a bad play-fellow or because he is planning some mischief. Thus, one cause is *kama*[2]. It is man's evil thoughts which drive him to evil deeds. The second cause is anger. We get angry when we do not get the thing we want. Anger has its source in *rajas*. These two great enemies of man drive him to sin. The reign of *kama* is different in its effect from the reign of Rama. Those who prosper under Rama's reign understand the sport of God which this creation is. Those, on the other hand, who are swayed by desire and anger will see, in the creation, not Rama's sport, but Satan's. Like Kumbhakarna[3] *kama* is ever waiting, openmouthed, for its prey. When its appetite is not satisfied, its victim is filled with anger. Know, Shri Krishna tells Arjuna, that this is your enemy. Since the two are twins, He has used the singular pronoun *enam*.

As fire is obscured by smoke, a mirror by dirt, and the embryo by the amnion, so is knowledge obscured by this.[4]

If there is any smoke, it stays only for a while. As soon as it has gone, the fire gives full heat. The mirror will have to be cleaned, and only then will it give service, provided of course we know that the thing is a mirror. But the foetus covered by the placenta can do nothing about it, it cannot even cry. The man who is under the sway of desire and anger passes through these three stages.

Knowledge is obscured, O kaunteya, by this eternal enemy of the wise man in the form of Lust, the insatiable fire.[5]

This *kama* harms, like an enemy, even a man of spiritual knowledge.

Notes

1. III, 37.
2. Desire.
3. Ravana's brother in the *Ramayana*, a voracious eater who slept for days at a stretch.
4. III, 38.
5. III, 39.

[60] May 4, 1926

The senses, the mind and the reason are said to be its seat; by means of these it obscures knowledge and stupefies man.

Therefore, O Bharatarshabha, bridle thou first the senses and then rid thyself of this sinner, the destroyer of knowledge and discrimination.

Subtle, they say, are the senses; subtler than the senses is the mind; subtler than the mind is the reason; but subtler even than the reason is He.[1]

Shri Krishna now explains the various stages. It is true indeed that the senses are powerful—they control the body. The mind is stronger than the senses and the intellect stronger than the mind. But stronger still than the intellect is the *atman* which dwells in the body.

The senses, the mind and the intellect, these three are the dwelling places of desire and anger. But the *atman* in you, Shri Krishna tells Arjuna, is higher than all of them. If we seize the house in which the enemy lodges, we shall be able to kill him, or he will leave the place and run away. Occasionally, one may forget Him who is the Lord over these three, but that need not worry us, since the moment we think about that Lord we shall be able to overcome all of them.

Thus realizing Him to be subtler than the reason, and controlling the self by the Self (*Atman*), destroy, O Mahabahu, this enemy—Lust, so hard to overcome.[2]

"Subduing the *atman* by the *atman*" means overcoming the baser, the demoniac impulses in the mind through the *atman*, that is, through the godward impulses; in other words, Arjuna should, Shri Krishna tells him, master his egotistic instincts by striving for spiritual welfare and, assured that his real self was more potent than the intellect, he should storm the fort and seize it. The senses are the gatekeepers and the mind is the minister. What the senses tell the mind is reported by the latter to the intellect, and the intellect decides and issues its order. If, however, we regain the sovereignty which is rightfully ours, then we would be able to subdue the mind, the intellect and the senses whom at present we have accepted as our masters, as in our country we have accepted foreigners as our masters and believe that we get the food we eat because of them.

Our *atman* should be vigilant day and night. One whose *atman* is so awake will not have dreams in his sleep. But we are bound to have them if we are slaves of sleep. Shri Krishna thus assures Arjuna that, if he keeps constant watch, he will be harassed neither by thieves coming in from outside nor by those that dwell within. If we do not establish our rule over the body, it will yearn for things which we do not approve of and we shall forfeit our authority over it.

Notes

1. III, 40, 41 & 42.
2. III, 43.

[61] May 5, 1926

If we wish to deal worthily by even the most wicked person, we should assume that he has no evil intention. He is bound to have good feelings somewhere deep in his heart. The *atman* never gets angry. It remains unattached and unmoved. If we cannot overcome desire or anger in us even in some measure, we should tolerate them when they invade us.

No one has yet succeeded in laying down a universal rule about how we should act towards a thief. We should, however, bear in mind that however we act we should be inspired by love for him. We must think and find out how we may win him over with love. We should assume that it is not in human nature to steal. Even as rational beings we should be convinced that there is no human being in the world who is beyond all hope of change. Love is a kind of force of attraction. Science tells us that even dust has the property of attracting other things. Even a particle of dust possesses some kind of power of attraction; that is why Mirabai sings about the bond of love. That bond is much stronger than that of a slender thread can ever be.[1] Why should we be filled with passion or get angry whenever we lose anything?

Such is the yoga described in this third chapter. There is ceaseless movement and change. We cannot choose but work with the body as ceaselessly as the ball of this earth rotates. What is the way, then, of saving ourselves from work? The *Gita* replies that, by shedding all attachment and aversion, we escape the fruits of our actions.

[Chapter Four]

I expounded this imperishable yoga to Vivasvan; Vivasvan communicated it to Manu, and Manu to Ikshvaku.

Thus handed down in succession, the royal sages learnt it; with long lapse of time it dwindled away in this world, O Parantapa.[2]

We are doing things every moment, but it is God who has placed us on his wheel and is moving it like a potter, producing ever new shapes. "This yoga was known from the beginning of time, but has perished in this age. People have forgotten the art of working without attachment and aversion. Were it not so," Shri Krishna said, "I would not have had to be a witness to this battle."

The same ancient yoga have I expounded to thee today; for thou art My devotee and My friend, and this is the supreme mystery.[3]

The highest truth may be imparted only to a *bhakta*[4], for such a person will serve the world's good.

Notes

1. Mirabai's lines read: Hari has tied me with a slender thread/ And I turn as He pulls me.
2. IV, 1 & 2.
3. IV, 3.
4. A devotee of God.

[62] May 6, 1926

Shri Krishna says,

This yoga, "was known in ancient times, I taught it to Vivasvan, he taught it to Manu, and Manu taught it to Ikshavaku. At this Arjuna wonders. You and I, he says, live in the present age, and you say you taught this to people in former times; how can that be?

Later was Thy birth, my Lord, earlier that of Vivasvan. How then am I to understand that Thou didst expound it in the beginning?

Many births have we passed through, O Arjuna, both thou and I; I know them all, thou knowest them not, O Parantapa.[1]

When we sing about the succession of births for human beings through 84,00,000 living forms, we refer to our having had countless lives before the present one, and we state our inference that death is only a change from an old house into a new one. But it is only a person who remembers his previous lives that can say this with certainty. Shri Krishna states categorically that, being a yogi, he remembered his previous existences but that Arjuna could not remember his. He could say this; we cannot.

Though unborn and inexhaustible in My essence, though Lord of all beings, yet assuming control over My nature, I come into being by My mysterious power.[2]

The Hindu belief in avatars may present a difficulty to some of us. Avatar means descent. Our descent means God's descent too, for He is present in every creature and in every object. All this is His *maya*. All concrete things—our body, the material objects, all these—exist at definite points in space and time, but the *atman* was not born in time, it pervades all space and exists through all time. We do not know it by direct experience. If we wish to understand the principle known as God, either with the help of reason or through faith, we should first know the *atman*. What is it? So long as we live in ignorance, it is more distant than even the sky, but in our awakened state we cannot say that it is removed from us by even so much as an inch. It is that through which we came into being and through which we exist if you believe that you are that, then "I" and "you" are identical—but only a person devoid of egotism can assert that. "I" and "you" are identical in the sense in which the ring and chain are in the final analysis but gold. Name and form are only for a moment; while things have them, they are no more real than a mirage. That into which things merge when they cease to have name and form is ever the same.

And so Krishna says:

"Though I was never born in time, though I am the Lord of all creatures, I incarnate Myself and am born as a human being."

This is the essential nature of the *atman*. If we realize this truth, we would always act in conformity with that nature; we then act, though born as human beings, as if we were never born. If the *atman* in each of us is identical with the *atman* in everyone else, one *atman* born in a body means all of them born, and all others born means that one born too. This is a difficult idea to grasp. "This is *maya*,"says Shri Krishna, "and through it I incarnate Myself in this world time and again."

We can follow reason only up to a point. What, then, does avatar mean? It is not as if God comes down from above. It would be right to say, if we can say it without egotism, that each one of us is an avatar.

The *atman* in every body is as potent as the *atman* in any other, though outwardly we see differences. In our awakened state all are one, though in our ignorant state we may seem separate existences. In real truth, there are not several, there is only one.

If we constantly reflect over this essence named the *atman*, we shall regard no one as an enemy to be killed and shall have nothing to get angry about. We shall then see that anyone who hits us hits himself too.

When Krishna says that He incarnates Himself as a human being, he only uses the idiom of common speech. God never incarnates

Himself as an *atman* and is never born as a human being. He is ever the same. When, from our human point of view, we see special excellence in some individual, we look upon him as an avatar. In God's language there is no such word as avatar; it exists only in the language of human beings.

Notes

1. IV, 4 & 5.
2. IV, 6.

[63] May 7, 1926

Arjuna asked Shri Krishna how He could have expounded this yoga to other people of olden times, to which Shri Krishna replied that they had had many previous existences, which He remembered but Arjuna could not. He added that, though He was not subject to birth and change, though He was the Lord who dwelt in the hearts of all creatures, He submitted to the action of *prakriti*, which was His creation, and through the power of his *maya* came down to live on the earth.

He then proceeds to explain in what circumstances God incarnates Himself as a human being.

For whenever Right declines and Wrong prevails, then O Bharata, I come to birth.[1]

In these lines Shri Krishna held out an assurance to the entire world. If God remained inactive when dharma was eclipsed, man would be helpless. In this *Kaliyuga,* all human efforts produce results contrary to what was intended. Hindus and Muslims, for instance, continue to fight among themselves. Can anyone prevent this? I was passionately eager to do such penance that they should never fight.

But all my efforts failed. Does that mean that this fighting will go on for ever? Assuredly not. Will God let human beings overindulge their senses with impunity? He tells us that He will tolerate our selfindulgence within limits, for He knows that we would weary of it. I will tolerate, He says, a little fighting and will not incarnate on the earth just because of that. But when men recognize no limits in fighting, demolish temples and kill people indiscriminately, that would mean eclipse of dharma. That would be wickedness in the name of dharma, it would mean the spread of *adharma* and disorder. Do not, God says to comfort men, give way to despair when such things happen. "It is good," He says, "that you feel helpless at such a time, for by making you feel so I humble your pride." We remember what Surdas[2] says:

"I have tried my strength in one way and another, till I am weary and can do no more; you must save me now;" that is how man thinks in his pride, that he will do this, and he will do that, but God humbles his pride. Man, however, has this promise from the Lord. He need not despair and feel that, if he fails in some task, it will not be done. Let him have faith that God will have it done. So the Lord has said in these lines that, whenever necessary, He comes down to live on the earth, and sets everything right. If He did not do that, He would not enjoy our worship and reverence. What dishonour can there ever be for a man who lives as God's slave? It is the slave's master who will be judged from the manner in which the slave lives. Is it, therefore, ever likely that God will let dharma be eclipsed? If *adharma* prevails, God will forfeit our reverence and worship. He has, therefore, no choice but to incarnate Himself as a human being.

To save the righteous, to destroy the wicked, and to re-establish Right I am born from age to age.[3]

Shri Krishna has told us that we do nothing, nor does He. Who, then, destroys the wicked, and how are they destroyed? It is God's inviolable law that karma never fails to produce its effect. We can say that a human being may be able to counter-act the effects of karma, and yet assert that karma never fails to produce its effect. The point is not that a person may not have to suffer the fruits of his actions, but that, if he cultivates non-attachment, even while in fact suffering the fruits of action, he would not inwardly feel that he suffered them. But suffer them he must. No karma is ever forgiven. It is, therefore, the wickedness of the wicked which destroys them. When, in this world, one human being kills another, the former is only an instrument.

Arjuna was a bowman of prowess and brave warrior. When he killed his enemies, it was not his strength which prevailed against Duryodhana.

The latter was destroyed by his own sins. Hence the saying, "The pot of sin is bound to break on day." If it was true that God comes down from above and destroys the wicked, He would be as much under the sway of ignorance as we are. But that is not what happens. If we have faith and understand God's law, we would be sure that the wicked would be destroyed through their own sins.

Destruction of the wicked does not mean their physical destruction. Physically, both the wicked and the virtuous perish. It may be that a *bhakta* will pass away in the prime of his youth, and a wicked person will live up to the age of 76; shall we say that this was an instance of God's injustice? Kesar Bhagat was bitten by a serpent yesterday and died; should we, therefore, believe that he was a wicked man? In fact he was a good man;

he was, though a mere labourer, a *bhakta* and a man of upright character. We would be punished with degradation if we believed that a man must have been wicked because he died early.

Yes, it is true in one sense that the good do not die, for we sing their glory ever afterwards. Everyone sings the glory of Rama, but no one of Ravana. If we think of him still, it is in order that we may keep ourselves free from his sins, run away from them. On the contrary, if we sing the virtues of a man and assimilate them, let them sink into our very soul, they are bound to become stronger in us day by day.

Virtues never die. If we see the contrary in the world, that is but God's *maya*. It is true that virtues are cultivated with effort, and that vices require no such effort; but ultimately vices perish and virtues prosper.

The appearance to the contrary is the effect of *maya*. If that were not so, what is said here about "destruction of the wicked" would not be true.

Shri Krishna does not mean here physical destruction of the wicked. While the *vasana*[4] with which a man died exists, he cannot but be born again. It is stated, it is true, that a good man will not be born again, but only if he rises above the place of *gunas*. There is, beyond the *gunas* of good and evil, a state which is characterized by no *guna*.

It is not an undesirable state, but a desirable one. It is the state of *moksha*, a state which endures for ever. But the assurance which God holds out here is not that goodness never perishes, but that evil most certainly does. When evil seems to prevail in the world, He, the Witness within, manifests Himself and shows that in truth it does not, shows it by the example of His own life. When evil spreads in the world, some persons, inspired by God, feel in their hearts that it is not enough for them to be a little good, that they must do *tapascharya* and be exceptionally good, so good that people would look upon them as perfect manifestation of the Divine in man. That is how Shri Krishna came to be worshipped as the fullest avatar. God has in these verses assured man that whenever dharma is eclipsed and the reign of *adharma* spreads, He comes into the world to protect the good, to destroy the wicked and restore the rule of dharma. This means that dharma is never destroyed. Shri Krishna did not say that while the wicked are destroyed, the good are not. He himself passed away, and that too meeting an untimely death.

If we take a total view, we shall see that it is not wickedness but goodness which rules the world. The wicked can prevail only when they number crores, but goodness will rule when embodied to perfection even in one person. Non-violence has been described as so powerful that all forces of violence subside in its presence. Under its influence, even beasts forget their nature. Even one good person can change the world. Such a one enjoys an empire over people's hearts; we do not, because we follow goodness only as best we may. The type of good man I have mentioned has but to send a message, and people will do what he wants them to do, such is the power of goodness.

Where wickedness prevails, there is disorder in every field of life, but where goodness rules, order prevails and people are happy. They are happy not in the sense that their material needs are satisfied but in the sense that they lead virtuous and contented lives. As for material possessions, some men have crores of rupees and yet live a distracted life; that is no sign of being happy.

This verse, then, means that when *adharma* spreads, some men undertake *tapascharya* and, through their *tapascharya*, generate goodness in the world. Even the wicked bow in reverence before goodness. Its power is felt by beasts too. This can happen even in the present age. Anyone who has completely shed hatred and ill will, who has succeeded in making his life a perfect embodiment of truth, can command everything in life. He does not have to ask that anything be done. He has only to wish and the wish will be fulfilled.

God does not have to be born and to die, to incarnate Himself on earth as a human being. It is but His *maya* that we see in the world. That *maya* is described here and we are reassured that wickedness prevails only for a while but goodness endures for ever. We should, therefore, cultivate goodness in ourselves and see that we do nothing whereby we may become wicked.

Notes

1. IV, 7.
2. A 16th-century saint-poet of Northern India.
3. IV, 8.
4. Desire clinging to one's self even after the death of the physical body.

[64] May 8, 1926

God destroys evil and restores goodness by inspiring man's heart with noble ideals. On the balance goodness must prevail in the world, otherwise the world would perish. We see that a family in which evil increases is ruined, like, for instance, the Yadava race, which perished. It had taken to evil ways. Though a man like Krishna dwelt among them, the Yadavas took to immorality and drinking, fought among themselves and were killed. Even a strong and self-willed man whom no one dares attack will sooner or later fall at someone's hands; this is so true that no member of the Yadava race survived. When there is so much evil in the world that on the balance there is more of it than good, that their sum is a minus quantity, the destruction of the world is certain. The body endures only so long as there is vitality in it; in the same way, the world would perish if at any time there should be less of goodness and more of evil in it. That is why the Lord said that He appeared in the world in every age.

He who knows the secret of this My divine birth and action is not born again, after leaving the body; he comes to Me, O Arjuna.[1]

Is there any reason why such a person should not merge into God? He would see that his body was perishable, and that it was not worthwhile to waste his energy on it. Was it not better, he would ask himself, to strive to realize the immortal *atman*? The *atman* is confined in the cage of this body, held in the prison of the body like a criminal. All of us have committed a crime, so to say, and are, therefore, imprisoned in the body; witness, for instance, Tulsidas and Surdas saying in their poems that there was no greater sinner in the world than they. We sin from the moment we are born, and that is why we are born again and again. Being confined in the cage of this body, we cannot soar as high as we wish. But we can do so if we reflect over the mystery of God's incarnations and actions in the world of men. If we realize the truth about the atman which is a lion, we shall become lions. How can we realize that truth? To explain that, Shri Krishna says:

Freed from passion, fear and wrath, filled full with Me, relying on Me, and refined by the fiery ordeal of knowledge, many have becone one with Me.[2]

"Those who know the mystery of God's incarnations and actions become free from attachments, from fear and anger," says Shri Krishna. "They become absorbed in Me. (If you open their hearts, you will find the image of Rama inside.) They live in complete surrender to Me. Purified by knowledge and *tapaschaprya* they have become as I am, have lost themselves in Me." Shri Krishna has explained here how we may know that a person has understood the mystery of God's incarnations and actions.

Notes

1. IV, 9.
2. IV, 10.

[65] May 9, 1926

In whatever way men resort to Me, even so do I render to them. In every way, O Partha, the path men follow is Mine.[1]

In other words, people reap as they sow. As the quality of your *bhakti*, so is its reward. If there is any motive behind your *bhakti*, if you seek anything through it, you will get what the quality of your *bhakti* entitles you to. You will get, not what you wish to get, but what you deserve to get. We may wish to become God, but that does not mean that we shall become God. We shall get only that which we have earned by our manner of life. We shall get what we deserve. If you walk a distance of four miles, you will get only what is at the end of it.

If you eat *kariatu*[2] to have a purge, it does not mean that the effect will follow. *Kariatu* will at the most cure a mild fever. If you swallow castor oil and then wish that you should get no motion, you cannot have it so. This is the meaning of the line: In whatever way men resort to Me, even so do I render to them.

Shri Krishna then says: *mama vartmanuvartante manushyah Partha sarvashah.*

"Everyone follows a path which leads to Me." This verse has a history behind it. When Tilak Maharaj was alive, he had cited this verse in the course of a discussion about violence and non-violence. I had argued that we should bear with a person who might have slapped us. In reply, he cited this verse to prove that the *Gita* upheld the principle of "tit for tat". That is, we should act towards a person as he acts towards us. I cling to the reply which I gave to him then.[3] I had argued that this verse could not be used in support of his contention.

We should not act towards a person as he acts towards us. If he is bad to us, we may not therefore be bad to him. This verse merely lays down God's law. Shri Krishna says that He will worship a person as the latter worships Him. That means, we reap as we sow. One cannot do evil to others and expect good for oneself. Man has no right to return two slaps for one. But a principle quite the opposite of this prevails in the world, and as education spreads the position becomes worse. Uncivilized people may return two slaps for one, may fight back when attacked, and among them the relation of father and son may not be always sweet. If, however, a father behaves as a civilized man, he would use wisdom and endure the son's misconduct in patience, and so teach him to behave with humility. If the son is good, then he would suffer his parents' weaknesses in patience, and that is the better way of the two. We prefer the second to the first. Besides, we read in the preceding verse about the type of man who can realize God. It says that those serene persons who are *vitaragabhayakrodhah,* that is, who are free from all attachment, fear and anger, realize God.

The present verse cannot contradict that one, but completes its meaning. The previous verse says that a person who yields to attachment and anger will not realize God. If one yields to anger, one will reap the fruit of anger. We are thus taught not to yield to anger but to banish attachment, fear and anger from us.

In the second line, therefore, the Lord says that men are governed by His law. He means that law, the law of karma, which rules the world. We can truly say that God is law. God created His law and left the world to its governance, reserving to Himself no right to interfere with its operation. He then told men to decide for themselves whether they would or would not continue to be born in the world, as though making the position clear to them in advance so that they might not blame Him afterwards.

If we worship God, He would be pleased; but it does not mean that, if we do not worship Him, He would be displeased and would change His law. The law is immutable. Ishvar[4] is not a ruler though literally the word means "a ruler". But, then, since God does nothing, he suffers nothing either. He neither acts nor suffers the consequences of action. He stands apart, detached. We have given free rein to our imagination and employed all manner of epithets to describe God, and we quarrel about Him needlessly. Take the instance of the Jain and the Vedanta philosophies. According to the latter, all things are pervaded by God, whereas the former holds that no such being as God exists. We adopt a third attitude,—one which is the right one for laymen to adopt—namely, that God both exists and does not exist.

God is not a ruler; He is all-pervasive, He is life, He is unconditioned and devoid of form. His rule consists in the rule of His law. No one has questioned the existence of His law. Not a single school of philosophy has done so. That law is of course a living law. If we equate it with God, recognize that it is God, people will then have no reason for quarrelling. That is the implication of this verse.

The principle of "You will reap as you sow" is part of even man-made law. Anyone who steals is punished. Even a thief has to submit to the law. He is not a rebel. The person who defies a law with deliberate intention to do so is an outlaw, but the murderer who is punished for his crime is not an outlaw. We become outlaws when we commit civil disobedience, for our disobedience is deliberate. Those who commit civil disobedience, and do so deliberately, are also outlaws, but the person who steals in abject helplessness is still ruled by the country's law. In the same way, man too is ruled by God's law, whether he submits to it willingly or not. That immutable truth is stated in this verse:

> Those who desire their actions to bear fruit worship the gods here; for in this world of men the fruit of actions is quickly obtainable.[5]

Every desire bears its proper fruit. So long as any desire is left in us, we cannot escape the round of birth and death. If we strive for yogic powers, our effort will certainly be rewarded, though not necessarily in the manner described in books on yoga. Chanting a *mantra*[6] is not necessarily rewarded in exactly the same way as described in the Shastras. Men try to discover God's laws, they conclude that certain actions will have certain results. If they get hold of the truth, may be there will be some efficacy in the *mantras* which they employ; but, then, even self-seeking and insincere men use this method. Or, it may be that the ceremonies accompanying the chanting of the *mantra* were not correctly performed; if so, the hoped-for result would not follow. I do not know anything about *mantras* for counteracting the effects of snake-bite, but there may be something in these claims. Some persons assert that we still know very little about the laws underlying the efficacy of such *mantras*. In this age they are discovering the laws of the visible world, but the number of such laws is infinite. Shall we ever succeed in discovering them all? Similarly, there are laws governing the invisible world too. In future, the laws of that world—the powers of the mind—may also be discovered. *Mantras* originated in the discovery of such laws. But, like the hypotheses about the visible world, the principles behind particular *mantras* may or may not be true and, according as they are true or not, the *mantras* may succeed or fail.

The author of the *Gita* knew this and, therefore, advised us to take no interest at all in these things. If we go after them, we may perhaps have our desires fulfilled, and so he said that people who hanker after worldly success worship various gods. But that, he said, will profit them little in the end. It will not increase the sum of happiness in the world. If, however, we decide to work in a spirit of disinterested service, we would not concern ourselves with *mantras*, nor shall we be required to study innumerable Shastras. Just one little Shastra will suffice, the practice of *bhakti*—Ramanama. We shall not even have to study the whole of the *Gita*, it will suffice if we understand its substance. We should find out and take the place appointed for us in this world-machine created by God. A man who has no desires, how well his work shines! We suffer because of our innumerable desires. People do not keep to their places of duty and that creates disorder and confusion in the world. That man who, instead of being absorbed in his work, is always discontented has not found his right place in the world-machine. If even in a family every member is discontented, the family would be disrupted. In similar circumstances there would be chaos in a country's government, too. If everyone working in this world-machine seeks a reward for his work and, therefore, constantly changes the spheres of his work, there will be no order anywhere; the condition of such a person is like that of one who wastes himself in pleasures and then runs about in search of tonics and pills. With our minds full of cravings, we run after things in the world. While our attachment to the ego remains, we shall never taste the sweet ambrosia of Self-knowledge. The *Gita*, therefore, tells us that if, giving up attachment to the ego, we attend to the best of our ability to the task which has fallen to our lot, an emperor's work and that of one who cleans lavatories will be esteemed of equal worth in God's court. There, King Janaka and the man who cleaned lavatories in his palace have an equally honoured place. Suppose, however, that a present-day ruler and Janaka's Bhangi were to present themselves in God's court at the same time, in all likelihood, the Bhangi would be given an exalted place and the ruler would be left out. In God's court a man with a crown is not esteemed as of greater worth than one who has nothing on his head. The latter will be regarded worthy of a crown while a man with a jewelled crown will receive no attention. Hence the *Gita* says that he who works without attachment to the ego works best and becomes qualified for *moksha*.

Notes

1. IV, 11.
2. *Chiretta*.
3. *Vide* "Note on Tilak's Letter", after 18-1-1920.
4. God.
5. IV, 12.
6. Formula with magical efficacy.

[66] May 11, 1926

The order of the four *varnas*[1] was created by Me according to the different *gunas* and karma of each; yet know that though, therefore, author thereof, being changeless I am not the author.[2]

"I have," Shri Krishna says, "created four *varnas* on the basis of character and work." These are Brahmin, Kshatriya, Vaisya and Sudra. What should be the character of a Brahmin? What is distinctive of him? He is a Brahmin who knows *Brahman*, who lives most in the consciousness of God. And a Brahmin's work in life is to teach and help people to realize God. Besides this particular gift, he will also have the qualities of character which mark the other *varnas*. The Kshatriya's special dharma is protection of society. He should, above all, be a brave man. The Vaisya occupies himself with commerce. That is his special dharma. If he did not follow it, perhaps the world would not go on as it does. The Sudra's special dharma is service. If he combines with his service the spirit of *yajna* or the motive of public good, he will win the reward of his life. There is here no question of higher and lower. If we regard the person who cleans lavatories as lower and another who reads the *Gita* as higher, that will be the end of us. The majority in the world are engaged in the work of service. If a man combines the spirit of *yajna* with such work, he will be a *mumukshu*. A Sudra is expected to have humility, but humility does not mean abjectness. He serves no one except God. Anyone for whom action is a necessity is subject to continual change. God is spotless and without form. He has no need to sleep or eat and drink. He does not move, and yet it is He who does everything. The weather expert will tell us that the storm was produced by changes in atmospheric pressure, but as he looks back for antecedent causes, he will reach a point beyond which he will not be able to go. God is an expert law-maker, for He is the author of all laws, though, being perfect, He is under no necessity to act or do anything. He never violates His law. God is present in everything that exists and, therefore, He and His law are one. He is spirit. That is, His law is spirit, it is God Himself. He is, and also is not, the doer of things.

Since the universe displays some order in its running, we may assume that God is the author of that order. But the Lord has told us here that He is its author and yet is not its author—that is His mystery beyond human understanding.

Actions do not affect Me, nor am I concerned with the fruits thereof.[3] "Fruits of action do not cling to me, for I have no desire for them," says Shri Krishna. Once a machine is set in motion, every part in it works automatically. When we have learnt to function in this manner, like a machine, we shall have gained the true end of human effort. We shall then be fit for direct realization of God.

Notes

1. Divisions of society.
2. IV, 13.
3. IV, 14.

[67] May 12, 1926

God works like a machine. He is His law. He is the author of law and He it is who administers it. What perfect order this represents!

There is never a question of His suspending His law or of deciding to uphold it. The machine has been going on from eternity. God's law exists and has been in operation since the time that He came into being, if we can say such a thing about Him. We indeed conceive such a necessity for Him. He never suffers the effects of karma, for He has no wish to be fulfilled through any karma. Every part in a machine goes on working ceaselessly; it is the man behind the machine who operates it. In regard to God, we also imagine that He is Himself the machine and its operator. Can anyone say of a machine that it suffers the effects of karma or has any wish to be fulfilled through karma? A machine simply goes on working. If, in the same manner, we become totally immersed in our work, so that we are one with our work, we lose ourselves in that work. But, then, we should first ascertain our duty. The man of lust loses himself in his lust, so much so that he becomes the very embodiment of lust. Even simple contact with such a person is dangerous. We should not lose ourselves in our passions in that manner. Our duty is to strive for self-realization and we should lose ourselves in that aim. Such a person can never be disturbed by evil desire and, at last, he becomes one with God. If we lose ourselves in God, become machines, make ourselves as clay in God's hands, is it any wonder that we may become one with Him? We should lose ourselves in God so completely that we do not remain separate from Him at all. This verse explains how we can do so. It is to explain this that the Lord says here that karma has no effect on him, for he desires nothing through karma.

"Anyone who knows this truth about Me is never bound by karma."[1] How can he be? He who knows God's law will work but will desire nothing through work. Why do we feel the strain of work?

Because, as we work, we remain attached to the "I" within us; were it not so, we would never feel impatient or worried. We should be so absorbed in our work that we do not even notice the time when we should stop it. We should thus work on like machines. I once saw a beautiful painting in a Roman Catholic Church, the work of a gifted painter. It is the time of prayer. Women have been working in the fields, pickaxes in hand. As one of them was about to dig with her pickaxe, the bell tolled for prayer and the pickaxe fell from her hand, she bent her body as though kneeling for prayer and started praying.

The poet—for the painter is a poet—had imagined the woman as working like a machine. For these women work was woship. There is a saying in Latin which means that bodily labour is a form of worship.

Anyone who believes that it is so will automatically kneel down at prayer time. A person who has resolved that he will always get up at four will roll up his bed as the clock strikes four. If such a person misses praying at prayer time, he will feel weary and oppressed and will not be able to concentrate on any work.

A person who works with such devotion, how can he suffer the effects of karma? That is, he never feels the strain of work. He is ever fresh. There are so many who cannot be happy unless they are working.

They never feel the need to stop work for a moment and stretch themselves for rest. If any visitors interrupt them in their work, they feel miserable. Such persons never feel the effects of karma.

The man of lust loses himself in his lust, but he wearies of his indulgence because he seeks pleasure from it. Anyone who seeks pleasure is bound to weary of it sooner or later. If a person indulges his palate, he cannot but fall ill; he is bound to suffer from some disease. But what disease can he suffer from who never indulges his palate, who does not eat for enjoyment? One should do the task on hand without expecting pleasure from doing it, do it merely as one's duty. He who approaches his work in this spirit, who desires nothing through it, will not have to suffer the effects of karma. God does not suffer the effects of karma though He controls this vast machine. The signs which indicate that we suffer such effects are the need we feel for food and water and the wearing out of our bodies. God.is ever awake. We are awake for some time and then sleep, we eat and feel hungry. But God, though He is ever awake, does not have to make an effort to keep Himself awake, He does not sleep and does not eat.

Though He acts, He does nothing. Behind every act of ours, there is a trace of egotism and attachment to the "I",—an action of the will. We will to act, we have to do so, before we do anything. God keeps awake for ever without a moment's interruption. We cannot do so. If, however, we keep such a state before us as our ideal, we can do the best work. That is why

Shri Krishna said: yoga is skill in action.[2] That is, the man who is firmly established in yoga always does better work than one who is restless and impatient in his work.

Knowing this did men of old, desirous of Freedom, perform action; do thou, then just as they did—the men of old in days gone by.[3] The seekers of *moksha* in old days knew this truth and worked in such a spirit. To realize God means to work like God, with singleminded devotion and ceaseless vigilance. Though living in the human body, we should imitate God as much as we can. "Our forefathers did this. You too," Shri Krishna tells Arjuna, "should act in the same manner" (Man is ruled by vows. God has no need to take any. Everyone should resolve that he or she will not fall asleep here. You ought not to give me pain by dozing here.) How is it that Arjuna thought about dharma when he was required to kill his relations? Shri Krishna, therefore, rebuked him and said that he should not think on those lines, for in old times people worked without thinking of any reward for work. If one works in that spirit, one is not bound by the effects of karma. "Think how I act," says Shri Krishna. "I create society with its four classes, but I am not bound by the effects of karma, for I remain unattached.""You too", He tells Arjuna, "should act in that manner."

You, students, should study with the same devotion as the *brahmacharis*[4] of old days. They bore themselves in such a manner that, though mere boys, they seemed to be grown-up, mature men. I speak of more than forty years ago. I distinctly remember that, at our place, in the absence of the priest his young son read the *Bhagavata*, and he read it very well indeed; so good was the education he had received at home. He must have been barely fifteen. Those whom we describe as *brahmacharis* today must behave as the *brahmacharis* of old did. You should sit upright, like a pole. Practise prayers for a whole month, and then you will discover that you are making some progress. What is the meaning of your feeling restless as you sit here?

What is the good if you feel that, when you leave this place, you will get back into bed?

"Do your work and leave the responsibility to me," says Shri Krishna. "What is it you can do? Everything is done by me. Left to yourself, you will remain slumbering. On your own, you do only evil. You cannot say that I incline you to remain slumbering or to do evil. I inspire you to do only good. It is

Satan who inclines you to remain slumbering, to abuse people, to behave disrespectfully to others and to cheat people in the name of spinning."

Notes

1. IV, 14.
2. II, 50.
3. IV, 15.
4. Students attached to preceptors in hermitages.

[68] May 13, 1926

'What is action? What inaction?'— here even the wise are perplexed. I will then expound to thee that action knowing which thou shalt be saved from evil.[1]

"I will explain to you what right karma is and, having understood it, you will save yourself from evil, from the round of birth and death."

Our eyes are closed with bandages, like those over the eyes of the bullock in the oil-press. These bandages are not eternal, but we let them stay because we have grown used to them as natural, as fear is natural to us. There was a lion cub who, having always lived among goats, would tremble with fear like a goat, Then a real lion happened to meet him, and he held a mirror before him. The cub roared, and escaped from the company of the goats. This cub had not been forced to put a bandage over its eyes, the bandage had just grown of itself. In the same way, everyone of us has the bandage of ignorance grown over the eyes, and we do not know that it is not our dharma to live in evil, to submit to the round of birth and death. Our dharma is to rise ever higher until at last we can rise no more. We can have no rest till we have reached the goal. There will be eternal peace when we have reached it, that is, the peace of *moksha*. If you are on the top of the Himalayas, you are certain to fall from there, the top itself will crumble one day. It will crumble because it is ever changing. There is no changing in the state of *moksha* and no falling from there. *Moksha* means destruction of the shackles of birth and death, getting out of that round, it means deliverance from evil. If we meet a worthy guru, and he loosens the bandage of ignorance over our eyes and holds before us the mirror of knowledge, we would know what we are, would know whether we deserve to go from birth to birth or are fit for something else. In truth we deserve better than to follow this round, we belong to a higher station. We shall become fit for that station when the darkness of ignorance has vanished. The Lord told Arjuna that He would show the way by following which he could save himself from evil, that his actions till then were only a means of binding him. Shri Krishna wished to help Arjuna to deliver himself from that bondage, but what could He have taught him if the latter had not questioned Him eagerly, had not shown that he thirsted for knowledge, if he had not told Him: "I am like one sunk in ignorance; I do not know what my duty is; I have faith in you; show me what my dharma is?"

For it is meet to know the meaning of action, of forbidden action, as also of inaction. Impenetrable is the secret of action.[2]

One should know what karma is, what *vikarma*—that is, forbidden karma—is, what *akarma*—that is, ceasing from karma—is.

The truth about karma is a deep mystery.

Who sees inaction in action and action in inaction, he is enlightened among men, he is a yogi, he has done all he need do.[3]

The aim of this verse is to show that one who does karma may still not be doing anything. I have already in a previous discourse mentioned my own example and told you that if I worked with attachment to my ego there were occasions when I would become mad. But things go on and leave me unaffected because I do everything merely as my duty. Even if every boy here were to leave me, I would not shed one tear. I would, on the contrary, dance with joy like Narasinh Mehta and sing "Happy am I that the net is no more". If we work in such a disinterested spirit, we can follow the example of the Lord who said that, though He had created society with its four classes, He was not their creator. That is so because of the principle that one may do karma and still not have done it.

We are caught in the motion of the wheel of this world. Our duty is to work ceaselessly as a part of this machine. We should spend every minute of our waking life in doing work which has fallen to our lot, and do it as if we are impatient over it and yet not be so, be calm in fact. The bullock that keeps the water-wheel in motion goes round and round, but no bucket falls from its place. If it were not a bucket but our heart in that place, it might even fall off; the bucket, however, does not fall off, it remains in its place, calm. We should be filled with such calm. On the other hand, if our heart is agitated, we may rest from work but shall not have ceased from action, we would still be working. The bonds tighten round such a person and there is but misery in store for him. If he believes that those who let themselves be entangled in the affairs of life weave bonds of karma round them and that he himself is free, he will be under a delusion, for every thought is a form of karma. That is why the Lord has said that the truth about karma is a deep mystery. Those who do karma through their thoughts load themselves with burdens so heavy that they will never be able to throw them off. On the other hand the man who becomes absorbed in work, does it as duty, and, if he finds that he cannot do a particular thing, leaves it alone,—such a person weaves no bond of karma round him.

Last evening, I rebuked . . . [4] and other boys. On that, . . .[5] told me that there was harshness in my voice and asked me if it was not a sign of anger in me. I said that I was not God. I only strive for perfection, but I am not fit to be anyone's guru. I am full of desires, and so, when I am excited, my voice is naturally raised. If I had succeeded in banishing every desire from me, I would be able to do as much work as I am doing now, but my voice would ever be the same.

I aspire to reach such a state. It is true that sometimes my voice is raised and there is a little flash of anger in my eyes. This is the state Arjuna had in mind when he asked the Lord how a person is overcome with evil desire against his will.[6] I am still swayed by desire and anger. I say this to illustrate the truth that we cease from karma in the measure that we do karma without any thought of its fruit. If I run away from a task in despair, if I get upset or raise my voice because. . .[7] does not listen to me, I weave the bonds of karma round me. Having undertaken a duty, having agreed to look after some children entrusted to me and sharing the responsibility of bringing them up, how can I now run away from the task? If I retire to the heights of the Himalayas and live there in peace, I would be indulging my body in idle comfort and weave round myself the bonds of karma. I must, therefore, remain in the midst of these responsibilities, and win *moksha* through them. If I become free from anger and shake off ignorance, if I become more vigilant and alert, I would be doing no karma even when occupied in some karma. This illustration explains both the ideas, of a person doing no karma even when occupied in karma and of another who, though he believes that he is doing no karma, is in fact weaving the bonds of karma round himself.

Everyone should apply this illustration to himself, forgetting all about me as an individual. I have mentioned my own example merely in order to explain that we are all imperfect. I say, not merely out of modesty or as a matter of form, but with detachment, that I am imperfect. This is not my modesty, but the simple truth. When I am completely free from the sway of desire and anger, you will always see me calm, more so than you see me today. I am striving to be free from these. I feel that one day I shall attain such a state of calm. In this age, we do not have the means with which to measure ourselves. The *Gita* was composed to help us. It says that we should work like machines and pour out our life in our work.

Notes

1. IV, 16.
2. IV, 17.
3. IV, 18.
4. The names are omitted in the source.
5. *Ibid.*
6. III, 36.
7. The names are omitted in the source.

[69] May 23, 1926

We should think further about the first line of the verse[1] beginning with *karmanyakarma*. We saw in a previous verse that no human being ceases from karma altogether even for a moment. That means that the very process of living is a form of karma. Eating, speaking, thinking, sleeping, all these are forms of karma (. . . .[2] said that, when he retired to that place to seek peace, he had tried to stop even thinking, for thinking, too, is a form of karma). Thus, no one can escape doing karma. Still the *Gita* distinguishes between karma and *akarma*, between the yogi and ordinary human beings, between night and day, and explains that the involuntary processes in the body are not karma; that is, even though we do such karma, we weave no bond round us through it. I have an aim in this discussion of the *Gita*, and that is that children should understand some of the ideas and act accordingly, and, therefore, the discussion is certainly a form of karma for me. If I had accepted the work of teaching and if explaining the *Gita* came naturally to me, then this very work would perhaps deserve to be described as *akarma.* Even so, the idea of *akarma* is like the Euclidean definition of a straight line, and the work of explaining the *Gita* would be *akarma* only in a relative sense. Karma becomes relatively *akarma* when it is undertaken for the service of others, for the sake of our higher good. We may be said to eat and breathe with that aim only if we have voluntarily and deliberately dedicated our body to the service of Shri Krishna. He who lives with the knowledge that his body is not his, that God makes it dance as He wills, may be said to have realized God. All karma done in that spirit is *akarma*. Anything else, though seeming *akarma,* is in truth karma. A yogi may have ceased riding fancy's horses, and still his *samadhi* may be a form of karma for him if he has sought it for better health. Some persons suffering from consumption learn to enter into such *samadhi*; it is plain that their aim in doing so is to cure themselves of their disease. Their karma in this case is not inspired by the motive of higher good. Only that karma is so inspired in which our aim is realization of God and nothing else, when this aim, too, is pursued with spontaneous naturalness. The person who is inspired by it is not in the least conscious of it. In all that he does, there is only the yearning for realizing God and no other thought. Such a person loses the very consciousness of his body, as the *gopis* did. Even those who are possessed by lust lose the consciousness of their bodies, but they go to hell because they have given themselves up to the pursuit of lust and do not yearn to see God. When such a person, after he has had enough of pleasure, experiences the joy of devotion to God, he realizes that this latter joy is far superior to the pleasure he got by giving himself up to lust, that by losing himself in the pleasure of lust he grew weaker, whereas by losing himself in the joy of God he was filled with strength. After this experience, he is no more negligent in work but learns to be proficient in it. He who does everything for the sake of the higher good and dedicates all his work to God has ceased from karma. Just as the judge dispenses justice and the hangman hangs the condemned man in the name of the king, so if we feel that in this empire of the universe we are God's slaves and are prompted by Him to do what we do, all our actions will be for our higher good.

He whose every undertaking is free from desire and selfish purpose, and he who has burnt all his actions in the fire of knowledge—such a one the wise call a *pandita.*[3]

That person whose undertakings are never inspired by selfish desire or personal aims but are altogether spontaneous, whose karmas have been burnt up by the fire of knowledge (everything that exists and will cease has life in it, which means that a piece of stone has life in it, but, though it does no karma it has no knowledge either)—such a person will not be like a stone in regard to karma but, on the contrary, may do all manner of karma and will still have his karmas burnt up by the fire of knowledge. For instance, this earth created by God is in unceasing motion and yet seems at rest; it seems so though it is spinning with a speed which would make us giddy if we could see it.

When typing on a typewriter has become mechanical work with the typist, the finger will alight on the right letter even when he is not looking at the keyboard; he who is able to work in such spontaneous manner and is fully alert, like the typist, in everything he does, may be described as the Buddha.

Notes

1. IV, 18
2. The name is omitted in the source.
3. IV, 19.

[70] June 2, 1926

We may be doing much work, but without any consciousness that we are working.[1] We wish to know the *atman* dwelling in this human body—wish to know it directly so that its knowledge may become a part of our being as it was with Sudama[2]. An experienced carpenter will make a board effortlessly, whereas one with only a theoretical knowledge of the craft will not be able to make one. He who has learnt to work effortlessly in this manner goes on working mechanically and still remains detached. The verse beginning with *yasya sarve samarambhah*[3] describes the character of such a person.

We do not have to make any effort for winking the eye; all our actions should become spontaneous like this. Anyone who has acquired control over his thoughts to this degree will never have an evil thought; such a person will move in the world as if he was no more than a corpse. He will seem so to us because he has no desire and no aim, is not subject to attachments and aversions; he is a man who has ceased from karma.

This work of explaining the *Gita* which I am doing is prompted by a personal motive, the wish to see that the boys understand it.

He who has renounced attachment to the fruit of action, who is ever content, and free from all dependence,—he, though immersed in action, yet acts not.[4]

He who has given up desire for the fruits of karma, who is ever contented, not more so at one time and less at another time, who is always satisfied with what he has—such a person may be ever so deeply engrossed in work but in truth he does nothing. As Narasinh Mehta has said, an ascetic and a perfectly chaste woman do not know the pleasure of earthly love; if any such person were to come and see us plying the charkha all the hours of the day, he would think that we had become mad, that we were so occupied with work that we paid no attention to performing daily worship. But, according to the *Gita,* we can say that we were doing no work, for we had no selfish aim in our work and did it simply as our dharma, did it merely because of our faith [in the value of spinning]. With scepticism all round us, to go on spinning with the faith that it would bring swaraj indicates the state of unvarying inner content in which we live. This is true, of course, of only those people who attribute all this power to the charkha and devote themselves whole-heartedly to it.

Expecting naught, holding his mind and body in check, putting away every possession, and going through action only in the body, he incurs no stain.[5]

He alone does not feel the body to be a burden who hopes for nothing, whose mind is ever steady and who has completely given up the desire for possessions. How does this become possible? The body, too, is a kind of property which we possess. We should so use it that we would not mind its perishing today rather than tomorrow. If we cultivate such an attitude, we would not feel the body to be a burden.

Ladha Maharaj had given up all concern with this particular form of property, the body, and kept repeating the name Siva all the hours of the day; anyone who works in that spirit, with the sole aim of giving the body its hire and not for the sake of pleasures, may be doing karma all the time and still he stores up no sins.

Notes

1. The remark was prompted by the sight of a mad man who came towards the meeting, muttering the word "Prabhu", God.
2. An indigent Brahmin friend of Krishna.
3. IV, 19.
4. IV, 20.
5. IV, 21.

[71] June 3, 1926

That person who is described as doing *shariram* karma does not have to suffer the fruits of karma. This does not mean that his karma bears no fruit, but only that he seeks none. In other words, he does not attribute the karma to his *atman*. For instance, I listen to the *Gita* being read out. I should do so with humility, for listening to it is my duty; the fruit of listening to it will follow of itself, whether we think of it or not, in the same way that a seed which has been sown grows by itself into a tree. This seed has no ego. We are animals to the extent that we have some needs in common with them, but in certain respects we are different from them. The consciousness that we do things should disappear from us. A person who writes his diary every day does not think about how much his hand worked during the day; in that way all our work should be done mechanically.

Even an action which one took to be most virtuous karma may turn out to be sin. Supposing one is born a prince through the virtue of meritorious work, how does it profit one? What good is there in being born a prince? To be born poor and to be born a prince, these are two extremes of the same state. We say that we should try to make do with less sleep, and that may seem contrary to the teaching of the verse we are discussing. But we make the effort in order that by and by sleeping less may become natural to us, just as we try to rise above *rajas* and *tamas* by engaging ourselves in *sattvik*[1] activity.

Shariram karma means karma for keeping the body alive.

Observance of *brahmacharya* and other rules has become difficult for us because we pamper the body too much. We have made difficult what should be quite natural to us. It is not natural for human beings to violate *brahmacharya*. We seek pleasures because we live as if the body and the *atman* were identical. If, instead, we look upon the body as only a material object and think merely of keeping it alive somehow, we would not run after pleasures. How can we be ever disturbed by evil desires if we look upon our body as the temple of the *atman*? Should anyone maintain himself merely by doing half an hour's writing every day? No. Anyone who does so is a thief. The mind works for the *atman*, and so does the body, but we ought to undertake physical labour to maintain the body. Even the work of teaching cannot serve as a means for this purpose. Only agriculture or similar work can count as work for the sake of the body.

Content with whatever chance may bring, rid of the pairs of opposites, free from ill will, even-minded in success and failure, he is not bound though he acts.[2]

He who is satisfied with what he gets in the ordinary course of things, who has risen above the pairs of opposites, such as happiness and suffering, has no ill will in him and bears an equal mind towards success and failure, is indifferent towards them or is not affected by them—such a person does not dance with joy on getting something which is welcome to him and does not start lamenting his lot when disagreeable things happen—he may do karma and still be not doing it, that is, will not be bound by the effects of his karma.

Of the free soul who has shed all attachment, whose mind is firmly grounded in knowledge, who acts only for sacrifice, all karma is extinguished.[3]

That person who works without attachment is free, that is, he is not bound by the effects of karma. He whose mind has become steady through knowledge and who always works in the spirit of *yajna* has all his karmas burnt up in the fire of knowledge.

It would be far better that we die than that we eat merely to serve ourselves. That is, if we cultivate a state of mind such that we eat and drink in order that we may serve God, serve the *atman*, that is, eat and drink in the spirit of *yajna*, then we shall have ceased from karma.

Notes

1. Characterized by *sattva.*
2. IV, 22.
3. IV, 23.

[72] June 4, 1926

If we recite certain verses thousands of times over and over again and with faith, they acquire great power for us. A Muslim should not tire of reciting *kalamas*[1] and a Hindu should not tire of reciting the *gayatri* or of repeating Ramanama or the *dwadash mantra*. I have discussed today's verses at great length with Vinobaji, too, but I am not sure of their meaning. The *Gita* was composed after the time of the Vedas, and the different sects have tried so to interpret its teaching that it may support their own tenets. It is too much to believe that the *Gita* condemned Vedic rituals. I have, therefore, tried again and again to get a meaning which would not conflict with the Vedic practices. Not that this was necessary for myself. My task is to find in them a meaning that would satisfy you.

The teacher of the *Gita* did not lay down that those who came after him should always read in it only the meaning which he himself had in mind. Now, it says that every karma done in the spirit of *yajna* leaves no effects behind it. Any action done without reference to one's own interest is a form of *yajna*. The next verse follows as a consequence from this, and also explains the manner of doing such *yajna*.

The offering of sacrifice is *Brahman*; the oblation is *Brahman*; it is offered by *Brahman* in the fire that is *Brahman*; thus he whose mind is fixed on acts dedicated to *Brahman* must needs pass on to *Brahman*.[2]

That which is thrown into the *yajna* is *Brahman* and so is the oblation (*arpan* has been interpreted to mean all the materials used for the purpose of the *yajna*). If that oblation is thrown by *Brahman* into the fire which is also *Brahman*, it is bound to act as *Brahman*.

Anyone who relates all his karmas to *Brahman* will merge into the latter. How can a person who sees God in every aspect of a *yajna* have to suffer the fruits of karma? He becomes both the ladle used in the *yajna* and the oblation poured out by its means. He looks upon God as a potter and offers himself as clay to Him and lets Him make from it any pot He pleases. The verse thus explains how there may be *akarma* in karma.

Notes

1. The creed of Islam as expressed in the verse from the Koran: There is no God but Allah and Mohammed is His apostle.
2. IV, 24.

[73] June 5, 1926

Shri Krishna now explains the different types of *yajna*:

Some yogis perform sacrifice in the form of worship of the gods, others offer sacrifice of sacrifice itself in the fire that is *Brahman*.[1]

I have been told by Vinoba that there is support in the Vedas for the view that a person who has attained to knowledge of the *Brahman* need not worry about performing *yajna*. One who has made his life itself a long *yajna,* why should he undertake any other *yajna*?

A woman who is nearly blind has come among us. She has a fine voice and sings *Raghupati Raghav Raja Ram*. She is a Tamilian. She has come here with her husband's permission. She appears intelligent. We should feel that anyone who serves her performs a *yajna*. Such service serves our higher good. But to a person who performs a *yajna* by means of a *yajna*, that is, who has made his whole life a *yajna,* doing a *yajna* comes most naturally. Such a person is ever engaged in doing *yajna* with ceaseless vigilance. He identifies himself with all creatures in their suffering. The meaning here is not that he gives up doing *yajna*. Rather, it becomes his very nature to engage himself in *yajna,* just as it is natural for God to dwell in the heart of the basest of human beings. Some persons make a sacrificial offering of sense organs, hearing and others, into the fire of self-control; that is, they stop hearing with their ears, speaking with their tongues, savouring food and drink with the palate and seeing with their eyes.

Others make a sacrificial offering of sound and other objects of sense into the fire of the sense-organs. Here the process is reversed. Since we cannot stop our ears altogther, we should hear only what is good.

Since we cannot keep our eyes shut for ever, we should use

them only to see the glory of God everywhere. This is what is meant by saying that some persons sacrifice the objects of sense into the fire of the organs of sense.

Notes

1. IV, 25.

[74] June 6, 1926

When Kishorelal was living apart from others in a cottage, he tried to cultivate self-control. He was disturbed by the noise of passing trains while reading the *Jnaneshvari*[1]. I made the suggestion to him that he should block his ears with pieces of rubber. But he got used to the situation and declined to use any such pieces.

But what about children? The only course for them [in such circumstances] is to take measures to stop the functioning of the organ in question, for the state of inward concentration is not easy for them to cultivate. That is how we should act in regard to sound and other objects of sense.

Proceeding, Shri Krishna says:

Others again sacrifice all the activities of the senses and of the vital energy in the yogic fire of self-control kindled by knowledge.[2]

Others stop the functioning of all sense organs, stop even the movement of *prana*, that is, breathing, make themselves motionless and enter into *samadhi*, become firmly established in the *atman* and, lighting this yoga with the fire of knowledge, make a sacrificial offering of all the organs into it.

If a person cannot control his mind by any other means, he may adopt this way. Or one may get angry with oneself and stop the functioning of all one's organs. Some persons become angry with themselves because they do not succeed in their efforts to observe *brahmacharya*. Those who sail to the North Pole sacrifice money in millions over and over again, without gatting disheartened. The man who tries to observe *brahmacharya* but fails in his efforts becomes desperate and undertakes an indefinite fast, resolving in his mind that he will not let any organ of the body function because, so long as even one of them is functioning, his mind revels in evil thoughts; he, therefore, decides that it is best to stop all organs from functioning.

This is lighting up the fire of the yoga of control of the *atman*. This is no mere *samadhi* of the body, it is *samadhi* illumined by knowledge.

A man striving for success in *brahmacharya* suffers pain as a woman in labour does. If a person cannot bear obstruction to his efforts to cultivate self-control, we see that he gets upset. This is why I often say that such a person is like a milch cow and that we should bear his kicks.

Some sacrifice with material gifts; with austerities; with yoga; some with the acquiring and some with the imparting of knowledge. All these are sacrifices of stern vows and serious endeavour.[3]

There are people in this world who perform the *yajna* of money (who let their wealth be shared by others). Some others perform *tapas*[4] and imprison the monkey which is our mind. Some others, still, practise yoga or devote themselves regularly to holy studies, to the study of the Vedas. Some perform the *yajna* of the pursuit of knowledge. They do not read, but devote themselves to reflection and meditation. Ascetics who put themselves under strict vows perform a *yajna* in that manner.

Notes

1. Commentary on the *Gita* by Jnaneshvar, a Maharashtrian saint of the thirteenth century.
2. IV, 27.
3. IV, 28.
4. Austerities.

[75] June 8, 1926

Others absorbed in the practices of the control of the vital energy sacrifice the outward in the inward and the inward in the outward, or check the flow of both the inward and the outward vital airs.[1]

Some throw *pranavayu*[2] as sacrifice into *apanavayu*[3], while others hold the latter in the former. Some others still hold both. All these are practitioners of *pranayama*[4].

Yet others, abstemious in food, sacrifice one form of vital energy in another. All these know what sacrifice is and purge themselves of all impurities by sacrifice.[5]

Notes

1. IV, 29
2. Vital air in the lung.
3. Vital air in the abdomen.
4. Breath control.
5. IV, 30.

[76] June 9, 1926

Those who partake of the residue of sacrifice—called *amrita* (ambrosia)—attain to everlasting *Brahman*. Even this world is not for a non-sacrificer; how then the next, O Kurusattama?[1]

To strive and conquer desire is also a form of *yajna*. The *Gita* teaches us to look upon all activities for *paramartha*[2] as forms of *yajna*. *Paropakar* means working for others; but the idea that we work for others is only an illusion. We always work for ourselves. We shall attain deliverance only if we work exclusively for our higher self. All activities for *paramartha*, therefore, aim at one's own good.

Coming back to the verse, those who consume what remains after the *yajna* is over, that is, those who utilize for themselves only the time which remains after they have completed the *yajna*, enjoy *amrita* and attain to the timeless *Brahman*. The person who has done no work during the day but, like a heifer idling in mud, has spent his time in bed, steals the sleep which he enjoys at night. The man who does no *yajna* can win nothing in this world; what then can he win in the other world? He is lost in both.

Note

1. IV, 31.
2. Literally, the Supreme good; the term also means altruism.

[77] June 10, 1926

The verse which we have been discussing has a wide meaning. It means that we should eat only after all others have had their food. So long as the embodied soul lives in this world, it has no choice but to have relations with others. To become disinterested in the body, therefore, means that one should devote oneself exclusively to the service of others so that one may attain the *Brahman* beyond time. We should be as impatient to attain it as a lost sheep is to get back to its fold. Those who, on the contrary, live only for themselves prosper neither in this world nor in the next. Therefore, Shri Krishna tells Arjuna: stop thinking of some people being and others not being your relations. If you may kill any people, you should kill these too.

Even so various sacrifices have been described in the Vedas; know them all to proceed from action; knowing this thou shalt be released.[1]

One meaning given to this verse is that there are these different types of *yajna* in the sight of the *Brahman* [*sic*]. This interpretation omits any reference to the Vedas, for the *Gita* has actually denounced them. And, moreover, the verses[2] in question are found nowhere in the Vedas. Ordinarily, of course, the verse should mean this: "The Vedas describe these different types of *yajna*. You should know that all of them exist through karma; only so can you win *moksha*." After explaining the meanings of karma and *akarma*, the Lord makes it clear in this verse that it is simply impossible for anyone to live without doing karma. That of course does not mean that a state of *akarma* is impossible. Every karma done for the good of the *atman*, though it appears to be karma, is in reality *akarma*. If we can renounce the fruits of karma, that is, work only for others, then we may work like horses. On the other hand, when working for ourselves, we should be like a piece of inert matter, have no interest in the work at all. This is a state of the heart, an attitude of mind. Anyone who cultivates that attitude towards everything he does, sleeping, eating, drinking or cleaning the lavatory, will attain to *moksha*.

The words *evam bahuvidhah* in this verse mean that the different types of *yajna* are enumerated only as illustrations. Others can also be included if they satisfy the *Gita*'s definition of *yajna*.

Knowledge-sacrifice is better, O Parantapa, than material sacrifice, for all action which does not bind finds its consummation in Knowledge (*jnana*).[3]

The person who performs the *yajna* of knowledge makes a greater sacrifice than another who performs the *yajna* of money, for the *yajna* of knowledge includes everything, money and all other things. Knowledge covers everything, which exists in the world, without reference to the distinction between living and non-living. If we understand the terms *dravya*[4] and *jnana* in a wide sense, a *yajna* of knowledge includes *yajna* of every kind of *dravya*. Anyone who imparts the highest knowledge to us, convinces us to the very depth of our being that the body is not the *atman,* performs a very great *yajna* indeed.

Notes

1. IV, 32
2. That is, the verses in the *Gita* enumerating the different types of yajna; IV, 24 to 30.
3. IV, 33
4. Any material; in a restricted sense, the term means "money".

[78] June 11, 1926

The masters of knowledge who have seen the Truth will impart to thee this Knowledge; learn it through humble homage and service and by repeated questioning.[1]

"You can obtain this knowledge,"Shri Krishna tells Arjuna, "by bowing before a guru in utmost humility,—by prostrating your-self before him, fuel in hand,—by serving him and by frequent questioning, by harassing him with questions, and in no other way.

The enlightened ones who have seen the truth will impart this knowledge to you."

Note

1. IV, 34.

[79] June 12, 1926

When thou hast gained this knowledge, O Pandava, thou shalt not again fall into such error; by virtue of it thou shalt see all beings without exception in thyself and thus in Me.[1]

"When you have received that knowledge," proceeds Shri Krishna, "your understanding will never again be clouded by the darkness of ignorance and you will make no distinction like that between kinsmen and others, you will learn to regard all beings with an equal eye so that you will see them all as existing in you and in Me; in other words, for you everyone will be a kinsman. The entire universe is filled by Me, and, therefore, you will see Me in all objects.

When the 'I' in you has melted away, then it will be *jale Vishnu, sthale Vishnu, Vishnu Parvatamastake*[2] for you." Once we have realized that this whole universe exists in God, how can there be any problem of violence and non-violence for us? We would feel even thieves and tigers to be ourselves. Till we feel in that way, we may be sure that we have not attained to a state of knowledge at all.

Notes

1. IV, 35
2. "Vishnu in water, Vishnu on land and Vishnu on the tops of mountains".

[80] June 13, 1926

Can we claim that we have the knowledge described in the verse which we have been discussing? Suppose that we learn in one day to recite it; do we then become seers of truth? Do we become so when we teach that verse to others? Of course not. We cannot have this knowledge merely by talking about it. We understand with our reason that the universe is the same as ourselves, but we can only imagine what that means. We cannot grasp the idea or feel its truth. The moment we leave this place, we shall treat all others as different from us. Only that person in whom this idea has sunk from the intellect to the heart—even an intellectual nincompoop can have a heart which is an ocean of compassion—can feel its truth in direct experience. Shri Krishna says to Arjuna: "When I say that men of knowledge will impart this knowledge to you, I do not mean that they will convince your reason; I mean that they will awaken in you the faith that it is so.

You will then realize that it is because of your reason that you see things as separate from one another, that in truth they are one" God, ourselves and all objects in the universe are in essence one Reality.

Even God vanishes and we have only *neti, neti*. When a person has realized this, his ignorance will have completely vanished.

Even though thou be the most sinful of sinners, thou shalt cross the ocean of sin by the boat of knowledge.[1]

"Even if you are the most wicked of sinners," says Shri Krishna, "you will cross the sea of darkness and ignorance with the ship of knowledge"—crossing the Swayambhu-Raman[2] sea of *moha*[3] sang Raychandbhai.

Hunger cannot be satisfied by the knowledge that there is food in the vessel, or even when that food is swallowed down into the stomach; it is only when it is digested in the stomach and converted into blood that we may say that our hunger is satisfied.

As a blazing fire turns its fuel to ashes, O Arjuna, even so the fire of knowledge turns all actions to ashes.[4]

First, knowledge was compared to a ship, and now it is compared to fire. It burns up the bonds of karma.

Notes

1. IV, 36.
2. The name given in Jain literature to the farthest sea, which was believed to be so vast that no one could cross it.
3. The state of delusion in which the self takes the phenomenal existence as real.
4. IV, 37.

[81] June 15, 1926

For me, the *Gita* is the ship, not because it is a learned work but because I have liked it, it has appealed to me in my old age, or because some verse in it has been a great support to me, put it any way you like.

Man does not live by bread alone, whereas the lower creatures need only food to live. Anna Kingsford used to say that men seemed like tigers and snakes. Certainly, the lower creatures are as brethren to us. We all come from the same source. But they need only food to live, whereas man lives by performing *yajna*.Everyone performs *yajna* in one way or another. The spinning-wheel is one type of *yajna*.

Prayers, too, are a *yajna* for us. They represent a mode of spiritual cleansing. Till we have performed that *yajna*, we should feel uneasy inside us. Only those who attend to these readings of the *Gita* in that spirit, not others, may be said to be really interested in it. If we were not thus interested in these readings, we would engage a teacher more learned than even Vinoba and with his help, study the *Gita* in order to learn Sanskrit or be honoured as pundits in society. Instead, we join these prayers in order that they may sustain us in our life. Man's need for prayer is as great as his need for bread. A bad man will use his ears to hear evil of others and see sinful things, but the good man says that, had he a thousand eyes and ears, he would use them to contemplate the vision of God for ever and to heat devotional songs, and employ his five thousand tongues to sing His praises. It is only after I have prayed here every day that I feel the bliss of having tasted the *amrita* of knowledge. For that man who wishes to be a real human being, dal and *roti* are not his food. They count little to him. His real food is prayer. On Sundays, I need to lie in bed till late in the morning, and in vain would Ba[1] try to get me out of it. She used to spoil my mornings, which was not right. Many women do this sort of thing. They should not. Actually I had an excuse for what I did, for in those days I did not pray (as I do now). Even so, I tell you of my mistake. Sleeping for longer hours on Sundays did not make me the less drowsy on Mondays. You are *brahmacharis*. You ought to get up in time and attend prayers every day. You may excuse yourselves from other duties, but never from prayers. You should cultivate such a state of mind that for half an hour you will have only one thought in your mind, and no other. Everyone should set apart some time in this manner for reflection. It provides an opportunity to feel one with all living creatures. That is enough for today by way of introduction to the *Gita*.

Note

1. Kasturba Gandhi.

[82] June 16, 1926

There is nothing in this world so purifying as Knowledge. He who is perfected by yoga finds it in himself in the fulness of time.[1]

We see nothing in this world as holy as this knowledge (The purest *yajna*, therefore, is the *yajna* of knowledge.). He who has become fit for *moksha* through the practice of yoga comes to this knowledge in the course of time by his own effort. That knowledge is realization of the self. As soon as this realization is attained, all the burden of this body and of karma will melt away.

It is the man of faith who gains knowledge—the man who is intent on it and who has mastery over his senses; having gained knowledge, he comes are long to the supreme peace.[2]

Anyone who has unshakable faith will win deliverance with the help of Ramanama only. Parents purposely give their children the names of the Lord. That also may save them. That person who is for ever devoted to the Lord, who is self-controlled and who can fall into sleep any time he chooses, who has perfect control over every sense attains this knowledge and soon wins peace—*moksha* through it.

Notes

1. IV, 38.
2. IV, 39.

[83] June 17, 1926

We do a sum in mathematics with the help of our reasoning faculty. It does not matter whether or not we have faith in mathematics. But, for spiritual knowledge, faith is essential. Does a child have to train his intellect in order to love its mother or father? An illiterate mother loves her child with her heart. We may have a love relationship of any kind with God. The poet has presented to us only a few aspects of Divine love. A person who has no conception of the vast sea may be given some idea of it by telling him of rivers and streams.

But the man of doubt, without knowledge and without faith, is lost; for him who is given to doubt there is neither this world nor that beyond, nor happiness.[1]

That person who does not value knowledge, who lacks faith, that is, who is a sceptic, will perish. He prospers neither in this world nor in the other.

He who has renounced all action by means of yoga, who has severed all doubt by means of knowledge—him self-possessed, no actions bind, O Dhananjaya![2]

"Therefore," Shri Krishna says, "the doubt in your heart, born of ignorance, destroy it with the sword of knowledge and take up yoga—karmayoga[3] —and get ready."

Notes

1. IV, 40.

2. IV, 41.
3. The yoga of disinterested work

[84] [Chapter V] June 18, 1926

Thou laudest renunciation of actions, O Krishna, whilst at the same time thou laudest performance of action; tell me for a certainty which is the better.[1]

Shri Vyasa uses the figure of Arjuna to make it clear that he wrote the *Mahabharata* only as a *yajna* and that those who read it for their spiritual good would also be performing a *yajna*.

Note

1. V, 1.

[85] June 19, 1926

When can we say that a person who is eating is, nevertheless, not eating? Can we say that because, while eating, he absentmindedly puts a morsel into his nostril? Anyone who thinks about play while he is eating is merely inattentive; we cannot say that he is disinterested in eating. But a person may be eating with proper attention and yet we may say of him that he is, nevertheless, not eating. Of whom can we say this? Of one who eats as though he was performing a *yajna*, who offers up his action of eating to Shri Krishna, who eats with the feeling that he does so in obedience to the Lord's command. Or, such a person may also tell himself that it is not he, but his body, that is eating—the *atman* does not eat, or drink or sleep; he will then eat to serve others, to serve the lame, the crippled and the afflicted. That will be service of God, for God who dwells in the afflicted is also like them. That person's karma of eating will be in truth *akarma,* and will not bind him. If we aspire to be good, we must ceaselessly work to serve others, serve them in a perfectly disinterested spirit. We should not serve anyone with the hope that he, too, will serve us one day, but we may serve him because the Lord dwells in him and we serve that Lord. If we hear anyone crying in distress for help, we should immediately run to him and help him. We should help the Lord crying in distress. After doing what was needed, we should feel that it was all a dream. Would the Lord ever cry in distress? In this way, all our acts of service will seem to us as dreams.

Those who offer delicacies to the Lord before partaking of them, do they really perform an act of dedication to Shri Krishna? No, they don't. They themselves eat those delicacies. They do not eat them in the spirit of *yajna.* if a person offers the best part of such dainties to others to eat and himself eats only the indifferent items which remain behind, we may describe him as *yajnashishtamritabhuj*1.

Renunciation and performance of action both lead to salvation; but of the two, *karmayoga* (performance) is better than sannyasa (renunciation).[2]

Notes

1. One who eats the *amrita* left behind in a *yajna*; IV, 31.
2. V, 2.

[86] June 20, 1926

When Shri Krishna said *nehabhikramanashosti*[1] He assured us that no effort undertaken to follow dharma is ever wasted. Man cannot completely refrain from karma, and therefore, it is easy for everyone to follow karmayoga. Renunciation of karma, on the other hand, is a difficult matter, for it requires knowledge, whereas karmayoga can be followed even by an ordinary person. To retire into a cave in the Himalayas and sit there for ever doing nothing—it is extremely difficult to succeed in such an effort. It is a hard task to cultivate such stillness that one would not be tempted by anything even in one's thoughts. The Lord, therefore, tells us that karmayoga is a better path, since the other one is beset with obstacles and is likely to encourage hypocrisy, while the karmayogi runs no such risk.

Him one should know as ever renouncing who has no dislikes and likes; for he who is free from the pairs of opposites is easily released from bondage.[2]

Why should a karmayogi be looked upon as superior to a sannyasi? A karmayogi is necessarily a sannyasi. But a karmayogi of what type? One who has no ill will, who desires nothing and is ever devoted to his duty, who is not affected by the pairs of opposites, easily becomes free from the binding effects of karma.

It is the ignorant who speak of *sankhya* and yoga as different, not so those who have knowledge. He who is rightly established even in one wins to the fruit of both.[3]

Sankhya here means sannyasa and yoga means karmayoga. Men of little understanding think them to be distinct from each other, but not so the wise. In truth, they are two sides of the same coin. Anyone who becomes established in either reaps the fruit of success in the other too.

A thing at rest and another in intense motion seem alike. The earth, for instance. Rest and motion are a pair of opposites. But he who remains unaffected by such opposites reaps the fruit of both.

The goal that the *sankhyas* attain is also reached by the yogis. He sees truly who sees both *sankhya* and yoga as one.[4]

The state which is attained through *sankhya,* that is, through renunciation of karma, is attained by the karmayogi too. He alone has true knowledge who understands that *sankhya* and karmayoga are the same thing. That is, if we consider the essence of the two, we shall find no difference between them at all. Hence work done in the spirit of *yajna,* done without egotism for our higher good and for the service of others, has a place in both.

Notes

1. In, II, 40.
2. V, 3.
3. V, 4.
4. V, 5.

[87] June 22, 1926

Karma means work which circumstances make it necessary for us to undertake, not that which we do of our own choice. We should feel that we need not even pray for *praninam artinashanam*[1] or wish to work ceaselessly with that aim. When the 'I'in a person has vanished and he has merged into God, he feels no need to pray for anything. He will do only such work as circumstances make necessary for him. If he has no inclination of his own, only the purest type of work will come to him, and he will do it with the feeling that Narayana[2] does everything. When Harishchandra got ready to put the knife to his wife's throat, was it really Harishchandra who was acting?

It was the Lord who prompted him to act as he did, and Harishchandra only carried out His order. The unhappy man, he had made himself a mere servant. Having made ourselves servants of the Lord, it is not for us to choose what we shall do and what we shall not. We should do any work which comes to us and at the same time leave the burden of such work to Narayana to shoulder.

But renunciation, O Mahabahu, is hard to attain except by yoga; the ascetic equipped with yoga attains *Brahman* ere long.[3]

For him who has not learnt to offer all his actions to Shri Krishna, sannyasa is extremely difficult to practise. The truth is that sannyasa is impossible to practise except through karmayoga. Really speaking, therefore, sannyasa is karmayoga, and nothing else. He who has become free from attachments and aversions, who has shed the "I" in him, has become a true sannyasi.

The yogi who has cleansed himself, has gained mastery over his mind and all his senses, who has become one with the *atman* in all creation, although he acts he remains unaffected.[4]

He who is established in yoga soon attains the *Brahman*. Anyone who successfully follows karmayoga becomes established in yoga. He who has become pure, he whose evil impulses have all been burnt away and become reduced to a burnt thread in which only the twists of the original material are visible, will act mechanically in everything he does. That of course does not mean that he pays no attention to what he is doing; it only means that he has no egotistic feeling that he himself is doing anything, though the thread which he draws out will be as straight as that drawn by a machine. An unthinking person works mechanically and the Lord's servant, too, does merely what he is asked to do. But he does not work for payment and, therefore, his work shines out, whereas the hired labourer's work does not shine out as he works for money. No supervisor is required to keep watch over a Lord's servant at work. Outwardly, he seems dull, but inwardly he ever lives in the *Brahman*. He will have all the virtues of a machine and none of its defects. Besides, the man who lives in the *atman*, who has subdued the demons in him and mastered the senses, who sees himself in all creatures and all creatures in himself, will make no distinction between relations and others. He will ever live as a servant of all, and will partake only of what remains after others have had their share. Of such a person it can be said, *kurvannapi na lipyate*, that he works, but is not bound by the effects of karma.

The yogi who has seen the Truth knows that it is not he

that acts whilst seeing, hearing, touching, smelling, eating, walking, sleeping, or breathing.

Talking, letting go, holding fast, opening or closing the eyes—in the conviction that it is the senses that are moving in their respective spheres.[5]

These two verses are a commentary on the preceding verse. The man who knows the Truth acts as if he himself did nothing. Whether seeing or hearing, smelling, eating, walking, lying down to sleep, breathing, speaking, parting with or accepting anything, winking—in all these he will feel that it is his senses which are functioning according to their nature. Such a person acts but does not do anything. A yogi can take up this attitude, and so can a rogue, as also a devotee of the Lord. He who has consecrated his heart to the Lord will feel no desire to do anything for himself. Even when he retires to sleep, he will say that it is his body which will fall into sleep. The functions of the body are not evil in themselves. We make them so. If the body works without interference by us, it will emit nothing but fragrance. We can thus take it as a mathematical truth that our work will tend to evil in proportion as we are conscious of the 'I' in us and it will tend to good in proportion as we shed that 'I'.

Notes

1. "End to the suffering of all creatures", from the verse: I do not desire a kingdom nor that I may go to heaven or win liberation. I only desire that the suffering of all creatures in pain may end.
2. Vishnu.
3. V, 6.
4. V, 7.
5. V, 8 & 9.

[88] June 23, 1926

If we keep loudly reciting the two verses which we have been discussing, we do not become yogis thereby. We should cultivate such a state that we wholly cease to be conscious of the 'I' in us. Only that person can apply these verses to himself who is always completely absorbed in the task on hand, whose every action is dedicated to Shri Krishna and who seeks no benefit for himself from anything he does.

If he uses his ears, it is to hear praise of God. If he uses his eyes, it is to have *darshan*[1] of the Lord. Nor does he ever suffer. Whenever anything happens which might cause him pain, he would think that the pain was not felt by him. 'If', he would tell himself, 'I forget the 'I' in me when suffering this pain and think of Rama, no one would be able to know that I had been stung by a scorpion.' He would feel that it had stung his body and that there was a red spot on it, that is all.

He works mechanically, and still everything he does shines out. His actions grow ever more beautiful. He never tires of work, never feels upset and confused.

He who dedicates his actions to *Brahman* and performs them without attachment is not smeared by sin, as the lotus leaf by water.[2]

Shri Krishna says this to guard against anyone making unworthy use of the preceding two verses. Such a person remains untouched by sin, as the lotus leaf remains untouched by water. The term "sin" is used here in a wide sense, and covers both sin and virtue.

Such a person does not have to suffer the consequences of either sinful or virtuous action. He goes on working, but remains unaffected by work. Leaves of other plants get wet and decay, but the lotus is not moistened by water.

Only with the body, mind and intellect and also with the senses do the yogis perform action without attachment for the sake of self-purification.[3]

The yogis work, but only with their bodies, with their minds or their intellectual faculties or their senses, and feel that they themselves are not working since they work without attachment and with the aim of self-purification. To work with this aim means to dedicate one's work to the *Brahman*.

We worked for self-purification in 1921, but afterwards strayed from that path and so found ourselves in difficulties.

He who works for self-purification goes on working with his machine in a disinterested spirit.

A man of yoga obtains everlasting peace by abandoning the fruit of action; the man ignorant of yoga, selfishly attached to fruit, remains bound.[4]

Renouncing the fruits of karma, the yogi wins the peace which is the reward of faith and devotion, the peace which brings *moksha*—the peace enjoyed by the man established in *Brahman*.

That is not the peace of a stone or the peace which the unthinking man enjoys, or that which the man of lust absorbed in the pursuit of lust enjoys for a while; it is the peace of the man established in *Brahman*, the bliss which belongs to the *atman*.

The man who is not established in yoga stays in the grip of desire. He who works under the sway of ignorance must be a man attached, that is, one who is bound through attachment to fruits of work or with the snake-like coil of expectation and sense-cravings.

When a snake is provoked, it can coil round us and crush us to death, but at the most it breaks our bones. To Mirabai, however, the snake in front of her seemed Shaligram[5] dancing. At the worst it would have harmed her physically, but the snake which bites the man of lust destroys his very soul.

Notes

1. Sight of an object, place or person regarded as holy.
2. V, 10.
3. V, 11.
4. V, 12.
5. Shri Krishna.

[89] June 24, 1926

We should understand the meaning of the words of the *Gita* not merely to satisfy our curiosity but with the aim of putting its teaching into practice. In my case, the constant reading of the *Gita* has filled my life with prayer. We should leave alone what we cannot put into practice. It is a misuse of our intellectual energy and a waste of time to go on reading what we cannot put into practice. I have to say this because of a complaint Shri Vinoba has made. As the students do not go to bed early, they find it difficult to rise early and their health suffers. The students complain that the teachers, too, do not retire early but keep awake talking till midnight. This does not accord well with the spirit in which we have been reading the *Gita*. We should be *sarvabhutatmabhutatma*[1] or *atmavat sarvabhuteshu*[2]. For the sake of our neighbour, we should desist from making noise or, if we talk, talk in low whispers, as thieves do. I, too, should retire early in the evening.

What does the phrase *brahmanyadhaya karmani*[3] mean? God

does not arouse him who does not wish to wake up. That means that we should adjust ourselves to the weakest limbs in society; or eliminate them, destroy and burn or bury them. If we are not ready for this, we should not exert ourselves to reform or raise any class of people.

Renouncing with the mind all actions, the dweller in the body, who is master of himself, rests happily in his city of nine gates, neither doing nor getting anything done.[4]

The self-controlled man, that is, the man established in the *atman*, mentally renounces all karma and lives in peace. To renounce all karma mentally means to make the mind indifferent to them, to withdraw it into an attitude of detachment towards work and feel that we are not doing what we are engaged in, that it is God who impels us to do it. Surely we do not feel, as we breathe, that we are breathing. We have mentally renounced that karma. It becomes necessary to breathe with a conscious effort of mind only when natural breathing is obstructed. At all other times, it goes on mechanically. The *atman* dwells, ever at rest, in this body with nine doors[5] doing nothing and causing nothing to be done. Though it may be working or acting to make others work, it will not be doing so if it has mentally renounced karma.

Notes

1. Who sees his *atman* as one with the *atman* in every creature; in V, 7.
2. Who sees himself in all creatures.
3. In V, 10.
4. V, 13.
5. Eyes, ears, nostrils, mouth and two organs of excretion.

[90] June 25, 1926

This life is a play proceeding before us. If we devote ourselves to our work without taking interest in the play or letting our mind be distracted by it, we would be *karmasannyasis*[1]. Suppose that a prisoner is asked to attend and witness another being whipped. He attends without any interest. His eyes see what is happening, but his mind may not be attentive. I would see a thing to which I become a witness by chance, but I would leave the place without stopping even a moment longer.

We recognize relationships, that this is a son and that is a brother, regard it as our duty to see that the bonds endure, and act accordingly—in all this we are involved with our minds. There is no mental renunciation of karma.

The Lord creates neither agency nor action for the world; neither does He connect action with its fruit. It is nature that is at work.[2]

The Lord says: "Ultimately I am the Creator of all beings. That means that, when you see I see, and when you do not see I, too, do not see."[3] That is [His] nature. This is a truth before which speech fails.

We may assert, from different points of view, that God is the Doer, and also that He is not.

If you withdraw interest from the functioning of your senses, they will never feel any strain and you will not feel exhausted. Of course, some exhaustion you will always feel, since complete annihilation of the 'I' sense is impossible. We discussed yesterday the idea that we should speak not of "self-realization" but of "self-purification". Self-purification is to be achieved through the body. We act through the *atman* to the degree that we have to act through the body.

In truth, however, the *atman* does nothing, nor does it cause anything to be done.

Notes

1. Those who have renounced action.
2. V, 14.
3. The second sentence is placed within brackets in the source.

[91] June 26, 1926

When God the Artist painted this human eye, He so made it that the *atman* should shine through it. He certainly could not have intended it to cast lustful glances. The function of the eye is to ensure the safety of the body and to see God. What are the thoughts which come to your mind when you look upon the image of Hanuman? Of *brahmacharya, bhakti* and service. And of strength, for he was Ramachandra's servant and Ramachandra always gives his servants the strength they need. In this way the moment we look at anyone's eyes we should be able to see the *atman* behind.

The Lord does not take upon Himself anyone's vice or virtue; it is ignorance that veils knowledge and deludes all creatures.[1]

Man's real nature is to serve others and to work for selfpurification, and so we should not cherish the 'I' in us. This is why it is said here that God does not take upon Himself anyone's sin.

But to them whose ignorance is destroyed by the knowledge of *atman*, this their knowledge, like the sun, reveals the Supreme.[2]

When a man's ignorance, which envelops the knowledge in him, has been destroyed by that knowledge, the light of God is revealed to him. God is the witness of all that occurs. The idea that we should live in obedience to Him, act only as prompted by Him—that is knowledge.

We can experience its truth directly only when all the twists in the heart have straightened out and the *atman* alone shines there forever.

Notes

1. V, 15.
2. V, 16.

[92] June 27, 1926

When the night in one's mind has turned to dawn, one comes in the presence of God.

Those whose intellect is suffused with That, whose self has become one with That, who abide in That, and whose end and aim is That, wipe out their sins with knowledge, and go whence there is no return.[1]

He whose intellect has become fixed on the Lord, who has merged in Him, who is exclusively devoted to Him and who ever lives absorbed in Him, who has dedicated his all to the Lord and trusts to Him alone, such a person, attains deliverance; the sins of such a one are washed away by knowledge.

The men of Self-realization look with an equal eye on a Brahmin possessed of learning and humility, a cow, an elephant, a dog and even a dogeater.[2]

Pundits, that is, men of knowledge, see all things with an equal eye. They have the same regard for a Brahmin rich in learning and gentleness, for a cow, an elephant, a dog or a

Chandal. They feel that the *atman* in each of these is identical with the *atman* in themselves.

The only difference is that in some the *atman* is enveloped by layers upon layers of ignorance, and in others these layers have fallen off.

What was said earlier, that the yogi sees himself in others, means the same thing as this. Ganga water in separate vessels is Ganga water after all.

In this very body they have conquered the round of birth and death, whose mind is anchored in sameness; for perfect *Brahman* is same to all, therefore in *Brahman* they rest.[3]

They have conquered the world on this very earth, in this very life, who are equal in mind to all human beings, who have no taint of impurity in them, who abide in God and live ever devoted to Him.

When can we say of a person that he is *samadarshi*? Can we say so of that man who would give equal quantities to an elephant and an ant? Indeed no. We can say it of him who gives to each according to his or her need. A mother will give nothing to her child who is ill and will give another who is well as much as he can eat. A person who is filled with the spirit of non-violence, with compassion, will so act that the world will say of him that he behaved towards all as if they were himself, did justice to all; that he gave water to him who needed water and milk to him who needed milk.

No one can be like God, absolutely free from impurity and equal towards all. One can, therefore, become *samadarshi* only by losing oneself in Him.

Notes

1. V, 17.
2. V, 18.
3. V, 19.

[93] June 29, 1926

Let us describe some instances of equal regard for all. One is that of the elephant and the ant. Second, if an enemy and a friend arrive at his place together, both hungry, the *samadarshi* will offer food first to the enemy. He would feel that to be justice. He would be afraid lest there be some hatred for the enemy lurking in his heart, and he would satisfy him first. The friend, too, would appreciate his motive.

A pundit[1] does not mean one who is merely learned, but one who is both learned and wise. If anyone warns him that feeding an enemy would be like giving milk to a snake, he would cite in reply this verse from the *Gita* and say that he was man of faith, that his father was a lover of the *Gita* and so was he, that they had never come to harm by following its teaching. 'Why should I, therefore, not continue to do so?,' he would ask.

One rule of swadeshi is that in serving people we should give priority to those who live near us. There is also an opposite rule, that we should serve first those who are distant from us and then those who are near us. Near in the first rule means physically near, and distant in the second rule means distant from us mentally. Both may mean the same thing. An enemy may be physically near and distant mentally; we should, despite his being distant, serve him first.

The reason behind this rule of swadeshi is that we cannot reach all human beings in this world. If you ignore your neighbour and seek to serve someone living far away, that would be pride on your part.

We display good manners, culture and learning in serving first those who are mentally distant from us.

In this very body they have conquered the round of birth and death, whose mind is anchored in sameness; for perfect *Brahman* is same to all, therefore in *Brahman* they rest.

Those who follow this rule in their conduct have won the battle of this life. They hold enemy and friend in equal regard. The enemy is the elephant and the friend is the ant of our illustration.

We should make ourselves like that with which we wish to be one. If we wish to lose ourselves in *Brahman*, we must become *samadarshi* as *Brahman* is.

He whose understanding is secure, who is undeluded, who knows *Brahman* and who rests in *Brahman*, will neither be glad to get what is pleasant, nor sad to get what is unpleasant.[2]

Notes

1. The reference is to V, 18.
2. V, 20.

[94] June 30, 1926

He who has detached himself from contacts without finds bliss in *atman*; having achieved union with *Brahman* he enjoys eternal bliss.[1]

The person, who has become liberated into unity with *Brahman* and who is not attached to the objects of his outgoing senses, experiences true happiness in his *atman*. One can have peace only by remaining unattached. It is impossible to prevent the impact of senseimpressions; that is why Shri Krishna speaks of the need to become unattached. If we constantly meditate on the holy feet of Rama, the impact of external impressions will have no effect on us. The *atman* that is united in yoga with *Brahman*, that is, which has attained to the state of *samadhi* in which it merges into *Brahman* and abides in it for ever, such an *atman* enjoys undying bliss.

For the joys derived from sense-contacts are nothing but mines of misery; they have beginning and end, O Kaunteya; the wise man does not revel therein.

The man who is able even here on earth, ere he is released from the body, to hold out against the flood-tide of lust and wrath,—he is a yogi, he is happy.[2]

Shri Krishna is repeating here what he has already explained in Chapter II.

He who finds happiness only within, rest only within, light only within,—that yogi, having become one with Nature, attains to oneness with *Brahman*.[3]

That yogi who finds his happiness and his peace within him, who does not need external objects to make him happy, who is ever self-absorbed and is inspired by the light which shines within him, such a yogi has merged into *Brahman* and attains nirvana in it.

We should read the *Bhagavad Gita* in order that its poetry may be revealed to us.[4] There are two types of nirvana. One is destruction of one's body, after which, however, the necessity of being born again and again remains as ever. The other nirvana is *brahmanirvana*, which is a state of void. But the void is in regard to the external world; within it is all bliss of illumination.

They win oneness with *Brahman*— the seers whose sins are wiped out, whose doubts are resolved, who have mastered themselves, and who are engrossed in the welfare of all beings.[5]

Rishis who are sinless and pure attain to *brahmanirvana, Rishis* of what description? Those whose doubts have vanished, who hold their *atman* a prisoner (have control over it) and who rejoice in the good of all creatures.

Such a *rishi* can bear ill will to no one. He is ever ready to serve the welfare of even the most wicked. He serves the whole world. A person can become the very embodiment of selfless service only if Rama dwells in his heart. Anyone who is earnestly concerned for the good of another cannot bear any real suffering on the part of the latter. We have heard of fathers who get cholera if their sons are infected by it, though of course their concern was only for their sons.

A father may not be happy with his son, and still he cannot bear when the latter suffers. A *rishi* like this would be moved to profuse tears by the suffering of others, and he would strive ceaselessly to end it.

Notes

1. V, 21.
2. V, 22 & 23.
3. V, 24.
4. This sentence is in square brackets in the source.
5. V, 25.

[95] July 1, 1926

Sarvabhutahite ratah: We have an instance of this in the story of Yudhishthira and his dog.[1] We should not merely cure the fever of a member of our family, but try to discover the cause of the fever from which the whole world is suffering and remove that cause. All beings in the world are sunk in ignorance.

Do you know anything about the *atman*? Perhaps a little. Well, a *rotla*[2] is unbaked before it is baked.[3]

The cause of disease is not in the stomach, it is indulgence of the palate, and the cause of that, again, is the mind.

Rid of lust and wrath, masters of themselves, the ascetics who have realized *atman* find oneness with *Brahman* everywhere around them.[4]

Those yogis who are free from desire and anger, whose minds have become steady and who are ever absorbed in their *sadhana*[5] who have realized the self, are always and in all circumstances in a state of *brahmanirvana*.

That ascetic is ever free—who having shut out the outward sensecontacts, sits with his gaze fixed between the brows, outward and inward breathing in the nostrils made equal; his senses, mind, and reason held in check; rid of longing, fear and wrath; and intent on Freedom.[6]

Outward action is a symbol of inner action. It is not enough that breathing is regular and the eyes are focused on a point between the brows; these actions should be symbols of an inner state.

The first verse here runs on into the second one.

Knowing Me as the Acceptor of sacrifice and austerity, the great Lord of all the worlds, the Friend of all creation the yogi attains to peace.[7]

Since God is the Friend of all creatures, why need such a person fear Him?

Since He accepts all service and all our karmas, they can never be fruitless. In dedicating everything to Him, we necessarily act without thought of self. And we are convinced in the heart of our hearts that nothing that we do will remain fruitless.

Notes

1. In the *Mahabharata*, Yudhishthira refused to enter Heaven unless a dog that followed him was also allowed to go, with him.
2. Thick, round cake of unleavened bread, made of coarse millet.
3. This paragraph is placed within brackets in the source.
4. V, 26.
5. Single-minded effort for self-realization.
6. V, 27 & 28.
7. V, 29.

[96] Chapter VI, July 2, 1926

The last chapter raised the question, "Of sannyasa and karmayoga, which is superior?" Shri Krishna has tried to answer the question, but the problem is not one which can be easily solved. The personal God and the impersonal *Brahman*, both are real; and likewise he who rests in absolute peace and he who is ceaselessly occupied in work, both are right, for the sannyasi is in fact working and the other one who is always working rests in absolute peace. One person may feel that there is nothing he need do, that he is already in the presence of God; such a person can cease from work. He who has free access to the king's court, what more need he do? When the subjects themselves know the king's will and carry it out, what work need the king do? It would surprise the subjects only if he came forward to work. I have still to remind you again and again that you should not doze here, that you should be attentive, and so on; but a day will come when it will not at all be necessary for me to do this, for all of you will have then learnt to work methodically. It is, therefore, right and proper that at present I keep telling you these things and take interest in these matters; it will be equally right if, by and by, I stop doing so and let myself rest in peace.

But Arjuna does not say yet that he has understood the point, and so Shri Krishna takes up the same argument again in Chapter VI.

He who performs all obligatory action, without depending on the fruit thereof, is a sannyasi and a yogi—not the man who neglects the sacrificial fire nor he who neglects action.[1]

He who deposits all his works in God's treasury, and goes on doing his duty without looking for reward—for, as we know, God is the enjoyer of *yajna* and *tapas*,—is both a sannyasi and a yogi. But that person who never lights the fire for *yajna*—originally it was an act of public service to keep a fire burning in the home for performing a *yajna*—or never works, is neither a sannyasi nor a yogi.

Such a person would in fact be a prince of idlers.

What is called sannyasa, know thou to be yoga, O Pandava; for none can become a yogi who has not renounced selfish purpose.[2]

Shri Krishna says: "Know that yoga is the same thing that the learned describe as sannyasa. For you, it is not sannyasa to run away from the battle; sannyasa for you lies in fighting—it is I that enjoy a *yajna*—for the person who has not renounced personal motives for action can never be a yogi. Sannyasa is not something which can be demonstrated outwardly; it is a matter of the spirit within. The restless play of desires and fancies should cease; only then can one be a sannyasi."

Notes

1. VI, 1.
2. VI, 2.

[97] July 3, 1926

For the man who seeks to scale the heights of yoga, action is said to be the means; for the same man, when he has scaled those heights, repose is said to be the means.[1]

For the *muni* who aspires to master yoga, the only means is work (For yoga has been defined as skill in action). If a person lets himself be beaten for a long time on the anvil of work, some day he may be shaped into a yogi. For him who has established himself in yoga, who has attained to a state of spiritual equipoise, whose mind has become steadfast, for such a person the right means [of continuing in this state] is *shama,* that is, resting in peace.

The argument here is the same that we discussed yesterday.

Today, I have to try and explain my meaning in different ways. To succeed in my effort, I have to see that my meaning sinks into you, so that you understand it as clearly as I do. This effort is a kind of yoga and will be rewarded with success. When you learn to understand my meaning through a mere gesture, then the right means for us will be silence. A factory is filled with noise the whole day, but, when the time for closing it arrives, complete peace reigns in it. That machine required the means of work in order to be a yogi; afterwards, peace became the means. That is how a well-ordered machine acts. Such peace is not the peace of the grave or the peace of lethargy or inertness; it is the peace of conscious life, the peace of the sea.

When a man is not attached either to the objects of senses or to actions and sheds all selfish purpose, then he is said to have scaled the heights of yoga.[2]

When a person remains unattached to objects of the senses or to work, but uses his senses and works in a detached spirit, such a person, then, who has renounced all personal motives for work, is said to have established himself in yoga.

By one's Self should one raise oneself, and not allow oneself to fall; for *Atman* (Self) alone is the friend of self, and Self alone is self's foe.[3]

You can win *moksha* only by your own effort. Today, we

simply act as enemies of our *atman*. The *atman* is self-effulgent, and so it must win its freedom by its own effort. Who can light the divine sun?

He rises into freedom as soon as it is dawn. He comes, established in yoga, and sinks into peace in the evening (But does the sun really sink into peace? Shall I have sunk into peace even when I die?).

Notes

1. VI, 3.
2. VI, 4.
3. VI, 5.

[98] July 4, 1926

In our ordinary language we say that God grants freedom to the *atman*, for we do not know how to express the idea in any other way.

But can the *atman* ever merge in God except through its own power?

It has all the attributes of God, and that is why it can merge in Him. As the *atman* is self-effulgent, so is God. A thing cannot merge in something else with unlike attributes. We are advised to take care and see that our atman does not destroy itself, for it is in the power of the *atman* to do so, though, of course, it cannot annihilate itself completely because it is imperishable. The man who says "I am an atheist" contradicts himself in that very statement. We cannot add a single moment to the life of this universe, and so also we can never succeed in destroying the *atman*.

His Self alone is friend who has conquered himself by his Self; but to him who has not conquered himself and is thus inimical to himself, even his Self behaves as foe.[1]

While we live, there are two sides in us: the demoniac and the divine, the God-like and the Satanic. So long as this strife goes on, it is our duty to fight Satan and protect ourselves. In the war between gods and demons, it is the former who always win in the end. When the world is no more, God will laugh and ask where Satan was. The *atman* of the atheist acts as his enemy. The truth is that the *atman* of each of us does so, thanks to the evil of *kaliyuga*.

Of him who has conquered himself and who rests in perfect calm the Self is completely composed, in cold and heat, in pleasure and pain, in honour and dishonour.[2]

That person who has overcome the lower self in him and who is ever unperturbed, in heat or cold, pleasure or pain, honour or dishonour,—any praise or censure given to us is like a stream which flows away towards God and disappears—the *Paramatman* is such a person becomes *samahita*[3]. Even in him who is the very image of unquiet, who is filled, not with non-violence, but with violence, who is not truthful but untruthful—even in such a one the Supreme Self abides in perfect equipoise.

Notes

1. VI, 6.
2. VI, 7.
3. Gandhiji has not indicated the meaning which he attaches to it.

[99] July 6, 1926

We can say that the *atman* dwells in perfect equipoise when what is outside of us is a reflection of what is within. It will not do if the body is erect but the mind is not so. Today our minds are not erect.

The dog has four legs, and we have two, and yet our minds behave like those of four-legged creatures.

The yogi who is filled with the contentment of wisdom and discriminative knowledge, who is firm as a rock, who has mastered his senses, and to whom a clod of earth, a stone and gold are the same, is possessed of yoga.[1]

Jnana here means listening to readings from the Shastras, meditating over them, studying them, and *vijnana* means realizing the *atman* in direct experience. *Jnana* is understanding through reason, and *vijnana* is that knowledge which sinks through reason into experience. *Jnana* is knowledge obtained from the Shastras, whereas *vijnana* is knowledge which is part of one's experience. Non-violence will have become direct experience for us in this sense when our whole life comes to be permeated with the spirit of compassion, when non-violence manifests itself in us in its true essence. That boy who comes to feel compassion as his own experience will to that extent have purified himself, or attained knowledge of the self.

He whose *atman* is filled to perfect contentment with such *jnana* and *vijnana*, who dwells firmly like *kuta*—he is a *kutastha* that is, who endures blows, as the anvil does without ever breaking into pieces, remains unshaken in the midst of even extreme suffering—who has subdued his senses completely, such a one may be described as a yogi who has attained freedom. He has become united with God, has become inwardly purified. To such a yogi, clay, stone and gold, all are equal. All three come from earth. Earth which has hardened is stone.

Gold, silver, diamonds, sapphire, all these are transformations of earth. But they are all without any worth—everyone of them is but dust. If we shed greed, we would look upon all these articles with the same eye.

He excels who regards alike the boon companion, the friend, the enemy the stranger, the mediator, the alien and the ally, as also the saint and the sinner.[2]

He who has the same regard for friend and foe, for one who deserves to be hated and one who is a kinsman, for the sadhu and the sinner, as he would have for clay and gold, he may be said to have won the battle of this life. The same law applies to the world of the living which applies to the world of inert matter. As clay and gold are ultimately the same substance, so the sadhu and the sinner are ultimately one.

The sadhu and the sinner are forms of the same reality. They are both manifestations of the *atman*. The layer of uncleanliness has disappeared from over the sadhu's *atman* and is becoming ever thicker over the sinner's. We shall have risen above the ordinary level only when we learn to have equal regard for either. Tulsidas has shown by his example how we can do that.

Let the yogi constantly apply his thought to *atman* remaining alone in a secluded place, his mind and body in control, rid of desires and possessions.[3]

A yogi should constantly live in a solitude and be in union with the *atman*. To live in solitude means to withdraw the mind from the outside world. He who lives by himself and seeks to control his mind should shed all desires and, having renounced all possessions, yoke the *atman* to the *Paramatman* in contemplation. Renunciation of possessions includes renunciation of the desire for possessions too. He who practises *japa*[4] in solitude in the hope of winning a kingdom is no yogi. A man who possesses a few lakhs of rupees may be less acquisitive than another who daily gives away money in charity and sacrifices wealth but is constantly thinking of money.

Notes

1. VI, 8.
2. VI, 9.
3. VI, 10.
4. Constant repetition of a name or formula believed to have spiritual power.

[100] July 7, 1926

Rahasi[1] means in a quiet place free from noise and *ekaki*[2] means living by oneself. One can live in solitude and by oneself even in the midst of the bazaar in Ahmedabad.

Even so, one must have physical solitude. One can go to a cremation ground and, thinking on the perishable body, experience the feeling of solitude. *Yatachittatma*[3] means one who is free from physical or mental restlessness. A man can make do with a mere *langoti*[4], which even a flying kite may bring him. Can anyone, however, do without some possessions for the comfort of the body?

We should supply the body its minimum needs and not seek to multiply them. If we go on multiplying bodily needs, we shall ever be going from birth to death and from death to birth. So long as the turban is there, we may use it but we should not buy another to replace it; likewise, we may look after the body, but only to supply its minimum needs. We shall not then have to be born and to die again and again. *Atmanam unjita*[5] means yoking the *atman* to the *Paramatman* fixing it on the *Paramatman.*

Fixing for himself, in a pure spot, a firm seat, neither too high nor yet too low, covered with *kusha* grass, thereon a deerskin, and thereon a cloth.[6]

One should place a seat in a holy spot—*desha* may mean even "country", for it was supposed that Bharat was *karmabhumi*—a country in which people engage themselves in *karma* with ceaseless vigilance is a *karmabhumi*—whereas one is born in other countries to enjoy the fruits of one's actions (though India is no longer such a country today)—One should place a firm seat, neither too high nor too low. One should spread out *kusha* grass and *ajin,* and then cover the spot with a piece of cloth. *Ajin* means deerskin. This is mentioned because in those days deer used to be hunted. A yogi devotes himself to his practice for quite a long time. He should, therefore, protect himself carefully lest he should feel cold and his limbs become cramped.

He should place himself on such a seat and remain there motionless.

Sitting on that seat, with mind concentrated, the functions of thought and sense in control, he should set himself to the practice of yoga for the sake of self-purification.[7]

Notes

1. In VI, 10.
2. *Ibid.*
3. *Ibid.*
4. Codpiece.
5. In VI, 10.
6. VI, II.
7. VI, 12.

[101] July 8, 1926

I gave a wrong meaning yesterday to the phrase *yatachittendriya*.[1] To control the activity of the *chitta* and the senses means to restrain such activity. *Yogah chittavrittinirodhah*[2]. If the waves are continually rising, we describe the sea as stormy. There is no essential difference between the sea and the waves in it. All souls are like waves in water, that is, they are but different forms of that water. We need not ask why we should let waves rise in ourselves. Human beings conceive God as a kind of doll; respectable people even make gold images of Him. All this goes on. The rising of a wave means being born, and the wave subsiding means death. Telling himself this, a man may become steady in mind and let the wave of desire subside in it. Patanjali tells us that if we restrain the waves from rising, we shall know whether the master of the *chitta* is desire or whether it is God. Expanding the phrase *chittavriti*, Shri Krishna sopke of *chitta* and *indriyas* in this verse.

Keeping himself steady, holding the trunk, the neck and the head in a straight line and motionless, fixing his eye on the tip of his nose, and looking not around.

Tranquil in spirit, free from fear, steadfast in the vow of *brahmacharya*, holding his mind in control, the yogi should sit, with all his thoughts on Me, absorbed in Me.[3]

Notes

1. In VI, 12.
2. "Yoga is controlling the activity of the mind"—Patanjali in *Yogasutra*.
3. VI, 13 & 14.

[102] July 9, 1926

These four verses describe processes of yoga. I remember to have read in jail that they would take not less than six months to learn.

These processes are physical actions, and we cannot be certain that everyone will profit from them. The body and the mind, however, are so difficult to control that in our country people attach special importance to these processes. When such ideas are given importance in theory, all kinds of experiments are undertaken, as, for instance, climbing Dhavalgiri as a holy effort. Two Italian boys had decided to tour round the whole earth walking. They were just young boys. They were happy with what they had undertaken. When I asked them what they hoped to learn from their tour, one of them got very angry. They would acquire a venturesome spirit, from which they themselves would profit, but in other ways they would have simply thrown away their lives. The same is true about *pranayama* and other processes which have been mentioned. There is no fraud behind them,and no intention to impose on people; they are a means of fixing our mind on God. If I resolve to observe silence even when in the midst of a bazaar, why should I let my mind be distracted by the noise around me? Similarly, while attending these prayers, too, we are at once in the midst of society and in solitude.

The yogi, who ever thus, with mind controlled, unites himself to *atman,* wins the peace which culminates in *Nirvana,* the peace that is in Me.[1]

We may attain the peace which follows our merging in *Brahman* if we are good children of God.

Yoga is not for him who eats too much, nor for him who fasts too much, neither for him who sleeps to much, nor yet for him who is too wakeful.[2]

Yoga is not meant for the person who eats too much. He will not succeed in his efforts for spiritual discipline. Nor will the person who eats nothing, who takes a vow of total abstinence from God, succeed in his yoga. Similarly, the man who sleeps or keeps awake too long also will not succeed.

It should be borne in mind that this is said in continuation of the preceding four verses. It is true that anyone who eats or sleeps too much can achieve nothing. Some persons live merely on the physical level; they can achieve nothing worth while. But the converse requires a little thinking about. He who has undertaken spiritual discipline but cannot bear hunger will be in the same mental condition as the starving millions in the country. He will not be able to provide his *chitta* the nourishment it needs and so he will not succeed in fixing his thoughts on God. And the same is true about keeping awake.

There is no fear that anyone here intends to abstain from food or to keep awake too long in this manner. This verse refers to a person who imposes such discipline on himself for progress in yoga. But a person who, however hard he tries, cannot acquire control over his senses, whose eyes always open to cast lustful glances and whose other senses, too, crave indulgence—let such a person certainly undertake long fasts, even if his body should perish in consequence. He should do nothing for outward show. We look upon truth as the chain which binds us all together here. Any of us here who fasts will not deceive himself. He may fast if he feels that he cannot curb his cravings in any other way. An idea has come to prevail nowadays that in this world one must satisfy one's desires. Hence my advice to you that you should not spare yourself any harshness in striving for selfpurification.

If a person loves to boast about secretly gratifying his eye, ear or palate, it would do him much good to take any number of vows to curb the body and cultivate vigilance. If we wish to, we can certainly control the senses. But we do not wish do so, and then look for excuses. The *Gita* advises such persons not to eat or sleep too much.

The four verses we have discussed describe a method which serves as a kind of help like that with which a child may learn to walk.

They advise one to follow the golden mean. Having adopted

such a method, one's effort should be to do or to die. If people sacrifice so much to discover the North Pole, will it be too much if we lay down our lives in the effort to discover the North Pole of the *atman*?

Notes

1. VI, 15.
2. VI, 16.

[103] July 10, 1926

Shri Krishna advised moderation in the beginning, the avoiding of excess in all matters. It is only by and by that one can judge what constitutes excess. He said, therefore, that in the beginning one should proceed slowly.

A time may come, however, when we shall not feel as excess what may seem to be so to an ordinary person. When a person is distracted by innumerable evil impulses and feels himself helpless to curb them, he may employ satyagraha against his body and against God. We should scrupulously practise non-violence towards others, but we would come to grief if we adopt it in dealing with our body.

Against our body we must employ non-co-operation. That is, we must begin by non-co-operating with the evil impulses in our heart. We must tell the body that we have been paying it hire in the form of food for working as our watchman, but that we have decided to stop paying it from today because it is not doing its duty properly. We may pay rent only for a house which serves to protect us, of which the roof does not leak and the walls are not dilapidated. Why pay for a house which is rotten inside? The other one with a leaking roof and dilapidated walls can be repaired, but what can we do with a house the air in which has become poisoned? Thus, if the body does not fulfil the conditions of our leasing it, we have a right to go on an indefinite fast.

To him who is disciplined in food and recreation, in effort in all activities, and in sleep and walking, yoga (discipline) becomes a relief from all ills.[1]

The man who avoids excess, what does he gain? He who is regular in food, rest and so on, who acts with due moderation in everything, who is moderate even in his sleep, will find that his practice of yoga ends all his suffering.

When one's thought, completely controlled, rests steadily only on *atman*, when one is free from longing for all objects of desire, then one is called a yogi.[2]

When the mind has come under our complete control, when it is easily restrained by us, when it is fixed constantly on the *atman*, that is, acts in everything in obedience to the *atman*, when it has become completely disinterested, that is, become free from all desires, then the person may be said to be established in yoga.

As a taper in a windless spot flickers not, even so is a yogi, with his thought controlled, seeking to unite himself with *atman*.[3]

The condition of the yogi who is regularly practising yoga and who has acquired control over his mind is like that of a lamp in a windless place, which does not flicker. If we are unsteady in mind, the storm of the cravings of the senses blows out the *atman* as a breeze blows out the lamp. As the latter gets its food from air, so the *atman* gets the food it needs through the senses and the mind. The lamp gets its food from air which is motionless; likewise the *atman* gets nourishing food from the mind if we keep the air of its impulses still.

Where thought curbed by the practice of yoga completely ceases, where a man sits content within himself, *atman* having seen *atman*.[4]

When the impulses in a persons' mind have subsided and the mind is filled with peace, when through the practice of yoga the mind has come under one's control and its impulses have subsided, when the person sees the *atman* through the *atman*, that is, when his mind has become absorbed in the *atman* and he lives for ever content in the *atman*,—such a person has become a yogi.

Notes

1. VI, 17.
2. VI, 18.
3. VI, 19.
4. VI, 20.

[104] July 11, 1926

Watt discovered that if we collect steam and let it escape through a pipe, it will draw a load of any weitht. Similarly, those boys who restrain all their outgoing impulses and concentrate them in one direction will be able to carry any weight on their shoulders. How much, then, would we benefit if we restrain all these impulses and let them subside and be transformed into devotion to God.

Where he experiences that endless bliss beyond the sense which can be grasped by reason alone; wherein established he swerves not from the Truth;[1]

When compared with the highest bliss—the bliss which abides for ever—the pleasures of the senses are but momentary. That bliss cannot be felt through the senses, it can be experienced only by the intellect. If a person has perceived with his intellect the reality which God is, if he has understood with it his duty and then yoked himself to the chariot of God, if, shaking off lethargy, he has entered his name in God's office for duty—such a person will never be shaken from his purpose.

A person whose mind has become fixed in this manner does not cease even for a moment to be conscious of the reality which is God.

He is a yogi.

Where he holds no other gain greater than that which he has gained; and where, securely seated, he is not shaken by any calamity however great;[2]

Having attained this state, the person does not even dream that he can gain anything better still. Such a condition is possible only if one thinks about nothing but Ramanama even in one's dreams, if one has worked the whole day in a disinterested spirit of service. If we have not spent the night in sound sleep, if we have had a bad dream, we may understand that our mind is still full of greed, attachment, etc.

He whose mind does not sleep at all during any hour of the day is firmly established in yoga, he is single-minded in his devotion.

I once saw in Pretoria jail a Negro who had a mind so strong, like a demon's, that he never shrank back, no matter how much he was flogged. The yogi's mind, however, becomes like a god's; his skin glows and the mind never wavers. If the mind of a person who dwells in solitude is wandering in all directions, though physically alone he lives amidst a crowd. That state should be known as yoga (union with the Supreme), the disunion from all union with pain. This yoga must one practise with firm resolve and unwearying zeal.[3]

What has been described as yoga means complete absence of suffering. The state beyond happiness and suffering cannot be described in words. We speak of it as peace. When we are in that state, we are said to be in yoga. We should establish ourselves in such yoga with a determined mind, without getting tired of the effort.

Notes

1. VI, 21.
2. VI, 22.
3. VI, 23.

[105] July 13, 1926

Anyone who depends for his happiness on external circumstances makes it plain that in fact he does not want to be happy. In the end such a person becomes unhappy. But he who feels neither happiness nor misery—we should throw both into the river Sabarmati—if we become glad on getting something which is to our liking and feel miserable when we get something which we do not like, either state of mind is bad—he who rises above both happiness and misery has achieved yoga. Yoga means absence of suffering, never feeling miserable. If anyone abuses us, we should lay the abuse at God's feet.

Likewise, if anyone praises us, the praise too we should lay at His feet.

This is the meaning of non-possessiveness. He is a yogi who cultivates such a state of mind and feels himself as light as a flower. Shaking oneself completely free from longings born of selfish purpose; reining in the whole host of senses, from all sides, with the mind itself;

With reason held securely by the will, he should gradually attain calm and with the mind established in *atman* think of nothing.[1]

Such a person is a yogi; that is, he escapes from the dualities of happiness and suffering.

Wherever the fickle and unsteady mind wanders, thence should it be reined in and brought under the sole sway of *atman*.[2]

Proceeding, Shri Krishna explains in different words the idea of the preceding verses. He has asked Arjuna to fix the mind on the *atman*. What more can He say? But He tries to explain the idea still more clearly.

One should withdraw the mind from any object or thought to which it wanders, hold it in check and bring it under the control of the atman.

The speed of air can be measured by a meterologist and that of electricity by a scientist. But no machine has yet been invented to measure the speed of the mind. It is unsteady and restless. We should withdraw it from every direction in which it flies and fix it in the right place, that is, in the *atman*.

For, supreme bliss comes to this yogi, who, with mind becalmed, with passions stilled, has become one with *Brahman*, and is purged of all stain.[3]

Such a yogi, whose mind has become stilled, whose *rajasik* impulses, whose egotism and pride, have all completely subsided, and who has become merged in *Brahman*—such a yogi will experience the supreme bliss.

The yogi, cleansed of all stain, unites himself ever thus to *atman*, easily enjoys the endless bliss of contact with *Brahman*.[4]

The yogi who has thus learnt to yoke his *atman* constantly [to God], who has been purified of his sins, who has felt the contact of *Brahman*, enjoys everlasting bliss.

The man equipped with yoga looks on all with an impartial eye, seeing *atman* in all beings and all beings in *atman*.[5]

He who is established in yoga, who looks upon all with an equal eye, sees himself in all other creatures and all other creatures in himself—such a yogi with an equal eye for all can enjoy the bliss of merging in *Brahman*.

Notes

1. VI, 24 & 25.
2. VI, 26.
3. VI, 27.
4. VI, 28.
5. VI, 29.

[106] July 14, 1926

The verse which we took up yersterday is an important one. The yogi is not one who sits down to practise breathing exercises;

he is one who looks upon all with an equal eye, sees other creatures in himself.

Such a one attains *moksha*. To look upon all with an equal eye means to act towards others as we would towards ourselves. That idea is explained still further in the following verse.

He who sees Me everywhere and everything in Me, never vanishes from Me nor I from him.[1]

"He who sees Me everywhere and sees all creatures and objects in Me, I am never absent from such a person. He is always dear to Me, he is never far from Me",—as Hanuman was never far from Ramachandra.

Note

1. VI, 30.

[107] July 15, 1926

It is not easy to see all creatures in ourselves. The key with which to achieve this is given in the next verse, and that is, that one should see others in oneself by seeing them and oneself in God. As ice becomes what it is from water, so we have all come from the same water and shall turn again into that water. The hailstone which realizes that it is water in substance will feel itself as water. God and God's *maya* are one; what distinction, then, can there be between a Brahmin, a *Chandal* and a Sudra? That is why the sage Bharadwaja asked Rama whether the latter had killed Ravana or only his own *maya*. Rama is never absent from us and we are never far from Rama.

The yogi who, anchored in unity, worships Me abiding in all beings, lives and moves in Me, no matter how he live and move.[1]

"The yogi," says Shri Krishna, "who worships Me the dweller in all creatures, who, after merging in *Brahman*, feels that he is *Brahman* and that the world exists in *Brahman* and who worships Me with that feeling, such a yogi, though ever enganged in outward activities, lives in Me."

As they say, "walking with unsteady steps on the earth but fixing the mind on the sky", so a person who has his eyes always fixed on the sky of his heart dwells in God every moment, whether walking or eating or drinking, or in any condition whatever. There are impostors who claim that, though they may indulge in immoral pleasures, they are still yogis. They tell us that, being victims of *maya,* we may hold that some things are permitted and others forbidden, but that they themselves are bound by no rules. If we ask them to exchange their gold for our stone, they will not agree. They will answer that they are learned men and the gold had better be with them. But about the actions of a person who has banished all evil from his heart, the world will say—he himself will not claim it—that though doing karma he dwells in God.

He who, by likening himself with others, senses pleasure and pain equally for all as for himself, is deemed to be the highest yogi. O Arjuna.[2]

He who acts towards others as if they were himself will meet their needs as if they were his own, will do to others what he would to himself, will learn to look upon himself and the world as one. He is a true yogi who is happy when others are happy and suffers when other suffer.

Only that person who has reduced himself to a cipher, has completely shed his egotism, can claim to be so. He alone may be said to be such a person who has dedicated his all to God. But this is a difficult state to achieve, and so Arjuna puts a question.

I do not see, O Madhusudana, how this yoga, based on the equal mindedness that Thou hast expounded to me, can steadily endure, because of fickleness (of the mind).[3]

When we are travelling in a train, we cannot see clearly the things outside. That is how it is.

For fickle is the mind, O Krishna, unruly, over-powering and stubborn; to cub it is, I think, as hard as to curb the wind.[4]

Arjuna says: "O Krishna, the mind is fickle, it unsteadies the heart, it is strong, and obstinate in its fickleness. We can see this truth if we can curb it, but it is as difficult to curb it as it is to curb air."

Undoubtedly, O Mahabahu, the mind is fickle and hard to curb; yet, O Kaunteya, it can be held in check by constant practice and dispassion.

Without self-restraint, yoga, I hold, is difficult to attain; but the selfgoverned soul can attain it by proper means, if he strive for it.[5]

Notes

1. VI, 31.
2. VI, 32.
1. VI, 33.
2. VI, 34.
3. VI, 35 & 36.

[108] July 16, 1926

We may have studied the *Gita* with great care and attention, but we can achieve nothing if we lack strength of heart. We should strive for self-purification in respect of all our attachments. We should overcome ignorant attachments and carry out self-purification. Arjuna has become a bridge between Shri Krishna and the world. Possessing such knowledge and after having enjoyed, the privilege of Shri Krishna's company for so long a time, he should have no question to ask. It is for the benefit of the world that he puts all the questions.

If one, possessed of faith, but slack of effort, because of his mind straying from yoga, reach not perfection in yoga, what end does he come to, O Krishna?[1]

He who does not persevere in his effort to be a yogi, who does not strive hard enough, who has faith but whose mind has wandered away from yoga—he may have retired into a secluded spot in a forest but his thoughts dwell in the world without—what becomes of such a person who has failed to reach the goal of his yoga? Does he rise or does he fall?

Without a foothold, and floundering in the path to *Brahman*, fallen from both, is he indeed not lost, O Mahabahu, like a dissipated cloud?[2]

A person may have read a number of books and been struggling for some spiritual progress. But afterwards he thinks and tells himself: No, I feel inclined to retire into solitude and put my head in God's lap and offer satyagraha to him." One, however, who has let his mind wander in all sorts of ways and has become full of doubts perishes like a scattered cloud. He becomes like a jug without a bottom. Because he has strayed from the path towards *Brahman* which he has been following, does such a person perish?

This my doubt, O Krishna, do Thou dispel utterly; for there is to be found none other that Thou to banish this doubt.[3]

Notes

1. VI, 37.
2. VI, 38.
3. VI, 39.

[109] July 17, 1926

Shri Krishna answers this question with a solemn assurance.

Neither in this world, nor in the next, can there be ruin for him, O Partha; no well-doer, oh loved one, meets with a sad end.[1] Shri Krishna says: "No, Arjuna, such a person is destroyed neither in this world nor in the other, for a weak yogi who strives halfheartedly is certainly not destroyed. No one who strives for good ever comes to harm." In these words, Shri Krishna assured the whole world that He would always welcome those who sought Him as persons engaged in a good effort, no matter with what energy they pursued their aim. Every action bears fruit and in particular no effort for realizing God is ever wasted. A person making such an effort never falls, but always rises. If he has faith, what does it matter if he connot strive with determination? Whatever his achievement, he will be counted as a soldier in God's army.

Fallen from yoga, a man attains the world of righteous souls, and having dwelt there for numberless years is then born in a house of pure and gentle blood.[2]

Such a person rises, after his death, to the world which men of good deeds attain and, after dwelling in it for a long time, is born in a family of men who are holy and possess *shri*—that is, men who enjoy God's grace, not necessarily posses riches—for it is difficult for one born in a rich family to practise yoga or chant Ramanama. Is Vishnu, with whom dwells Lakshmi, believed to be the Lord of Lakshmi because He owns a mint? No. Lakshmi means *bhakti*. The sage Agastya may be described as a man who enjoyed *shri*, for he had obtained from Shiva the boon of *bhakti*. Shri Krishna ate a dish of green leaves offered by Vidura.[3] It is in the family of such a person that one who has fallen from the path of yoga, a weak yogi who none the less has faith, is born.

Or he may even be born into a family of yogis, though such birth as this is all too rare in this world.[4]

Or he is born in the family of a wise yogi. Born in such a family, he learns to have an equal mind in all things right from his childhood. *Bhakti* is a daily practice in the family of such a yogi. We may say that Sudhanva and Narad were so fortunately born.

There, O Kurunandana, he recovers the intellectual stage he had reached in his previous birth, and thence he stretches forward again towards perfection.[5]

He acquires in this family the state of equal-mindedness which I explained to you. He acquires in this life the state which he had failed to acquire in his previous life, whether or not he remembers his effort in that life.

In Itlaly, there is an eight-year-old boy who plays on the Sitar [*sic*] as if he was born with the skill.

Similarly, if a boy of eight can look upon all with equal regard, we shall conclude that that is the effect of his mode of life in a previous birth. He will then strive fruther in the same direction and ultimately reach his goal.

By virtue of that previous practice he is borne on, whether he will it or not; even he with a desire to know yoga passes beyond the Vedic ritual.[6]

Because of his experience in the previous life, such a person is spontaneously drawn towards God. He who is a yogi and yearns for knowledge crosses the *shabdabrahman*, that is, goes beyond the endless forms of karma and rituals enjoined in the Vedas, not beyond the karma which we undertake with a view to service or in a disinterested spirit but beyond the karma prompted by personal motive and activities undertaken fot the sake of various personal gains.

But the yogi who perseveres in his striving, cleansed of sin, perfected through many births, reaches the highest state.[7]

Perserving in his effort, such a yogi destroys the effects of his sins and, succeeding in his aim after many lives, attains *moksha*.

Notes

1. VI, 40.
2. VI, 41.
3. Character in the *Mahabharata* known as "the wisest of the wise", he gave good advice to both the Pandavas and the Kauravas, but in the war he sided with the former.

4. VI, 42.
5. VI, 43.
6. VI, 44.
7. VI, 45.

[110] July 18, 1926

The capital of self-purification acquired in this life will never be wasted.

The yogi is deemed higher than the man of austerities; he is deemed also higher than the man of knowledge; higher is he than the man engrossed in ritual; therefore be thou a yogi, O Arjuna!.[1]

Shri Krishna says: "I ask you to be a yogi, for the yogi is superior to the person who performs *tapascharya,* and he is considered superior even to the man who is a *jnani*. Here *jnani* does not signify a person who is merely learned in Shastras or is wise in practical affairs. The yogi is superior also to one who spends all his time in rituals and similar pursuits. You should, therefore, be a yogi."

And among all yogis, he who worships Me with faith, his inmost self all rapt in Me, is deemed by Me to be the best yogi.[2]

Among all classes of yogis, the best of course is the one who has faith in God. As the rays of the moon are the only thing which will make the *chataka* bird happy, so nothing is as effective as constant repetition of the Lord's name for ending man's threefold suffering in this world.

A Swami from Pushkar Raj[3] once came to visit me. He asked me: "Why have you taken up the spinning-wheel now in your old age?" In a region in which water is scarce, anyone who digs with a shovel—digs for water so that he may serve others—is repeating Ramanama though he may not be literally doing so, and reaps the fruit of repeating it. There are many in the world for whom food is the only *Brahman*. It is dharma to undertake physical labour and make such a starving person laour too, till he can get food. That sannyasi put his question to me, but he did not know that I was practising *akrama* through karma.

In this sixth chapter, Shri Krishna has explained how one may cultivate the spirit of sacrifice through work; he has explained the means of learning self-control. As the method, however, is difficult to practise—though it is not essential that everyone should follow it—, the question is raised whether a person who fails in such an effort does not get the worst of both the worlds. Replying, Shri Krishna says:

"No; nothing done with a spiritual motive is lost."

Notes

1. VI, 46.
2. VI, 47.
3. A holy place in Rajasthan, sacred to *Vaishnavas*.

[111] Chapter VII, July 20, 1926

Hear, O Partha, how, with thy mind rivetted on Me, by practising yoga and making Me the sole refuge, thou shalt, without doubt, know Me fully.

I will declare to thee, in its entirely, this knowledge, combined with discriminative knowledge, which when thou hast known there remains here nothing more to be known.

Among thousands of men hardly one strives after perfection; among those who strive hardly one knows Me in truth.[1]

That is, this knowledge is of supreme worth and not everyone can acquire it.

Earth, Water, Fire, Air, Ether, Mind, Reason and Ego—thus eight-fold is my *prakriti* divided.

This is My lower aspect; but know thou My other aspect, the higher—which is *Jiva* (the Vital Essence) by which, O Mahabahu, this world is sustained.[2]

[Shri Krishna says to Arjuna,] "There is also another *prakriti* of Mine which you may call *para prakriti*. It exists in living creatures, and is superior to the *prakriti* in inert matter; through it the entire universe exists."

Notes

1. VII, 1, 2 3.
2. VII, 4 & 5.

[112] July 21, 1926

We should regard an enemy as one with us. We should reflect how we with someone who is afraid of us to behave towards us. Even if it is in his power to cut us to pieces, we want him to be fair to us. If we have imprisoned someone, we should not put him under greater restraint than necessary, though he may be our enemy. In any case, we cannot torture him to death. This is no more than the law of the world.

Even obeying that law, though we fear snakes and do not wish to die, we also want to complete the reading of the *Gita* and to acquire the highest knowledge, to serve a few people in the world and bring the spinning-movement to success, to work in the cause of cow-protection. With this aim, we may wish to protect ourselves. I don't wish to suggest that you cruelly tortured the snake. But certainly you did not simply lift it and remove it elsewhere. This is a difficult matter. We may catch a snake and remove it, but should do so gently. We should not inflict pain on it. We should think on this matter not because Kishorelalbhai wants us to do so, but because we want to put the teaching of the *Gita* into practice. We should certainly not beat up a snake for our pleasure. We must not derive pleasure from tossing a kitten. This is ignorance and cruelty. Even a child should think how he or she would feel if someone treated him or her in the same manner.

Why does the *Gita* counsel us to treat *Chandals* and *Bhangis* in the same manner as we do others?

We should actually feel towards them in the same manner. It is in vain that one reads the *Gita* if one does not try to live in such a spirit. We should not get pleasure in torturing snakes and other creatures like them. We catch a snake and hold it tight with sticks, but we may do this because we have no choice in the matter. Our attitude should be the same as when we take special care of the body and even pamper it, but feel how much better it would be if we did not do this.

We should adopt a fixed attitude of mind, that in such matters we should do the minimum necessary and no more. Do not tell yourselves that you will think about these matters when you have white hair on your heads. You must make the best use of your youth right now. As Lord Krishna said, among thousands only one person strives for self-realization, that is, for self-purification, and among the thousands who strive only a rare person comes to a right knowledge of Him. Hence we should strive hard and long. We should look upon ourselves as those exceptional persons among thousands. We should try to become philosophers. We should aspire to be the rare individuals among those thousands, and hope that we shall succeed.

Know that these two compose the source from which all beings spring; I am the origin and end of the entire universe.[1]

Shri Krishna says: "The *apara prakriti*, the soul that lives in the visible world, and the *para prakriti*, the invisible world, believe these to be the cause of all creatures that live. For I am the source of the whole universe, and am that in which it subsides. That is, I am the cause of creation and destruction. Do not think, therefore, that you kill anyone."

There is nothing higher than I, O Dhananjaya; all this is strung on Me as a row of gems upon a thread.[2]

"As the beads are held together by the string, so this universe is held by Me."

In water I am the savour, O Kaunteya; in the sun and the moon I am the light; the syllable AUM in all the Vedas; the sound in ether, and manliness in men.

I am the sweet fragrance in earth; the brilliance in fire; the life in all beings; and the austerity in ascetics.[3]

Know Me, O Partha, to be the primeval seed of all beings; I am the reason of rational beings and the splendour of the splendid.[4]

Notes

1. VII, 6.
2. VII, 7.
3. VII, 8 & 9.
4. VII, 10.

[113] July 22, 1926

Of the strong, I am the strength, divorced from lust and passion; in beings I am desire undivorced from righteousness.[1]

"I am the strength of the strong, but that strength which is used without selfish motive or attachment. Such was King Janaka's strength. I am the *kama* in creatures which is not contrary to dharma." "Kama not contrary to dharma" means the desire for *moksha*, or the desire to end the suffering of creatures.

If we desire to end the suffering of others, our suffering, too, will end. This is true in the ordinary sense of the words.

But in Sanskrit the desire to end the suffering of others is described as a *mahaswartha*.[2] It means interest in the *moksha* of all creatures.

Anyone who feels such a desire would be striving hard for his own *moksha*.

Know that all the manifestations of the three *gunas, sattva, rajas*, and *tamas*, proceed from none but Me; yet I am not in them; they are in Me.[3]

We say that we should offer up everything to God, even evil. The two, good and evil, are inseparable, and so we should offer up both. If we wish to give up sin, we should give up virtue too. There is possessiveness in clinging even to virtue.

We say of the physical Rama that he both had and did not have a body. He had contradictory attributes, he was personal God and impersonal *Brahman*, he had attributes and was beyond attributes. For the evil, God is evil. He is in truth the very image of compassion, but He cannot violate His law and so we say that He destroys evil.

Befogged by these manifestations of the three *gunas*, the entire world fails to recognize Me, the imperishable, as transcending them.[4]

Truly speaking, even those who are ruled by *sattvik* impulses may be said to be under their power because of their ignorance.

For this My divine delusive mystery made up of the three *gunas* is hard to pierce; but those who make Me their sole refuge pierce the veil.[5]

It is said in the *Bhagavat* that in *Kaliyuga* anyone who constantly repeats *Om namo Bhagavate Vasudevaya* will cross this sea of becoming and reach the other shore. This is true of Ramanama, too.

The deluded evil-doers, lowest of men, do not seek refuge in Me; for, by reason of this delusive mystery, they are bereft of knowledge and given to devilish ways.[6]

Notes

1. VII, 11.
2. Literally, supreme self-interest.
3. VII, 12.
4. VII, 13.

5. VII, 14.
6. VII, 15.

[114] July 23, 1926

Four types of well-doers are devoted to Me, O Arjuna; they are, O Bharatarshabha, the afflicted, the spiritual seeker, the material seeker, and the enlightened.[1]

My worshippers whose actions are ever the holiest fall into four classes, says Shri Krishna. They are: (1) those in distress, (2) those who yearn for *jnana* or seek *moksha*, (3) those who worship Me for worldly benefits, and (4) the *jnanis* who worship God as His servants and seek nothing from Him. They tell God that it was simply their duty, as His subjects, to worship Him, and that it made no difference to them whether or not He rewarded them.

Of these the enlightened, ever attached to Me in single-minded devotion, is the best; for to the enlightened I am exceedingly dear and he is dear to Me.[2]

Among them all, the *jnani*, who always lives in union with Me, yoked with Me, calls upon Me *"tunhi, tunhi"* 3 and lives as a *bhakta*, keeps repeating My name as if he was reciting a *kalama* from the Koran, is the best.

Mirabai was a great devotee of the Lord, but she belonged to the class of *jnanis*. "I am," Shri Krishna says, "very dear to such *jnanis* and they to Me. We are thus like the lover and the beloved."

All these are estimable indeed, but the enlightened I hold to be My very self; for he, the true yogi, is stayed on Me alone, the supreme goal.[4]

All these four classes are noble people, though maybe some of them believe in *mantras* and worship God through them. Is it not better that, instead of spending their time in sin, they should worship God?

Is not a man who begs before the king's palace better than another who enters it to rob? The self-respect of a suffering man is fully preserved only if he approaches the king and no one else for help. There are people in the world who, when they suffer, seek succour not from God but from others. The Lord, therefore, is certainly pleased when people go to Him. "All these are certainly worthy men," says Shri Krishna, "but of them all the *jnani* is My very soul, Myself as it were. He who has yoked himself to Me has risen to the highest state."

At the end of many births the enlightened man finds refuge in Me; rare indeed is this great soul to whom 'Vasudeva is all'.[5]

After many lives, the *jnani* seeks refuge in Me."After many lives" means after a long and hard struggle. Such a person is always saying, not with his tongue merely but with his very heart, that this whole universe is a manifestation of Vasudeva.[6] A mahatma of that greatness is very rare.

Men, bereft of knowledge by reason of various longings, seek refuge in other gods, pinning their faith on diverse rites, guided by their own nature.[7]

Selfish men whose minds are clouded by all kinds of worldly desires and who seek the help of witch-doctors worship lower deities.

Some, for instance, vow to make a gift of so much rice or so many coconuts to the Mother-goddess at Khodiar; they obey their nature and worship her in that manner.

We may say that Ladha Maharaj belonged to the class of men who are driven by suffering to worship God, but he may also have been a *jnani*. We do not know his mental state.

Notes

1. VII, 16.
2. VII, 17.
3. "Thou, Thou".
4. VII, 18..
5. VII, 19.
6. Vishnu.
7. VII, 20.

[115] July 24, 1926

Whatever form one desires to worship in faith and devotion, in that very form I make that faith of his secure.[1]

If they think that they of their own accord worship the gods whom they do, they are ignorant. They do not get their faith from those deities. What help can a mere courtier give to one who has direct access to the king? For instance, Sudama went straight to Shri Krishna, and then the courtiers' attitude towards him changed. Such a person need not worship any other deity.

Possessed of that faith he seeks to propitiate that one, and obtains therethrough his longings, dispensed in truth by none but Me.[2]

If there were many independent deities who could act on their own, there would be no God.

But limited is the fruit that falls to those short-sighted ones; those who worship the gods go to the gods, those who worship Me come unto Me.[3]

Short-sighted worshippers of gods reap perishable fruits. Only one type of person wins deliverance. Those who worship the lower gods rise so far as the world of those gods. Those who worship Me come direct to Me.

Not knowing My transcendent, imperishable, supreme character, the undiscerning think Me who am unmanifest to have become manifest.[4]

"These persons of little intelligence do not know My unmanifest state," says Shri Krishna. "They mistake the manifest universe for the invisible reality behind. They do not know the best part of Me at all (the part beyond the manifest), do not know Me as the changeless, supreme Purushottama." If, for instance, we worship the Sun, who gives light and heat, we divide the divine power of God into its several aspects and worship one of them. Instead, we should try to know the highest, the invisible state of God. This visible universe is ever taking new shapes. The gods change their forms but God is ever the same.

Notes

1. VII, 21.
2. VII, 22.
3. VII, 23.
4. VII, 24.

[116] July 25, 1926

Our intellect has not the power to tear up the veil from before the *atman* and set it free. One who has felt the desire to do this has no little intellectual power. So long as we have not reflected deeply over these matters, we imagine beings with as many as ten heads. Then someone may wake up and ask whether the *atman* can ever have heads. He would then remember his study [of the *Gita*], remember the verses in the Second Chapter and realize that the *atman* was unmanifest and could not be pierced or wetted. "Unthinking men," Shri Krishna says, "wish to measure Me with their little yardsticks, they make an image of Me and act as if it was Myself."

Veiled by the delusive mystery created by My unique power, I am not manifest to all; this bewildered world does not recognize Me, birthless and changeless.[1]

"I do not vouchsafe light to all. Everyone cannot know Me, for I am veiled by the *maya* of My yoga." If God had not created such *maya*, we could not have existed in this visible universe. But, then, one may ask, why did God create this universe at all? To ask this question is like a clock asking why its maker made it. A creature must have complete faith in its creator."The unthinking man enveloped in *maya*," says Shri Krishna, "does not know Me, the Unborn and the Immutable."

Notes

1. VII, 25.

[117] July 27, 1926

"I am not luminous to all, that is, everyone cannot see Me.

Human beings are blinded by My light. Such is the power of My *maya* that people can truthfully say that at this moment some lives are being born and some are dying." But we should understand that these transformations are not real. Who can know that Reality which is veiled behind objects with name and form? If someone told us that in his country rivers get frozen and that human beings and vehicles pass over them, we would not easily understand his statement; this idea of Reality veiled behind these objects with name and form is similar to that. It is true, nonetheless. The Lord says that this is due to the power of His *yogamaya*, that His real essence is the Unmanifest.

I know, O Arjuna, all creatures past, present and to be; but no one knows Me.

All creatures in this universe are bewildered, O Parantapa, by virtue of the delusion of the pairs of opposites sprung from likes and dislikes, O Bharata.

But those virtuous men whose sin has come to an end, freed from the delusion of the pairs of opposites, worship Me in steadfast faith.

Those who endeavour for freedom from age and death by taking refuge in Me, know in full that *Brahman, adhyatma* and all karma.

Those who know Me, including *adhibhuta, adhidaiva, adhiyajna,* possessed of even-mindedness, they know Me even at the time of passing away.[1]

Those who think of Me, even at the moment of death, as *adhibhuta, adhidaiva* and *adhiyajna,* are men who have become steady. They who know Me as the Lord of all creatures, of the gods and of *yajnas,* that is, as the Creator and Preserver of the whole universe, and know that this world of flux has no effect on Me whatever, are men united to Me in yoga."

Note

1. VII, 26, 27, 28, 29 & 30.

[118] Chapter VIII, July 28, 1926

In Chapter VII, Shri Krishna fulfilled his promise, explained both *jnana* and *vijnana* and assured Arjuna that once he had understood these he would never be touched by evil.

The *apara prakriti,* the world of visible objects, can be perceived with the senses and known through the intellect, but the *para prakriti* can be apprehended only when we go beyond the senses, the intellect and the ego. If we wish to know God's transcendent essence, we should in some measure be what He is. We, too, have the two essences, *apara* and *para,* in us, of which we should subdue the *apara* and acquire better knowledge of the *para*.

The main question raised in Chapter I was, how can one kill one's kinsmen? The answer to this extended to seven Chapters. And now begins the eighth. Shri Krishna is making all this effort with the aim of removing the confusion of thought and the ignorance which had unsettled Arjuna's mind. He has been brought to the point of distinction between the *apara* and the *para prakriti*.

What is the *Brahman*? What is *adhyatma*? What karma, O Purushottama?

What is called *adhibhuta*? And what *adhidaiva*?

And who here in this body is *adhiyajna* and how? And how at the time of death art Thou to be known by the self-controlled?[1]

Arjuna asks Shri Krishna, "You have told me about *Brahman, adhyatma,* karma, *adhibhuta* and so on. But what do these terms mean? And what is *adhiyajna*? What is meant by saying that he whose mind is yoked to the Lord can know all this at the moment of death?"

Note

1. VIII, 1 & 2.

[119] July 29, 1926

Shri Krishna answers Arjuna's question.

The Supreme, the Imperishable is *Brahman;* its manifestation is *adhyatma;* the creative process whereby all beings are created is called karma.[1]

That which never perishes and is the ultimate Reality is *Brahman.* Our nature is *adhyatma.*

The Lord of us all is the power which creates this *adhyatma.*

Creating all beings and keeping them in existence is an act of renunciation and is known as karma.

Note

1. VIII, 3.

[120] July 30, 1926

We cannot have personal relation with all beings in the world, but can have spiritual relation with them.

Anyone who feels no desire to do good to others harms not only himself but others too. If a woman expecting a baby does not protect, it she may die and the baby, too, may die. To protect it is her karma, which is a form of renunciation. If such a woman is not regular in eating, if she thinks evil thoughts and eats unwholesome food, both she and the baby would be harmed. We are continually harming ourselves in this manner. Some of us may be inclined to ask how the world is concerned if we harm ourselves. But in harming ourselves, we harm both ourselves and the world.

Karma here certainly does not mean an act of creation. Vyasa's writing of the *Gita* and the *Mahabharata* was a great *visarga* (an act of renunciation). It is impossible that the jewel of a work like the *Gita* would signify by the term karma the merely physical act of creation.

Adhibhuta is My perishable form; *adhidaivata* is the individual self in that form; and O best among the embodied, *adhiyajna* am I in this body, purified by sacrifice.[1]

That is, Shri Krishna says that He is the Lord of *yajnas* and grants their fruit. The modes of being which belong to the living creatures in the world are perishable modes.

Note

1. VIII, 4.

[121] July 31, 1926

There is a saying in Latin which means that the way to Hell is paved with good intentions. Good intentions by themselves do not succeed, but the person doomed to Hell believes that they do, without his having to strive to realize them. We cannot give all that we with to, but we can receive everything we would. However much I try, if you do not receive what I give, what can I do? If all of you make a serious effort, you can stop wasting others' time. If you but try to get up at four, you will most certainly not fail. What does it matter even if the effort breaks us? *Moksha* is for those who strive till they break.

Krishna is the Lord of *yajna*, and we worship Him because, though in human form, He worked all His life. He was awake every moment, awake even when the Pandavas slept. The latter's eyes were always fixed on Him. He did not wish to harm the Kauravas or help the Pandavas; His only aim was to see that right prevailed. He spent his body working ceaselessly all His life, but it retained its light till the last. The word *prayatna*[1] in just an ordinary word, but the thing itself is such that the moment you resolve on it you will begin to reap the fruit. Krishna had resolved that the Pandavas should win and, therefore, their victory was certain. He was the very embodiment of disinterested service, and wished to harm none. When Parashuram[2] was lying with his head in Karna's lap, the latter was bitten by some deadly creature and was bleeding profusely, but he did not move an inch. Surely, he too was a human being, like any of us. We should, similarly, make good resolutions and strive to realize them, offering up the fruit of our effort to Shri Krishna.

By describing Arjuna as the best among beings endowed with a body, Shri Krishna suggests that he need not fear anyone at all.

Notes

1. Effort, striving.
2. A Brahmin-warrior, one of the incarnations of Vishnu, from whom Karna.

[122] August 1, 1926

And he who, at the last hour remembering Me only, departs leaving the body, enters into Me; of that there is no doubt.

Or whatever form a man continually contemplates, that same he remembers in the hour of death, and to that very form he goes, O Kaunteya.[1]

Hence they say, you will reap as you sow.

We should let no impurity enter our thoughts. Perents give us the human form, sometimes a form like their own. The subtle changes which take place within us become visible through our eyes. If we get a disease, we should believe that we ourselves are the cause of it. A person whose mind is so strong that he influences his surroundings, learned the art science of fighting instead of being influenced by them, gets no disease. It is for our good, therefore, to believe that our illness is the result of our sins. If we have been repeating Ramanama from the depth of our heart, how can even a dream, if it is evil, leap over that protecting wall and enter our mind? If any does, we may believe that we have been uttering Ramanama only with our lips. If we have any fear whatever in our heart, that too is a form of evil and we suffer from many serious diseases because of it. Hence, as we free ourselves more and more from evil impulses and desires, we become less and less subject to disease. Even persons whose ears and noses and all other limbs had been infected are known to have recovered. The body possesses a natural power of recovery. Recovery brought about with the help of herbs lasts for some time only; and the man who has overcome his evil desires and cultivated devotion to God will refuse to be cured with the help of herbs and say that, when the evil in him has disappeared, he will be all right. If, as a result of this attitude, he dies, he will welcome death.

Anyone who thinks wicked thoughts will find that in one day his body has become ugly. Once a person charged with murder came to me. I merely looked at him and told him that he was trying to deceive me. He left at once.

Note

1. VIII, 5 & 6.

[123] August 3, 1926

Thinking is a form of karma. Thoughts have such power that sometimes their effects are more terrible than those of actions. If someone finds a pistol placed in his hand by another person and is forced to fire it, he cannot be said to have committed violence because he had acted under force. But he who harbours violence in his thoughts and, keeping himself in the background, incites others to do violence, is guilty of terrible violence. Besides, there are also enemies within which prompt us to commit violence. Despite our effort to think the best thoughts and act upon them, we are driven to commit sin. It is the desire and anger in us which are responsible for this. All the same, our efforts at self-control and good thoughts help us. If the God of death himself puts a pistol in a person's hands and forces him to commit violence, such violence will not harm him. He will ever have the name of Narayana on his lips and, when he dies, his end will be good. Ordinarily we do not see this happen, for our thoughts are those of miserable wretches. They ought ever to flow in a self-controlled stream. A person whose thoughts are of this kind repeats the name of Narayana while engaged in any work. His actions are not his, they are prompted by the Lord within.

Shri Krishna has packed in these two verses the essence of all philosophy: man will reap as he thinks.

Therefore at all times remember Me and fight on; thy mind and reason thus on Me fixed thou shalt surely come to me.

With thought steadied by constant practice, and wandering nowhere, he who meditates on the Supreme Celestial Being, O Partha, goes to Him.[1]

No one should believe that it will suffice if he does this at the moment of death. He who has been striving in this direction from his childhood will win the battle and the other will lose. We boarded a ship at Delagoa Bay to see Gokhale off. The latter was playing billiards. I had not joined him. He thought I did not like his playing that game and asked me: "Do you think I enjoy playing this?"

"No," I said, "you are trying to prove the ability of our countrymen." In this way, even his playing was dedicated to Lord Krishna. I of course knew it. I am sure in my mind that my effort to learn dancing was also not prompted by love of dancing. At that time, my only thought was to acquire all the accomplishments which make a gentleman. The point is that everything we do should be dedicated to Shri Krishna. We can so dedicate only the work which comes to us unsought, not that which we undertake of our own choice. Though the inmates of the Ashram attend to different tasks, dedicating them to Shri Krishna, in reality all of them are doing the same work if there is complete harmony in their thoughts. If that is not so, and only one person is earnest about spinning and others let their minds wander, then they cannot be said to join the former in spinning.

Note

1. VIII, 7 & 8.

[124] August 4, 1926

Who so, at the time of death, with unwavering mind, with devotion, and fixing the breath rightly between the brows by the power of yoga, meditates on the Sage, the Ancient, the Ruler, subtler than the subtlest, the Supporter of all, the Inconceivable, glorious as the sun beyond the darkness,—he goes to that Supreme Celestial Being.[1]

He who knows all attains to that supreme, divine Purusha. At the moment of departing, that is, when dying, one should think on that Purusha Who is beginningless, Who rules the world and Who is in essence finer than the finest we can conceive.

In the sixth century B.C., there ruled in Lydia a king named Croesus[2]. He had immense wealth. The Greek saint and law giver, Solon[3] once went to see him. Croesus asked him whether anyone could be happier than he himself was. Solon's reply was that only after a man has died can we say whether he had been happy. This same Croesus was afterwards attacked and defeated by King Cyrus of Persia. He was sentenced to be hanged. As he was being taken to the gallows, he shouted Solon's name thrice. On being asked by Cyrus why he did that, he repeated Solon's reply to his question. Cyrus freed him and kept him as his adviser. When the King died, he left his son in the care of Croesus. In much the same way, it is only after a man's death that we can say whether he has passed into a higher world.

Proceeding, Shri Krishna describes that supreme Purusha, Who is the Creator of everything that exists, Whose essence cannot be comprehended by our minds, Whom only the yogis see in their contemplation, Who has the glory of the sun (shines like the sun, with the light of timeless consciousness) and Who is beyond the darkness of ignorance. Our reason cannot conceive how infinitely small and how infinitely vast He is. He who, when leaving this world, thinks with a fixed mind on this Purusha,—only his mind is fixed who has yoked himself to the Lord in *bhakti* and who possesses the strength acquired by long *sadhana*—thinks of Him with *bhakti* and with the power of his yoga, who refuses any treatment or medicine to save his life—keeps his mouth shut,—who knows that he is leaving for a world where there is no darkness and no suffering or happiness, and who focuses his *prana* on the point midway between his brows and meditates,—such a person attains to the realm of the Supreme, the Divine Purusha described in this verse.

Notes

1 VIII, 9 & 10.

2 The last king of Lydia, 560-546 B.C.

3 *c.* 638-558 B.C.; Athenian statesman and poet. The story of their meeting is narrated by Herodotus, but is chronologically impossible.

[125] August 5, 1926

That which the knowers of the Vedas call the Imperishable (*or* that word which the knowers of the Vedas repeat), wherein the escetics freed from passion enter and desiring which they practise *brahmacharya*, that Goal (*or* Word) I will declare to thee in brief.

Closing all the gates, locking up the mind in the hridaya, fixing his breath within the head, rapt in yogic meditation;

Who so departs leaving the body uttering *AUM—Brahman* in one syllable—repeatedly thinking on Me, he reaches the highest state.[1]

While in the previous verse Shri Krishna referred to other states of mind, here He speaks only of meditation on the Lord.

That yogi easily wins to Me, O Partha, who, ever attached to Me, constantly remembers Me with undivided mind.

Great souls, having come to Me, reach the highest perfection; they come not again to birth, unlasting and (withal) an abode of misery.[2]

Why is it misery to be born over and over again?

A STUDENT: One may not be born a human being—in every life. But what does it matter if one is born a monkey. We may enjoy our life dancing and jumping about all the time.

ANOTHER STUDENT: Can one be sure that, after one dies, in the next life, one will be born a Brahmin?

Should we not welcome that state in which there is no death?

Are there any who like dying? Those who do, die again and again. He who does not want death gives up his attachment to bodily life, closes all the bodily doors without much thinking. If he forgets the body, mortifies it every moment, he will not have to die. It is because there is death for everyone who is born that life is a cause of suffering. The birds are ever happy, but then they have no knowledge and are not free. Would you like it, if someone changed all the boys into birds?

That state in which there is no death and no birth, no disease, no attachment and no aversion, that supreme state is known as *moksha*.

Notes

1. VIII, 11, 12 & 13.
2. VIII, 14 & 15.

[126] August 6, 1926

Even big mountains, sun and moon and stars, all things are transient. If our lives were as long as one crore years, perhaps we would not feel the transience of our existence. We are not conscious of the transience of the sun, but science tells us that it is not eternal.

Both from a profound and from a superficial view, it is transient. Ramanama alone is imperishable. Life and death are both transitory states; not only are they so, they are the cause of all suffering.

Why? It is not because the *Gita* says so that we should regard them as the cause of suffering; we should feel in our own lives that they are so. The best way of ensuring that after death we pass to a higher world is to feel every moment that life in this world is from its very nature full of suffering, so that we give up attachment to it and free ourselves from the dualities of love and hatred.

We can understand even with our reason that life in this world is full of suffering. If we but think, we shall realize that the very process of birth of all creatures is something repulsive. This is what is meant by saying "I am sin", "I have my source in sin". This existence being enveloped in *maya*, we take pleasure every moment in what should repel us. We have no sense through which we can feel in all its intensity this pain [which the process of birth means]. Even our state after birth is, from the beginning to the end, one long imprisonment.

We love fondling a child, because it smiles and laughs with pleasure.

But, then, prisoners also laugh. We take pleasure in this slavery because it is a part of our existence, but in truth it is a state in which we can not rest in peace even for a moment. Look at the physical frame of this body. It excretes dirt through countless pores, such dirt as we cannot bear touching. If only we reflect, we shall find nothing to attract us in this body. But, then, even this prison is a house through which we can win our freedom. If we come to regard it in that light, we shall make the minimum necessary use of it. The way to freedom, of course, does not lie in committing suicide. Anyone who kills himself will certainly be born again. He will yearn all the more to return to life. The ideal of self-control had its origin in the knowledge of the manner in which life comes into existence and of other facts of our physical life. This body is not to be pampered, but to be mortified and subjugated. If it sees that it does not get what it craves, it will on its own leave us in terror. If, Shri Krishna says, people realize the misery of this existence, the state to which

He will raise them will be a little better than their present one. That supreme state is not to be conceived as one in which the higher bliss which we experience in this life will also vanish. On the contrary, we shall have it thousand fold in that other state. With this thought constantly in one's mind, one should get absorbed in the duties of this life, forget oneself altogether in them. One should see oneself in the whole world and the world in oneself, and act towards others accordingly. The ideal of non-violence also had its origin in this realization that, when human life as such is full of suffering, we should cause suffering to none.

From the world of Brahma down, all the worlds are subject to return, O Arjuna; but on coming to Me there is no rebirth.[1]

All the worlds, including the world of Brahma[2] will return to their source. The sun, the moon, Brahma, Vishnu, all will perish.

"But," Shri Krishna says, "once a human being comes to Me, he never perishes."

This is what I have tried to explain in my talk today.

Notes

1 VIII, 16.

2 One of several heavens, distinct from the absolute, impersonal Brahma.

[127] August 7, 1926

There is great poetry in this verse. This little drop contains knowledge as vast as the sea, and the more that knowledge becomes part of our experience the more we discover its poetry. In such a verse, the poet soars on the wings of his imagination, released from the bondage of the body and the senses. His imagination works on what he has heard with his ears and seen with his eyes and, going beyond the certainties of reason, he says that all that is known through the senses is a product of the human mind; that is, he imagines that since we ourselves perish, this whole universe will perish too. All that the human mind can imagine or conceive is perishable, is subject to ceaseless change. He who has dedicated himself to truth will not be prepared to forsake it merely because the world does not agree with him, as if his truth depended on the world and he was acting in a play.

Shri Krishna, therefore, the Prince of Yogis that He is, says here that we believe there is happiness in the world of Brahma but that there is no happiness even there.

He asks Arjuna to go to the world beyond all these worlds, the world in which He Himself dwells. This is simply beyond our imagination.

But what is beyon our imagination does exist, nevertheless. If a person dies striving to reach that world, there is no rebirth for him.

Those men indeed know what is Day and what is Night, who know that Brahma's day lasts a thousand *yugas* and that his night too is a thousand *yugas* long.[1]

Note

1. VIII, 17.

[128] August 8, 1926

A day and a night of ours are made up of 24 hours. They say that anyone who focuses his eyes on the tip of his nose and meditates will find bliss, but it is necessary to go beyond this. In order to become become a *jnani* one must learn to look deep into things.

Anyone who practises this method but goes beyond it will study his self and draw far-reaching conclusions, will realize that things are not what they seem. We do not, thus, require a *Gita* to tell us that Brahma[1] must have a day different in length from ours; we can see this ourselves if we use our brains. It seems to us an absolute certainty that the Sun will always be there. He will be a *jnani* who understands the nature of time from a study of one object existing in time. Such a person will take into account all the factors, which ordinary men and women fail to do. The latter would generally reason that, since no one practises control of the senses, it is impossible to practise and ought not to be attempted; if we reason thus, we shall invite ruin upon ourselves. This is fallacious reasoning.

If we want to know what is a day and what a night, we should have a standard of measurement. How can we measure infinite time?

A day as long as a thousand *yugas* and a night of equal length! We should know that there is a day and night of such length in order that we may learn patience, and that, if the result of our effort takes time to show itself; we may not give way to despair. We may have faith in the spinning-wheel, but what progress can we expect from devoted work of only four or five years? We may see no tangible result in our own life-time. Nonetheless, we should have faith and go on working.

Having devoted ourselves to this work, we should not give way to despair, nor be proud of ourselves. Let us remember that a thousand *yugas* make one day, and out of a thousand Parvatis one succeeds.

There were a great many Parvatis and Shambhus who failed, before one Parvati and one Shambhu succeeded. We should know that this is how the power of *tapas* works.

At the coming of Day all the manifest spring forth from the

Unmanifest, and at the coming of Night they are dissolved into that same Unmanifest.[2]

When Brahma's day[3] begins, the Unmanifest becomes manifest.

All these creatures, which had vanished into nothingness, come to life again. When his night begins, the whole creation vanishes, that is, merges into the Unmanifest. In this way, all creation appears and vanishes, and does so endlessly. We have no reason to believe that the universe is fixed and motionless; in fact it is revolving, with a speed a thousand times greater than that of a spindle. The Earth will return into nothingness, will perish, but there will certainly be some who will survive that final destruction.

This same multitude of creatures come to birth, O Partha, again and again; they are dissolved at the coming of Night, whether they will or not; and at the break of Day they are reborn.[4]

When the night comes, whether we wish it or not, the universe returns into nothingness, and when the day comes a new creation appears.

How long shall we remain caught in this endless cycle? To reassure us on this, Shri Krishna says:

But higher than that Unmanifest is another Unmanifest Being, everlasting, which perisheth not when all creatures perish.[5]

There is another Unmanifest Reality beyon this Unmanifest[6] and it is immutable; it is the immutable Reality immanent in all perishable creatures. Everything which exists will perish, but the ground of all this existence is imperishable. Thus, we go a good deal further than the tip of our nose.

This Unmanifest, named the Imperishable, is declared to be the highest goal. For those who reach it there is no return. That is My highest abode.[7]

Shri Krishna says: "You can come to Me by patient striving and living in this world only as a witness. Have faith and, devoting yourself to duty, work out the welfare of your soul." The substance of all this is that the supreme *Brahman* never perishes, everything else does.

Notes

1. The Creator in the Hindu Trinity.
2. VIII, 18.
3. A day and a night of Brahma consist of 8,640,000,000 years or 2,000 *mahayugas*.
4. VIII, 19.
5. VIII, 20
6. The source to which the visible universe returns at the end of the cycle; *vide* verse 18 above.
7. VIII, 21.

[129] August 10, 1926

The form in which the timeless essence which is God manifests itself is known as His incarnation. We can know that essence in every creature. The principle of oneness does not mean that all of us should become beasts; it means, on the contrary, that God is present in the heart of even the most wicked of creatures, and that the latter awakes to His presence when the time comes. Ramachandra's picture as a child is a product of the poet's imagination, but we may believe it as true, knowing that higher consciousness is present even at that age. If a little child is a *jnani* and still behaves as we know children do, we should say, "The *Brahman* sports before the *Brahman*."[1] Such a child would be a visible form of the *Brahman*, in the same sense that Parvati was the embodiment of *tapascharya* and Krishna of yoga, of the *Brahman*.

Note

1. The line is from a poem by Narasinh Mehta.

[130] August 11, 1926

This Supreme Being, O Partha, may be won by undivided devotion; in It all beings dwell, by It all is pervaded.[1]

"That supreme state, to be attained in yogic contemplation, is beyond my reach": so sang Raychandbhai.

Now I will tell thee, Bharatarshabha, the conditions which determine the exemption from return, as also the return, of yogis after they pass away hence.[2]

"I shall now describe that state" (the word may also mean time) "after reaching which, or that path after treading which, there is no returning."

Fire, Light, Day, the Bright Fortnight, the six months of the Northern Solstice—through these departing men knowing *Brahman* go to *Brahman*.[3]

It is often said that this and the next verse do not fit into the teaching of the *Gita*, but we will treat them as if they did.

The *Gita* did not drop down from heaven, nor is it as if every work that Krishna said to Arjuna was written down. Vyasa has given what the Lord said to a seeker and, in doing so, he would include even things which he himself did not understand from his own experience.

It may have been a general belief in those times which made people particular that they did important things at particular hours of the day only, or welcomed death during a certain part of the day. The favourites of a king can approach him only at a fixed hour, and no one else can go to him at that time. Similarly, it may have been the prevalent belief in those days that only people who died in an auspicious hour would reach God; this, of course, did not mean that those who died in some other hour had not aspired and striven in their lives to reach God after death.

Those who die when there is fire and light, on any day in the bright half of one of the six months following the winter solstice, will reach the *Brahman*. This statement may be intended to have either a literal or an allegorical meaning. If the latter, it means, that anyone who has attained a state like the bright half of the month, a state of knowledge as bright as light, will not return to this world after death.

On the other hand:

Smoke, Night, the Dark Fortnight, the six months of the Southern Solstice—therethrough the yogi attains to the lunar light and thence returns.[4]

Such a person lives in heaven and, when the merit earned by his virtuous deeds is exhausted, he returns to the earth.

We may, therefore, take either of the two meanings. Anyone who has not attained to full illumination will have to return to this earth; in other words, he who spends his life in disinterested work and prays daily to the Lord with love and devotion will not have to return, for he will have cut asunder the bonds of karma. Anyone who departs after a life of disinterested *bhakti* will not have to return.

Notes

1. VIII, 22.
2. VIII, 23.
3. VIII, 24.
4. VIII, 25.

[131] August 12, 1926

Some persons treat these two verses as interpolated; we cannot do so, for the copies of the *Gita* which we use contain them. If the meaning of any verse contradicts the very meaning of the *Gita*, we may reject that verse, otherwise we should try to reconcile it with the rest of the teaching, as we did yesterday. *Kala* [in these verses] means state, condition. We do not know whether, in the age when the *Gita* was composed, the North and the South Poles were discovered. For those who live in the region of the North Pole, the day and the night are as long as our six months. The period following the winter solstice is a time of light and signifies a waking state, whereas the period following the summer solstice signifies a state of ignorance. We have compared the latter state with the state full of desire and the former with that which is free from desire.

The Lord, Shri Krishna, now proceeds:

These two paths—bright and dark—are deemed to be the eternal paths of the world; by the one a man goes to return not, by the other he returns again.[1]

These two paths, the bright and the dark, that which leads to a state from which there is no returning and the other which leads to a state which is impermanent, have existed from the beginning of time.

The bright state is that of the illumination of knowledge and the dark state is that of ignorance. Dying in one state, a person never returns; dying in the other, he is bound to return.

The yogi knowing these two paths falls not into delusion, O Partha; therefore, at all times, O Arjuna, remain steadfast in yoga.[2]

The yogi who knows the distinction between these two paths never succumbs to darkness. He realizes that disinterested *bhakti* is the best form of *bhakti*. If we have faith in the Lord and *bhakti* for Him, why should we forever be begging things from Him? Anyone who is filled with faith and love will feel that there is nothing for him to beg.

He will have offered everything to the Lord, placed himself at His mercy. He may say: "All that is mine is yours." Such single-minded *bhakti* is *uttarayana*[3], it is light, and so on. What, again, is the significance of Krishna's advice to remain yoked to Him at all times?

It means that one should cling to knowledge and single-minded devotion.

The gods are immortal, but only compared to human beings. They, too, will perish in time."Therefore," says Shri Krishna, "instead of going to the gods who will perish, if you come to Me, then alone will you get knowledge and in no other way." Arjuna should, Shri Krishna says, keep the knot in his heart, the little grains of dust which cover the knowledge within, so thoroughly cleaned that at the moment of death he will spontaneously have the right thoughts.

Whatever fruit of good deeds is laid down as accruing from (a study of) the Vedas, from sacrifices, austerities, and acts of charity—all that the yogi transcends, on knowing this, and reaches the Supreme and Primal Abode.[4]

We saw in the verse beginning with *yavanartha udapane*[5] that he who has acquired this light and knowledge is in the condition of one who has secured that beyond which nothing else remains to be obtained.

Notes

1. VIII, 26.
2. VIII, 27.
3. Northward course of the sun.
4. VIII, 28.
5. II, 46.

[132] Chapter IX, August 13, 1926

I will now declare to thee, who art uncensorious, this mysterious knowledge, together with discriminative knowledge, knowing which thou shalt be released from ill.

This is the king of sciences, the king of mysteries, pure and sovereign, capable of direct comprehension, the essence of dharma, easy to practise, changeless.[1]

There was a man who, whenever he got very angry, sat down to do sums in algebra; anyone else who tried to do this, when he ought to be repeating Ramanama, would find the effort a burden-some task. If somone is dying and cries for help, it would be unfeeling arrogance to tell him that you were busy doing sums in algebra, for it would be moment when the Shastras could well be thrown into the sea. Doing a sum in algebra is not in itself a duty, but the aim behind it may be a duty. Through it, I may know who and where I am. Doing a sum is not by itself a duty, the first duty is service. For instance, eating is never a duty in itself. He is a true man who leaves the dinner table and runs to do an act of service.

The knwoledge of this duty is *rajavidya*. It is the king of all secrets, it is sacred and the highest knowledge, it is dharma and worthy to be followed in action, and easy to follow besides; once acquired, it is never destroyed. "I will impart that knowledge to you," says Shri Krishna.

Note

1. IX, 1 & 2.

[133] August 14, 1926

Men who have no faith in this doctrine, O Parantapa, far from coming to Me, return repeatedly to the path of this world of death.

By Me, unmanifest in form, this whole world is pervaded; all beings are in Me, I am not in them.[1]

So long as our eyes of knowledge have not opened, we have no choice but to see with the eyes of faith.

And yet those beings are not in Me. That indeed is My unique power as Lord! Sustainer of all beings, I am not in them; My Self brings them into existence.

As the mighty wind, moving everywhere, is ever contained in ether, even so know that all beings are contained in Me.[2]

Air fills space, but space is not identical with air. We can say that air fills space. Though space is empty, we can say that it is filled with air. And yet space is not air. The air which fills space is still not in it, so God who dwells in all creatures is still not in them. In one sense, He is not in them, for we can see other things with our eyes but not Him.

He who has faith and he who lacks it, both are sincere in their beliefs. God exists for him who has faith, but does not exist for him who lacks it.

A Shastri will be able to explain the point of these two verses.

The Ganga water does, and yet does not, contain dirt. Similarly, even the most wicked of beings exists in God. The cruellest of men, even a *Chandal*, exists in Him, and yet does not. God is above good and bad. Vyasa puts these contradictory statements together, for our reason knows its limitation in trying to describe the truth. It is enough if we understand that God pervades the entire universe.

Notes

1. IX, 3 & 4.
2. IX, 5 & 6.

[134][1] August 15, 1926

Innumerable ways of falling are open to a man, he need not make any effort for the purpose; it is for rising that one has to strive.

We may revere and always keep in a proper place a holy book which we believe helps us on the path of good; but anyone who goes no further than showing it outward reverence will find such reverence a means of bondage. There should, therefore, be discrimination even in reverence; only so will that reverence help us to advance. Outward reverence for a holy book is not all. We should go further than that.

We should try to follow the teaching of the book in our life. God is omnipotent and we are His creatures. When, however, we, who are mere ants in His sight try to eat Him up, He uses a part of His infinite power. He is so near that we feel we can touch Him this very moment, and yet we never do, so far away He is. As space and air exist one in the other, so do God and the universe. He who has faith certainly exists in God; he who lacks it does not. God does not force Himself on anyone, but He does not close the door, either, against anyone who aspires to be united to Him—such is His nature.

All beings, O Kaunteya, merge into my *prakriti,* at the end of a *kalpa,* and I send them forth again when a *kalpa* begins.[2]

The holy books speak of such rise and disappearance of the worlds.

The individual soul, of course, passes through birth and death.

But the universe, too, comes into existence and disappears. If the soul, therefore, wishes to know its essence, it will have to transcend the universe. We know for certain that this lamp will one day be destroyed, and yet it is the only thing we can use; it is essential, therefore, that we take care to keep it clean. This Ashram has buil-dings, which are its body, so to say. They will be destroyed one day. But the Ashram's soul, which is its ideals, will never perish. To realize that imperishable essence, we may even need to put up buildings of brick and mortar. In this way, we must use our reason and discrimination and keep working. If we wish to live in this world, we must put to use even things which will perish, but only with the aim of realizing the imperishable essence beyond them.

Resorting to my *prakriti,* I send forth again and again this multitude of beings, powerless under the sway of *prakriti.*[3]

Notes

1. The notes of this discourse were taken by Punjabhai.
2. IX, 7.
3. IX, 8.

[135] August 17, 1926

But all this activity, O Dhananjaya, does not bind Me, seated as one indifferent, unattached to it.[1]

God acts according to His *prakriti,* and yet He does nothing since He is above even His *prakriti.*

If a king does sinful things, his subjects too suffer. But God, being omniscient, can do nothing without thought. Sin means only what is done without taking thought. How can a person who thinks before acting commit a sin? Likewise, how can one who is by nature inclined to sin act virtuously? If one does good spontaneously, in the same way that our eyes wink automatically, one will not have to suffer the fruits of such good actions. It is man's nature to do good, for all selves are one. That being so, the apparent separateness of each self has no significance. When this is realized, man's ego melts away.

Man's essence, which is *atman,* is all-pervading, for he who has realized it will not see himself as different from others, but will see all in himself. For such a person, therefore, doing good becomes his nature. When he seems to be serving other creatures, he is doing so not out of kindness to them but is merely following his own nature.

To us who are enveloped in *maya,* it may seem that he is practising virtue, but in truth it is not so; he is acting only according to his nature towards all creatures.

Note

1. IX, 9.

[136] August 18, 1926

With me as Presiding Witness, *prakriti* gives birth to all that moves and does not move; and because of this, O Kaunteya, the wheel of the world keeps going.

Not knowing My transcendent nature as the sovereign Lord of all beings, fools condemn Me incarnated as man.[1]

"Creatures sunk in darkness, dwelling in the human body, do not know Me," says Shri Krishna, "they disregard Me"(Has not

Tulsidas said that those who make a distinction between Rama and God are ignorant and know nothing? We project our ignorance on to God too.) "They do not know My supreme state, do not know Me as the Lord of all creatures. Labouring under the illusion that I am a human being, they do not know My real essence."

Note

1. IX, 10 & 11.

[137] August 19, 1926

Vain are the hopes, actions and knowledge of those witless ones who have resorted to the delusive nature of monsters and devils.

But those great souls who resort to the divine nature. O Partha, know Me as the Imperishable Source of all beings and worship Me with an undivided mind.[1]

The mahatmas, who are ruled by their divine *prakriti,* like Vibhishana[2] and others, worship Me with their minds illumined by knowledge and with single-minded devotion—Me who am the Creator of all beings.

Always declaring My glory, striving in steadfast faith, they do Me devout homage; ever attached to Me, they worship Me.

Yet others, with knowledge-sacrifice, worship Me, who am to be seen everywhere, as one, as different or as many.[3]

"Others worship Me by striving for knowledge. Some of them worship Me as the only One (that is, believing that all this is Vasudeva), some others worship My different manifestations and others still worship Me in everything which exists.

We may take *vishvatomukham* to go with *mam*, and understand the line to mean that "they worship Me who am the same in all or dwell in all"; or we may interpret *ekatvena* to mean "with devotion" and *prithaktvena* to mean that "they look upon Me as the Lord and themselves as My devotees and worship Me in that spirit". Or, *ekatvena* may mean "worshipping Me as Impersonal Absolute" and *prithaktvena* may mean "worshipping Me as personal God". In any case, *vishvatomukham* taken as an independent, third term, yields no sense.

Notes

1. IX, 12 & 13.

2. In the *Ramayana*; he tried to persuade his brother, Ravana, to restore Sita to Rama. Failing in this effort, he went over to Rama and was accepted by him.
3. IX, 14 & 15.

[138] August 20, 1926

I am the sacrificial vow; I am the sacrifice; I the ancestral oblation; I the herb; I the sacred text; I the clarified butter; I the fire; I the burnt offering.

Of this universe I am Father, Mother, Creator, Grandsire; I am what is to be known, the sacred syllable *AUM*; the *Rig*, the *Sama* and the *Yajur*;

I am the Goal, the Sustainer, the Lord, the Witness, the Abode, the Refuge, the Freiend; the Origin, the End, the Preservation, the Treasurehouse, the Imperishable Seed.[1]

I am *gati* which means *moksha*—the state which human beings strive to attain. I am the sustainer, the Lord, and the witness. I am the abode, and the shelter. I am *suhrid* which means a kind friend who serves me without expectation of reward.

I give heat; I hold back and pour forth rain; I am deathlessness and also death, O Arjuna, Being and not-Being as well.[2]

I give heat, but in the form of the sun which gives happiness and the light of knowledge to all creatures. I draw the rains and release them. I am death and I am immortality; I am being and also nonbeing.

That is, every object and every state which we can think of in this universe are God. This means that God is not merely all that is good, He is also the evil. Nothing exists unless He wills it. It is not true that God is the Lord of light and Satan of darkness. While we live in this body, we may believe in these dualities. We should engrave Tulsidasji's words in our hearts, that while we are enveloped in *maya* all this, which is false, will seem as true. The nacre will appear as silver and the sun's rays will appear as the mirage. We shall continue to think in this way till a *jnani* opens our eyes and convinces us that the appearance of the rope as the serpent, of the nacre as silver and of the sun's rays as mirage, is but the work of our imagination. We believe that God is both good and evil and, believing that, some of us ask what harm there is in following evil. But it is quite wrong if we argue thus.

The point is not that we should act like scorpions or centipedes, but that we should have goodwill for them, without ourselves becoming poisonous like them. The Lord has here stated a profound truth which is beyond the capacity of our reason to comprehend. What He has stated cannot possibly be true in this world. We can only imagine that it must be true in some sense. Being and non-being, virtue and sin, immortality and death, these are contradictory things. They cannot be true for human beings, they can be so only for God. That third state [in which contraries are reconciled] is not a mere mixure of the two.

Hydrogen and oxygen together yield water, but water does not display the separate properties of either; it has characteristics of its own.

Similarly, we must not imagine that God has in Him the qualities of both virtue and sin, but should think that He has something else which is different from either. If we had both virtue and sin in us, there would be an explosion, but Siva swallows both. The existence of the two in God is a miracle, and He alone knows its mystery. We should make no attempt to cultivate such a state. If we try to combine the two in us, such an attempt to imitate God will simply destroy us.

Followers of the three Vedas, who drink the *soma* juice and are purged of sin, worship Me with sacrifice and pray for going to heaven; they reach the holy world of the gods and enjoy in heaven the divine joys of the gods.[3]

Those who perform the rituals enjoined in the three Vedas, who drink *somarasa* (in the region of the North Pole *somarasa* was food and it would be a crime to refuse it to anyone, for if given to a dying man it saved life), who wash away their sins and worship the Lord by performing sacrifices, pray that they should go to heaven. They go to the sacred realm of Indra and there enjoy divine pleasure such as gods do.

Notes

1. IX, 16, 17 & 18.
2. IX, 19.
3. IX, 20.

[139] August 22, 1926

They enjoy the vast world of heaven, and their merit spent,

they enter the world of the mortals; thus those who, following the Vedic law, long for the fruit of their action earn but the round of birth and death.

As for those who worship Me, thinking on Me alone and nothing else, ever attached to Me, I bear the burden of getting them what they need.[1]

Yoga means realization of God and *kshema* means safeguarding of the means which help us to attain it.

Even those who, devoted to other gods, worship them in full faith, even they, O Kaunteya, worship none but Me, though not according to the rule.[2]

The right method is to have no intermediary between oneself and God. "But," Shri Krishna says, "those who seek Me through the gate-keepers that stand between, they too worship Me, for they worship these in order to reach Me."

For I am the Acceptor and the Director of all sacrifices; but not recongnizing Me as I am, they go astray.[3]

"I am," says the Lord "the recipient and the Lord of all *yajnas.*" That is, he who does everything without thinking that he himself does it can say that not he but the Lord does everything.

"Those, however, who do not know the truth and, therefore, do not know Me, return again to the world."

The sinful man, so long as he is conscious of his ego, describes himself as the most wicked of men. Tulsidas says, on the one hand, that there could be none as lustful, lecherous, degraded and adulterous as he was and, on the other hand, attributes all his sins to God, for, since he had no ego in him, how could he have committed those sins?

The river Ganga washes away all kinds of sins, but she receives no stain. Likewise, the timeless body in Rama is sinless. The physical Rama, of course, is subject to sin. If we prevert this idea and start committing sins and then say that sins cannot touch us, we shall be like the frog in the fable who tried to blow his body into the size of an ox and so burst. A *bhakta* will say: "I am a sinful man, but I am in your hands." Beyond this, our reason does not work. "Do not describe man as God; he is not God, but he is not different from the light of God."

Notes

1. IX, 21 & 22.
2. IX, 23.
3. IX, 24.

[140] August 24, 1926

Those who worship the gods go to the gods; those who worship the manes go to the manes; those who worship the spirits go to the spirits; but those who worship Me come to Me.

Any offering of leaf, flower, fruit or water, made to Me in devotion, by an earnest soul, I lovingly accept.[1]

The Lord did not accept the fruit sent by Duryodhana, for he had not sent it with love. His motive was to get his own aim served through Shri Krishna. He wanted the Lord's help on his own terms.

He had not mastered the self. But Vidura, who was a man of simple heart, offered a plain dish of leafy greens and the Lord accepted it with love, for Vidura's *bhakti* was unrivalled and his heart was straightforward and clean. He felt no awe for the wealth of the mighty.

Whatever thou dost, whatever thou eastest, whatever thou offerest as sacrifice or gift, whatever austerity thou dost perform, O Kaunteya, dedicate all to Me.

So doing thou shalt be released from the bondage of action yielding good and evil fruit; having accomplished both renunciation and performance, thou shalt be released (from birth and death) and come unto Me.[2]

"If you live thus, you will be free from the bonds of karma which are sometimes good and sometimes evil in their fruit, for I shall be the recipient of all that you enjoy." He who has purified himself through *sannyassa-yoga*—who dedicates to the Lord all that he does, who keeps on doing useful work right till the end of his life, but in a spirit of dedication to the Lord,—such a one goes to Him after death.

I am the same to all beings; with Me there is none disfavoured, none favoured; but those who worship Me with devotion are in Me and I in them.[3]

If we seek refuge in the Lord, He will give us all that we can wish. If we go to the Ganga, we can have the Ganga water, but we shall have only as much as fills our cupped palm if that is all we seek. The Lord provides a grain for the ant and a cart-load for the elephant.

Notes

1. IX, 25 & 26.
2. IX, 27 & 28.
3. IX, 29.

[141] August 25, 1926

A sinner, however great, if he turns to Me with undivided devotion, must indeed be counted a saint; for he has settled resolve.[1]

A man like Ajamila may have resolved to purify himself of the evil in him, and he may sit down in a firm posture for yoga; maybe his thoughts do not leave him, but he is none the less a sadhu who keeps repeating *Om* and is firm in his resolution. But another person who is not firm in his mind and not regular in practice, who follows no method in his work, may be a good man and still he does not deserve to be called a sadhu.

For soon he becomes righteous and wins everlasting peace; know for a certainly, O Kaunteya, that My *bhakta* never perishes.[2]

Such a person soon becomes a holy man, and attains inviolable peace of mind. We should not, therefore, regard even the most wicked of men as wicked. He can become good in this very life. Shri Krishna says: "Be certain, O Arjuna, that no *bhakta* of mine ever perishes."

This body perishes, but he dies after becoming a good man rather than a wicked one.

For finding refuge in Me, even those who though are born of the womb of sin, women, Vaisyas, and Sudras too, reach the supreme goal.[3]

"Anyone who surrenders himself or herself to Me," assures the Lord, "whether man or woman, Vaisya or Sudra, or one born among wicked people—in a family of the most wicked *Chandals*—even then such a person will attain the supreme state."

The Lord has given a great assurance to the world in these verses. This is His reply to those learned in the Vedas. Such persons argue that those who have not studied the Vedas cannot realize God. It was believed in those days that women, Vaisyas and Sudras cannot attain *moksha*. In fact, Krishna tended cows as a boy in Nanda's family and did the work of a Sudra. The Vaisya's function was rearing cows and agriculture. But in course of time those who were engaged in agriculture came to be regarded as Sudras. Shri Krishna says here that, even if Vaisyas and Sudras are not able to study the Vedas, they can certainly attain the blessed state. Anyone who, though ignorant of the Vedas, knows the *Brahman*, and has a pure heart is certain to attain this state.

How much more then, the pure Brahmins and seer-kings who are my devotees? Do thou worship Me, therefore, since thou hast come to this fleeting and joyless world.

On Me fix thy mind, to Me bring thy devotion, to Me offer thy sacrifice, to Me make thy obeisance; thus having attached thyself to Me and made Me thy end and aim, to Me indeed shalt thou come.[4]

"Forget yourself in Me," says Shri Krishna, "meditate constantly on Me, let your *atman* be in ceaseless communion with Me, and live with your heart ever united with Me; if you live thus, I shall draw you towards Me."

"You need only allow yourself to be drawn, and shall not resist.

You may not draw Me, but I can draw you. You will be able to understand this riddle, no one else will."

This chapter has also been named *Rajavidya*[5] and *Rajaguhyayoga*[6].

Shri Krishna tells Arjuna that He has explained the highest knowledge and expounded the highest mystery—the meaning of yoga and *kshema*. The union of yoga is to be achieved with the Lord; one should not aspire to earn great riches or rise to a position of honour or win an empire in this world. All that is needed is a fixed determination to realize God. What is the good of any pleasure we can get through the senses—the eyes, the nose, the ears and so on? We should not be allured by it, for such pleasure is short-lived. There were emperors, but they have passed away. He whom we seek dwells in our hearts, and the holy temple in which He sits opens only by the means of prayer. The Lord explained this by saying *manmana bhava madhakto madyaji*[7]. "I am," He says, "the author and sustainer of all, I am the friend, I am the source, the cause of existence and of the final destruction—I am all this. There is nothing else. I am all that there is.

You are of no consequence. The other gods in the worlds in between will also perish, like you. I alone never perish. If you wish that you should not perish, you should come to My world, and that you can do by surrendering your whole mind to Me. Whether you are engaged in bathing or washing or any other like activities, if you are repeating my name the while and if you dedicate to Me all that you eat, if you worship Me as you give your body its hire, you will surely come to Me."

Notes

1. IX, 30.
2. IX, 31.
3. IX, 32.
4. IX, 33 & 34.
5. The sovereign science.
6. The yoga of sovereign mystery.
7. In IX, 34.

[142] Chapter X, August 26, 1926

Yet once more, O Mahabahu, hear My supreme word, which I will utter to thee, gratified one, for thy benefit.

Neither the gods nor the great seers know My origin; for I am, every way, the origin of them both.

He who knows Me, the great Lord of the worlds, as birthless and without beginning, he among mortals, undeluded, is released from sins.[1]

Those who know Me as the Unborn, the Beginningless and the Supreme Lord of all creatures do not sink into the darkness of ignorance. A person who has sunk in darkness knows the night as day and the day as night. Among all these creatures who are bound to perish, the *jnani* becomes free from all sins, for he will have no vestige of aversion and attachment, no trace of egotism; he will remain unaffected by the pairs of opposites, will ever be humble and believe that it is the Lord who provides for his living.

Discernment, knowledge, freedom from delusion, long suffering, truth, self-restraint, inward calm, pleasure, pain, birth, death, fear and fearlessness;[2] Non-violence, even-mindedness, contentment, austerity, beneficence, good and ill fame,—all these various attributes of creatures proceed verily from Me.[3]

All the qualities mentioned in these two verses, intellect, knowledge, the absence of ignorant attachment, forgiveness, truthfulness, control of the senses, serenity, happiness and suffering, birth and death, fear and absence of fear, ahimsa, inward poise and contentment, *tapas*, making gifts, good name or evil reputation among men—these conditions exist in all creatures and I am the cause of each one of them.

The Creator of all beings is also the cause of all the good and evil which we see in these beings.

Notes

1. X, 1, 2 & 3.
2. X, 4.
3. X, 5.

[143][1] August 27, 1926

The seven great seers, the ancient four, and the Manus too were born of Me and of My mind, and of them were born all the creatures in the world.

He who knows in truth this My immanence and My yoga becomes gifted with unshakable yoga; of this there is no doubt.[2]

Everything which exists is created by the Lord. He who believes, not merely with his reason but with his heart, that no creature can live or act without His permission or except as He wills, yokes himself to Him in single-minded devotion, but he who forgets the Lord and believes in his pride that he rises by his own efforts labours under a delusion. There is no doubt at all that he who believes in God from the depth of his heart and obeys the Lord who dwells in him attains to a state of serenity which is never perturbed.

I am the source of all, all proceeds from Me; knowing this, the wise worship Me with hearts full of devotion.

With Me in their thoughts, their whole soul devoted to Me, teaching one another, with Me ever on their lips, they live in contentment and joy.

To these, ever in tune with Me worshipping Me with affectionate devotion, I give the power of selfless action, whereby they come to Me[3].

In this way, knowledge comes spontaneously to a *bhakta*. He does not have to wade through big volumes. But he who believes that he will acquire knowledge first and cultivate *bhakti* afterwards will fail miserably in his aim. No one can acquire knowledge in that way. Such knowledge breeds, if anything, pride. But he who lovingly cultivates devotion for the Lord and constantly thinks on Him gets knowledge without any special effort to that end.

Out of every compassion for them, I Who dwell in their hearts, destroy the darkness, born of ignorance, with the refulgent lamp of knowledge.[4]

Notes

1. The notes of this discourse were not taken by Mahadev Desai.
2. X, 6 & 7.
3. X, 8, to 10.
4. X, 11.

[144] August 28, 1926

Lord! Thou art the supreme *Brahman*, the supreme Abode, the supreme Purifer! Everlasting Celestial Being, the Primal God, Unborn, All-pervading.

Thus have all the seers—the divine seer Narada, Asita, Devala, Vyasa—declared Thee; and Thou Thyself dost tell me so.

All that Thou tellest me is true, I know, O Keshava, verily, Lord, neither the gods nor the demons know Thy manifestation.

Thyself alone Thou knowest by Thyself, O Purushottama, O Source and Lord of all beings, God of gods, O Ruler of the universe!

Indeed Thou oughtest to tell me of all Thy manifestations, without a remainder, whereby Thou dost pervade these worlds.

O Yogi! constantly meditating on Thee, how am I to know Thee? In what various aspects am I to think of Thee, O Lord?

Recount to me yet again, in full detail, Thy unique power and Thy immanence, O Janardana! For my ears cannot be sated with listening to Thy life-giving words.[1]

One who does engraving work every day does not tire of it. He returns to it whenever he is free. Similarly, Arjuna, who loves repeating Krishna's name in devotion, requests Him again and again to describe His powers till the latter can say no more.

Note

1. X, 12 to 18.

[145] August 29, 1926

Yea, I will unfold to thee, O Kurushreshtha, My divine mainifestations,—the cheifiest only; for there is no limit to their extent.[1]

I am the *Atman*, O Gudakesha, seated in the heart of every being; I am the beginning, the middle and the end of all beings.

Of the *Adityas* I am Vishnu; of luminaries, the radiant Sun; of *Maruts* I am *Marichi*; of constellations, the moon.

Of the Vedas I am the *Sama* Veda; of the gods, Indra; of the senses I am the mind; of beings I am the consciousness.

Of *Rudras* I am Shankara; of *Yakshas* and *Rakshasas* Kubera; of *Vasus* I am the Fire; of mountains Meru.

Of priests. O Partha, know Me to be the chief Brihaspati; of army captains I am Kartikeya; and of waters, the ocean.

Of the great seers I am Bhrigu; of words I am the one syllable '*AUM*', of sacrifices I am the *Japa* sacrifice; of things immovable, the Himalayas.

Of all trees I am Ashvattha; of the divine seers, Narada; of the heavenly choir I am Chitraratha; of the perfected I am Kapila the ascetic.

Of horses, know Me to be Uchchaihshravas born with *Amrita*; of mighty elephants I am Airavata; of men, the monarch.

Of weapons I am *Vajra*; of cows, *Kamadhenu*; I am Kandarpa, the god of generation; of serpents I am Vasuki.

Of cobras I am Ananta; of water-dwellers I am Varuna; of the menes I am Aryaman; and of the chastisers, Yama.

Of demons I am Prahlada; of reckoners, the Time; of beasts I am the lion; and of birds, Garuda.

Of cleansing agents I am the Wind; of wielders of weapons, Rama; of fishes I am the crocodile; of rivers, the Gangas.

Of creations I am the beginning, end and middle, O Arjuna; of sciences, the science of spiritual knowledge; of debaters, the right argument.

Of letters, the letter A; of compounds I am the *dvandva*; I am the imperishable Time; I am the creator to be seen everywhere.

All-seizing Death am I, as also the source of things to be; in feminine virtues I am *Kirti* . (glory), *Shri* (beauty), *Vak* (speech), *Smriti* (memory), *Medha* (intelligence), *Dhriti* (constancy) and *Kshama* (forgiveness).

Of *Saman* hymns I an *Brihat Saman*; of metres, *Gayatri*; of months I am *Margashirsha*; of seasons, the spring.[2]

"I am *Brihat Saman* among *Saman* hymns and *Gayatri* among metres. Among the months, I am *Margashirsha* (when in old times the Aryans lived in the region of the North Pole, this was regarded as the first month of the year and that is why it is mentioned here). Among the seasons I am Spring."

Notes

1. X, 19.
2. X, 20 to 35.

[146] August 31, 1926

Of deceivers I am the dice-play; of the splendid, the splendour; I am victory, I am resolution, I am the goodness of the good.[1]

"I am the gaming of those who indulge in gambling." (This is merely intended to point out that God exists not only in what is good in the world, but also in what is evil. Shri Krishna could also have said that He was the sin of the wicked. He could certainly have said that He was Ravana among the demons, for He let Ravana have his way and enjoy himself only as long as He chose. The author's intention is only to assert that God is omnipotent. God's creation contains both good and evil. By saying this, Shri Krishna gives us some freedom to choose between the two. To us who are confined in the prison of this body, he grants that freedom. He gives us the freedom to shake off our bonds. If a prisoner condemned to imprisonment for life is permitted a seemingly unimportant condition by fulfilling which he can be free, it will be a great thing for him, for he can secure his freedom through it. We are in the same condition, for the Lord has assured us that we can be what we wish to be.) I am the splendour of the splendid. I am victory, resolution and the goodness of the good.

Of *Vrishnis* I am Vasudeva; of Pandavas Dhananjaya; of ascetics I am Vyasa; and of seers, Ushanas.

I am the rod of those that punish; the strategy of those seeking victory; of secret things I am silence, and the knowlege of those that know.

Whatever is the seed of every being, O Arjuna, that am I; there is nothing, whether moving or fixed, that can be without Me.

There is no end to my divine manifestations; what extent of them I have told thee now is only by way of illustration.

Whatever is glorious, beautiful and mighty know thou that all such has issued from a fragment of My splendour.

But why needst thou to learn this at great length, O Arjuna? With but a part of Myself I stand upholding this universe.[2]

If we have an idea of the infinite powers of the Lord, we shall become humble. We will not then follow the example of Narad who once felt proud of the one power which he possessed. The Lord has said that even being proud is His privilege. The substance of all that He has said is that we should learn to be the humblest of the humble.

Knowing that there is no limit to the power of God, we should submit to violence if anyone attacks us, without offering violence in return. If we attenpt to resist him with violence, God will humble our pride, for there has been no demon, from Ravana downwards, whom the Lord has not destroyed.

Notes

1. X, 36.
2. X, 37 to 42.

[147] Chapter XI, September 1, 1926

This is regarded as an important chapter. The *Gita* is poem with a profound meaning, and the eleventh Chapter is the most poetic of all. If we wish to learn true *bhakti,* we should know this Chapter by heart. If we do so, we shall feel, when reciting it, that we are bathing in a sea of *bhakti*.

Out of Thy grace towards me, Thou hast told me the supreme mystery revealing the knowledge of the Supreme; is has banished my delusion.

Of the origin and destruction of beings I have heard from Thee in full detail, as also of Thy imperishable majesty, O Kamalapatraksha!

Thou art indeed just as Thou hast described Thyself, Parameshvara! I do crave to behold now that form of Thine as Ishvara.

If, Lord, Thou thinkest it possible for me to bear the sight, reveal to me, O Yogeshvara, Thy imperishable form.

[148] September 2, 1926

Behold, O Partha, my forms divine in their hundreds and thousands, infinitely diverse, infinitely various in colour and aspect.

Behold the *Adityas*, the *Vasus*, the *Rudras*, the two *Ashwins*, and the *Maruts*; behold. O Bharata, numerous marvels never revealed before, Behold today, O Gudakesha, in my body, the whole universe, moving, and unmoving, all in one, and whatever else thou cravest to see.[1]

"See the *Adityas*," Shri Krishna says, "the *Vasus*, the *Rudras*, the *Ashwins* and the *Maruts*, all together. See the entire world, animate and inanimate, all as one reality."

This cosmic form includes, good and evil, Hindus and Muslims, believers and atheists, all.

"You may also see," Shri Krishna adds, "anything else you wish to see."

But thou canst not see Me with these thine own eyes. I give thee the eye divine; behold My sovereign power!

With these words, O King, the great Lord of Yoga, Hari, then revealed to Partha His supreme form as Ishvara.[2]

Notes

1. XI, 1 to 7.
2. XI. 8 & 9.

[149] September 3, 1926

The teaching of the *Gita* was not meant to be merely preserved in a book; it was meant to be translated into action. Mahadev and Punjabhai take notes of what I speak, but had we arranged recording on a gramophone plate, every word could have been taken down.

Could we have said, then, that the gramophone machine had understood the *Gita*? It is an inanimate object. Similarly, what will this knowledge profit us if we merely take down notes and do not put the teaching into practice? We should, therefore, serve the people among whom we live, and help our elders in their domestic chores. Why should Ba find it necessary to send for Kusum to help her? Why should she request Ramachandra, who is a guest here just for a few days, to help her wash the kitchen? Why should she, who is at present under a vow of eating only once a day, not get some time for rest? If you give her no help, you are like the gramophone in our example.

With many mouths, and many eyes, many wondrous aspects, many divine ornaments, and many brandished weapons divine;

Wearing divine garlands and vestments, anointed with divine perfumes, it was the form of God, all marvellous, infinite, seen everywhere.

Were the splendour of a thousand suns to shoot forth all at once in the sky that might perchance resemble the splendour of that Mighty One.

Then did Pandava see the whole universe in its manifold divisions gathered as one in the body of that God of gods.[1]

VOL. 37 : 11 NOVEMBER, 1926 - 1 JANUARY, 1927 273

The whole universe, despite its manifold divisions, is gathered there in Him (Like a tree and its leaves. The tree is like the cosmic form of the Lord, the root and the leaves being one. The root contains the whole world of the tree, and the leaves represent that world divided into many forms.). Arjuna saw thus the [cosmic] form of the God of gods.

Then Dhananjaya, wonderstruck and thrilled in every fibre of his being, bowed low his head before the Lord, addressing Him thus with folded hands:[2]

Notes

1. XI, 10 to 13.
2. XI, 14.

[150] September 4, 1926

Within Thy form, O Lord, I see all the gods and the divers

multitudes of beings, the Lord Brahma on his lotus-throne and all the seers and the serpents divine.

With many arms bellies, months and eyes, I see Thy infinite form everywhere. Neither Thy end, nor middle, nor beginning do I see, O Lord of Universe, Universal-formed![1]

(On the one hand, Arjuna says that Shri Krishna has a definite form and, on the othe, he says that He is formless. In other words, His form is so vast that in truth He is formless.)

With crown and mace and disc, a mass of effulgence, gleaming everywhere I see Thee, so dazzling to the sight, bright with the splendour of the fiery sun blazing from all sides,—incomprehensible.[2]

You bear crown, mace and disc. You are a mass of radiance which glown at all piaces.

(The sun gives some faint idea of the Lord's light, but it is no more than a dim point of light in comparison with the Lord's.) Thou art as lustrous as fire and the sun. Thou art dazzling to the sight because of thy immeasurable effulgence.

Thou art the Supreme Imperishable worthy to be known; Thou art the final resting-place of this universe; Thou art the changeless guardian of the Eternal Dharma; Thou art, I believe, the Everlasting Being.[3]

Cannot we say that the rains yesterday were an aspect of this infinite cosmic form of God? He has placed the sun at such a great distance from us; what would have been our condition if it had been a little nearer? Can we, then, imagine Arjuna's condition wih Shri Krishna standing near him, Krishna glowing with the light of a thousand suns.

Thou hast no beginning, middle nor end; infinite is Thy might; arms innumerable; for eyes, the sun and the moon; Thy mouth a blazzing fire, overpowering the universe with Thy radiance.[4]

By Thee alone are filled the spaces between heaven and earth and all the quarters; at the sight of this Thy wondrous terrible form, the three worlds are sore oppressed, O Mahatman![5]

(This Sabarmati, too, is an aspect of the infinite power of God. If the warning received yesterdys comes true and there is a heavy flood, we would simply shake with fear.)

Here, too, the multitudes of gods are seen to enter Thee; some awestruck praise Thee with folded arms; the hosts of great seers and *siddhas*, 'All Hail'on their lips, hymn Thee with songs of praise.[6]

Notes

1. XI, 15 & 16.
2. XI, 17.
3. XI, 18.
4. XI, 19.
5. XI, 20.
6. XI, 21.

[151] September 5, 1926

One feels as though these verses were specially written for us. We had information from the Collector that there would be a heavy flood in the Sabarmati. Naturally, I was agitated in my heart, not knowing what to do. But I reminded myself of the verses which I daily recite before the women: *"Govind, Dwarkavasin"* and so on.

Krishna would be welcome if he flew to our help on His Garuda.

Otherwise, if all these things were carried away in the flood, our honour would be saved. Let anyone who survives to witness the destruction live on faithful to our vows.

I had advised them to construct the loom-shed as far away as the road. "The weak will pretend to be good" as the saying goes, and so we have nothing to do but wait in patience. If the authorities of the [Sabarmati] jail invite us to take shelter in it, I will ask them if they have invited the people of Vadaj too. I will tell them that they should offer shelter to all others before they invite us.

You should eat, not to gratify your palate, but to keep yourselves alive to keep up your strength. As I sit here in peace, we heard the blowing of the mill whistles, and so I remarked, "No one can escape work." It is the same story: "We seek refuge with the Lord who is the ship that ferries us across this sea of creation." Shall we never be free from this affliction [of work]? When afflicted with other deseases, we may keep repeating the Lord's name, or the *dwadash mantra* or any other prayer which will bring us peace of mind. Which is a greater storm, the inward storm in the heart or this outward storm of work? Is this latter storm more of an affliction than that our eyes and ears should disobey us and attend to things which they ought to shun? Every inmate of the Ashram has wings. I should like even the women to have them. Anyone who wihses to leave is certainly free to do so, either by train or to the city on the other side. As the headman of a village, this is all I can tell you. If you can think of anything better, please do.

The *Rudras, Adityas, Vasus, Sadhyas,* all the gods, the twin *Ashwins, Maruts,* Manes, the hosts of *Gandharvas, Yakshas, Asuras* and *siddhas*—all gaze on Thee in wonderment.

At the sight of Thy mighty form, O Mahabahu, many-mouthed, with eyes, arms, thighs and feet innumerable, with many vast bellies, terrible with many jaws, the worlds feel fearfully oppressed, and so do I.

For as I behold Thee touching the sky, glowing, numerous-hued with gaping mouths and wide resplendent eyes, I feel oppressed in my innermost being; no peace nor quiet I find, O Vishnu!

And as I see Thy mouths with fearful jaws, resembling the Fire of Doom, I lose all sense of direction, and find no relief. Be gracious, O Devesha, O Jagannivasa!

All the sons of Dhritarashtra, and with them the crowd of kings, Bhishma, Drona, and that Karna too, as also our chief warriors— Are hastening into the fearful jaws of Thy terrible mouths. Some indeed, caught between Thy teeth are seen, their heads being crushed to atoms.

As rivers in their numerous torrents run headlong to the sea, even so the heroes of the world of men rush into Thy flaming mouths.

As moths, fast-flying, plunge into blazing fire straight to their doom, even so these rush headlong into Thy mouths, to their destruction.

Devouring all these from all sides, Thou lappest them with Thy flaming tongues; Thy fierce rays blaze forth, filling the whole universe with their lustre.

Tell me, Lord, who Thou art so dread of form! Hail to Thee, O Devavara!

Be gracious! I desire to know Thee, Primal Lord; for I comprehend not what Thou dost.[1]

Note

1. XI, 22 to 31.

[152] September 7, 1926

Doom am I, full-ripe, dealing death to the worlds, engaged in devouring mankind. Even without thy slaying them, not one of the warriors, ranged for battle against thee, shall survive.[1]

Therefore, do thou arise, and win renown! Defeat thy foes and enjoy a thriving kingdom. By Me have these already been destroyed; be thou no more than an instrument, O Savyasachin![2]

"Savyasachin" means one who can use a bow with the left hand, that is, with either hand.

Drona, Bhishma, Jayadratha and Karna, as also the other warrior chiefs—already slain by Me—slay thou! Be not dismayed! Fight! Victory is thine over thy foes in the field.

Hearing this word of Keshava, crown-wearer Arjuna folded his hands, and trembling made obeisance. Bowing and all hesitant, in faltering accents, he proceeded to address Krishna once more.

Right proper it is, O Hrishikesha, that Thy praise should stir the world to gladness and tender emotion; the *Rakshasas* in fear fly to every quarter and all the hosts of *Siddhas* do reverent homage.[3]

"And why should they not bow to you? You are the destroyer of the demons." The demons are our enemies, external and internal.

What even if the river should swallow us and destroy us? How much more fearful is the flood inside us? Who will destroy the demons inside? And so Arjuna said:

And why should they not bow down to Thee, O Mahatman? Thou art the First Creator, greater even than Brahma. O Ananta, O Devesha, O Jagannivasa, Thou art the Imperishable, Being, not-Being, and That which transcends even these.

Thou art the Primal God, the Ancient Being; Thou art the final restingplace of this Universe; Thou art the Knower, the 'to-be-known', the supreme Abode; by Thee, O myriad-formed, is the Universe pervaded.

Thou art *Vayu, Yama, Agni, Varuna, Shashanka, Prajapati,* and

Prapitamaha! All hail to Thee, a thousand times all hail! Again and yet again all hail to Thee![4]

Notes

1. XI, 32.
2. XI, 33.
3. XI, 34 to 36.
4. XI, 37 to 39.

[153] September 8, 1926

There was once a woman in Madras who was a devotee of the Lord. She used to worship Him with her back towards the idol. A learned man rebuked her for doing so, but she cited this verse in reply, and the learned pundit was speechless. If all space is pervaded by God, when we find his eyes, ears and noses on all sides, why should we sit facing in a particular direction to worship Him?

All hail to Thee from before and behind! All hail to Thee from every side, O All; Thy prowess is infinite, Thy might is measureless! Thou holdest all; therefore Thou art all.

If ever in carelessness, thinking of Thee as comrade, I addressed Thee saying, 'O Krishna!', 'O Yadava!' nor knowing Thy greatness, in negligence or in affection.

If ever I have been rude to Thee in jest, whilst at play, at rest-time, ot at meals, whilst alone or in company, O Achuta, forgive Thou my fault—I beg of Thee, O Incomprehensible one!

Thou art Father of this world, of the moving and the unmoving; Thou art its adored, its worthiest, Master; there is none equal to Thee; how then any greater than Thee? Thy power is matchless in the three worlds.

Therefore, I prostrate myself before Thee, and beseech Thy grace, O Lord Adorable! As father with son, as comrade with comrade, so shouldst Thou bear, beloved Lord, with me, Thy loved one.

I am filled with joy to see what never was seen before, and yet my heart is oppressed with fear. Show me that original form of Thine, O Lord! Be gracious, Devesha, O Jagannivasa!

I crave to see Thee even as Thou wast, with crown, with mace, disc in hand; wear Thou, once more, that four-armed form, O thousand armed Vishvamurti!

Ir is to favour thee, O Arjuna, that I have revealed to thee, by My own unique power, this My Form Supreme, Resplendent, Universal, Infinite, Primal—which none save thee has ever seen.

Not by the study of the Vedas, not by secrifice, not by the study of other scriptures, not by gifts, nor yet by performance of rites or of fierce austerities can I, in such a form, be seen by anyone save thee in the world of men, O Kurupravira!

Be thou neither oppressed nor bewildered to look on this awful form of Mine. Banish thy fear, ease thy mind, and lo! behold Me once again as I was.[1]

Note

1. XI, 40 to 49.

[154] September 9, 1926

Beholding again Thy benign human form I am come to myself and am once more in my normal state.

Very hard to behold is that Form of Mine which thou hast seen; even the gods always yearn to see it.

Not by the Vedas, not by penance, nor by gifts, nor yet by sacrifice, can any behold Me in the Form that thou hast seen.

But by single-minded devotion, O Arjuna, I may in this Form be known and seen, and truly entered into, O Parantapa![1]

First we should know the Lord, then see Him and then merge into Him. We may tell Him: "You may eat me up, I will not resist if You do. I am Yours, and I want to be one with You. What harm can it do even if You eat me up?" Telling us that He can grind us into paste with his teeth and throw it out, He tells us that we can know Him through *bhakti*. We can pass His test only through faith. When we know that everything takes place through Him and that we live and die as He wills, how can we be affected by anything?

He alone comes to Me, O Pandava, who does My work, who has made Me his goal, who is My devotee, who has renounced attachment, who has ill will towards none.[2]

The Lord has given the whole substance of Chapter XI in this last verse. "He who works for Me is ever devoted to Me, who is attached to nothing and bears ill will to none—not even to a person who may have committed a heinous sin—but ever blesses him instead,—such a person comes to Me."

Notes

1. XI, 51 to 54.
2. XI, 55.

[155][1] Chapter XII, September 10, 1926

To love God means to be free from attachment to any work. We should of course do work, but without egotistic attachment to it, simply for the love of God. A lustful man forgets his love for parents and children when seeking gratification of his lust and abandons himself blindly to it. This also is a form of non-attachment. But the cause is a filthy one, whereas love for God is good. And now for the meaning of the verse [with which we began].

Of the devotees who thus worship Thee, incessantly attached, and those who worship the Imperishable Unmanifest, which are the better yogis?[2]

The Lord replies:

Those I regard as the best yogis who, riveting their minds on Me, ever attached, worship Me, with the highest faith.

But those who worship the Imperishable, the Indefinable, the Unmanifest, the Omnipresent, the Unthinkable, the Rock-seated, the Immovable, the Unchanging, Keeping the whole host of senses in complete control, looking on all with an impartial eye, engrossed in the welfare of all beings—these come indeed to Me.[3]

Notes

1. The notes of this discourse were not taken by Mahadev Desai.
2. XII, 1.
3. XII, 2 to 4.

[156][1] September 11, 1926

Greater is the travail of those whose mind is fixed on the Unmanifest; for it is hard for embodied mortals to gain the Unmanifest Goal.[2]

Those who have fixed their minds on the Unmanifest, that is, who worship the formless *Brahman*, experience greater difficulty in their effort, for it is extremely difficult for us, embodied souls, to know the unmanifest state.

It is very difficult to meditate on *shunya*. The moment we attribute a single quality to God, we cease to worship the Unmanifest.

We must all, nevertheless, realize that beyond the Personal God there is a Formless Essence which our reason cannot comprehend. The consummation of *bhakti* lies in the *bhakta* merging in God, so that ultimately nothing but One Formless God remains. Since, however, it is easier to reach this state through the worship of the Personal God, the Lord says that the other path of seeking the Formless Essence directly is difficult to follow.

But those who casting all their actions on Me, making Me their all in all, worship Me with the meditation of undivided devotion,of such, whose thoughts are centred on Me, O Partha, I become ere long the Deliverer from the ocean of this world of death.[3]

Notes

1. The notes of this discourse were not taken by Mahadev Desai.
2. XII, 5.
3. XII, 6 & 7.

[157] September 12, 1926

The verse beginning with *kleshodhikatarastesham*[1] has given me great light; for it says that devotion to the Unmanifest is difficult to cultivate and that it is a harder path to follow. The reason given is very significant. If one retires to a forest and meditates on God, one can certainly realize Him. Likewise, one who serves as an accountant or clerk or manager in a firm can also do that. Both may be in the same state of mind and can, therefore, reach the same goal.

If we are sincere in our devotion to the cause of the spinningwheel movement, the country is bound to embrace it in course of time. This faith is an illustration of the path which human beings should adopt, this is the path of *bhakti*, of the worship of a Personal God, for the spinning-wheel is visible to us and we see power in it. If, however, we worship the spinning-wheel for itself, our worship will be like the worship of the Unmanifest *Brahman*. It will be so, that is, if we merely worship the spinning-wheel without spinning on it. In my view, however, even if a time comes when we decide to withdraw into complete silence, it will not mean that we have abandoned the spinning-wheel or forsaken our aspiration for the *Brahman*. If indeed we ever retire to some high peak on the Himalayas, it will not be because we shall have lost interest in the spinning-wheel or been disillusioned with the people. To retire with such a motive will be no way of worshipping the Unmanifest. Of course, we shall benefit in some way even if we do so. If a man decides out of disgust to observe *brahmacharya* or to give up immorality, he will certainly benefit. But his action will not nave been prompted by true knowledge. Similarly, this idea of retirement is not meant for anyone who is disgusted with the spinning-wheel or with the people.

If a person, however, feels that there is an Essence beyond this universe of objects with name and form and that he must know it, and if he leaves this world and withdraws into solitude with that aim, that also is a legitimate path. But it is a difficult one even if one is sincere in one's aspiration to cultivate *bhakti* or the Unmanifest. The idea that the *Brahman* is real and that the visible universe is illusory is simply beyond the capacity of our reason to comprehend. How difficult it must be, then, to live according to it? It is only when our body is completely transformed into an armour that nothing will pierce it. The Shastras narrate the stories of Prahlad[2] and Sudhanva[3]. As these stories show, it is possible, even while one is physically alive, to live as if one had renounced one's body. It is extremely difficult for a man to cultivate such a state of mind and live for ever absorbed in the *atman*.

All but one in a crore live in illusion and error. They will not break away from their ignorant attachment and will have to be born again in this world.

The path of karma is the easiest to follow. The path of reason can lead one into great error. The path along which we have the least danger of falling into error is the one described in the verse beginning with *nehabhikramanashosti*[4]. Neither Christians nor Muslims, nor certainly Hindus, have risen above the worship of the Personal God.

There is a book by Shibli[5] in which he has discussed the question whether or not God has a body. Even a person who aspires to cultivate devotion exclusively for the Unmanifest worships some visible symbol. We can of course understand with our intellect the idea that the body is unconnected with the *atman*. To say that one can attain *moksha* while physically alive only means that, after death, one will not have to be born again. Has anyone ever been able to say what his state after death will be? The spiritualists and Theosophists are not correct, in my view, about what they say concerning spirits, in the sense that no one has been able to know and tell the whole truth.

For this reason, Shri Krishna told Arjuna that it would be better for him to take no interest in the problem at all. "Silence is golden in this matter," he says. "Don't you see, you dear simpleton, that I Myself have taken on a human body? And you ask Me, of all persons, whether worship of the Unmanifest is better, or that of the Personal God. You had better stop asking such questions and do as I tell you.

Free yourself from all thoughts of violence and act towards all creatures with equal love and regard." If we understand this truth, we would escape many problems. We should not mind if, because we worship the Personal God, we are called idolaters and criticized for being so. And, therefore, proceeding, Shri Krishna says:

On Me set thy mind, on Me rest thy conviction; thus without doubt shalt thou remain only in Me hereafter.

If thou canst not set thy mind steadily on Me, then by the method of constant practice seek to win Me, O Dhananjaya.[6]

What is the difference between *abhyasayoga* and meditating on God? I think the former means listening to readings from holy books, reflecting on them and letting the mind dwell on their teachings. It means associating ourselves with men who are engaged in doing these things and listening to prayer songs and group devotions, for every little offering we make, leaf, flower, fruit or water, ultimately reaches God.

Notes

1. XII, 5.
2. A devotee of God who was persecuted by Hiranyakashipu, his unbelieving father.
3. Son of king Hansadhwaj in the *Mahabharata*, who defying his parents and adhering to truth and God, smilingly threw himself into a cauldron of boiling oil.
4. II, 40.

5. Presumably, *Life of the Prophet* by Maulana Shibli.
6. XII, 8 & 9.

[158][1] September 14, 1926

If thou art also unequal to this method of constant practice, concentrate on service for Me, even thus serving Me thou shalt attain perfection.

If thou art unable even to do this, then dedicating all to Me, with mind controlled, abandon the fruit of action.[2]

"Do not," Shri Krishna says, "be impatient to reap the fruit of your efforts."

Better is knowledge than practice, better than knowledge is concentration, better than concentration is renunciation of the fruit of all action, from which directly issues peace.[3]

Here *jnana* does not mean mere learning, but it means genuine experience of truth in however limited a measure. Meditation, which means concentration of the mind [on God], is better than such *jnana*, but renunciation of the fruit of action is said to be better even than such meditation. Shri Krishna says this because a person practising meditation may possibly be deceiving himself. Moreover, *jnana* does not mean ultimate self-realization. *Jnana* and meditation are compared here in their restricted meanings and one is described as better than the other. Renunciation of the fruits of action is mentioned last, but in truth it should be the first step. One who practises it becomes free from attachment to the ego.

Shri Krishna then proceeds to describe the characteristics of a man of this type.

Who has ill will towards none, who is friendly and compassionate, who has shed all thought of 'mine' or 'I', who regards pain and pleasure alike, who is long-suffering;[4]

Friendship can exist only between equals, but one should feel compassion towards all. We cannot throw a cricket bat at a dog to hit it. How would we feel if our parents or teachers did that to us? Even if we are obedient sons of our parents, how would we feel towards them if they threw a bat at us to hit us? We shall not discuss here what our duty towards a dog is. It is certain, however, that it is not right for us to hit one. Forgiveness lies is not being angry even with a dog which may have bitten us. Tit for tat is a wrong principle. It is certainly not based on forgiveness. What can we gain by being wicked with the wicked? The good of both lies only in our showing love and compassion even for such persons.

We should understand the difference between selflessness and freedom from egotism. The first means not making a distinction between ourselves and others. It describes a person who regards the entire world as his family. The second term describes a person who believes that it is not he who has done a particular thing, that it is God who has done it.

Notes

1. The notes of this discourse were taken by Punjabhai.
2. XII, 10 & 11.
3. XII, 12.
4. XII, 13.

[159] September 15, 1926

Who is ever content gifted with yoga, self-restrained, of firm conviction, who has dedicated his mind and reason to Me—that devotee (*bhakta*) of Mine is dear to Me.

Who gives no trouble to the world, to whom the world causes no trouble, who is free from exultation, resentment, fear and vexation,—that man is dear to Me.[1]

The meaning of this verse is already contained in the term *adweshta*[2]. Who expects naught, who is pure, resourceful, unconcerned, untroubled, who indulges in no undertakings,—that devotee of Mine is dear to Me.[3]

The whole of Chapter XII describes the characteristics of a *bhakta*. If we compare the verses[4] which describe a *sthitaprajna* with these, we shall find them similar.

On whom does a *bhakta* of God rely except on Him? *Shuchi* means a person who is pure both in body and mind. *Daksha* means a person who does everything which he undertakes, wholly in a spirit of dedication to God. *Udasin* means one who remains unaffected even if all his many plans come to nothing. One who is a *sarvarambhaparityagi* will not go in search of work, work will come seeking him.

God Himself will appoint his work and call him to it. Such a person, knowing that God shoulders the burdens of us all, leaves everything to Him. A slave need not go looking for work.

Who rejoices not, neither frets not grieves, who covets not, who abandons both good and ill—that devotee of Mine is dear to Me.

Who is same to foe and friend, who regards alike respect and disrespect, cold and heat, pleasure and pain, who is free from attachment; Who weighs in equal scale blame and praise, who is silent, content with whatever his lot, who owns no home, who is of steady mind,—that devotee of Mine is dear to Me.[5]

"He does not get elated, though an emperor may bow to him," so sang Raychandbhai.

They who follow this essence of dharma, as I have told it, with faith, keeping Me as their goal,—those devotees are exceedingly dear to Me.[6]

All of us have our appointed tasks, as Brahmins or Kshatriyas, Vaisyas or Sudras. Anyone who does his work without hope of reward and in a disinterested spirit is a *bhakta* of God. The Second Chapter contains verses describing a *sthitaprajna*. They describe the state of mind of a yogi living absorbed in a mystic world. This Chapter XII describes, in our ordinary language, the state of mind of a bhakta.

Notes

1. XII, 14 & 15.
2. In XII, 13.
3. XII, 16.
4. In II, 55 to 72.
5. XII, 17 to 19.
6. XII, 20.

[160] Chapter XIII, September 16, 1926

From Chapter XIII begins a new subject. It discusses the body and its nature.

This body, O Kaunteya, is called the Field; he who knows it is called the knower of the Field by those who know.[1]

Pandavas and Kauravas, that is, divine and demoniacal impulses, were fighting in this body, and God was watching the fight from a distance. Please do not believe that this is the history of a battle which took place on a little field near Hastinapur; the war is still going on.

This is the verse we should keep in mind in order to understand the meaning of the phrase *dharmakshetra*.

And understand Me to be, O Bharata, the knower of the Field in all the Fields; and the knowledge of the Field and the knower of the Field, I hold, is true knowledge.[2]

Our bodily life will have been lived to some purpose if it is spent in thinking which of these two we should serve and which we should go to for refuge.

Notes

1. XIII, 1.
2. XIII, 2.

[161] September 17, 1926

What that Field is, what its nature, what its modifications, and whence is what, as also who He is, and what His power—hear this briefly from Me.

This subject has been sung by seers distinctly and in various ways, in different hymns as also in aphoristic texts about *Brahman* well reasoned and unequivocal.[1]

This theme has been expounded analytically by seers in manifold ways in various hymns. It has been discussed in the *Brahmasutras*[2] with steps logically arranged and clearly explaining the connection between cause and effect; and every word has been weighed so that not a syllable could be altered.

The great elements, Individuation, Reason, the Unmanifest, the ten senses, and the one (mind), and the five spheres of the senses; Desire, dislike, pleasure, pain, association, consciousness, cohesion—this, is sum, is what is called the Field with its modifications.[3]

The five *mahabhutas, ahamkar*, which sustains those *bhutas, buddhi*, the *avyakta* (*prakriti*), the ten sense, the mind and the objects of the five senses, so also desire, ill will, happiness, misery, association, consciousness, cohesion—this, in brief, is the Field with its modifications.

Sanghat means the power of the different elements in the body to co-operate with one another. *Dhriti* does not mean the abstract virtue of patience, but the property of the atoms in physical bodies to cohere. This property is made possible by *ahamkar*, which is latent in the unmanifest *prakriti*.

Freedom from pride and pretentiousness, non-violence, forgiveness, uprightness, service of the Master, purity, steadfastness, self-restraint;

Aversion from sense-objects, absence of conceit, realization of the painfulness and evil of birth, death, age and disease;

Absence of attachment, refusal to be wrapped up in one's children, wife, home and family, even-mindedness whether good or ill befall;

Unwavering and all-exclusive devotion to Me, resort to secluded spots, distaste for the haunts of men;

Settled conviction of the nature of the *atman*, perception of the goal of the knowledge of Truth,—

All this is declared to be knowledge and the reverse of it is ignorance.[4]

Shauch means outer and inner purity. It can be achieved by repeating Ramanama. This purity can be properly preserved only if the heart is constantly kept clean by repeating Ramanama. Every morning, we should weep with tears streaming from our eyes and ask ourselves why we did not remember to start repeating Ramanama, and why we, of all people, had a bad dream.

Absence of interest in the objects of senses means the awareness that certain things ought to be treated as forbidden by us, that they ought to be unacceptable to us.

The attributes described include the realization of the evils of birth and death, of old age, disease and suffering. One who realizes this starts with the thought: "I am sin." Why is it, we should ask ourselves, that we are afflicted with all manner of diseases? We ought to learn to cultivate equanimity of mind towards everything which may happen, good and evil. What does living in solitude mean?

Retiring into a cave to live there alone by oneself? Our effort will have been worthwhile only if we can feel solitude even in the midst of a huge crowd. To live in solitude means to sit in a spot meditating on one single thought.

Notes

1. XIII, 3 & 4.

2. Aphorisms on Vedanta philosophy by Badarayana.
3. XIII, 5 & 6.
4. XIII, 7 to 11.

[162] September 18, 1926

I will (now) expound to thee that which is to be known and knowing which one enjoys immortality; it is the supreme *Brahman* which has no beginning, which is called neither Being nor non-Being.[1]

Why does Shri Krishna say this, when they say that the *Brahman* is *sachchidananda* and that it alone is real? What he means to say is that *Brahman* does not mean being, the contrary of non-being. When we use the word *sat* in connection with the *Brahman*, its meaning transcends the two opposites and it signifies neither being nor nonbeing.

It is, so to say, a neutral term. God cannot be described as evil, nor as good. He is above either. The reality which is God is beyond the three categories of time.

Everywhere having hands and feet, everywhere having eyes, heads, mouths, everywhere having ears, It abides embracing everything in the universe.

Seeming to possess the functions of the senses, It is devoid of all the senses; It touches naught, upholds all; having no *gunas*, It experiences *gunas*.

Without all beings, yet within; immovable yet moving; so subtle that

It cannot be perceived; so far and yet so near It is.

Undivided, It seems to subsist divided in all beings; this *Brahman*—That which is to be known is the Sustainer of all, yet It is their Devourer and Creator.[2]

Though indivisible He seems to be there divided in all beings.

He is worth knowing. He sustains all the creatures. He is their destroyer and yet the Creator of them all.

Notes

1. XIII, 12.
2. XIII, 13 to 16.

[163] September 21, 1926

All contrary qualities are attributed to God because we cannot free our minds from dualities. Light of all lights, It is said to be beyond darkness; It is knowledge, the object of knowledge, to be gained only by knowledge; It is seated in the hearts of all.[1]

He is the Superlight. He is beyond darkness, that is, He is selfeffulgent.

. . .

He is Himself Knowledge. He is also the object of Knowledge to be realized only by Knowledge.

Thus have I expounded in brief the Field, Knowledge and that which is to be known; My devotee, when he knows this, is worthy to become one with Me.

Know that *prakriti* and *purusha* are both without beginning; know that all the modifications and *gunas* are born of *prakriti*.

Prakriti is described as the cause in the creation of effects from causes;

Purusha is described as the cause of the experiencing of pleasure and pain.[2]

Karya (anything done under compulsion of desires) and *karan* (the desires)—*prakriti* is the cause of their creation. *Purusha* is the cause of the experience of happiness and misery.

God is described as having two aspects. Under one aspect we should know Him as *prakriti* and under the other as *purusha*. The world is ever changing, and is therefore *maya*. The *purusha* is not transient, for He is the witness.

For the *purusha*, residing in *prakriti*, experiences the *gunas* born of prakriti; attachment to these *gunas* is the cause of his birth in good or evil wombs.[3]

Notes

1. XIII, 17.
2. XIII, 18 to 20.
3. XIII, 21.

[164] September 22, 1926

It is enough if we look upon God as a king and if all of us become His slaves, that is, disclaim any right over our bodies.

What is called in this body the Witness, the Assentor, the

Sustaner, the Experiencer, the Great Lord and also the Supreme *Atman*, is the Supreme Being.[1]

The *purusha* dwelling in this body is *para,* that is, beyond *maya* but He witnesses and gives consent. He is the *bharta* who sustains everything, and also the Enjoyer. He is, moreover, the God of gods and is described as *Paramatman*.

Fire has the power of burning, but it can burn nothing without God's consent.

He who thus knows *purusha* and *prakriti* with its *gunas*, is not born again, no matter how he live and move.[2]

If anyone claims that he is a *bhakta* of God and that, therefore, the sins he may commit are committed by God, he is wrong. But it would be right if the world said of him that he was a man of God and that everything he did was done through him by God. If anyone asks us whether we have attained spiritual knowledge, our reply should be:

"Only God knows; I do not know." Our reason may be carried away by pride at any time and become evil, but the man who has attained to perfect knowledge will never be misguided by his reason. Our belief is that Rama and Krishna were incarnations of God. How can we be sure that King Rama was not a hypocrite and his rule was not evil? How do we know that Krishna was not the most wicked of men? But we have no right to indulge in such doubts. Whomsoever we worship, we should look upon as *Purna Purushottam*,[3] that is best. If we believe that the people of India have faith in God, we should worship Him accordingly.

This verse does not sanction self-indulgence, but points out the great value of *bhakti*. Every karma has the effect of binding the soul, but one can become free from the bonds of karma by dedicating all one's karmas to God. Thus, anyone who has become free from the egotistic idea of being the author of anything and who recognizes every moment of his life the authority of the Dweller within will never commit sin. It is in egotism that sin has its source. There is no sin where there is no consciousness of the "I". This verse explains how to act so that one may commit no sin.

Some through meditation behold the *atman* by themselves in their own self; others by *Sankhya* Yoga, and others by Karma Yoga.[4]

Notes

1. XIII, 22.
2. XIII, 23.
3. Perfect incarnation of God; the description is generally limited to Shri Krishna.
4. XIII, 24.

[165] September 23, 1926

Yet others, not knowing (Him) thus, worship (Him) having heard from others; they too pass beyond death, because of devoted adherence to what they have heard.[1]

If, having heard it explained that we shall be saved by dedicating all our work to God, we act in this spirit, then we can say that "he who . . . is not born again, no matter how he live and move" applies to us.

Wherever something is born, animate or inanimate, know, thou Bharatarshabha, that it issues from the union of the Field and the knower of the Field.[2]

If we examine things separately, human beings, grains of dust, water, and so on, out conclusions [about their origin] will be different in each case. If, instead, we go to the very first cause, we shall no more think of objects having their distinctive forms and names. The Ravana who invests things with such charm that we willingly submit to its spell is far more dangerous than the other one of the story who killed people physically.

Who sees abiding in all beings the same *Parameshvara*, imperishable in the perishable, he sees indeed.[3]

Though things are ever perishing, there is an indestructible element in everything which remains unaffected by any change, He alone sees who sees this.

When he sees the same *Ishvara* abiding everywhere alike, he does not hurt himself by himself and hence he attains the highest goal.[4]

When he sees the same God abiding alike at all places he does not destroy the self by the self-*believes that, with the destruction of his body, he himself does not perish*—and consequently he achieves the highest status.

Who sees that it is *prakriti* that performs all actions and thus (knows) that *atman* performs them not, he sees indeed.[5]

Who realizes that *prakriti* is the doer of all actions and sees that *atman* is not the doer—*though all things take place through God's* maya, the Supreme Purusha involved in the process is not their *author*— he alone who does so sees indeed.

When he sees the diversity of beings as founded in unity and the whole expanse issuing therefrom, then he attains to *Brahman*.[6]

Notes

1. XIII, 25.
2. XIII, 26.
3. XIII, 27.
4. XIII, 28.
5. XIII, 29.
6. XIII, 30.

[166] September 24, 1926

The *Gita* is a work intended to be a guide in life and we should be able to find in it support for all our actions in practical life. Not all can understand Dr. Tribhuvandas's book[1]; a vaid or a doctor can understand it more easily than laymen. We are in the same position as the latter [in relation to the *Gita*].

This Imperishable Supreme *Atman*, O Kaunteya, though residing in the body, acts not and is not stained, for He has no beginning and no *gunas*.

As the all-pervading ether, by reason of its subtlety, is not soiled, even so *atman* pervading every part of the body is not soiled.

As the one Sun illumines the whole universe, even so the Master of the Field illumines the whole field.

Those who, with the eyes of knowledge, thus perceive the distinction between the Field and the knower of the Field, and (the secret) of the relese of beings from *prakriti*, they attain to the Supreme.[2]

Who knows the difference between the Field and the knower of the Field, and who knows how creatures may become free from the bonds of *prakriti* and *maya*, he realizes *moksha*.

Notes

1. *Ma-ne Shikhaman* (Advice to a Mother).
2. XIII, 31 to 34.

[167] September 25, 1926

In Chapter XIII Shri Krishna explained the nature of the Field and the knower of the Field, the means of understanding the nature of each and the different characteristics of such knowledge. The very first characteristic of knowledge is stated to be *amanitva*. Hence, however great one's knowledge, if one is proud of that knowledge, one has read the *Gita* in vain. Where there is pride, there is no knowledge. A man who has knowledge is always free from pride and ostentation, is straightforward, serves his guru, is pure and steady, is a man of self-control and is free from egotism, and he does not suffer because of old age and disease. He is not attached to his son or wife or home, is filled with unswerving devotion for the Lord, lives in solitude, takes interest in spiritual studies and is devoted to the pursuit of philosophic truth.

[168] Chapter XIV, September 26, 1926

We assemble here for studying the *Gita*, that is, for learning to follow its teaching in daily life. When we have a stomachache, we consult a book of home remedies and use the medicine suggested.

The *Gita* is such a book of home remedies for us. We find in it medicines for our spiritual disease. If we want to make the *Gita* our *Kamadhenu*, we should make it our only source as far as possible. We may consult any number of books in the world in support of what we derive from the *Gita*, but should be satisfied with its sole authority.

For this, we should have singleminded devotion to it. Such devotion should become spontaneous in us.

In a certain place, people used secretly to catch fish from the village pond. The village committee decided that, since in any case people caught fish,—did so in secret and were then afraid of being discovered—they should be required to take out licences for catching fish and some revenue raised by that means. This led to a dispute between two parties and the dispute was brought to me for settlement.

I was afraid to give a decision, for people are not content to leave it to others to exercise discrimination in religious matters and faith on their behalf. If we are guided by some other person's ideas about dharma, we would be lost when he was dead. It would have been much better if those village people had decided to consult the *Gita* or the Veda or the Koran, instead of asking me. We should look upon any of these works as the means of solving our spiritual problems. But I was told afterwards in reply [to my suggestion] that one could find support from a book for any idea. The true meaning of *Kamadhuk*, however, is that it satisfies a pure wish only. If the *Gita* satisfies any wish, it would not be a *kamadhuk* but would be aunt *Putana*[1]. When the authors of the Shastras said that Sudras and others should not read Vedas and other [sacred] works, probably their reason was that the latter might interpret these works to justify their own wishes in particular matters. Anyone who approaches the Shastras without scrupulous regard for truth and non-violence will derive no benefit from them. It is possible to draw any number of evil ideas from the Bible, the Vedas, the Koran and other scriptures. I have come across persons who justified even murder on the authority of these works.

The *Gita,* however, will serve as a safe guide to anyone who reads it with truth and non-violence as his guiding principles. Everyone should decide for himself with its help. The work will not be a *Kamadhenu* to any person who consults Kishorelal or me, and accepts our interpretation of it. Instead of borrowing faith from others, one should have one's own faith and come to decisions accordingly. If the intention is sincere and there is no desire for outward show, any error that the decision may contain will be forgiven. A person acting in this manner learns a lesson from his error and discovers the right path.

Yet again will I expound the highest and the best of all knowledge, knowing which all the sages passed hence to the highest perfection.

By having recourse to this knowledge they became one with Me. They need not come to birth even at a creation, nor do they suffer at a dissolution.[2]

Notes

1. A female demon who attempted to kill the infant Krishna by suckling him, but was herself sucked to death by the child.
2. XIV,1 & 2.

[169] September 28, 1926

The great *prakriti* is for me the womb in which I deposit the germ; from it all beings come to birth, O Bharata.[1]

Among the very first sentences in the Bible is; God said let there be light, and there was light; [that is,] let there be a universe, and a universe came into existence. A potter has to mould clay into a shape on his wheel and then put the thing into fire to bake; God does not have to act in that manner. He is a magician, He simply puts the seed in his imagination—which is *prakriti*, Lakshmi or Mother Goddess of the world—and the universe comes into existence.

Whatever forms take birth in the various species, the great *prakriti* is their Mother and I the seed-giving Father.[2]

I am the *mahadyoni* of all the forms which take birth in the various species, as also the source of the seed— *Sattva, rajas* and *tamas* are the *gunas* sprung from *prakriti*; it is they, O Mahabahu, that keep the imperishable Dweller bound to the body.

Of these *sattva*, being stainless, is light-giving and healing; it binds with the bond of happiness and the bond of knowledge, O sinless one.[3]

Those persons whose food, recreation and thoughts are *sattvik* are healthy. A person who merely eats *sattvik* food but is not *sattvik* in his general way of living and in his thoughts should be looked upon as a diseased person.

Rajas, know thou, is of the nature of passion, the source of thirst and attachment; it keeps man bound with the bond of action.[4]

Know that *rajas* is associated with desire. This may mean either that it has its source in, or that it is the cause of, desire. It creates attachment for cravings. It keeps the embodied one (i.e., living being) bound with the bond of karma.

Tamas, know thou, is born of ignorance, of mortal man's delusion; it keeps him bound with heedlessness, sloth and slumber, O Bharata.[5]

Pramad means all kinds of unworthy wishes arising in us. *Alas* is *pramad* in a worse form still. *Nidra,* which is next, is the state of mind natural to those sunk in darkness. A man who is established in *Samadhi* and is always awake feels no need to recline for rest or stretch his limbs for relaxation. A lethargic person would not get up even from a place which had caught fire. It is his slumber that is referred to as part of the meaning of *tamas*.

Notes

1. XIV, 3..
2. XIV, 4.
3. XIV, 5 & 6.
4. XIV, 7.
5. XIV, 8.

[170] September 29, 1926

Sattva attaches man to happiness, *rajas* to action, and *tamas*, shrouding knowledge, attaches him to heedlessness.[1]

Sattva leads to happiness and the quality of *rajas* to karma. (This is not karma as it is defined in the *Gita;* it is the karma of him who is always doing something or other without pausing to think.)

Tamas covers up knowledge and leads to *pramad*. *Sattva* prevails, O Bharata, having overcome *rajas* and *tamas; rajas,* when it has overpowered *sattva* and *tamas;* likewise *tamas* reigns when *sattva* and *rajas* are crushed.[2]

If a person overcomes *rajas* and *tamas,* he can create *sattva*.

(All the three exist in us. We should make a special effort to cultivate that which we want to strengthen.) If we wish to strengthen *rajas,* we should subdue the other two and, if the quality of *tamas,* we should stop the activity of both *sattva* and *rajas*.

When the light—knowledge—shines forth from all the gates of this body, then it may be knwon that the *sattva* thrives.

Greed, activity, assumption of undertakings, restlessness, craving— these are in evidence when *rajas* flourishes, O Bharatarshabha.

Ignorance, dullness, heedlessness, and delusion—these are in evidence when *tamas* reigns, O Kurunandana.

If the embodied one meets his end whilst *sattva* prevails, then he attains to the spotless worlds of the knowers of the Highest.[3]

That is, he attains spiritual welfare. When he is nearing death, such a person refuses to take any medicine which may be offered, and says that he will have nothing but Ganga water. He who awaits death in peace in this manner is a *sattvik* man.

If he dies during the reign within him of *rajas,* he is born among men attached to action; and if he dies to *tamas,* he is born in a species not endowed with reason.[4]

The world of beings of action means the human world. The dark world means the world of brutes.

The fruit of *sattvik* action is said to be stainless merit; that of *rajas* is pain and that of *tamas* ignorance.

Of *sattva,* knowledge is born, of *rajas,* greed; of *tamas,* heedlessness, delusion and ignorance.

Those abiding in *sattva* rise upwards, those in *rajas* stay midway, those in *tamas* sink downwards.

When the seer perceives no agent another than the *gunas* and knows Him who is above the *gunas,* he attains to My being.[5]

When the *atman* dwelling as witness in this body sees none else, but knows only Him who is above the *gunas,* that person comes to Me.

When the embodied one transcends these three *gunas* which are born of his contact with the body, he is released from the pain of birth, death and age and attains *moksha.*[6]

Notes

1. XIV, 9.
2. XIV, 10.
3. XIV, 11 to 14.
4. XIV, 15.
5. XIV, 16 to 19.
6. XIV, 20.

[171] September 30, 1926

Arjuna asks:

What, O Lord, are the marks of him who has transcended the three *gunas*? How does he conduct himself? How does he transcend the three *gunas*?

He, O Pandava, who does not disdain light, activity, and delusion when they come into being, nor desires them when they vanish.[1]

The Lord replies:

He who transcends the three *gunas*, does not suffer because of light or activity or darkness—that is, when any of them predominates over the others—and does not wish that it should prevail or subside.

This is one of the few difficult verses in the *Gita*. Should not one wish to have knowledge? In fact, in the *gayatri mantra* itself—in the best Vedic prayer—we pray to the shining Being to purify our intellect, to make it *sattvik*. We also pray: *tamaso ma jyotirgamaya*[2].

We aspire to be lifted from the darkness of attachment to illumination, from darkness to light. What, then, should we make of the statement in this verse? If we, living in the Ashram, did not cherish the aspiration which we do, we would fail in our aims. We must teach every child to say this prayer the very first thing in the morning. We should pray, tears streaming from our eyes, to be saved from the army of Kauravas, the army of deep slumber.

What, then, does the *Gita* teach? That we should not mind even if the slumber becomes deeper, should not even wish to get out of it?

Should we say, I have no wish, the three states are the same to me? If anyone feels thus, you may be sure he will be totally ruined. Either we should regard this verse as an interpolation, or as the very key to the meaning of the *Gita*. If you remember, in the beginning Arjuna does not ask whether or not it is proper to kill, but asks what good he could expect from killing his kinsmen. And so the Lord asks him: "What is this distinction you make between kinsmen and others? Your duty is to do the job of killing, irrespective of whether they are your kinsmen or others." Similarly, Arjuna does not hear ask Shri Krishna which of the three *gunas* is best. He knows that ultimately one must transcend all the three. We can know a person who possesses one of the three *gunas*. It is not difficult to distinguish among the three classes. But can we find anyone in this world who has risen above the *gunas* altogether? This verse gives the Lord's reply to that question. What other reply could He give? A person who has risen above the three *gunas* will not let himself be deceived by the threefold distinction of good, bad and indifferent, and we shall not see in him the effects of any of the three *gunas*, so rare will be his state of mind. But this is an important chapter, and we shall think more about it tomorrow.

Notes

1. XIV, 21 & 22.
2. "Take me from darkness to light," an Upanishadic prayer.

[172] October 1, 1926

We discussed one idea yesterday. Talking of a person who does not feel concerned whether light, activity or darkness prevails or subsides, we saw that we find no one of the sort in the world. We come across no person who does not wish to get rid of what we regard as evil—lethargy, inertia or excessive activity—or does not wish to acquire pure knowledge. On the contrary, we pray for such knowledge.

The word *jijnasu*[1] came into use because of our aspiration for knowledge, and we should pray that this aspiration may ever grow.

This verse, therefore, should fill us with greater enthusiasm for doing our duty. Our aim is to strive to end the suffering of the entire world.

It is a general rule that we should not take any statement of a writer in isolation, but should consider it in its total context.

Now, then, for whom is this verse meant? Well, it is meant for one who has risen above the *gunas*. It enumerates the characteristics of such a person. This is what he would appear to us to be. We do not know how he in fact acts. We say, for instance, that the sun is a blazing fire, but scientists say that it is utterly black. An English poet has said that things are not what they seem. This is Sankara's theory of *maya*.

It means that things do not appear as they are, that they are not what they seem to be, for everything is known to us through the medium of the waves in our minds.

Surely, the rainbow is not in truth what it seems to be. It is mere appearance. That is why it has been said that this world is like waves in water, or like a rainbow.

By what sign shall we, who live in the three-coloured world, recognize the man who has transcended the three *gunas*? He will not feel unhappy if the world mistakenly labels a man bad, or regards him as a man of knowledge or a lethargic man. What does it matter if the world thinks that we are mere agitators?

Thus, one who has risen above the three *gunas* will not seem to the world to be happy when one sees activity or unhappy when one sees lethargy. Such a person has come out of the duality of happiness and misery. He has risen above the pairs of opposites. A person like this should seem to us untouched, unconcerned, by anything. He should be absolutely free from egotism.

There is, thus, a state which is different even from the middle one. The *Bhagavad Gita* has stressed this point again and again. It teaches you just one thing, to shed the thought of "I" in such matters. We say *neti, neti*. You think I am such a person. In truth, I am "yes" and you are "no".[2] A person who has risen above the three *gunas* should appear to the world to be a cipher, a mere stone. That is, he sould have got rid of his "I". The world has looked upon Rama as God incarnate, for it could not do otherwise. Shankara asked Parvati how she could suppose that Rama felt miserable because of separation from Sita. He was, he said, pained to see that she had attributed ignorance to Rama, who had shed his egotism and worked like a cipher.

Note

1. One who seeks knowledge.
2. Gandhiji meant that one was more conscious of one's own "I" than the "I" of another.

[173][1] October 2, 1926

Every day we are born anew. *Ayurved* tells us that every seven years the whole body of a person changes into a new one, but that we are not aware of the change because it takes place slowly. The body does not change all of a sudden at the end of the seventh year, as if by magic, but the old body gradually wears out and is replaced by a new one. Thus, creation and destruction follow upon the heels of each other. There is no point of space so completely empty that you can put anything there without displacing something else, that is, you cannot create without destroying. Even the mind becomes either stronger or weaker day by day. Everything in the world is in a state of flux. Nothing is fixed. Only God is both fixed and changing.

A person who has risen above the three *gunas* is one who has become a cipher. But when can one be in such a state? In his poem beginning with the words *apurva avasar*, Shri Rajchandra sings:

"When the body has become as the burnt rope". That should be our condition. When a rope is burnt, only its form remains, and none of its other properties survive. Such a rope may be said to have risen above the three *gunas*, for it no longer has the property in virtue of which it can be used for connecting or binding things or drawing water from a well. A person who has risen above the three *gunas* is like such a rope.

As a rope may produce on us the illusion of a snake, so we may think of such a person as being like inert stone or having no interest in any activity, but he does not care. It is our dharma to be like such burnt rope.

The only way of rising to this state beyond the three *gunas* is to cultivate the *sattvik* quality, for in order to rise to that state one is required to cultivate the virtues of fearlessness, humility, sincerity, and so on. So long as we live in the body, there is some evil, some violence. The most, therefore, that we can do is to be *sattvik* in the highest degree possible.

The state beyond the three *gunas* can only be imagined. It does not seem possible to maintain it in action. In concrete action, our state must be *sattvik* in the highest degree. We cannot say even of a seemingly perfect man that he has risen beyond the three *gunas*. We can only say that he seems to be like one who has so risen. Someone has said in English that, outwardly, we shall find no difference between a sinner and a man of virtue, but that the greater a sinner the more virtuous he can be. He ever thinks of his sinful life and gives up his vices one by one. To such a sinner, even a beautiful temptress like Rambha is but a wooden or stone figure. In this way, he becomes pure in no time.

If we wish to attain *moksha* any time, to rise above the three *gunas*, we should cultivate in us the *sattvik* qualities. That is why we pray: *tamaso ma jyotirgamaya*. So long as a person feels that he serves others, he is selfish. If he believes that he has risen above the three *gunas*, he is a great hypocrite. If we really serve others, people will certainly know that. How can we ourselves know it? It is said in the Bible: "Let not thy left hand know what thy right hand does." That is the mark of a person being *sattvik*. The characteristics of such a person are almost similar to those of one who has risen above the three *gunas*, though, of course, the latter is undoubtedly on a higher level than the former since he knows neither what his right hand nor what his left hand does.

He, who, seated as one indifferent, is not shaken by the *gunas*, and stays still and moves not, knowing it is the *gunas* playing their parts;

He who holds pleasure and pain alike, who sedate, who regards earth, stone and gold, as all the same, who is wise and weighs in equal scale things pleasant and unpleasant, who is even-minded in praise and blame;

Who holds alike respect and disrespect, who is the same to friend and foe, who indulges in no undertakings—that man is called *gunatita*.[2]

A person who has risen above the three *gunas* knows what it is to be in that state but cannot describe it. If anyone can describe his state, he is not a person who has so risen, for he is still conscious of his "I".

He who serves Me with an unwavering and exclusive *bhaktiyoga* transcends these *gunas* and is worthy to become one with *Brahman*.

For I am the very image of *Brahman*, changeless and deathless, as also of everlasting dharma and perfect bliss.[3]

A person who struggles ceaselessly and hard to overcome his shortcomings may not perhaps succeed, in this birth, in overcoming them all, but in the end he will surely benefit. Today the world will censure him for his shortcomings; if, however, he bears all that in patience, and strives ever harder, he is sure ultimately to get peace of mind. Peace lies in the very fact of struggling. It is a source of great reassurance. Hence, we should strive to cultivate *sattvik* qualities.

Notes

1. The notes of this discourse were not taken by Mahadev Desai.
2. XIV, 23 to 25.
3. XIV, 26 & 27.

[174][1] Chapter XV, October 3, 1926

The Lord Said:

With its root above and branches below, the *ashvattha* tree, they say, is imperishable; it has Vedic hymns for leaves; he who knows it knows the Vedas.[2]

Shvah means "tomorrow". *Ashvattha,* therefore, means this transient world which will not last beyond tomorrow. It is changing every moment. That is why it is *ashvattha*. He is a man of spiritual knowledge who knows the real nature of this world and also knows dharma.

Notes

1. The notes of this discourse were not taken by Mahadev Desai.
2. XV, 1.

[175] October 5, 1926

Above and below its branches spread, blossoming because of the *gunas,* having for their shoots the sense-objects; deep down in the world of men are ramified its roots, in the shape of the consequences of action.[1]

In the first verse, Shri Krishna shows the means of going beyond this world. In this verse, he has described the world from another point of view, that of the ignorant man.

Its form as such is not here perceived, neither is its end, nor beginning, nor basis. Let men first hew down this deep-rooted *Ashvattha* with the sure weapon of detachment:

Let him pray to win to that haven from which there is no return and seek to find refuge in the Primal Being from whom has emanated this ancient world of action.[2]

We shall remain apart from this world, while working in it, when we no longer look upon it as God's sport but, regarding it as the sphere in which people run after enjoyments, cut it off at the root with the weapon of non-co-operation. In no other way is it possible to cut it off at the roots, for it is without beginning and without end. That is why Shri Krishna has advised non-co-operation.

To that imperishable haven those enlightened souls go—who are without pride and delusion, who have triumphed over the taints of attachment, who are ever in tune with the Supreme, whose passions have died, who are exempt from the pairs of opposites, such as pleasure and pain.[3]

They who crave to win that haven are indifferent to honour or insult. They are absolutely free from delusion. They have scored triumph over the taints of attachment. Those who are always *atmarthi* (that is, who are aware every moment that they are not their physical bodies but are the *atman*), whose cravings for objects of senses have subsided (who look not fear-struck but serene at the moment of death) are the enlightened souls that go to that imperishable haven.

On every leaf of the banyan tree are inscribed the Vedas, which means that Ramanama is inscribed on its every leaf. The world is a holy gift made by God out of His grace; the tree of the world grows from the navel of Brahma. But there is another world with its root below, whose leaves are the various objects of sense-pleasure; that world is the world of desire.

Adhyatmanityah means those whose thoughts dwell with love on Rama, who repeat His name and do His work.

Notes

1. XV, 2.
2. XV, 3 & 4.
3. XV, 5.

[176] October 6, 1926

Neither the sun, nor the moon, nor fire illumine it; men who arrive there return not—that is My supreme abode.[1]

Its light is not borrowed from the sun or the moon or the fire, for it shines with its own light, men who reach it return not—that is my supreme abode.

A part indeed of Myself which has been the eternal *Jiva* in this world of life attracts the mind and the five senses from their place in *prakriti*.[2]

"Every hair on the body chants the Vedas," so sang Tulsidas.

When the Master (of the body) acquires a body and discards it, He carries these with Him wherever He goes, even as the wind carries scents from flower-beds.

Having settled Himself in the senses—ear, eye, touch, taste, and smell—as well as the mind, through them He frequents their objects.

The deluded perceive Him not as He leaves or settles in (a body) or enjoys (sense-objects) in association with the *gunas*; it is only those endowed with the eye of knowledge that see Him.[3]

We see only the world, but do not see God who is immanent in it.

Notes

1. XV, 6.
2. XV, 7.
3. XV, 8 to 10.

[177] October 7, 1926

Yogis who strive see Him seated in themselves; the witless ones who have not cleansed themselves see Him not, even though they strive.[1]

The first thing necessary, therefore, is the observance of the rules of *yama-niyama*.

One who has not observed them is apt to give wrong meanings to the verses of the *Gita*. Such a person would tell himself that, since the objects of senses are created by God, we should accept and enjoy them. They alone, who have become purified, who have suffered in the furnace of *tapas*, will read the right meanings.

The light in the sun which illumines the whole universe and which is in the moon and in the fire—that light, know thou, is Mine.[2]

There is a story in an Upanishad which tells how some gods took the form of *yakshas* and went to test *Agni, Vayu*, etc., but were worsted.[3]

It is I who, penetrating the earth, uphold all beings with my strength, and becoming the moon—the essence of all sap—nourish all herbs.[4]

Pervading the earth, I uphold all beings with my strength, and becoming the moon, the producer of all sap, nourish all herbs, foodcrops and all else that grows in the fields.

It is I who, becoming the *Vaishvanara* Fire and entering the bodies of all that breathe, assimilate the four kinds of food with the help of the outward and the inward breaths.[5]

Vaishvanara means the heat which digests food. The four types of food are what is sucked, what is licked, what is drunk and what is eaten.

And I am seated in the hearts of all; from Me proceed memory, knowledge and the dispelling of doubt[6]; it is I who am to be known in all the Vedas, I, the author of Vedanta and the knower of the Vedas.[7]

Notes

1. XV, 11.
2. XV, 12.
3. Gandhiji had probably the *Kenopanishad* in mind. If so, he did not recollect the details of the story correctly.
4. XV, 13.
5. XV, 14.
6. In his rendering Gandhiji has used the word "intellect" in place of "the dispelling of doubt".
7. XV, 15.

[178] October 8, 1926

There are two Beings in the world: *kshara* (perishable) and *akshara* (imperishable). Kshara embraces all creatures and their permanent basis is *akshara*.[1]

In this world there are two Beings—*kshara* and *akshara*. *Kshara* means all beings which are subject to death, which have a name and form. The immutable reality behind them, the power of which sustains all, is *akshara*.

The Supreme Being is surely another—called *Paramatman* who as the Imperishable *Ishvara* pervades and supports the three worlds.

Because I transcend the *kshara* and am also higher than the *akshara*, I am known in the world and in the Vedas as *Purushottama* (the Highest Being).[2]

Because I transcend *kshara*, that is, the world of name and form and am also higher than *akshara*, the world and the Vedas know Me as the highest among all beings.

He who, undeluded, knows Me *Purushottama*, knows all, he worships Me with all his heart, O Bharata.[3]

He is above all opposites. Once we have risen above this world, which is but *maya*, need we think of God as its author?

Thus I have revealed to thee, sinless one, this most mysterious Shastra; he who understands this, O Bharata, is a man of understanding, he has fulfilled his life's mission.[4]

I have disclosed to thee this most secret (the best even of the best) Shastra; he who understands this becomes a man of understanding, fulfils his life's mission and also becomes free from his debt.

Notes

1. XV, 16.
2. XV, 17 & 18.
3. XV, 19.
4. XV, 20.

[179] Chapter XVI, October 9, 1926

The Lord said:

Fearlessness, purity of heart, steadfastness in *jnana* and yoga— knowledge and action, beneficence, self-restraint, sacrifice, spiritual study, austerity, and uprightness;[1]

Non-violence, truth, slowness to wrath, the spirit of dedication, serenity, aversion to slander, tenderness to all that lives, freedom from greed, gentleness, modesty, freedom from levity; Spiritedness, forgiveness, fortitude, purity, freedom from ill will and arrogance—these are to be found in one born with the divine heritage, O Bharata.[2]

Sattvasanshuddhi means purity of the self or inner purity. *Jnanayogavyavasthiti* means certainty of knowledge; *jnanavyavasthiti* means unceasing direct experience, and *yogavyavasthiti* means constant awareness of God, sense of identity with Him. Ahimsa also embraces violence deliberately committed out of compassion (When Dr. Nangi was to perform an operation, he used to fast on the day previous, so that no emotional disturbances in him, like anger, etc., might affect the patient). A teacher who punishes his pupils without anger will have tears streaming from his eyes as he canes him.

Consider Yudhisthira's forbearance—when, in King Virata's court, the King struck him, he did not let the drops of blood fall from his nostrils on the ground. Forbearance means returning good for evil, so profound is its significance.

Notes

1. XVI, 1.
2. XVI, 2 & 3.

[180] October 10, 1926

Pretentiousness, arrogance, self-conceit, wrath, coarseness, ignorance— these are to be found in one born with the devilish heritage.[1]

Dambha means pretending to possess what one does not. *Darpa* means boasting about something which one possesses in only a small measure. *Abhiman* means being proud of a quality which one possesses. Narad showed pride when he had vanquished Kamadeva[2] and he fell because of his pride. *Parushya* means harshness.

The divine heritage makes for Freedom. The devilish for bondage.

Grieve not, O Partha; thou art born with a divine, heritage.

There are two orders of created beings in this world—the divine and the devilish; the divine order has been described in detail, hear from Me now of the devilish, O Partha.

Men of the devil do not know what they may do and what they may not; neither purity, nor right conduct, not truth is to be found in them.[3]

Those who lack purity and truthfulness and whose conduct is not moral are diseased men and women. There can be no disease unless there is mental evil or bodily error. A person whose *atman* is awake every moment of his life constantly prays that his body be filled with light. How did Ladha Maharaj overcome his leukoderma?

Every time he applied the *bel* leaves on the affected parts, he prayed that light should enter his body. We can prevent unhealthy emotions from disturbing our body only if we daily pray for the flow of light into it. I would ask every person who suffered from a disease if he was free from attachments and aversions. Outwardly we may be clean and our conduct may be moral; but, in the absence of truthfulness, it is all as hollow as a drum. We gather here to cultivate that truthfulness.

Notes

1. XVI, 4.
2. God of love.
3. XVI, 5 to 7.

[181] October 12, 1926

'Without truth, without basis, without God is the universe' they say; 'born of the union of the sexes, prompted by naught but lust.'

Holding this view, these depraved souls, of feeble understanding and of fierce deeds, come forth as enemies of the world to destroy it.

Given to insatiable lust, possessed by pretentiousness, arrogance and conceit, they seize wicked purposes in their delusion, and go about pledged to unclean deeds[1] .

Given to boundless cares that end only with their death, making indulgence or lust their sole goal, convinced that that is all.

Caught in a myriad snares of hope, slaves to lust and wrath, they seek unlawfully to amass wealth for the satisfaction of their appetites.[2]

How can desire and anger overcome him who is protected by willing submission to holy authority?

Anger consumes many times more energy than does joy. It is because people spend more energy than they can afford that injustice and tyranny prevail in the world.

Notes

1. Gandhiji's rendering has "of sinful bent of mind" in place of "pledged to unclean deeds".
2. XVI, 8 to 12.

[182] October 13, 1926

Anger involves expenditure of energy by thirteen muscles, whereas laughter by only ten. Enjoyment of sense-pleasure leads to death. *Brahmacharya* leads to immortality. Once Raychandbhai was suffering from headache. I asked him to which theatre he had been to see a play. He replied that he had been witnessing a play at night, lying at home, and said that he did not wish to consume his energy in trying to cure his headache. It was good, he told me, that I saw him as he was. He was, he said, less powerful than God's law.

Sexual indulgence necessarily leads to death. If people gave themselves up to it, God's rule in the world would end, and Satan's prevail.

This have I gained today; this aspiration shall I now attain; this wealth is mine; this likewise shall be mine hereafter.

This enemy I have already slain, others also I shall slay; lord of all am I; enjoyment is mine, perfection is mine, strength is mine, happiness is mine.

'Wealthy am I, and high-born. What other is like unto me? I shall perform a sacrifice! I shall give alms! I shall be merry!' Thus think they, by ignorance deluded.[1]

Living in this way, man gambles away the *ratnachintamani*[2] of his body. Even Yudhishthira had gambled, and lost Draupadi too in the throw. We can, however, say that he had less of anger and desire in him than Duryodhana. We ourselves are full of that mixture. We must strive our best to raise ourselves to a higher level.

And tossed about by diverse fancies, caught in the net of delusion, stuck deep in the indulgence of appetites, into foul hell they fall.

Wise in their own conceit, stubborn, full of the intoxication of pelf and pride, they offer nominal sacrifices for show, contrary to the rule.[3]

Yajna is only a pretext; their real aim is to serve their own interests.

Notes

1. XVI, 13 to 15.
2. A precious stone which yields everything that is desired.
3. XVI, 16 & 17.

[183] October 14, 1926

Given to pride, force, arrogance, lust and wrath they are deriders indeed, scorning Me in their own and others' bodies.

These cruel scorners, lowest of mankind and vile, I hurl down again and again, into devilish wombs.

Doomed to devilish wombs, these deluded ones, far from ever coming to Me, sink lower and lower in birth after birth.[1]

Threefold is this gate of hell, leading man to perdition,—Lust, Wrath and Greed; these three, therefore, should be shunned.[2]

One who keeps himself free from these does not devote himself to the pursuit of worldly happiness, but follows the path of spiritual welfare.

The man who escapes these three gates of Darkness, O Kaunteya, works out his welfare and thence reaches the highest state.

He who forsakes the rule of Shastra and does but the bidding of his selfish desires, gains neither perfection, nor happiness, nor the highest state.

Therefore let Shastra be thy authority for determining what ought to be done and what ought not to be done; ascertain thou the rule of the Shastra and do thy task here (accordingly).[3]

In this context, we should say that we would obey our conscience. But, then, even Ravana would say that he obeyed his conscience.

He alone can use this plea whose mind has become purified by knowledge acquired from Shastras. So the question is, what is Shastra? The Vedas, the works of history, the *Puranas* all these are Shastras. They, however, contain contradictory statements. Shastra comes from the root *shas*. Someone has argued that the *Gita* teaches the principle of "tit for tat", and quotes Shaikh Sadi in his support, who said that he who was good to the bad would be bad to the good.

But Shastra is subject to the principles of truth and non-violence.

Shastra rules, and does not aim at spreading anarchy. But of this more tomorrow.

Notes

1. XVI, 18 to 20.
2. XVI, 21.
3. XVI, 22 to 24.

[184] October 15, 1926

Whenever we have a social problem to discuss, we should

think of authorities and consult them; as, for instance, in connection with the problem of dogs which is unnecessarily agitating me. If, however, our foundations are not strong, consulting a Shastra will avail us nothing.

If the foundations are strong, it should be our principle that we will cling to truth at any cost. We shall have read Shastras to some purpose if we are determined that, even if Yudhishthira told a lie, our ideal shall be truth.

If by Shastra we mean a book, the Bible, the Koran and other books have been before mankind for so many hundreds of years, but no one has come to the end of these problems. The intention in this verse is to tell us not to look upon ourselves as an authority, that is, not to be guided by our wishes and feelings. So long as one's intellect has not become vigilant and the heart is not filled exclusively with Ramanama, one should be ruled by the authority of the Shastras. Here Shri Krishna refers to the struggle in us between divine and demoniac impulses. So long as we are in that condition, we should be guided by the authority of the Shastras. That Shastra means *shishtachara*[1] that is, we should follow the example of those forefathers of ours who were holy and fearless. The ideal of conduct among shepherds may be stealing sheep, and among meat-eaters eating meat. A boy once wanted to discuss with me whether or not we can eat meat, but his mother did not let me discuss the subject with him. She was right. She thought that nothing could be brought about by force. If the boy became a vegetarian, she thought, there would be a quarrel in the family. One must certainly fear *shishtachara*. It may be disregarded only if it requires one to violate truth, etc. Where the tradition of guru and disciple has disappeared, men will follow their own wishes. The *Gita* has advised us: *tadviddhi pranipatena*[2] but it is not so easy to find a guru. If we keep on the search for a guru, we shall always have some wholesome fear in our heart. With the thought of a guru constantly in our mind, it will remain pure. The *Gita* tells us that, if the divine impulse has quickened in us, we should be humble. [One should think] "I know nothing. I want to ask God, or a guru, but how may I see either?" We should, therefore, pray. He who prays with faith in God will one day be saved. He who talks as if *Brahman* was in him will not be saved. The literal meaning of the verse is that we should be guided by the authority of the Shastras. The derived meaning is that we should be guided by *shishtachara*. To be *shishta* means that, in the absence of a guru, we should be humble, and to be humble means to worship our personal God. That is, we should look upon ourselves as insignificant creatures, like bugs and fleas, and worship God. If you are humble, you will be saved. If you are humble and sincere, the veils before your eyes will be lifted one after another.

Chapter XVII begins with the idea explained in this verse.

Chapter XVII

Arjuna said:

What, then, O Krishna, is the position of those who forsake the rule of Shastra and yet worship with faith? Do they act from *sattva* or *rajas* or *tamas?*[3]

By disregarding the manner enjoined in the Shastras means by disregarding the *shishtachara,* or without the guidance of a guru, and with faith means with some little humility. Shri Krishna's reply to this is indirect. Not to accept Shastra as an authority and to have faith are inconsistent with each other. Faith consists in accepting the authority of Shastra.

Shri Krishna replies:

Threefold is the faith of men, an expression of their nature in each case; it is *sattvik, rajas* or *tamas*. Hear thou of it.[4]

Arjuna and Shri Krishna are friends, but the former does not understand that Shri Krishna is playing with him. It is certainly not Arjuna's intention to corner Shri Krishna in argument. But the latter thinks that He might play with Arjuna a little. The Lord need not bother Himself why Arjuna put this question. He assumes that a person may disregard the manner enjoined in the Shastras, and then asks what kind of faith such a person has. Is it *sattvik* or *rajasik* or *tamasik*?

Notes

1. The prevailing social standard of right conduct
2. Acquire knowledge by prostrating yourself (before a guru); in IV, 34.
3. XVII, 1.
4. XVII, 2.

[185] October 16, 1926

The faith of every man is in accord with his innate character; man is made up of faith; whatever his object of faith, even so is he.[1]

Faith can be enlightened. Everyone needs faith, provided one is not misguided by it. If anyone clings to a straw, he will certainly fall, but he will not fall who clings to the branch of a tree. Mrs. Besant has said that a person needs steps till he has climbed to the top. Shastra is such a step. Once a person has climbed to the top, he needs neither steps nor banisters. The top appears so perfectly flat to him that he pays no attention to what is below.

Sattvik persons worship the gods[2], *rajasik* ones, the *Yakshas* and *Rakshasas;* and others—men of *tamas*—worship manes and spirits.

Those men who, wedded to pretentiousness and arrogance, possessed by the violence of lust and passion, practise fierce austerity not ordained by Shastra.

They, whilst they torture the several elements that make up their bodies, torture Me too dwelling in them; know them to be of unholy resolves.[3]

Those who do not even abide by the rules enjoined by Shastras but in their pride follow their self-chosen way fall into such a state.

If you put truth in one scale of the measure and *tapas,* Shastras and similar things in the other scale, the former will weigh heavier.

That Shastra which seeks to suppress truth is of little use. Those who follow such a Shastra are men of demoniac inclination. If truth is timeless, so is untruth; and, likewise, if light is timeless, so is darkness too. We should embrace what is timeless only if it is combined with truth.

Notes

1. XVII, 3.
2. In his rendering Gandhiji has added here: "Gods mean *sattvik* powers or impulses".
3. XVII, 4 to 6.

[186] October 17, 1926

If a Shastra is not supported by truth and non-violence, it may even be the means of our fall. As they say, we should swim in our father's well, not drown ourselves in it. Father in this context means *shishtachara*. It is said that one cannot get knowledge without a guru.

The moment you have found one, you know what the *shishtachara* is. But these are such hard times that one does not easily find a guru. If we are doing God's work, it is bound to be in harmony with *shishtachara*. That is why we are enjoined to keep repeating the Lord's name while doing any work. This verse explains in what spirit we should do this. Our faith must not be in ghosts and spirits or in demons. We ought to pray only to a beneficent deity.

Of three kinds again is the food that is dear to each; so also are sacrifice, austerity, and charity. Hear how they differ. Victuals that add to one's years, vitality strength, health, happiness and appetite; are savoury, rich, substantial and inviting, are dear to the *sattvik*.[1]

Victuals that are bitter, sour, salty, overhot, spicy, dry, burning, and causing pain, bitterness and disease, are dear to the *rajas*.

Food which has become cold, insipid, putrid, stale, discarded and unfit for sacrifice, is dear to the *tamas*.[2]

If we cling to this classification, we shall not come to the right conclusion. Shri Krishna has first explained the qualities of the *sattvik* man, and then his taste, etc. *Ladu*[3]-lovers have included *ladus* in *sattvik* food. They do not help one to safeguard one's *brahmacharya*.

In interpreting the meaning of *rasya*[4], too, we should use discrimination. There must have been a reason in that age for making such a classification, for there must have been persons even then who would eat a handful of chillies at a time. In the present age, there is no need for eating *snigdha*[5] foods. If here we start eating ghee, our food would be, not *sattvik* or *rajasik*, but such as a demon would love. The inclusion of bitter, sour and saltish foods is quite correct. Then the verse mentions food which has been left over. Stilton cheese (a food containing countless germs) is of this class. *Daliya*[6] and *mamara*[7] do not belong to this class.

Notes

1. XVII, 7 & 8.
2. XVII, 9 & 10.
3. A sweet shaped like a ball.
4. Relishing.
5. Containing fat.

6. & 7. Processed gram and rice.

[187] October 19, 1926

That sacrifice is *sattvik* which is willingly offered as a duty without desire for fruit and according to the rule.

But when sacrifice is offered with an eye to fruit and for vain glory, know, O Bharatashreshtha, that it is *rajas*.

Sacrifice which is contrary to the rule, which produces no food[1], which lacks the sacred text, which involves no giving up and which is devoid of faith is said to be *tamas*.[2]

A *yajna* without *dakshina* means one in which no gifts are made to the poor.

Homage to the gods, to Brahmins, to gurus and to wise men; cleanliness, uprightness, *brahmacharya* and non-violence—these constitute austerity (*tapas*) of the body.[3]

That is *tapas* in which one goes through physical discomfort or hardship.

Words that cause no hurt, that are true, loving and helpful, and spiritual study constitute austerity of speech.

Serenity, benignity, silence, self-restraint, and purity of the spirit—these constitute austerity of the mind.

This threefold austerity practised in perfect faith by men not desirous of fruit, and disciplined, is said to be *sattvik*.

Austerity which is practised with an eye to gain praise, honour and homage and for ostentation is said to be *rajas*; it is fleeting and unstable.

Austerity which is practised from any foolish obsession, either to torture oneself or to procure another's ruin, is called *tamas*.[4]

A person who fasts for a hundred days or keeps standing on one foot performs not *sattvik* but *tamasik tapas*.

Notes

1. Gandhiji's rendering has "grain" in place of "food".
2. XVII, 11 to 13.
3. XVII, 14.
4. XVII, 15 to 19.

[188] October 20, 1926

Charity, given as a matter of duty, without expectation of any return,[1] at the right place and time, and to the right person is said to be *sattvik*.[2]

It may not in all circumstances be right to give what it is right to give in certain circumstances. This is also true about recipients. It is but right to give food to one who has lost the use of his limbs altogether. But suppose there is a blind man who is suffering from fever and comes begging. He would be an unworthy object of our charity if we gave him food. If we give him a blanket and he sells it, then also will our gift have been made to an unworthy person. In one place, it may be right to give food, in another something else, and in still another a third thing, The principle is the same in all cases, but its application will vary according to place, time and person. The same is true about *yajnas*.

Charity, which is given either in the hope of receiving in return, or with a view to winning merit, or grudgingly, is declared to be *rajas*.

Charity given at the wrong place and time, and to an undeserving recipient, disrespectfully and with contempt, is declared to the *tamas*.

AUM TAT SAT has been declared to be the threefold name of *Brahman* and by that name were created of old the *Brahmanas*, the Vedas and sacrifices.

Therefore, with AUM ever on their lips, all the rites of sacrifice, charity and austerity, proceed always according to the rule, by *Brahmavadins*[3].[4]

Those who seek knowledge of the *Brahman* dedicate all their *yajnas*, gifts and *tapas* to Shri Krishna. They do everything in the name of Hari[5], in the name of *Aum*.

With utterance of TAT and without desire for fruit are the several rites of sacrifice, austerity and charity performed by those seeking Freedom.

SAT is employed in the sense of 'real' and 'good'; O Partha, Sat is also applied to beautiful deeds.[27][6]

Constancy in sacrifice, austerity and charity, is called SAT; and all work for these purpose is also SAT.[7]

Aum comes first in all these actions. *Sat* signifies the process of their performance. If we wish that we should be steady in our *yajnas* and gifts, then *Aum* signifies the commencement and *sat* signifies the process. *Sat* signifies process and also stands for Hari. *Brahma satyam jaganmithya* has been stated in this sense.

Whatever is done, O Partha, by way of sacrifice, charity or austerity or any other work, is called *asat* if done without faith. It counts for naught hereafter as here.[8]

Aum tat sat means that all that exists is *Aum*, that our "I" is unreal, that God alone is and nothing else is real, that we are all running after things in vain.

We should even eat our food in a *sattvik* spirit. There are persons who eat as an act of worship. We should resolve that we wish to live as ciphers in this world. The world may kick us from one place to another as if we were a ball, but we will not let ourselves be so kicked.

We will use our knowledge, our bodies, our strength and money, all for the service of others, and that too not with the desire to earn a good name for ourselves. Thus, *Aum tat sat* is a vow of humility. It teaches us to realize our utter insignificance, to be completely free from egotism. If the Imam Saheb[9] would recite it, here is a *kalama* for him.

Notes

1. Gandhiji's rendering has: "to one who is not in a position to do good in turn".
2. XVII, 20.
3. Expounders of *Brahman*.
4. XVII, 21 to 24.
5. Vishnu.
6. Gandhiji has not given a translation of this verse. He has, however, referred to its content in the comment which follows.
7. XVII, 25 to 27.
8. XVII, 28.
9. Abdul Kadir Bawazeer.

[189] October 21, 1926

The threefold classification of gifts, faith, *tapas,* etc., given in Chapter XVII is only an illustration. We can make as many categories as we like. The intention was to show that the reign of the three *gunas* prevails throughout the universe. A cooking or other utensil is an inert object, but it contains air inside; likewise, everything is pervaded by the spirit. Existing apart from the three *gunas* is God. We have to merge in Him. Even if we cultivate the *sattvik* qualities to their highest perfection in us, something of *rajasik* and *tamasik* will remain. But, without worrying ourselves about this, we should continue to strive and cultivate finer and finer *sattvik* qualities in us, for the impulses which agitate us the least and consume the least amount of our energy are *sattvik* impulses. Though Janaka was as good as a disembodied soul even while he lived in a body, the difference between him and us is only one of degree. It is true, of course, that for one like him there was no returning to this life after he was dead.

Chapter XVIII

In Chapter XVIII Arjuna requests Shri Krishna to explain to him the distinction between sannyasa and *tyaga*. He says: Mahabahu! I would fain learn severally the secret of *sannyasa* and of *tyga,* O Hrishikesha, O Keshinishudana.[1]

The Lord replies:

Renunciation of actions springing from selfish desire is described as *sannyasa* by the seers; abandonment of the fruit of all action is called *tyaga* by the wise.[2]

There is no real distinction between the two. *Kamya* karma seems to mean all karma—though I am not sure that I am right. Total renunciation of karma is not possible. The renunciation of all karma, then, is sannyasa, and *tyaga* means renunciation of fruits of karma.

Notes

1. XVIII, 1.
2. XVIII, 2.

[190] October 22, 1926

Yesterday I interpreted *kamya* karma to mean all karmas.

Surendra then reminded me of the explanation given by Vinoba, namely, karmas undertaken with definite motives. But every karma has some motive behind it. That we may be unattached to it is a different matter, but the motive is bound to be served. The existence of the body itself means karma. Though we live in the body, we can live unconcerned with it.

Some thoughtful persons say: "All action should be abandoned as an evil"; others say: "Action for sacrifice, charity and austerity should not be relinquished."

Hear my decision in this matter of *tyaga,* O Bharatasattama; for *tyaga,* too, O mightiest of men, has been described to be of three kinds.

Action for sacrifice, charity and austerity may not be abandoned; it must needs be performed. Sacrifice, charity and austerity are purifiers of the wise.

But even these actions should be performed abandoning all attachment and fruit; such, O Partha, is my best and considered opinion.

It is not right to renounce one's allotted task; its abandonment, from delusion, is said to be *tamas.*

He who abandons action, deeming it painful and for fear of straining his limbs, he will never gain the fruit of abandonment, for his abandonment is rajas.

But when an allotted task is performed from a sense of duty and with abandonment of attachment and fruit, O Arjuna, that abandonment is deemed to be *sattvik.*

Neither does he disdain unpleasent action, nor does he cling to pleasant action—this wise man full of *sattva,* who practises abandonment, and who has shaken off all doubts.

For the embodied one cannot completely abandon action; but he who abandons the fruit of action is named a *tyagi.*[1]

When we have resolved to renounce the fruits of all karmas, we will engage ourselves only in karma which is in the nature of a duty for us. By the sannyasa mentioned in the first verse, the poet meant renunciation of all karmas. The central idea of Chapter XVII was that one should work without selfish motives. The state of mind in which such motives will have disappeared most is the *sattvik* state.

Total renunciation of karma is impossible while we live in the body, and the *atman's* connection with the body will remain right till the moment of death. What a person who has fallen into a state of *samadhi* can do is to stop the movements of the heart so that the heart-beat will not be perceived even with a stethoscope. The practitioners of yoga tell us that the soul can leave the body at will and fly away for a while. But to what purpose? We can certainly reduce the pulse-rate at will. The truth is that if a yogi really wishes that his soul should leave his body, his faculty of speech and his mind, it will certainly do so. I have no doubt that, if we do not will that the body should endure, it will certainly fall. But our desire to give up the body is never intense, for we feel even a pin-prick. A person like Ramdas Swami can even dwell in another's body and feel his suffering, but he cannot be conscious of the bodies of all, except in imagination. All that we can do, therefore, is to shun karmas which have any trace of egotism in them.

Note

1. XVIII, 3 to 11.

[191] October 23, 1926

Harishchandra's actions belonged to the category of *tyaga*. He was equally ready, when duty required him, to perform apparently evil as well as good actions.

To those who do not practise abandonment accrues, when they pass away, the fruit of action which is of three kinds: disagreeable, agreeable, mixed; but never to the sannyasis.

Learn, from me, O Mahabahu, the five factors mentioned in the *Sankhya* doctrine,[1] for the accomplishment of all action:

The field, the doer, the various means, the several different operations, fifth and the last, the Unseen.[2]

When Fate was no longer favourable, Arjuna was robbed though he still had with him the same bow and arrows which he always had.

Whatever action, right or wrong, a man undertakes to do with the body, speech or mind, these are the five factors thereof.

This being so, he who, by reason of unenlightened intellect, sees the unconditioned *atman* as the agent—such a man is dense and unseeing.

He who is free from all sense of "I", whose motive is untainted, slays not nor is bound, even though he slay all these worlds.[3]

If I put a pebble in . . . 's[4] hand and incite him to fling it at . . .[5] would the sin be on his head or mine? Arjuna dragged Krishna all the way from Dwarka [to Hastinapur] and was now saying that he did not wish to fight. Was that right? Shri Krishna tells Arjuna: "I ask you to fight." What harm need Arjuna fear, then? The sword in Harishchandra's hand was not his, nor was it Kashiraja's.[6] Harishchandra could have resorted to satyagraha, but should he have done that simply because the person in question was Taramati? When one's selfinterest is involved, one should do an [unpleasant] thing irrespective of whether in itself it ought to be done. If, however, no self-interest had been involved, if it was not that the woman was his queen, if Harishchandra had been repelled by the deed itself, so much so that his hand would have refused to obey him, he could have resorted to satyagraha.

If read superficially, this verse is likely to mislead the reader. We shall not find anywhere in the world a perfect example of such a person; as in geometry we require imaginary, ideal figures, so in practical affairs, too, we require ideal instances when discussing ethical issues. This verse, therefore, can be construed thus only: "We may say [for the sake of argument] that he whose sense of 'I' has melted away altogether and whose reason is tainted with no trace of evil whatever can kill the entire world; but one who is completely free from the egotistic sense of 'I' has no body, and one whose reason is absolutely pure is simultaneously conscious of time in all its categories, past, present and future, and there is only one such being, God, Who does nothing though doing everything and Who is non-violent though He kills". Man, therefor, has only one course open to him, that of not killing and of following the *shishtachara*—of following Shastra.

Knowledge, the object of knowledge, and the knower compose the threefold urge to action; the means, the action and the doer compose the threefold sum of action.[7]

For instance, the idea that we must get swaraj is knowledge, and the person who deserves it is the knower. But this is not enough to bring us swaraj. There should be corresponding work for swaraj—the means of winning it. We can think out similar instances of any class of activities.

Knowledge, action, and the doer are of three kinds according to their different *gunas*; hear thou these, just as they have been described in the science of the *gunas*.

Know that knowledge whereby one sees in all beings immutable entity—a unity in diversity—to be *sattvik*.[8]

Things in this world seem distinct from one another, but in reality they are not so. If the jaundice in our eyes disappears, we would see all things as one, undivided reality.

That knowledge which perceives separately in all beings several entities of diverse kinds, know thou to be *rajas*.[9]

That knowledge is *rajasik* which perceives separately in all beings different entities of various kinds.

It is through the *rajas* spirit that we make these three classes: I, mine and others. Attachments and aversions arise from this. The *sattvik* state has no room for attachments and aversions.

And knowledge which, without reason, clings to one single thing, as though it were everything, which misses the true essence and is superficial is *tamas*.[10]

Tamas jnana is that in virtue of which a person does everything with attachment, without seeing any purpose in what he does and believing that it is without significance and of no consequence.

In *tamas* knowledge, all kinds of notions are mixed up and it is believed that there is no such Being as God. That action is called *sattvik* which, being one's allotted task, is performed without attachment, without like or dislike, and without a desire for fruit.

That action which is prompted by the desire for fruit or by the thought of 'I', and which involves much dissipation of energy is called *rajas*.[11]

A *sattvik* person does not go seeking work. A *rajasik* person is engaged one day in inventing an aeroplane and is busy the next in discovering how to reach India from England in five hours. Such a person sets apart half an hour out of twenty-four to deceive his *atman*, and devotes the remaining twenty-three and a half to his body. Is the charkha work *rajasik*, or is it *sattvik* too? This can be decided only by reference to the spirit in which it is done. If a person plies the charkha merely for the sake of money, his work is *rajasik*, but it will be *sattvik* if he does so for the good of the world, in the spirit of a *yajna*.

That action which is blindly undertaken without any regard

to capacity and consequences, involving loss and hurt, is called *tamas*.[12]

In *tamas*, a person plunges into work without thinking of the consequences. One who works without desiring the fruit of his work knows what that fruit will be, but does not yearn for it.

Notes

1. Gandhiji's rendering adds here: "in which karma has been discussed".
2. XVIII, 12 to 14.
3. XVIII, 15 to 17.
4. The names are omitted in the source.
5. *Ibid.*
6. Harishchandra was sold by sage Vishwamitra to recover the sacrificial gift due from him. When his wife, Taramati, came to the burning-ground to cremate her son, Harishchandra threatened to strike her with his sword because she prevented him from obeying his master and removing the shroud from the corpse.
7. XVIII, 18.
8. XVIII, 19 & 20.
9. XVIII, 21.
10. XVIII, 22.
11. XVIII, 23 & 24.
12. XVIII, 25

[192] October 26, 1926

That doer is called *sattvik* who has shed all attachment, all thought of 'I', who is filled with firmness and zeal, and who recks neither success nor failure.[1]

Free from the sense of "I" means one who works merely as an instrument. To say that he should have no attachment does not mean that he should be indifferent; on the contrary, such a person should be more active than others. The relation of God's devotee to God is, in one sense, that of the lover and the beloved, though in reality the two are as different from each other as north is from south. The devotee remains unattached [to sense-pleasures], whereas the lustful lover and beloved lose their vitality day by day. Do the British officials who come out to India lack anything in endurance and energy? They seem to be yogis, but they are not free from attachment. They believe in ends, and will adopt any means, fair or foul, for their sake. But one who is free from attachment is concerned with nothing but work and displays unfailing determination and energy. He displays determination and energy even in plying the charkha. A person who works in this spirit is a *sattvik* doer.

That doer is said to be *rajas* who is passionate, desirous of the fruit of action, greedy, violent, unclean, and[2] moved by joy and sorrow.

That doer is called *tamas* who is undisciplined, vulgar, stubborn, knavish, spiteful[3], indolent, woebegone, and dilatory.

Hear now, O Dhananjaya, detailed fully and severally, the threefold division of understanding and will, according to their *gunas*.

That understanding, O Partha, is *sattvik* which knows action from inaction, what ought to be done from what ought not to be done, fear from fearlessness[4] and bondage from release.

That understanding, O Partha, is *rajas*, which decides erroneously between right and wrong, between what ought to be done and what ought not to be done.

That understanding. O Partha, is *tamas* which, shrouded in darkness, thinks wrong to be right and mistakes[5] everything for its reverse[6].

Notes

1. XVIII, 26
2. Gandhiji's rendering has; "easily excited by joy or sorrow in success or failure".
3. In place of "spiteful", Gandhiji's rendering has: "lacking firmness of decision".
4. In place of "fear from fearlessness", Gandhiji's rendering has: "which things one should guard against and of which things one need have no fear."
5. Gandhiji's rendering has: "sees everything in a wrong light".
6. XVIII, 27 to 32.

[193] October 27, 1926

That will, O Partha, is *sattvik* which maintains an unbroken harmony between the activities of the mind, the vital energies and the senses.[1]

If a person clings to the decision he has made without being exercised about the consequences, does not change it from day to day, then we may say that he possesses a will that is unswerving. "By yoga" means in a spirit of dedication to God.

That will, O Partha, is *rajas* which clings, with attachment, to right-eousness, desire and wealth, desirous of fruit in each case.[2]

The first signifies dedication to God and the second attachment.

Because of that attachment, one pursues dharma, *artha*[3] and *kama*[4]. The decision of such a person may be faulty.

That will, O Partha, is *tamas*, whereby insensate man does not abandon sleep, fear, grief, despair and self-conceit.[5]

Everything we do involves grief and ignorance and, at any rate, disappointment and fear.

Hear now from Me, O Bharatarshabha, the three kinds of pleasure.

Pleasure which is enjoyed only by repeated practice, and which puts an end to pain.

Which, in its inception, is as poison, but in the end as nectar, born of the serene realization of the true nature of *atman*—that pleasure is said to be *sattvik*.[6]

One must do *tapascharya* for such happiness. It involves renunciation and, therefore, means hardship in the beginning.

Everything in which one must sacrifice sleep and give up lethargy, for instance, study and learning and teaching, is a kind of *tapascharya*.

But the reward is knowledge of the self. The bliss of knowing the *atman* is of the same character as the *atman*. The happiness of the body comes wholly from the satisfaction of desires, and because it depends on the satisfaction of desires it is transient. It is as transient as the life of a butterfly or a flash of lightning. The other happiness abides for ever. The happiness which springs from the serenity resulting from knowledge of the *atman* is like *amrita*.

That pleasure is called *rajas* which, arising from the contact of the senses with their objects, is at first as nectar but in the end like poison.[7]

Suppose we have been to a play or some such show. We enjoy witnessing it, but afterwards suffer for loss of sleep and also on account of the effect of the play on our mind.

That pleasure is called *tamas* which, arising from sleep and sloth and heedlessness, stupefies the soul both at first and in the end.

There is no being, either on earth or in heaven among the gods, that can be free from these three *gunas* born of *prakriti*.[8]

We should, therefore, strive to become free from these.

Notes

1. XVIII, 33.
2. XVIII, 34.
3. Wealth, power.
4. Pleasure.
5. XVIII, 35.
6. XVIII, 36 & 37.
7. XVIII, 38.
8. XVIII, 39 & 40.

[194] October 28, 1926

The duties of Brahmins, Kshatriyas, Vaisyas and Sudras are distributed according to their innate qualifications, O Parantapa.

Serenity, self-restraint, austerity, purity, forgiveness, uprightness, knowledge and discriminative knowledge, faith in God are the Brahmin's natural duties.[1]

Serenity, self-restraint, *tapas* (to keep body, speech and mind under control by hard discipline), purity, forgiveness (to wish well, from the heart, even to a person who may have hit us with a stone), straightforwardness (to have no impurity in one's eyes, to behave decently), knowledge and knowledge based on experience (not bookish, dry knowledge), faith in God—these are the natural duties of the Brahmin.

A person may have the qualities enumerated above, but may not believe in God, may be lacking in faith and devotion; if so, those very qualities will prove harmful. For instance, in Europe these days they train the body for prize competitions and wrestling matches. These persons, too, are required to exercise discipline over the body, but that is done without devotion to God and helps them in no way. Hence belief in and devotion to God should be among the most important characteristics of a Brahmin.

Valour, spiritedness, constancy, resourcefulness, not fleeing from battle, generosity[2] and the capacity to rule are the natural duties of a Kshatriya.[3]

A Brahmin, too, should have these qualities. For instance, Vashishtha and other sages had them. Likewise, a Kshatriya should have the qualities of a Brahmin; for example, Yudhishthira, Ramachandra, etc., were Kshatriyas but possessed the virtues of Brahmins. Bharata was the very ideal of what a Brahmin should be. In this way every individual should display, in varying measure, the qualities associated with all the castes, and a person will belong to the caste whose virtues he possesses in a predominant measure. These will determine his natural karmas.

Tilling the soil, protection of the cow and commerce are the natural functions of a Vaisya, while service is the natural duty of a Sudra.

Each man, by complete absorption in the performance of his duty, wins perfection. Hear now how he wins such perfection by devotion to that duty.

By offering the worship of his duty to Him Who is the moving spirit of all beings, and by Whom all this is pervaded, man wins perfection.[4]

Anyone who worships the *atman*—the *Brahman*—God that exists pervading the universe like its warp and woof,—reaches the goal; true success crowns him alone who sees prayer or worship in the karma which has fallen to his lot as his duty, who has made service and every karma of his a form of prayer.

Better one's own duty[5], though uninviting, than another's[6] which may be more easily performed; doing duty which accords with one's nature, one incurs no sin.

One should not abandon, O Kaunteya, that duty to which one is born,[7] imperfect though it be; for all action, in its inception, is enveloped in imperfection, as fire in smoke.[8]

This does not apply to actions like a stealing; it applies only to actions which have been described in the preceding verses as the natural karmas of the four castes. Even if one sees some evil in such karmas—as, for instance, Arjuna's shrinking from fighting because of his weakness of attachment— it is best to do them, for every karma, every beginning, is tainted with some evil.

He who has weaned himself from attachments[9] of all kinds, who is master of himself, who is dead to desire, attains through renunciation the supreme perfection of freedom from action.[10]

Here by sannyasa is meant, not renunciation of all karmas but only the renunciation of the fruit of all karmas and it is such renunciation alone which can be successfully practised.

Learn now from Me, in brief, O Kaunteya, how he who has gained this perfection, attains to *Brahman*, the supreme consummation of knowledge.[11]

Notes

1. XVIII, 41 & 42.
2. In place of "generosity", Gandhiji's rendering has: "being always ready to help the poor".
3. XVIII, 43.
4. XVIII, 44 to 46.
5. Gandhiji' rendering adds here: "karma which is one's duty".
6. Gandhiji' rendering adds here: "karma which is somebody else's duty".
7. Gandhiji' rendering has: "which has come to one unsought".
8. XVIII, 47 & 48.
9. Gandhiji's rendering has: "He who has given up attachment to everything that is, has become free from attachment".
10. XVIII, 49.
11. XVIII, 50.

[195] October 29, 1926

Equipped with purified understanding, restraining the self with firm will, abandoning sound and other objects of the senses, putting aside likes and dislikes.

Living in solitude, spare in diet, restrained in speech, body and mind, ever absorbed in *Dhyanayoga*, anchored in dispassion.

Without pride, violence, arrogance, lust, wrath, possession, having shed all sense of 'mine' and at peace with himself, he is fit to become one with *Brahman*.[1]

Ahankar, bala and *darpa* include one another, but it would not be like the *Gita* to use only one term. Its manner is to say the same thing over and over again in different ways. *Laghvashi*: I observe the vow of taking not more than five articles in my daily food, but, even if I keep it literally, I shall not have succeeded in keeping it well. Haridas mentioned dates and gave some good ones as gift. He watched my mood and offered me one to eat. I relished it, and immediately became conscious of a lapse. Even as it is, I told myself, you eat more than others do. I ate the date and it stuck in my throat. This is what should happen if we treat the body as something out of which we must take work. In this verse, we are asked to purify the intellect and to be *laghvashi*. To be *laghvashi* does not mean merely to be moderate in eating, but to be satisfied with one article when we feel we can make do with two. It is as though this misfortune befell me because we would be discussing the word *laghvashi* today. A person may take a vow that he would live exclusively on milk, and then consume fifteen pounds a day, or convert it into *mava*[2] and eat it. Why is it that such a person won't add water to milk and drink it? A barrister friend in England used to read for sixteen hours a day. He used to add water to his soup. Real hunger will prompt one to eat things that taste like amrita.

One with *Brahman* and at peace with himself, grieves not, nor desires; holding all beings alike, he achieves supreme devotion to Me. By devotion he realizes in truth how great I am, who I am; and having known Me in reality he enters into Me.

Even whilst always performing actions, he who makes Me his refuge wins, by My grace,[3] the eternal and imperishable haven.

Casting, with thy mind, all actions on Me, make Me thy goal, and resorting to the yoga of even-mindedness[4] fix thy thought ever on Me. Fixing thus thy thought on Me, thou shalt surmount all obstacles by My grace; but if possessed by the sense of 'I' thou listen not, thou shalt perish.

If obsessed by the sense of 'I', thou thinkest, "I will not fight", vain is thy obsession;(thy)nature will compel thee.

What thou wilt not do, O Kaunteya, because of thy delusion, thou shalt do, even against thy will, bound as thou art by the duty to which thou art born.[5]

"Hence," says Shri Krishna,"dedicate everything to me and, free from attachments and aversions and ever devoted to me, do the task which has fallen to your lot; so acting, you will remain untouched by sin."

Notes

1. XVIII, 51 to 53.
2. Milk boiled till it becomes a thick paste.
3. Gandhiji's rendering adds here: "not through his own strength".
4. Gandhiji's rendering adds here: "knowledge and meditation".
5. XVIII, 54 to 60.

[196][1] October 30, 1926

God, O Arjuna, dwells in the heart of every being and to His delusive mystery whirls them all,(as though) set[2] on a machine.[3]

We are sitting on this ball of earth, which does not stop from rotating or revolving even for a moment. It keeps rotating and revolving all the twenty-four hours. The stars and the sun do the same. Thus, nothing in the world is motionless. But things do not move through their own power; it is God's power which keeps everything in motion.

Just as we keep a machine in motion only as long as we choose and it has no power of its own to move, so also does God keep us in motion as He wills. We should not, therefore, be proud that we have done something. We should shed our egotism, become as a machine in God's hand and carry out His will, look upon Him as our all and obey His plan.

In Him alone seek thy refuge with all thy heart, O Bharata. By His grace shalt thou win to the eternal haven of supreme peace.

Thus have I expounded to thee the most mysterious of all knowledge; ponder over it fully, then act as thou wilt. Hear again My supreme word, the most mysterious of all; dearly beloved thou art of Me, hence I desire to declare thy welfare.

On Me fix thy mind, to Me bring thy devotion, to Me offer thy sacrifice, to Me make thy obeisance; to Me indeed shalt thou come—solemn is My promise to thee, thou art dear to Me.

Abandon all duties and come to Me, the only refuge. I will release thee from all sins, grieve not![4]

This verse is the essence of all Shastras and of the *Gita*. Shri Krishna tells Arjuna: "You should give up all arguing and take refuge in Me. That will be wholly for your supreme good. Only the service of the *atman* will advance a person's welfare."

Utter this[5] never to him who knows no austerity, has no devotion, nor any desire to listen, nor yet to him who scoffs at Me.

He who will propound this supreme mystery to My devotees, shall, by that act of highest devotion to Me, surely come to Me.[6]

All knowledge is preserved only when imparted to a person who is worthy of it, and not when imparted to one who is unworthy of it.

Nor among men is there any who renders dearer service to Me than he; nor shall there be on earth any more beloved by Me than he.

And who so shall study this sacred discourse of ours shall worship Me with the sacrifice of knowledge. That is My belief.[7]

That is, he who studies this intelligently will become free. Merely reciting the verses mechanically and without understanding their meaning will certainly not bring freedom.

Notes

1. The notes of this discourse were not taken by Mahadev Desai.
2. Gandhiji's rendering has "the clay of the potter's wheel", in place of "set on a machine".
3. XVIII, 61.
4. XVIII, 62 to 66.
5. Gandhiji's rendering has; "this knowledge".
6. XVIII, 67 & 68.
7. XVIII, 69 & 70.

[197] October 31, 1926

And the man of faith who, scorning not,[1] will but listen to it,—even he shall be released and will go to the happy worlds of men of virtuous deeds.

Hast thou heard this, O Partha, with a concentrated mind? Has thy delusion, born of ignorance, been destroyed, O Dhananjaya?[2]

Arjuna said:

Thanks to Thy grace, O Achyuta, my delusion is destroyed, my understanding has returned, I stand secure, my doubts all dispelled; I will do Thy bidding.[3]

Arjuna's memory, which had become clouded, has become clear. He has understood what his nature and his duty are, and his doubt has gone.

Sanjaya said:

Thus did I hear this marvellous and thrilling discourse between Vasudeva and the great-souled Partha.

It was by Vyasa's favour that I listened to this supreme and mysterious Yoga as expounded by the lips of the Master of Yoga, Krishna Himself.

O King, as often as I recall that marvellous and purifying discourse between Keshava and Arjuna, I am filled with recurring rapture.[4]

If we do not feel a new interest in this every time we read it, the fault must lie with us, it cannot be that of the author of the *Gita*.

And as often as I recall that marvellous form of Hari, my wonder knows no bounds and I rejoice again and again.

Wheresoever Krishna, the Master of Yoga, is, and wheresoever is Partha the Bowman, there rest assured are Fortune, Victory, Prosperity and Eternal Right.[5]

To Shri Krishna has been attached the epithet *Yogeshvar* and to Arjuna *Dhanurdhara;* this means that there are fortune, victory and eternal right only where there is perfect knowledge joined with light and power. He who has knowledge should have the fullest strength to use it; there should be perfection of knowledge and it should be fully translated into action.

We have taken this to be an imaginary conversation. The author of the *Mahabharata* has given us a wonderful work; he has displayed in it his perfect knowledge. He had entered into Krishna's heart.

Dhanurdhara means a person devoted to duty. Is there anyone who has attained to absolute knowledge? For that person, however, who has the strength of spirit to act upon what seems certain knowledge to him, there is no such thing as defeat; he may even have prosperity, and more than that he does not wish. If he goes on acting in that spirit, even his errors will be corrected in course of time. We know that we should always speak the truth, but manage to tell only half the truth but he who has pure knowledge and the necessary energy to act upon it, that is, has taken up a bow and arrow, will never depart from the path of morality.

We do not intend to give up the reading of the *Gita*; its reading at prayer time will continue, a few verses every day. We may also discuss some of them, if we wish to.

This is a work which persons belonging to all faiths can read. It does not favour any sectarian point of view. It teaches nothing but pure ethics.

Notes

1. Gandhiji's rendering adds here: "one whose faith is blind may scorn".
2. XVIII, 71 & 72.
3. XVIII, 73.
4. XVIII, 74 to 76.
5. XVIII, 77 & 78.

CONCLUSION

[1] November 4, 1926

The conclusion of our study of the *Gita* is that we should pray and read holy books, and know our duty and do it. If any book can help, it is this. Really, however, what help can a book or a commentary on it give? In the end, we achieve only as much as it is our good fortune to do. Our only right is to *purushartha*[1]. We can only strive and work. All human beings, and animals too, struggle. The only difference is that we believe that behind our struggle there is an intelligent purpose. What is the purpose, however? Merely to keep alive this body, or to know that which has taken on this body? To raise it or advance it, if that is possible? For the first object we work in any case, whether we wish or no. Our body itself is so made that it makes us work for it, even if we are unwilling. For instance, while the baby still in the mother's womb, its organs do function in one way or another. Though unconsciously, it does breathe. That also is a kind of effort. But it is not *purushartha*. Only effort aimed at the welfare of the *atman* can be described as *purushartha*. It has been described as the supreme *purushartha*. All else is futile expenditure of energy. For such *purushartha,* one of the means is reading the Shastras and reflecting and meditating on them. In order that our study may be really useful, it is necessary to repeat our recitation over and over again with attention to pronunciation, rhythm, etc. It is necessary to create an atmosphere of holiness round the *Gita*. If we are completely indifferent to it, then of course there is no question of attending to grammar, pronunciation, etc.

The truth about ourselves is that we strive for the supreme *purushartha* and know how to seek the means for it. We would honour and revere the *Gita*. It will certainly protect us. It is a deity of the mind. If so, we should read it daily as a part of our prayer.

What lesson shall we draw from all this? Today I will place before you only one idea. The *Gita* does not give the central importance to karma, nor to *jnana* nor to *bhakti*. It gives importance to all these. Oxygen is a very useful ingredient of air, but we cannot have only oxygen, other gases are equally necessary. Similarly, every element which the *Gita* includes is essential. Karma, *jnana* and *bhakti*, all three are essential, and each in its place is of central importance.

Without *bhakti* human effort by itself will not succeed, and, without *jnana*, *bhakti* will not bear fruit. Hence we see at places *bhakti* or *jnana* treated as a means which helps us in doing the right karma.

We can, however, do without any of the three elements, thanks to something else which has been explained. We cannot easily understand *jnana* and can understand *bhakti*[2], but we can understand karma more easily than either. Decorating the image, repeating Ramanama, all this is karma. Activity of every kind is karma. Karma means body. When any thought takes on a body, assumes form, it becomes karma. Body is a visible thing. To the degree that we can see the body, we can see karma. We cannot, therefore, live without karma, and that is why, we can say, the *Gita* has stressed karma. However, *bhakti* and *jnana*, too, are essential. Let us suppose that we have boarded the ship; who is to give it motion now? Who will start it? We feel happy at the sight of the ship and board it, with faith [that it will move]. Similarly, karma is indeed necessary, but we shall reach the goal only when an intelligent engineer starts and drives the ship. The idea of renouncing karma is a futile one. Even a sannyasi cannot live without karma. This argument, however, comes in later.

The *Gita*'s karma is not karma done under compulsion; it must be prompted by some little measure at any rate of knowledge.

Notes

1. Striving or determined effort.
2. The source has *jnana*, which seems to be a slip.

[2] November 5, 1926[1]

Following the path of non-violence, we discovered the value of the spinning-wheel, as also of *brahmacharya*. Beyond the river [Sabarmati] is *bhogabhumi*[2] while this is *karmabhumi*[3]. We wish to follow the path of renunciation. But no renunciation is truly such unless it gives us joy. We cannot live without joy. It is but proper that we should celebrate Diwali in a different manner from how it is done on that side of the river. We should today draw up a balance-sheet of our work. Our books of accounts are in our heart. We should have completely cleared the debit side. A business man always credits in his book at least one and a quarter rupee [on the New Year day]. We can follow him by making some good resolution. If we read the *Gita* regularly, we shall understand our duty easily.

The karma which the *Gita* advocates is done of one's own free will, and it is such karma as one cannot live without at all. There is another definition of karma besides this. Karma means body. So long as the body is connected with the soul, it has motion and acts. But karma also means violence. Hence comlete freedom from karma, which means from the body, is *moksha*. We should seek an existence that dispenses with this body and is beyond this world full of violence. In this world which is all karma, we should strive to cultivate a state of *akarma*. The *Gita* has shown how we can do this. We shall discuss this by and by.

Notes

1. This was Diwali day.
2. Place for enjoyment.
3. Place for duty.

[3] November 6, 1926

The peace of mind and the joy we feel when, with closed eyes, we recite the verses from memory are really great. We feel less joy when we read the verses.

Today is *padavo* (the New Year Day). May you succeed in

the good resolutions which you made before coming here. Anyone who has not made a single resolution should make one at least, that he or she will be sincere. If you do not become so, the bright outer surface will be no more than gilt and the inside will be base metal. Nothing will shine without truth; let everyone, there-fore, resolve that he will show himself as he is. The joy one can get by showing oneself as one is, is not to be had by decorating one's figure or beautifying oneself.

There is untruth in wearing your cap at an angle, in wearing the sari in a particular style and dressing your hair smartly. Anyone who dresses himself in various fashions so that he may appear more handsome than he is starts learning a lesson in falsehood. We can build a palace on the foundation of truthfulness.

Chapter III deserves special attention. We saw yesterday that karma means the body, it means violence, and I told you then that I would discuss this idea further today. This Chapter dwells on the necessity of *yajna*. *Yajna* means work for the benefit of others.

Afterwards, it is explained that every karma is tainted with evil, as it involves some measure of violence. However, violence committed for the sake of *yajna* is not violence. *Yajna* here does not mean that *yajna* in which they kill animals. There was a time when such *yajnas* were regarded as true *yajnas,* but now most people believe that they are not so. Since, however, every karma involves violence, I have divided violence into two categories. There is violence when the intention is to give pain, otherwise it is only an act of killing. Breathing involves killing, which is unavoidable violence, and is, therefore, forgiven.

Without such unavoidable violence, we cannot keep alive the body for its sacred pilgrimage. It is a principle of homoeopathy that the patient should take in the smallest possible quantity the very substance which has caused the disease. Similarly, if we wish to become non-violent in this violent world, we shall advance as we gradually become more and more non-violent. On the other hand, trying to overcome violence with violence leads to evil consequence. *Akarma* means reducing karma and the degree of violence involved in each karma. One who does that will not go seeking work to do. Such a person will ultimately reach a state in which his thought itself will be action. We cannot pursue even *bhakti* or *jnana* without some measure of karma—we shall see tomorrow how this is so.

[4] November 7, 1926

Since every karma involves violence, our ideal is to escape all karma, which means to win deliverance from this life. This does not mean that the world in which we live should vanish or be destroyed; it means that one should voluntarily renounce activity and sit at home quietly, that is, live in *Vaikunth*[1], knowing that this world of name and form is transient and that it is unprofitable to take pleasure in it. This, however, is not possible. We cannot, through force of will, have this world vanish from before us, or bring about the *moksha* of all people in it. Everyone, then, should seek his *moksha;* but how? By committing suicide? One who kills himself will not escape the body. It is opposing the law of nature to seek escape in this manner. It is with the mind that we have to renounce the body. If every karma involves violence and evil, we can mentally renounce karma. Does it mean that, after renouncing karma in that manner, one can do any karma one chooses? No. At present we mentally draw to ourselves innumerable things. When we have mentally renounced all karmas, a great many of them will fall off on their own. Such a person will then use to his benefit, as much as he can, the world from which all air will have escaped. "Only the outward form surviving, as of the burnt rope"; however, the burnt rope will also occupy a little space. Even if it is reduced to dust particles and they fly away into air, they will certainly occupy some space somewhere! It is our belief that if the outward form vanishes and the dust particles, too, vanish, then everything will have vanished. Like the sea, God neither increases nor decreases. The dust particles, obeying their nature, will have merged in Him. When we have renounced karma mentally, all attachment to it will have ceased.

Such a person will not even think what his duty is. He will be working only as directed by others. It is not he who will be doing the unavoidable, residual karma; God will be doing that. If I am not responsible even for my breathing, I am doing it under force, not willingly. A person who acts in such manner is non-violent. No one can be more non-violent than this while living in the body. Hence, as we saw in Chapter III, karma done in the spirit of *yajna,* that is, for the benefit of others, does not bind. To do karma for the benefit of others means to enlist ourselves as soldiers in God's army, to dedicate to Him our all, body, mind, wealth, intellect. I read a book by a protestant named

Wallace. He saw that their activity of converting others to Christianity did no good. He decided to mix with our people. He fell in love with the religions of India, but he could not forget Jesus. He then embraced the Roman Catholic Church, and felt that he was nothing as an individual, that the Church was all. He made an image, Parthiveshwar Chintamani, and resolved to surrender himself to it. As for the line of guru and disciple [to which he should belong], he looked upon society as a whole as his guru. This idea has appealed to me. If the Pope is immoral, there is bound to be corruption in society, but any person who has decided that he will do nothing on his own but do only what the Pope asks him to do, will only benefit himself. A protestant would say that one should obey one's conscience, but this Wallace kept his conscience out and surrendered himself to the Pope. His giving up concern for his conscience was a great idea. He has narrated a story. A Hindu once advised him[2] that repeating Ramanama was good and a Muslim advised the name Khuda. He repeated the names Rama and Khuda by turn. He once saw that another person uttering Ramanama was floating on water. Thereupon, he started saying Khuda-Rama and began to sink. God then told him: "My friend, I am both Khuda and Rama." This man, Wallace, thus wanted to cultivate single-minded devotion. His worshipping another person wholeheartedly was itself worship of his conscience. Everything becomes easy only when one surrenders oneself to God and lives as a cipher. A person who does so will have renounced all karma. Suppose a woman regularly goes to the *haveli*[3], and that the other women who go there are immoral. This woman, however, will be saved. The man who taught the *mantra* of Ramanama could not float, but the other one who learnt it and used it with faith did. Similarly, this woman who goes to the temple sees no immoral figure in the image, she sees only God. She would swim across and be saved; the others would be drowned. In the same way, anyone who mentally renounces all karma will be doing even the unavoidable, residual karma unwillingly and, therefore, will not be responsible for them. If he eats, he does so unwillingly; he breathes, too, unwillingly. How smooth everything becomes as soon as we mentally renounce all karma. We shall discuss tomorrow the meaning of violence and non-violence and of bondage and *moksha*.

Notes

1. The abode of Vishnu.
2. It is not clear from the source who is meant.
3. *Vaishnava* temple.

[5] November 9, 1926

A person can be free from karma only when he gives up his body altogether. Even the wish to live in the body must be renounced. If it is not, one will have to pass through many more lives. The wish to live in this body is what is termed *dehadhyasa*. That is the sea of existence.

While we remain in it, we shall ever be tossed about by the waves. In the course of time, then, we may perceive the deep truth that what we call happiness is not happiness but only an illusion of happiness, that misery is not misery but only an illusion of it. If a person mentally renounces karma, he becomes free from the sense of "I" and "Mine". He, therefore, resolves to work only in the spirit of *yajna* and for the benefit of others. Work done in such spirit is ahimsa, but only when two conditions are fulfilled by it. One is that there should be no element of selfishness in our motive, and the second is that there should be no self-interest of ours in it, that on the contrary it should be for the good and for the benefit of the world. If these two conditions are fulfilled then even the most dreadful-seeming act may be regarded as an act of ahimsa. We attribute ahimsa to an act, but we can do that only if the act is for the service of others. If a person can truthfully claim that he eats and performs other like acts in a disinterested spirit he is free from attachments. The wish to live in the body remains so long as I cling to it. We cannot hold a string in a disinterested spirit; holding it is an act of will. If a person has withdrawn his mind from the body as much as is humanly possible, he wins freedom from bondage to the body. What I am discussing is the question of violence and non-violence, of living in the body and being free from bondage to it. If this bodily life has no sense, use the body for the services of others, for a life of prayer to God. Those who advised us thus were not ignorant men, they spoke from experience. It is we who did not understand them. It is extremely difficult to give up our clinging to the body. Someone may well ask how we can explain this idea to a child. My reply is that it is only in young age that this idea is easily understood; one cannot understand it after one has lost one's teeth. A historian has said that there is no difference in outlook between youth and old age. Youth has desire and the capacity to satisfy it; in old age, the capacity is wanting and so the desire becomes stronger. If we do not follow the example of Menavati, who explained to Gopichand [the futility of attachment to bodily life], we shall invite misery upon ourselves. I go a step further and say that an old man is far more thoughtless than a young man. A prince is always surrounded by *hakims*[1] and consuming *yakutis*[2] but he is ever talking Vedanta[3]. Thus, boys and old men are the same in this regard.

Anyone who imbibes something, however little that may be, from these verses from the whole work, commencing with *Aum*—can attain complete peace. For him there will be only work undertaken for the service of others; the innumerable other karmas will have fallen away.

If, while we live in this body, we keep it yoked to work like a bullock to the cart, it will run after fewer things to do and with very much less intensity. We shall, then, seem to be doing nothing, but in fact we shall be working with energy which it is impossible to describe. We should seek out one activity or karma from among the countless in the world, or rather one activity or karma should come seeking us. Anyone who wants to serve will find objects of service anywhere. At the end of all discussion, Shri Krishna asked Arjuna in Chapter XVIII: "Surrender yourself to Me, do this very thing, but in obedience to My command. Dedicate your all to Me and go on with it," How this can be done, we shall discuss later.

Notes

1. Practitioners of *Unani* system of medicine.
2. *Unani* tonics.
3. Metaphysics (especially of the Upanishads).

[6] November 10, 1926

Today we are to have a bird's-eye view of the discussions, but I simply could not think out what to say. Right at the end of the work, in Chapter XVIII, Vyasa wondered what he had been making Krishna teach Arjuna, whether it was knowledge or ignorance, pure *bhakti* or something else. So he made Krishna brush aside all else and say:

"Abandon all duties and come to Me, the only refuge."[1] He later made Arjuna also say that he had forgotten what he had been taught.

The Lord replied that He, too, did not always remember the discussion and said that He would teach something new. And so He taught another *Gita*[2] which no one remembers.

Swami . . .[3] has been wandering for twenty-seven years, but till this day he has discovered nothing. Finally, now, he has joined the sect of . . . .[4] I am talking in a tone of despair, but what I am saying is true.

How does one, and how should one, seek refuge in the Lord?

Shri. . .'[5], the goldsmith, asked me to give him something, saying "Else, what could I carry back with me?" I looked at him for a while, unable to think of anything. Then I said: "Repeat Ramanama." What was it, however, that I gave him? And what did he receive? Things don't work that way. This is an old custom, but how many people following it seek refuge in Rama? The *Gita* was not the first work which advised us to seek refuge in the Lord. How, then, can we end our restless yearning? We must look inwards, not outwards, to discover the way. If we look outwards, where should we search? If God, on the other hand, is not outside of us but inside, how may we look inwards?

How shall we blow up the big rock that lies across our way as we look inwards? To seek God means to sink into ourselves, that is, to renounce all activities. Since, however, it is not possible to reno-unce all activities, we should engage ourselves in as few activities as possible, reduce ourselves to the utmost insignificance. To seek God is not a Herculean task, as the world may think it is; all that is necessary is to make oneself humble and yoke the mind to work every minute for the welfare of the *atman*. It is we who obstruct ourselves in this effort.

What should we do to overcome the obstructions? This is the first thing taught in the science of yoga. I have been thinking what education we should plan for boys and girls. They must get training in this. We should not deprive them of their right to get it. We wish to identify ourselves with the poor, but the children of the poor get nothing. From their infancy they work in the fields. Wherever the farmers' work is done systematically, their children are employed in such work right from their early years and few people think about the problems which exercise us. The way to realize God, which means the way to win swaraj too, is to do something which seems altogether unimportant, and that is, to show ourselves as we are even before children. If such behaviour becomes natural to us, the children will also watch it with admiration. I told you about Wallace. He said at the end: "I have still not surrendered my reason, and it is a protestant reason." But he did surrender his reason, his views, his all, and the salt was absorbed in the water of the sea. That is what the Buddha called nirvana. Such a person would not even remember that once he was an insignificant entity and think that he had now become the sea. We should, therefore, experience our insignificance, undertake the least important task and for its sake renounce everything, cultivate perfect disinterestedness.

We can achieve nothing by busily running about. The *Gita* advised Arjuna to give up concern with all dharma, that is, to take up the least important work and experience his insignificance. It tells us, in effect: "Live as a servant of the world; it is beyond your capacity to do more."

Notes

1. In XVIII, 66.
2. The *Mahabharata*, "Ashvamedha Parva"
3. The names are omitted in the source.
4. *Ibid*.
5. *Ibid*.

[7] November 12, 1926

Can procreation for *yajna* be described as consistent with *brahmacharya*? Yes, it can. In it, however, the desire for progeny is more important than concern for *yajna*. Whereas the world simply cannot go on without non-violence practised as *yajna*, we cannot say that procreation is essential. If the *smritis*[1] say, nevertheless, that *brahmacharya* is possible for a householder, they use the term *brahmacharya* in a restricted sense which we have completely rejected in our discussions.

Besides, there is one more argument. If destruction is violence, creation, too, is violence. Procreation, therefore, involves violence. The creation of what is bound to perish certainly involves violence.

Note

1. Sacred books prescribing rules for personal conduct and social life.

[8] November 13, 1926

The *Mahabharata* is a unique work and in it the *Gita* has a unique place. Describing a physical battle, it gives an account of an invisible fight and shows through it that in the physical battle not only those who lose but even those who win are defeated. The five or six who survived lived as though they were dead. Dhritarashtra becomes miserable, and so does Kunti[1]. We see in the Swargarohana Parva the fate which meets the five brothers and Draupadi. They die one after another. Yudhishthira, too, is hardly able to reach the end of the journey. And, therefore, Vyasa says that what they got from their victory was no better than dust.

This does not means that we should stop striving. In one sphere, Fate is all powerful, and in another *purushartha*. *Purushartha* means striving , and supreme *purushartha* means escaping from the pairs of opposites. Living in the world of opposites is no better than collecting dust with our hands. It is, however, the purpose of the *Gita* to show that every particle of dust can become as valuable as a jewel in certain conditions. The three *gunas* are aiming arrows at you from all sides.

If you remain unmoved as they pierce you, you can win. Those arrows may fall on the body and on the *atman* dwelling in the body, but, let them fall as long as they may, what harm can they do me so long as my *atman* is awake?

What is the condition under which this may be so? To explain who can understand this problem, Shri Vyasa gave the *Arjunavishadayoga*[2].

Arjuna here stands for the *atman* seeking knowledge. So long as the intellect is not aroused by circumstances, It will not feel the desire for knowledge. The *Gita* is not for the intellect so long as it remains ensnared by worldly allurements. Is the *Gita* for students? It is for all those who have faith, such faith that they wish to be Arjunas. A student who believes the statement of his teacher that India is 1,900 miles in length and 1,500 miles in breadth will not take up a rod and start measuring the distances. He takes the statement on trust. Similarly, when the teacher tells the pupils in the first standard that the earth is round, an intelligent pupil will believe him and start arguing with another who holds that it is flat. The pupil who is convinced of the truth of the statement will not question it. Such a pupil will also take on trust statements concerning dharma, which is also a kind of geography, as he does those about the physical science of geography.

He will exercise his curiosity in regard to many problems, but some things have to be accepted on trust. For instance, the definition of a straight line. Afterwards, such things become clear as day-light. The years of student-life are a time when one should take things on trust. Why students, even grown-up people take things on trust. We have no choice but to have faith in the ultimate things which remain unexplained by reason. A student's reason is virgin, and it is not taxed much. As it sharpens and acquires light and power, he goes on solving problems with its help by repeatedly putting questions, bowing humbly to the teacher as he does so. The only condition is that the pupil should feel curiosity and be eager to know. That is why Chapter I is called *Vishadayoga*. The term means the path which unites one to God through despondency. If we wish to be filled with exclusive devotion to God, to win *moksha,* we should go through despondency. . . . [3] told me: "Cannot we see God through fasting? Is it not right that we should punish the body severely if we feel all the time distracted by evil thoughts?" "There are," he said, "so many *bawas*[4] in the country. Some of them lie on spikes in the fierce sun and derive great contentment; surely they cannot be thinking evil thoughts at that time?" We shall find such persons in Europe too. Fakirs also have that experience. There have always been people in the world who did *tapas,* and theirs is not a crazy notion. I have merely put before you my humble view. I do not ask you to do such things. Our aim is to mortify the mind, to teach it patience in order to purify it. Fasting and similar lashes are sufficient for that. If we could be certain that we would always succeed in our aim by fasting, everyone would fast. Do you think there are only a few in this world who seek knowledge?

There are many such. People suffer a great many hardships to secure worldly things; do you think, then, that nobody would come forward to suffer being pierced with a nail in the neck for this purpose? I have seen persons who stabbed themselves with a knife as they begged for a pice. If people can do this to themselves for a pice, why should they not do it for a throne?

But that path is not easy. We have a middle way open to us, which is the only one worth following. But there is a point in what . . .[5] told me, and that is that we should have a burning aspiration in this direction. We should have the same impatience and yearning for *moksha* which lustful men and women display for the gratification of their lust. Let us renounce our yearning for worldly things and cultivate yearning for *moksha* instead. The first condition for one to be like Arjuna is that one should feel a burning aspiration. People start making distinctions between "mine" and "others". There is no doubt about whether we may kill or not. We know that we may not kill. The eternal law is not the law of killing.

Arjuna did not have the strength to follow that independent law, and merely asks how he could bring himself to aim his arrows at Drona and Bhishma. In this way, he made the false distinction between "his" and "others" and declared that he would not fight. But he is a mature man. He does not decide impulsively while sunk in darkness. He is all love for Krishna. Sinking with nervous fear, he asks Krishna to solve his problem. It is only when we feel nervous like him that we shall be cured. We shall not be cured till we feel a crisis. The experience is like the pangs of childbirth. Arjuna's experience is that which overwhelms one when one feels born again; may all of us have this experience. If the feeling endures, we would be saved.

Notes

1. Mother of the Pandavas.
2. Chapter I.
3. The names are omitted in the source.
4. Mendicant sadhus.
5. The names are omitted in the source.

[9][1]

In Chapter II, [we see that] the seeker should be eager. A person gets knowledge only when he suffers so much for it that his body becomes completely wasted and seems as if it would pass away any moment. We learn the same lesson from the story of *Gajendramoksha* and the narratives about Draupadi and others. When one has suffered so much, one gets knowledge and one's reason becomes purified.

When Pilgrim felt that he was surrounded by fire on all sides, he ran without worrying about his wife and children. When we have such a feeling, we may say that our reason has become purified, and all veils will then be lifted. Arjuna's heart is in the right place, but it is enveloped in ignorance and, therefore, it cannot help him to decide.

So Krishna explains the distinction between *atman* and the body. He advances one argument to convince Arjuna, till he is overwhelmed by it. Arjuna was worrying so much about the body; he should now worry equally for the *atman*. Krishna explains to him that the two things are distinct. The *atman* neither kills nor is killed. It is the body which perishes. Arjuna should know that in any case it will die, and should not worry about it. But this was only an argument. What should

Arjuna actually do? "If you do," Shri Krishna tells him, "what I ask you to do, you will have no cause to repent. Even if you make only a moderate effort, it will be rewarded. You should take my word that what you do, however small, will bear fruit." What type of person is he who works without worrying about the result? To answer this question, Shri Krishna describes the characteristics of such a person in Chapter II itself. The description creats so much interest in Arjuna, who was yearning for knowledge, that he feels eager to hear further.

He has no inkling yet of *bhakti*. One cultivates it only when one forgets everything else. Mira was filled with *bhakti* when she realized that having seen the light of the sun and the moon, she did not need the light shed by a glow-worm. If such a person still needs to do karma, it is only for serving others and not for his own sake. A *bhakta* may do exactly what we do, but his reason will show him how to do it in a different manner. And so the Lord explains how to do karma, and thereafter He explains the secret of *bhakti*. [Understanding that], one's attachment to the body falls away, the *atman* becomes stronger and awakens more fully day by day, and ultimately one sees it in a divine vision.

Note

1. The date of this discourse is not given in the source.

[10][1]

When Arjuna becomes utterly weak, his intellect is awakened. Shri Krishna then tells him: "Your intellect by itself will not serve you. You will need to do yoga, karmayoga." Tilak Maharaj has demonstrated this with many convincing arguments. He has shown that the intellect needs, as it were, to take a partner to itself and be a householder. When Arjuna asked Shri Krishna to explain to him the characteristics of the person practising both forms of yoga, the latter enumerated the characteristics of a *sthitaprajna.* This confused Arjuna. Would such a person be a man of karma or a *jnani*?

In Chapter III, therefore, Shri Krishna explains the meaning of karma. No one can live at all without karma. Mirabai begged of the Lord that she should think on Him with every breath she took. We do not breathe consciously, but do so instinctively. A healthy person does all karmas with detachment in the same manner as he breathes. Karma may be a sign of health and it may also be a sign of disease. For instance, the manner in which a person suffering from asthma breathes indicates that he has a disease. This is also true of a man who feels suffocated.

Similarly, one's karma may be a sign of health in some other person, but not in oneself. After this, Shri Krishna gave the example of Janaka and others. Citing His own example, He said that He, too, had to work and keep the machine going. He could not so much as stretch His limbs for rest. Arjuna could sleep, Shri Krishna said, but He could not.

Even then, He was always detached. If we follow this example, our intellect would retain its power till we are a hundred, or rather it would grow in strength with years. But human beings are attached to sense pleasures. If they were not, they would always attain perfect knowledge in course of time. If our experience is to the contrary, let us not pay attention to that. We are imperfect human beings and deduce imperfect principles from our imperfect experience. There should be, therefore, some flaw somewhere if experience tells us otherwise. Look at a fruit. As it grows bigger, it becomes more juicy and richer. The date has fallen off the tree and dried, but how sweet it is! Similarly, the intellect of a person who does not violate God's law should ripen and grow with years. In actual experience, however, we find that as a person grows older, he or she declines in strength and intelligence. Such a person has been a lover of gross pleasures in his life.

For an ordinary person, Chapter III is as valuable as a silver pot. It is extremely useful.

Note

1. The date of this discourse is not given in the source.

[11][1]

We have seen that God does not cease from karma even for a moment. How, then, can we win *moksha*? The reply was that the body should be left to do its karmas, that the *atman* was not involved in them. This teaching has been altogether misinterpreted by immoral people. But, truly speaking, it is easy enough to understand that the bond of the body itself involves karma. If there were no body, there would be no need to do karma, and God having no body He has no need to do karma. But the Lord says that, even though He has no body, He does not cease from karma. He should, therefore, be thought of as having one, for this entire visible creation is His body. When we think of Him as having no body, He is a Formless Reality. If the *atman* realizes that the body does its karma, it will be free from the bond of the latter. How can one feel that it is the body which goes on doing certain karmas? The body cannot do karma without the ego. Without the *atman*, the body itself can do nothing. This is one more problem.

This makes the *atman* a doer. It means, then, that the *atman*, joined to the ego, dwells in the body and does things. What we should do then was explained in Chapter III."Service of others brings holy merit to one, and through harassment of others one incurs sin." We may unhesitatingly do what is most for the benefit of others. We shall, of course, assume that the person doing that will be as detached from it as he can be. When we take the least credit for such work, it will be done with the most efficiency. A person walking with his natural speed of a mile an hour will outdistance another running at a speed of sixty miles, for the former will have his joy in his *atman*, whereas the latter will be full of doubts. His running will on the whole serve no purpose. If our work is free from egotism, though our speed may be slow, we are certain to reach the goal. Let us by all means work in the spirit of *yajna* and for the benefit of others. All that we should concern ourselves with is whether it is the body or the *atman* that we serve. To say that man is born for service of others is true in one sense only, because all his work is prompted by self-interest. If this selfinterest is the interest of the *atman*, then one's work is for the benefit of others. All the activities of such a person will be prompted by the motive of service.

Hence, the Lord concluded this part of the argument with the verse, "Better one's own duty, bereft of merit".[2] That means that, be one's own dharma what it is, even if it is seemingly without merit, it is better than another's which may have greater merit in it. Arjuna was attracted by the dharma of other people, and therefore, the Lord told him that, however good it was, it was not his dharma. Dharma well performed cannot be another's, for in fact such dharma cannot be well performed. Only one's own dharma can be well performed. The truth is that ultimately Arjuna will have to renounce both his own dharma and that of others, but he cannot have that *moksha* right now. *Swadharma* is what is natural to one. For him who works without egotism, his dharma lies clear before him. It grows and expands on its own. We can satisfactorily perform only our dharma, that which lies before us. We are deluded if we think that we can do teaching better than the work of cleaning lavatories which may have been assigned to us. We do as much good by cleaning lavatories as we would by teaching. From one point of view, the former is certainly without merit. What is cleaning lavatories in comparison with studies? The Ganga stands nowhere in comparison with the sea. The Ganga's dharma is to let boats sail over her, the sea's to let ships sail over it. The Ganga's may seem to have no merit, but that is her true dharma.

When we say that a dharma may be, or may seem to be, devoid of merit, "may be" is used ambiguously to mean "may seem to be".

From one point of view a certain task may be better than another, and yet for us the latter is superior.

This truth is the source of the idea of *varna*. Today all the four *varnas* have forsaken their functions, and yet we believe in the idea, for it helps to have an ideal even if it is no more than an ideal.

Anyone who wishes to become free from the body has no choice but to believe in *varna*, that is, in his own natural work. The Lord, therefore, told Arjuna that his work was to kill, and asked him to do it as *yajna*, without making a distinction between kinsmen and others.

The words *viguna* and *svanushthitat* have an equal and like force.

Notes

1. The date of this discourse is not given in the source.
2. III, 35.

[12][1]

The *Gita* is a valuable provision for the mind in one's lifejourney, as the spinning-wheel is for the body. It is a provision which I am able to supply. Continue to receive it. Remember the resolution of the committee about the verses included in the prayers. Even if they seem to be without merit, their recitation must be continued. The Chapters from the *Gita* [for recitation] should change every fortnight. You will find it difficult to keep up the practice till you have memorized the verses; if so, by all means read from a book. If by and by only one person remains to keep up this practice, he should imagine the entire world to be his listeners and go on reciting the verses. This is the only right course for anyone who has dedicated his life to non-violence. This is for those who wish to enjoy a spiritual empire, not for those who crave for empires of other kinds. Follow the practice with greater zest and put greater life into it day by day.

Today it is just a week-old baby. By and by it will, like the sun and the moon, rise and set periodically. Gradually, try to follow the meaning of the verses.

As I have told you, the *Gita* is a big knowledge-feast, it is the very *amrita* of knowledge. I must have had some point in saying that.

Many can memorize the verses. It is something within the power of both a god and a demon. I have suggested memorizing in order that you may make the right use of the *Gita* thereby, and not to enable you to make a show of your knowledge of it. If you know the verses by heart, you will get a little electrical energy from them at some hour of the day. You will think of some verse or other, and it will save you.

These verses are like oxygen. For those who read the *Gita* with faith, it is like the fabled wish-yielding tree. It can end all of our threefold sufferings. We may not see such a result in this life, but our faith should not be shaken on that account. If the result does not come, the reason will be deficiency of our own effort and not want of truth in the idea itself. It is only if we read the *Gita* in this spirit that it will prove the *amrita* of knowledge.

Note

1. The date of this discourse is not given in the source.

[13][1]

How should we define *swadharma*? The *varnashrama* had its origin in this idea. It is not peculiar to Hinduism, but prevails all over the world. In view of this, it is necessary to consider what *swadharma* means. In Chapter XVIII, we were even told that following one's *swadharma* one attains perfection; that is, following one's *swadharma* one attains equality with all. In this transitory world, we see equality nowhere. No two leaves are equal. But the *Gita* shows the way to equality. We shall see tomorrow how it does that.

Note

1. The dates of these discourses are not given in the source.

[14][1]

Swadharma, though devoid of merit, is better than *paradharma*, so much so that, if need be, one should prefer to die while doing one's *swadharma*. The reason is that *paradharma* may prove dangerous. We should be careful about this. No one should do work which belongs to another, for that may be dangerous. Suppose that there is a powerful minister in a country. Asquith was superior in authority to the commander-in-chief of the army, but his dharma was only to issue orders and it was for the latter to give effect to them.

Obeying his orders, the commander-in-chief would order the army to march to the battle-field. Suppose Asquith became vain and himself wanted to lead the army; if he did that, the country would be destroyed. The minister is of course next to the King in authority, but his taking upon himself this *paradharma* would be fraught with danger. Now think of the commander-in-chief. Suppose he wanted to rise to a higher position of authority and to become a minister, so that he might order the next commander-in-chief. If he did, there would be a great struggle for power in the country and it would be destroyed.

The commander-in-chief would lose the position he already enjoyed, without getting the one he wanted. One more condition is also essential. The commander-in-chief should do his work, and the minister his; neither is superior or inferior to the other. This requires a sense of dharma on the part of both. If they have it, neither would feel superior or inferior to the other, for each would do his own dharma well and earn 100 per cent marks.

In God's court, one's attitude to work will be given the highest importance. No one there will take into account who was superior and who inferior in status and authority. One should never believe that one's own dharma is superior and another's inferior. Or rather, one should believe that one's dharma is the best for one. Take the example of a mother's attitude to her child. If the latter is ugly, the mother will shower all the greater care on it and will quarrel with anyone who slights it. In the same way, one's own dharma helps one to win *moksha*. The *Mahabharata* contains many examples of this truth. In Tulsidas's work, too, Guha and Shabari were devoted to God as they did their own work, and so attained the supreme state.

Varnashrama had its origin in the idea of *swadharma*. We do not see today the true idea of *varna*. It is limited now to restrictions about inter-dining and inter-marriage. The idea of *varna* is not peculiar to Hinduism. Such dharma which was peculiar to one society would become narrow, and one need not die for it. If our dharma is universal and valid at all times, one should be ready to die for it.

Varna does not consist in customary practices regarding inter-dining and inter-marriage; the division of society into *varna*s is a division of functions. The idea of pollution by touch was a later accretion. The distinctions of *varna* prevail all over the world. We find them in every country. Most parents have to think what they will do about their children when they grow up, and the boys and the girls, too, have to think about their future. Exercised over these problems, we sacrifice our interests in this world and our welfare in the next. Worried by them, we lose sight of our means of deliverance. Can anyone else show us what our *swadharma* is? Doing *swadharma* does not mean the freedom of the individual and subordination of society. If a man seeks *moksha* and still believes that he is independent, he will utterly fail in his aspiration. One who seeks *moksha* behaves as society's servant. To win *moksha* means to merge in the sea. To attain that state means to be one with an infinitely vast sea. We are but germs in society. That word "germs" signifies our subordination to it. We are, in truth, free in such subordination. Our duty is what society assigns to us. Of three persons who work together, one is bound to be the leader.

A commander-in-chief must consult the minister in certain matters; and likewise the minister, too, should consult the former in some other matters. The definition [of *swadharma*], then, is that one must do the work assigned to one by one's superior. From this, we shall by and by rise to a higher stage.

Note

1. *Ibid.*

[15][1]

How is that in this *Gita* which is concerned with *moksha* we are asked to do work which may have no great significance, and to concern ourselves with *swadharma*? Can we win *moksha* in this manner? Yes, we can. In the *Mahabharata* there is Tuladhar's story.

The Brahmin in search of knowledge got it from a butcher. The devotee whom Mahadev [Desai] mentioned was a potter, and Bhojo Bhagat[2] was a cobbler. In saying, "better is death in the discharge of one's duty."[3] Shri Krishna has not laid down a principle very difficult to follow. The idea of *swadharma* involves restrictions on oneself.

Swa means that which one has been able to digest. If we are not able to digest [what we eat], many disturbances in the system will follow and we would get diseases. If, observing others round us consuming *dudhapak*[4] and growing fat, we also eat it, we would come to grief.

Swadharma indeed helps everyone to win *moksha*. But, till we have won it, what should we do as human beings living in these physical bodies? If we understand the body's dharma and do it, we shall have to voluntarily accept subordination in order that we may become perfectly ourselves. It is to God that we have to subordinate ourselves.

Can we hope that, because we recite *antar mama*[5] every day, God who is asleep in our hearts will awake? To wake Him, we shall have to seek someone's help. *Swadharma* means the work which falls to our lot from hour to hour. We should do the work assigned to us by others.

We have to submit ourselves to our conscience, but what will a person do if he has no conscience? When we have eliminated the "I" from us, then will God take the place vacated by it. We have to accept subordination for His sake. Having accepted a job anywhere, we should do it with single-minded devotion and sense of duty; we should do it even if this work which falls to our lot is unattractive to us, repels us or smells of violence. If in a world like ours full of violence, such work falls to our lot, we must do it. A task of this kind fell to the lot of Harishchandra. When he raised his sword to kill his wife, he had no violence in him. Did he wish ill to his wife? His heart was filled with compassion. The poet says that he had hardened his heart, but in truth he had hardened only his hand. If we were painters, we would not draw him with a face distorted by a feeling of aversion.

If he had in fact raised his sword with reluctance on his face, we would have to say that he was overcome by ignorant attachment and that, having risen so high, at last he fell; this blot would have remained on him. We cannot imagine any sign of suffering on his face. Following his example, we should do with perfect devotion and without hesitation any duty which falls to our lot. It is best, in the first instance, not to take up a task, but, having taken up one, we must not forsake it.

Consider, for instance, a large black ant whose feet, if stuck in jaggery, will not let go their hold of it; they remain stuck to it. Not to forsake the task undertaken, that is but the definition of satyagraha itself.

Everyone, from a child to an old man, should cling to the task undertaken till he or she breaks. This is internal meditation, this is Vedanta. Of course, the work done in this spirit should be dedicated to God. We should be totally absorbed in any work which we may be doing. If such absorption is inspired with a selfish interest in work, it will bring about our fall, and if with a sense of dedication to God it will lift us up.

Notes

1. The date of this discourse is not given in the source.
2. Gujarati poet, 1785-1850.

3. In III, 35.
4. Boiled, sweetened milk cooked with a little rice.
5. A Bengali *bhajan* included in the *Ashram Bhajanavali*.

[16][1]

So, then, this is one idea, that *swadharma* is better than *paradharma*.

The next question is: if no one can escape doing karma, what is the difference between the karma of a wise man and that of an ignorant man? The former performs *yajna* for others, the latter works for himself. If we do karma as *yajna*, it would be as if we did no karma. Shri Krishna then advanced the argument of society's good, and told Arjuna that he should work on without wasting a single moment in idleness, should work on without concern for the "I" and dedicating to God all that he did.

How does it happen that, though trying to act in this way, man sometimes commits sin? If, in doing *swadharma*, we follow our own wilful inclinations, do it in pride, we are not doing *swadharma*. What is the reason that, though most people in the world do their *swadharma*, the pile of sins in the world remains as huge as ever?

With Chapter III the *Gita* ends. It need not have been followed by anything more. Even in the third Chapter, there are five or six verses which are really important. The rest of the *Gita* is intended to explain more clearly what has been said in the first three chapters.

Shri Krishna tells Arjuna, in reply to his question, that desire and anger ride on our two shoulders. If they are with us while we do our *swadharma*, then we gain nothing. Can we say that many of those who enter the Councils act unworthily? They do it to serve others. But their action is prompted by desire, by the aim of getting the better of the Government; there is anger behind it and, therefore, it is not right.

Desire and anger are blood-brothers. They dwell in the senses and the mind. We can, therefore, overcome them only by subduing these.

Hence it is that the way to *moksha* is said to lie in becoming free from attachments and aversions. This is the reason why we are advised to become free from them. If we are enslaved by something, is there anything we would not do for its sake?

Vishvamitra[2] did hard *tapas*, but afterwards he felt that his *tapas* was superior to Vasishtha's[3]; from that arose desire, which provoked anger. One should understand this with one's reason at any rate and move as slowly as a snail; one may then work on without fear of any kind.

Notes

1. The date of this discourse is not given in the source.
2. Sages in the *Ramayana*.
3. *Ibid.*

[17] November 23, 1926

We ought to cultivate such a state of mind that on no day can we have peace unless we have recited verses from the *Gita*. What a contrast between the noise at the evening and the peace in the early morning! Wenshould not be satisfied merely with reciting the verses or leading their recitation anyhow. Day by day our recitation should improve in regard to pronunciation. One person's lapse in this matter is the lapse of all. As this is true of the music in a concert, so is it true of the music of life. If we pray with the heart and the mind in unison, why should we care for the perishable body? Why should we be concerned whether it lives or falls? We may not mind the distance from others which this material thing imposes on us; after all, how far apart can a material thing keep us? If we have cultivated the unity of our self with the selves of others, with God as witness, if we treat the lapse of one as the lapse of all, it will be very good indeed. If we also pronounce the words correctly, we shall approach God with water in a vessel as clean as possible. We shall have placed a *bel* leaf in the water with utmost attention to cleanliness, and filled the vessel with water from the purest source. Such outward attentions are meaningless in themselves; but they lend grace where there is faith. A man of faith will make his gift as artistic as he can. Today's craftsmanship is lifeless and no craftsmanship at all. How much patience must the craftsmanship of olden days have required? How many years must have been spent on learning it? We have come across no engineer of the old school, one who had built palaces in his time. Our effort to master correct pronunciation is a sign of our heartfelt love; we should not, thus, let our recitation of the *Gita* become dry at any time.

In Chapter III, Shri Krishna explained the supremacy of karma. After explaining that, if we wish to practise yoga through karma, we should dedicate to God every karma which we do, He explained what other things should accompany karma. It should be enriched with knowledge. Let us think about the path of knowledge and the path of karma. Anyone who follows the former exclusively becomes heartless; he who follows the latter exclusively becomes dull in mind. For the right choice of karma we should combine the methods of both the paths. Both are excellent, but neither can be practised without the other. Is there anything as humble as a stone, or anything which does as much karma as it does? How utterly dedicated to God is its karma? It goes on working for ever in the same, unchanging manner; but, as a mere piece of stone, it never wins *moksha*. A stone should cease to be a stone and should become Ahalya1, should come alive. On the one hand, we should be as inert as a stone, and, on the other, we should become the very image of knowledge, and this in such manner that no one can say whether the person is a man of karma or of knowledge. Then will his *purushartha* be complete. Where *jnana* and karma unite, *bhakti* will follow as a matter of course. For the moment, we have seen that there should be a combination of the two. When we have understood the meaning of both, we shall see no difference between *sankhya* and yoga. That is the substance of Chapter IV. I shall not go into a discussion of the different types of *yajna*.

Note

1. A character in the *Ramayana*. Her husband's curse had turned her into a stone, which regained her living form at the touch of Rama's feet.

[18][1]

Hathayogis[2] believe Chapter VI to have been written for them. Their belief is that it was written because *hathayoga* has a place in the practice of yoga. I do not share this view, though I admit that *hathayoga* has some utility. We should avail ourselves of all possible means which help in self-realization. It is said about the purely physical processes described in *hathayoga* that those who go through them will attain self-realization. Jnanadeva went riding on a wall to receive someone who was coming to see him riding a lion. But what then? He thereby brought yoga into discredit. These processes do not necessarily take one to God. The secret of rising towards God lies in the mind. In this very Chapter there is the verse: *Uddharedatmanatmanam natmanamavasadayet.*[3] That is, this Chapter teaches the importance of controlling the self. Mortification of the body is also as much for the control of the mind as for the control of the self.

Anyone who practises these processes, knowing that they help control of the mind, will certainly derive much profit from them. We have not taken them up because we have not met anyone who knows them. We have been visited by many who believed in them and recommended them to us, but none who knew them. Hence I have done nothing in that field. But I do have them in my mind. I mention this thing so that, if you come across a sadhu who is like me a seeker, you should avail yourselves of his services. Our bodies have become very weak. If we know these physical processes very well, they would be found to be far more effective exercises than what they teach in England. The sixth Chapter of course discusses the importance of rules. It also explains the means of doing karma in a disinterested spirit. *Jnana* signifies the knowledge of man who knows the Shastras and the term yogi means one who knows the science of karma.

This Chapter explains the conditions which must be fulfilled before we can do karma in a disinterested spirit. It is not possible to do karma in that spirit without control of the self. Those who control themselves from hour to hour, only they can work in that spirit.

Thieves, robbers and immoral men never talk about doing karma in a disinterested spirit. Many persons use the *Gita* to justify their actions.

But disinterestedness is a state of the mind, and such a state can never be cultivated without effort and without self-control. One whose left hand does not know what his right hand does, such a one knows what it is to be equal-minded. Our yardstick is the ability to see others as ourselves. We should think whether we should be happy if others did to us what we do to them.

Disinterestedness can never be cultivated without a spirit of renunciation. That is the true meaning of Chapter VI.

Notes

1. The date of this discourse is not given in the source.
2. Practitioners of yoga in its purely physical aspect.
3. In VI, 5.

[19][1]

The *Bhagavad Gita* is divided into three parts: six chapters for the syllable *tat*, six for *tvam* and six for *asi*[2].

In Chapter VI, Shri Krishna explains the means of controlling the senses. In the seventh chapter, he discusses the distinction between *jnana* and *vijnana*. *Vijnana* means knowledge of particulars. *jnana* embraces God's *para prakriti*, and *vijnana* relates to His *apara prakriti*. Chapter VIII discusses further what is included in *vijnana*.

The last verse in Chapter VII says that he who performs the three types of sacrifice, *adhiyajna*, *adhidaiva* and *adhibhuta*, goes to the Lord. Discussing *akshara*, Shri Krishna explained that one should meditate exclusively on that, for one becomes like that on which one meditates. He explained *adhidaiva* to mean that He was the *Parabrahman*, supreme above all, and asked why, since this was so, anyone should seek to please other deities lower or higher. It is God alone that one should worship and serve. But what does serving God mean? Shri Krishna said that He was both the invisible Reality and the visible world. If so, the karma which we do is also done by Krishna. If He is the master of the show, can we believe that we do anything? As the dirty water which falls into the Ganga is purified, so we should believe that the sins we commit are committed by God, for he who harbours no sinful thoughts cannot commit sin. Anything to which motion is imparted retains it for some time. If we fell a tree, for some time the leaves would remain green, but they would soon begin to wither. If a person has overcome both his conscious and unconscious desires, they will not rise again. In Chapters VII and VIII, Shri Krishna explains what Creation is and describes the visible world and the nature of karma, and shows that everything exists in God. Why does He lay so much stress on the necessity of doing karma in a disinterested spirit?

These two chapters sufficiently explain the reason. A person who has plunged into water goes on swimming in it, but the latter is in no way concerned. Similarly, God is a sea of compassion. This too, however, is merely a conception of our mind. Truly speaking, God is neither a generous-hearted Being nor a sea of compassion. It is in such a God that we lie and move.

Notes

1. The date of this discourse is not given in the source.
2. The three syllables constitute the great Upanishadic text *tat tvam asi*, "That thou art."

[20][1]

Chapters IX and X are to be taken together. Shri Krishna says:

"I dwell in all creatures, hence do all things for my sake." And so He said: "On Me fix thy mind, to Me bring thy devotion."[2] In Chapter X Arjuna asked Shri Krishna to show him His divine powers. The stream of *bhakti* which flows from Chapter VII onwards gathers volume from chapter to chapter. Shri Krishna shows Arjuna His divine powers and urges him again and again to dedicate everything to God. All the four chapters lead us towards *bhakti*. Chapter IX, especially, is about *rajavidya* and *rajaguhya*. It is really a great support for persons like us given to a life of sin. Even the most sinful person is promised help and support. The *Gita* would not approve anyone running down *mantras* from the Vedas. It says, on the contrary, that even the most sinful man will be saved if he dedicates everything to Shri Krishna.

This knowledge is *guhya* only so long as it has not touched the heart.

Notes

1. The date of this discourse is not given in the source.
2. In XVIII, 65.

[21] [November 27, 1926][1]

Shri Krishna showed His cosmic form to Arjuna and explained to him that it could be seen, not by those who had studied the Vedas and gained other like qualifications, but only by those whose hearts were steeped in *bhakti*. What a vision it must have been! My enthusiasm for the *Gita* grows day by day. I agreed to talk about the *Gita* and explain its meaning, and I liked the idea; but my pleasure in the discussion has grown from what it was when I started. I get daily more absorbed in it. We, who are given to self-indulgence, cannot always taste this joy. The real joy comes from *bhakti*, that is, it is spiritual. This interest is growing because it is like savouring food which is digested more and more completely from day to day, and it influences our conduct accordingly. Such is my state of mind. I feel that in this chapter the *Gita* reaches its highest point. We take twelve minutes to recite it, so that we are likely to feel tired by the time we have come half-way. If we let ourselves sink it it, we should be saved.

Shri Vyasa has described the vision so vividly that we feel as if we see it with our own eyes. Beholding it, we wonder what our own place in this universe is. It is nothing. It is as small as a grain of dust. Where are we in this universe of stars, suns and planets? If a hair could speak, it would describe its place thus: "I have value so long as I am a part of the body; separate me from it and my value is lost. The essence of life in me cannot vanish; as for the material substance, even the vast universe is transient, existing only as name and form." We are nothing, compared with that visible manifestation of God, this vast universe. Being what they are, whom can we kill? Even if we kill anyone, we too shall die simultaneously. As we understand this more and more, we should become steeped ever more fully in *bhakti*.

Even those who go out visiting other places should keep up the daily practice.

[From Gujarati] *Gandhijinu Gitashikshan*.

Note

1. This date is given on the title page of *Gandhijinu Gitashikshan*.

PART TWO

"ANASAKTIYOGA"[1]

THE MESSAGE OF THE "GITA"

It was at Kausani in Almora, on 24th June 1929, i.e., after two years' waiting, that I finished the introduction in Gujarati to my translation of the *Gita*. The whole was then published in due course.[2]

It has been translated in Hindi, Bengali and Marathi. There has been an insistent demand for an English translation. I finished the translation of the introduction at the Yeravda prison. Since my discharge[3] it has lain with friends, and now I give it to the reader. Those, who take no interest in the Book of Life, will forgive the trespass on these columns.

To those, who are interested in the poem and treat it as their guide in life, my humble attempt might prove of some help.

M.K.G.

Just[4] as, acted upon by the affection of co-workers like Swami Anand and others, I wrote *My Experiments With Truth*[5], so has it been regarding my rendering of the *Gita*. "We shall be able to appreciate your meaning of the message of the *Gita*, only when we are able to study a translation of the whole text by yourself, with the addition of such notes as you may deem necessary[6]. I do not think it is just on your part to deduce ahimsa, etc., from stray verses", thus spoke Swami Anand to me during the non-co-operation days. I felt the force of his remarks[7]. I therefore told him that I would adopt his suggestion when I got[8] the time. Shortly afterwards I was imprisoned.[9] During my incarceration I was able to study the *Gita* more fully. I went reverently through the Gujarati translation of the Lokamanya's great work[10]. He had kindly presented me with the Marathi original and the translations in Gujarati and Hindi, and had asked me,[11] if I could not tackle the original, at least to go through the Gujarati translation. I had not been able to[12] follow the advice outside the prison walls. But when I was imprisoned I read the Gujarati translation. This reading whetted my appetite for more and I glanced through several works on the *Gita*.[13]

2. My first acquaintance[14] with the *Gita* began in 1888-89 with the verse translation by Sir Edwin Arnold known as *the Song Celestial*. On reading it I felt a keen desire to read a Gujarati translation. And I read as many translations as I could lay hands on.

But all such reading can give me no passport for presenting my own[15] translation. Then again my knowledge of Sanskrit is limited; my knowledge of Gujarati too is in no way scholarly.[16] How could I then dare present the public with my translation?

3. It has been my endeavour, as also that of[17] some companions, to reduce to practice the teaching of the *Gita* as I have understood it. The *Gita* has become for us a spiritual reference book.[18] I am aware that we ever fail to act in perfect accord with the teaching. The failure is not due to want of effort, but is in spite of it.[19]

Even through the failures we seem to see rays of hope. The accompanying rendering contains the meaning of the *Gita* message which this little ban is trying to enforce in its[20] daily conduct.

4. Again this rendering is designed for women, the commercial class, the so-called Shudras and the like, who have little or no literary equipment, who have neither the time nor the desire to read the *Gita* in the original, and yet who stand in need of its support[21]. In spite of my Gujarati being unscholarly[22] I must own to having the desire to leave to the Gujaratis, through the mother tongue, whatever knowledge I may possess. I do indeed wish that, at a time when literary output of a questionable character is pouring in upon the Gujaratis, they should have before them a rendering, which the majority can understand, of a book that is regarded as unrivalled for its spirirtual merit and so withstand the overwhelming flood of unclean literature.[23]

5. This desire does not mean any disrespect to the other renderings. They have their own place. But I am not aware of the[24] claim made by the translators of enforcing their meaning of the *Gita* in their own lives. At the back of my reading[25] there is the claim of an endeavour to enforce the meaning in my own conduct for an unbroken period of 40[26] years. For this reason I do indeed harbour the wish that all Gujarati men or women[27], wishing to shape their conduct according to their faith, should digest and derive strength from the translation here presented.

6. My co-workers, too, have worked at this translation. My

knowledge of Sanskrit being very limited, I should not have full confidence in my literal translation. To that extent therefore the translation has passed before[28] the eyes of Vinoba, Kaka Kalelkar, Mahadev Desai and Kishorelal Mashruwala.

II

7. Now about the message of the *Gita*.

8. Even in 1888-89, when I first became acquainted with the *Gita,* I felt that it was not a historical work, but that, under the guise of physical warfare, it described the duel that perpetually went on in the hearts of mankind, and that physical warfare was brought in merely[29] to make the description of the internal duel more alluring[30]. This preliminary intuition became more confirmed on a closer study of religion and the *Gita*. A study of the *Mahabharata* gave it added confirmation. I do not regard the *Mahabharata* as a historical work in the accepted sense. The "Adiparva" contains powerful evidence in support of my opinion. By ascribing to the chief actors superhuman or subhuman origins, the great Vyasa made short work of the history of kings and their peoples. The persons therein described may be historical, but the author of the *Mahabharata* has used them merely to drive home his religious theme.

9. The author of the *Mahabharata* has not established the necessity of physical warfare; on the contrary, he has proved its futility. He has made the victors shed tears of sorrow and repentance and has left them nothing but a legacy of miseries.

10. In this great work the[31] *Gita* is the crown. Its second chapter, instead of teaching the rules of physical warfare, tells us[32] how a perfected man is to be known. In the characterstics of the perfected man of the *Gita,* I do not see any to correspond to physical warfare.[33]

Its whole design is inconsistent with the rules of conduct governing the relations between warring parties.[34]

11. Krishna of the *Gita* is perfection[35] and right knowledge personified; but the picture is imaginary. That does not mean that Krishna, the adored of his people, never lived. But perfection is imagined. The idea of a perfect incarnation is an aftergrowth.

12. In Hinduism[36] incarnation is ascribed to one who has performed some extraordinary service of mankind. All embodied life is in reality an incarnation of God, but it is not usual to

consider every living being an incarnation. Future generations pay this homage to one who, in his own generation, has been extraodrinarily religious in his conduct.[37] I can see nothing wrong in this procedure; it takes nothing from God's greatness, and there is no violence done to truth.

There is an Urdu saying which means: "Adam is not God but he is a spark of the Divine." And therefore he who is the most religiously behaved has most[38] of the divine spark in him. It is in accordance with this train of thought, that Krishna enjoys, in Hinduism, the status of the most perfect incarnation.

13. This belief in incarnation[39] is a testimony of man's lofty spiritual ambition. Man is not at peace with himself till he has become like unto God.[40] The endeavour to reach this state is the supreme, the only ambition worth having.[41] And this is self-realization. This selfrealization is the subject of the *Gita*, as it is of all scriptures.[42]

But its author surely did not write it to establish that doctrine. The object of the *Gita* appears to me to be that of showing the most excellent way to attain self-realization.[43] That which is to be found, more or less clearly, spread out here and there in Hindu religious books, has been brought out in the clearest possible language in the *Gita* even at the risk of repetition.

14. *The matchless remedy is renunciation of fruits of action.*

15. This is the centre round which the *Gita* is woven.[44]

This renunciation is the central sun, round which devotion, knowledge and the rest revolve like planets.[45] The body has been likened to a prison.[46] There must be action[47] where there is body. Not one embodied being is exempted[48] from labour. And yet all religions proclaim that it is possible for man, by treating the body as the temple of God, to attain freedom. Every action[49] is tainted, be it ever so trivial[50]. How can the body be made the temple of God?[51] In other words[52] how can one be free from action, i.e., from the taint of sin? The *Gita* has answered the question in decisive language: "By desireless action; by renouncing fruits of action; by dedicating all activities[53] to God, i.e., by surrendering oneself to Him body and soul."

16. But desirelessness or renunciation does[54] not come for the mere talking about it. It is not attained by an intellectual feat. It is attainable only by a constant heartchurn. Right knowledge is necessary for attaining[55] renunciation. Learned men possess a knowledge of a kind. They may recite the Vedas from

memory, yet[56] they may be steeped in self-indulgence. In order14 that knowledge may not run riot, the author of the *Gita* has insisted on devotion accompanying it and has given it the first place. Knowledge without devotion will be like a misfire. Therefore, says the *Gita*: "Have devotion, and knowledge will follow." This devotion is not mere lip worship, it is a wrestling with death.[58] Hence the *Gita's* assessment of the devotee's qualities is similar to that of the sages.

17. Thus the devotion required by the *Gita* is no soft-hearted effusiveness. It certainly is not blind faith. The devotion of the *Gita* has the least to do with externals. A devotee may use, if he likes, rosaries, forehead marks, make offerings, but these things[59] are no test of his devotion. He is the devotee who is jealous of none, who is a fount of mercy, who is without egotism, who is selfless, who treats alike cold and heat, happiness and misery, who is ever forgiving, who is always contented, whose resolutions are firm, who has dedicated mind and soul to God, who causes no dread,[60] who is not afraid of others[61], who is free from exultation, sorrow and fear, who is pure, who is versed in action and yet remains unaffected by it, who renounces all fruit, good or bad, who treats friend and foe alike, who is untouched by respect or disrespect, who is not puffed up by praise, who does not go under when people speak ill of him, who loves silence and solitude, who has a disciplined reason.[62]

Such devotion is inconsistent with the existence at the same time of strong attachments.[63]

18. We thus see, that to be a real devotee is to realize oneself.[64] Self-realization is not something apart.[65] One rupee can purchase for us poison or nector, but knowledge of devotion cannot buy us either salvation or bondage.[66] These are not media of exchange. They are themselves the thing we want. In other words, if the means and the end are not identical, they are almost so. The extreme of means is salvation. Salvation of the *Gita* is perfect peace.[67]

19. But such knowledge and devotion, to be true, have to stand the test of rununciation of fruits of action. Mere knowledge of right and wrong will not make one fit for salvation.[68] According to common notions a mere learned man will pass as a pundit. He need not perform any service. He will regard it as bondage even to lift a little *lota*.[69] Where one test of knowledge is non-liability for service, ther is no room for such mundane work as the lifting of a *lota*.

20. Or take *bhakti*.[70] The popular notion of *bhakti* is softheartedness, telling beads and the like, and disdaining to do even a loving service, lest the telling of beads might be interrrupted.[71] This bhakta[72] therefore, leaves the rosary only for eating, drinking and the like, never for grinding corn or nursing patients.

21. But the *Gita* says:[73] "No one has attained his goal without action. Even men like Janaka attained salvation through action. If even I were lazily to cease working, the world would[74] perish. How much more necessary then for the people at large to engage in action?"

22. While[75] on theone hand it is beyond dispute that all action binds, on the other hand it is equally true that all living beings have to do some work, whether they will or no. Here all activity, whether mental or physical, is to be included in the term action. Then how is one to be free from the bondage of action, even though he may be acting[76]? The manner in which the *Gita* has solved the problem is, to my knowledge, unique.[77] The *Gita* says: "Do your allotted work but renounce its fruit…be detached and work…have no desire for reward, and work."

This is the unmistakable teaching of the *Gita*.[78] He who gives up action falls. He who gives up only the reward rises. But renunciation of fruit in no way means indifference to the result. In regard to every action one must know the result that is expected to follow, the meansthereto, and the capacity for it. He, who, being thus equipped, is without desire for the result, and is yet wholly engrossed in the due fulfilment of the task before him, is said to have renounced the fruits[79] of his action.

23. Again, let no one consider renunciation to mean want of fruit for the renouncer. The *Gita* reading does not warrant such a meaning. Renunciation means absence of hankering after[80] fruit. As a matter of fact, he who renounces reaps a thousandfold. The renunciation of the *Gita* is the acid test of faith. He who is ever brooding over the result often loses nerve in the performance of his duty. He becomes impatient and then gives vent to anger and begins to do unworthy things; he jumps from action to action, never remaining faithful to any. He who broods over results is like a man given to objects of senses; he is ever distracted, he says goodbye to all scruples, everything is right in his estimation and he therefore resorts to means fair and foul to attain his end.

24. From the bitter experiences of desire for fruit the author

of the *Gita* discovered the path of renunciation of fruit, and put it before the world in a most convincing manner. The common belief is that religion is always opposed to material good. "One cannot act religiously in the mercantile and such other matters. There is no place for religion in such pursuits; religion is only for attainment of salvation", we hear many wordly-wise people say. In my opinion the author of the *Gita* has dispelled this delusion. He has drawn no line of demarcation between salvation and wordly pursuits. On the contrary, he has shown that religion must rule even our wordly pursuits. I have felt that the *Gita* teaches us that what cannot be followed out in daytoday practice cannot be called religion. Thus, according to the *Gita,* all acts that are incapable of being performed without attachment are taboo. This golden rule saves mankind from many a pitfall. According to this interpretation[81], murder, lying dissoluteness and the like must[82] be regarded as sinful and therefore taboo. Man's life then becomes simple, and from that simpleness springs peace.

25. Thinking along these lines, I have felt that in trying to enforce in one's life the central teaching of the *Gita,* one is bound to follow truth and ahimsa. When there is no desire for fruit, there is no temptation for untruth or *himsa.* Take any instance of untruth or violence, and it will be found that at its[83] back was the desire to attain the cherished end. But it may be freely admitted that the *Gita* was not written to establish *ahimsa.* It was an accepted and primary duty even before the *Gita* age.[84] The *Gita* had to deliver the message of renunciation of fruit. This is clearly brought out as early as the second chapter.

26. But if the *Gita* believed in ahimsa or its was[85] included in desirelessness, why did the author take a warlike illustration? When the *Gita* was written, although people believed in ahimsa, wars were not only not taboo, but nobody observed the contradiction between them and ahimsa.

27. In assessing the implications of renunciation of fruit, we are not required to probe the mind of the author of the *Gita* as to his limitations of ahimsa and the like.[86] Because a poet puts a particular truth before the world, it does not necessarily follow that he has known or worked out all its great consequences, or that having done so, he is able always to express them fully.[87] In this perhaps lies the greatness of the poem and the poet.[88] A poet's meaning is limitless. Like man, the meaning of great

writings suffers evolution. On examining the history of languages, we notice that the meaning of important words has changed or expanded. This is true of the *Gita*.

The author has himself extended the meanings of some of the current words.[89] We are able to discover this even on a superficial examination.[90] It is possible that, in the age prior to that of the *Gita*, offering of animals in sacrifice was permissible. But there is not a trace of it in the sacrifice in the *Gita* sense. In the *Gita* continuous concentration on God is the king of sacrifices. The third chapter seems to show that sacrifice chiefly means body-labour for service. The third and the fourth chapters read together will give us other meanings for sacrifice, but never animal-sacrifice. Similarly has the meaning of the word sannyasa undergone, in the *Gita*, a transformation. The sannyasa of the *Gita* will not tolerate complete cessation of all activity. The sannyasa of the *Gita* is all work and yet no work. Thus the author of the *Gita*, by extending meanings of words, has taught us to imitate him. Let it be granted that according to the letter of the *Gita* it is possible to say that warfare is consistent with renunciation of fruit. But after 40 years' unremitting endeavour fully to enforce the teaching of the *Gita* in my own life, I have, in all humility, felt that perfect renunciation is impossible without perfect observance of ahimsa in every shape and form.[91]

28. The *Gita* is not an aphoristic work; it is a great religious poem. The deeper you dive into it, the richer the meanings you get. It being meant for the people at large, there is pleasing repetition[92].[93] With every age the important words will carry new and expanding meanings. But its central teaching will never vary. The seeker is at liberty to extract from this treasure any meaning he likes so as to enable him to enforce in his life the central teaching.

29. Nor is the *Gita* a collection of Do's and Don'ts. What is lawful for one may be unlawful for another. What may be permissible at one time, or in one place, may not be so at another time, and in another place.[94] Desire for fruit is the only universal prohibition. Desirelessness is obligatory.

30. The *Gita* has sung the praises of knowledge[95], but is is beyond the mere intellect; it is essentially addressed to the heart and capable of being understood by the heart. Therefore the *Gita* is not for those who have faith. The author makes Krishna say:[96]

"Do not entrust this treasure to him who is without sacrifice, without devotion, without the desire for this teaching[97] and who denies Me. On the other hand, those who will give this precious treasure to My devotees will, by the fact of this service, assuredly reach Me.[98] And those who, being free from malice, will with faith absorb this teaching, shall[99], having attained freedom, live where people of true merit go[100] after death."

DISCOURSE I

No knowledge is to be found without seeking, no tranquility without travail no happiness except through tribulation. Every seeker has, at one time or another, to pass through a conflict of duties, a heart-churning.

Dhritarashtra said:

1. Tell me, O Sanjaya, what my sons and Pandu's assembled, on battle intent, did on the field of Kuru, the field of duty. The human body is the battle-field where the internal duel between Right and Wrong goes on. Therefore, it is capable of being turned into the gateway to Freedom. It is born in sin and becomes the seed-bed of sin. Hence it is also called the field of Kuru. The Kauravas represent the forces of Evil, the Pandavas the forces of Good. Who is there that has not experienced the daily conflict within himself between the forces of Evil and the forces of Good?[101]

DISCOURSE II

By reason of delusion, man takes wrong to be right. By reason of delusion was Arjuna led to make a difference between kinsmen and non-kinsmen. To demonstrate that this is a vain distinction, Lord Krishna distinguishes between body (not-self) and atman (self) and shows that whilst bodies are impermanent and several, atman is permanent and one. Effort is within man's control, not the fruit thereof. All he has to do, therefore, is to decide his course of conduct or duty on each occasion and persevere in it, unconcerned about the result. Fulfilment of one's duty in the spirit of detachment or selflessness leads to Freedom.

30. This embodied one in the body of every being is ever beyond all harm, O Bharata; thou shouldst not, therefore, grieve for anyone. Thus far Lord Krishna, by force of argument based on pure reason, has demonstrated that atman is abiding while

the physical body is fleeting, and has explained that if, under certain circumstances, the destruction of a physical body is deemed justifiable, it is delusion to imagine that the Kauravas should not be slain because they are kinsmen. Now he reminds Arjuna of the duty of a Kshatriya.

31. Again, seeing thine own duty thou shouldst not shrink from it; for there is no higher good for a Kshatriya than a righteous war.

32. Such a fight, coming unsought, as a gateway to heaven thrown open, falls only to the lot of happy Kshatriyas, O Partha.

33. But if thou wilt not fight this righteous fight, then failing in thy duty and losing thine honour though wilt incur sin.

34. The world will for ever recount the story of thy disgrace; and for a man of honour disgrace is worse than death.

35. The maharathas will think that fear made thee retire from battle; and thou wilt fall in the esteem of those very ones who have held thee high.

36. Thine enemies will deride thy prowess and speak many unspeakable words about thee. What can be more painful than that?

37. Slain, thou shalt gain heaven; victorious, thou shalt inherit the earth: therefore arise, O Kaunteya[101], determined to fight. Having declared the highest truth, viz., the immortality of the eternal *atman* and the fleeting nature of the physical body (11-30), Krishna reminds Arjuna that a Kshatriya may not flinch from a fight which comes unsought (31-32). He then (32-37) shows how the highest truth and the performance of duty incidentally coincide with expediency. Next he proceeds to foreshadow the central teaching of the *Gita* in the following *shloka*.

38. Hold alike pleasure and pain, gain and loss, victory and defeat, and gird up thy loins for the fight; so doing thou shalt not incur sin.

39. Thus have I set before thee the attitude of Knowledge; hear now the attitude of Action; resorting to this attitude thou shalt cast off the bondage of action.

41. The attitude, in this matter, springing, as it does, from fixed resolve is but one, O Kurunandana; but for those who have no fixed resolve the attitudes are many- branched and unending. When the attitude ceases to be one and undivided and becomes many and divided, it ceases to be one settled will, and is broken

up into various wills or desires between which man is tossed about.

42-44. The ignorant, revelling in the letter of the Vedas, declare that there is naught else; carnally-minded, holding heaven to be their goal, they utter swelling words which promise birth as the fruit of action and which dwell on the many and varied rites to be performed for the sake of pleasure and power; intent, as they are, on pleasure and power, their swelling words rob them of their wits, and they have no settled attitude which can be centred on the supreme goal. The Vedic ritual, as opposed to the doctrine of yoga laid down in the Gita, is alluded to here. The Vedic ritual lays down countless ceremonies and rites with a view to attaining merit and heaven. These, divorced as they are from the essence of the Vedas and short-lived in their result, are worthless.

45. The Vedas have as their domain the three *gunas*; eschew them, O Arjuna. Free thyself from the pairs of opposites, abide in eternal truth, scorn to gain or guard anything, remain the master of thy soul.

46. To the extent that a well is of use when there is a flood of water on all sides, to the same extent are all the Vedas of use to an enlightened Brahmana.

47. Action alone is thy province, never the fruits thereof; let not thy motive be the fruit of action, nor shouldst thou desire to avoid action.

48. Act thou, O Dhananjaya, without attachment, steadfast in Yoga, evenminded in success and failure. Even-mindedness is yoga.

49. For action, O Dhananjaya, is far inferior to unattached action; seek refuge in the attitude of detachment. Pitiable are those who make fruit their motive.

50. Here in this world a man gifted with that attitude of detachment escapes the fruit of both good and evil deeds. Gird thyself up for yoga, therefore. Yoga is skill in action.

Arjuna said:

54. What, O Keshava, is the mark of the man whose understanding is secure, whose mind is fixed in concentration? How does he talk? How sit? How move?

The Lord said:

55. When a man puts away, O Partha, all the cravings that

arise in the mind and finds comfort for himself only from atman, then is he called the man of secure understanding. To find comfort for oneself from *atman* means to look to the spirit within for spiritual comfort, not to outside objects which in their very nature must give pleasure as well as pain. Spiritual comfort or bliss must be distinguished from pleasure or happiness. The pleasure I may derive from the possession of wealth, for instance, is delusive; real spiritual comfort or bliss can be attained only if I rise superior to every temptation even though troubled by the pangs of poverty and hunger.

59. When a man starves his senses,[102] the objects of those senses disappear from him, but not the yearning for them; the yearning too departs when he beholds the Supreme. The *shloka* does not rule out fasting and other forms of selfrestraint, but indicates their limitations. These restraints are needed for subduing the desire for sense-objects, which however is rooted out only when one has a vision of the Supreme. The higher yearning conquers all the lower yearnings.

60. For, in spite of the wise man's endeavour, O Kaunteya, the unruly senses distract his mind perforce.

61. Holding all these in check, the yogi should sit intent on Me; for he whose senses are under control is secure of understanding. This means that without devotion and the consequent grace of God, man's endeavour is vain.

62. In a man brooding on objects of the senses, attachment to them springs up; attachment begets craving and craving begets wrath. Craving cannot but lead to resentment, for it is unending and unsatisfied.

63. Wrath breeds stupefaction, stupefaction leads to loss of memory, loss of memory ruins the reason, and the ruin of reason spells utter destruction.

64. But the disciplined soul, moving among sense-objects with the senses weaned from likes and dislikes and brought under the control of *atman*, attains peace of mind.

66. The undisciplined man has neither understanding nor devotion; for him who has no devotion there is no peace, and for him who has no peace, whence happiness?

69. When it is night for all other beings, the disciplined soul is awake; when all other beings are awake, it is night for the seeing ascetic. This verse indicates the divergent paths of the

disciplined ascetic and the sensual man. Whereas the ascetic is dead to the things of the world and lives in God, the sensual man is alive only to the things of the world and dead to the things of the spirit.

70. He in whom all longings subside, even as the waters subside in the ocean which, though ever being filled by them, never overflows - that man finds peace; not he who cherishes longing.

71. The man who sheds all longing and moves without concern, free from the sense of 'I' and 'Mine' - he attains peace.

72. This is the state, O Partha, of the man who rests in Brahman; having attained to it, he is not deluded. He who abides in this state even at the hour of death passes into oneness with Brahman.

DISCOURSE III

This discourse may be said to be the key to the essence of the Gita. It makes absolutely clear the spirit and the nature of right action and shows how true knowledge must express itself in acts of selfless *service*.

Arjuna said:

1. If, O Janardana, thou holdest that the attitude of detachment is superior to action, then why, O Keshava, dost thou urge me to dreadful action?

2. Thou dost seem to confuse my understanding with perplexing speech; tell me, therefore, in no uncertain voice, that alone whereby I may attain salvation. Arjuna is sole perplexed, for whilst on the one hand he is rebuked for his faint-heartedness, on the other he seems to be advised to refrain from action (II. 49-50). But this, in reality, is not the case as the following *shlokas* will show.

The Lord said:

3. I have spoken before, O sinless one, of two attitudes in this world - the Samkhyas', that of jnanayoga and the yogis', that of karmayoga.

4. Never does man enjoy freedom from action by not undertaking action, nor does he attain that freedom by mere renunciation of action. 'Freedom from action' is freedom from the bondage of acton.[103] This freedom is not to be gained by

cessation of all activity, apart from the fact that this cessation is in the very nature of things impossible (see following *shloka*). How then may it be gained? The following *shlokas* will explain:

5. For none ever remains inactive even for a moment; for all are compelled to action by the *gunas* inherent in *prakriti*.

6. He who curbs the organs of action but allows the mind to dwell on the sense-objects - such a one, wholly deluded, is called a hypocrite. The man who curbs his tongue but mentally swears at another is a hypocrite. But that does not mean that free rein should be given to the organs of action so long as the mind cannot be brought under control. Self-imposed physical restraint is a condition precedent to mental restraint. Physical restraint should be entirely self-imposed and not super-imposed from outside, e.g., by fear. The hypocrite who is held up to contempt here is not the humble aspirant after selfrestraint. The *shloka* has reference to the man who curbs the body because he cannot help it whilst indulging the mind, and who would indulge the body too if he possibly could. The next *shloka* puts the thing conversely.

7. But he, O Arjuna, who keeping all the senses under control of the mind, engages the organs in karmayoga, without attachment...than man excels. The mind and body should be made to accord well. Even with the mind kept in control, the body will be active in one way or another. But he whose mind is truly restrained, will, for instance close his ears to foul talk and open them only to listen to the priase of God or of good men. He will have no relish for sensual pleasures and will keep himself occupied with such activity as ennobles the soul. That is the path of action. Karmayoga is the yoga (means) which will deliver the self from the bondage of the body, and in it there is no room for self-indulgence.

8. Do thou they allotted task; for action is superior to inaction; with inaction even life's normal course is not possible.

9. This world of men suffers bondage from all action save that which is done for the sake of sacrifice; to this end, O Kaunteya, perform action without attachment. 'Action for the sake of sacrifice' means acts of selfless service dedicated to God.

10. Together with sacrifice did the Lord of beings create, of old, mankind, declaring: "By this shall ye increase; may this be to you the giver of all your desires."

11. "With this may you cherish the gods and may the gods cherish you; thus cherishing one another may you attain the highest good.

12. "Cherished with sacrifice, the gods will bestow on you the desired boons." he who enjoys their gifts without rendering aught unto them is verily a thief. "Gods" in *shlokas* 11 and 12 must be taken to mean the whole creation of God. The service of all created beings is the service of the gods and the same is sacrifice.

22. For me, O Partha, there is naught to do in the three worlds, nothing worth gaining that I have not gained; yet I am ever in action. An objection is sometimes raised that God being impersonal is not likely to perform any physical activity; at best He may be supposed to act mentally. This is not correct. For the unceasing movement of the sun, the moon, the earth, etc., signifies God in action.This is not mental but physical activity. Though God is without form and impersonal He acts as though He had form and body. Hence though he is ever in action, He is free from action, unaffected by action. What must be borne in mind is that just as all Nature's movements and processes are mechanical and yet guided by Divine Intelligence or Will, even so man must reduce his daily conduct to mechanical regularity and precision, but he must do so intelligently. Man's merit lies in observing divine guidance at the back of these processes and in an intelligent imitation of it rather than in emphasizing the mechanical nature thereof and reducing himself to an automation. One has but to withdraw the self, withdraw attachment to fruit from all action, and then not only mechanical precision but security from all wear and tear will be ensured. Acting thus man remains fresh until the end of his days. His body will perish in due course, but his soul will remain evergreen without a crease or a wrinkle.

27. All action is entirely done by the *gunas* of *prakriti*. Man, deluded by the sense of 'I', thinks 'I am the doer'.

28. But he, O Mahabahu, who understands the truth of the various *gunas* and their various activities, knows that it is the *gunas* that operate on the *gunas*; he does not claim to be the doer. As breathing, winking and similar processes are automatic and man claims no agency for them, he being conscious of the processes only when disease or similar cause arrests them, in a similar manner all his activities should be automatic, without

his arrogating to himself the agency or responsibility thereof. A man of Charity does not even know that he is doing charitable acts, it is his nature to do so, he cannot help it. This detachment can only come from tireless endeavour and God's grace.

30. Cast all thy acts on Me, with thy mind fixed on the indwelling *atman*, and without any thought of fruit, or sense of 'mine' shake off thy fever and fight! He who knows the *atman* inhabiting the body and realizes Him to be a part of the supreme *atman* will dedicate everything to Him, even as a faithful servant acts as a mere shadow of his master and dedicates to him all that he does. For the master is the real doer, the servant but the instrument.

33. Even a man of knowledge acts according to his nature; all creatures follow their nature; what then will constraint avail? This does not run counter to the teaching in II. 61 and II. 68 Self-restraint is the means of salvation (VI. 35, XIII. 7). Man's energies should be bent towards achieving complete self-restraint until the end of his days. But if he does not succeed, neither will constraint help him. The *shloka* does not rule out restraint but explains that nature prevails. he who justifies himself saying, 'I cannot do this, it is not in my nature,' misreads the *shloka*. True, we do not know our nature, but habit is not nature. Progress, not decline, ascent, not descent, is the nature of the soul, and therefore every threatened decline or descent ought to be resisted. The next verse makes this abundantly clear.

34. Each sense has its settled likes and dislikes towards its objects; man should not come under the sway of these, for they are his besetters. Hearing, for instance,is the object of the ears which may be inclined to hear something and disinclined to hear something else. Man may not allow himself to be swayed by these likes and dislikes, but must decide for himself what is conducive to his growth, his ultimate end being to reach the state beyond happiness and misery.

35. Better one's own duty, bereft of merit, than another's well-performed; better is death in the discharge of one's duty; another's duty is fraught with danger. One man's duty may be to serve the community by working as a sweeper, another's may be to work as an accountant. An accountant's work may be more inviting, but that need not draw the sweeper away from his work. Should he allow himself to be drawn away he would himself be lost and put the community into danger. Before God the work

of man will be judged by the spirit in which it is done, not by the nature of the work which makes no difference whatsoever. Whoever acts in a spirit of dedication fits himself for salvation.

40. The senses, the mind and the reason are said to be its seat; by means of these it obscures knowledge and stupefies man. When Lust seizes the senses, the mind is corrupted, discrimination is obscured and reason ruined. See II. 62-64.

41. Therefore, O Bharatarshabha, bridle thou first the senses and then rid thyself of this sinner, the destroyer of knowledge and discrimination.

42. Subtle, they say, are the senses; subtler than the senses is the mind; subtler than the mind is the reason; but subtler even than the reason is He.

43.Thus realizing Him to be subtler than the reason, and controlling the self by the Self(*atman*), destroy, O Mahabahu, this enemy - Lust, so hard to overcome. When man realizes Him, his mind will be under His control, not swayed by the senses. And when the mind is conquered, what power has Lust? It is indeed a subtle enemy, but when once the senses, the mind and the reason are under the control of the subtle-most Self, Lust is extinguished.

DISCOURSE IV

This discourse further explains the subject-matter of the third and describes the various kinds of sacrifice.

6. Though unborn and inexhaustible in My essence, though Lord of all beings, yet assuming control over My Nature, I come into being by My mysterious power.[104]

7. For whenever Right declines and Wrong prevails, then O Bharata, I come to birth.

8. To save the righteous, to destroy the wicked, and to re-establish Right I am born from age to age. Here is comfort for the faithful and affirmation of the truth that Right ever prevails. An eternal conflict between Right and Wrong goes on. Sometimes the latter seems to get the upper hand, but it is Right which ultimately prevails. The good are never destroyed, for Right...which is Truth...cannot perish; the wicked are destroyed because Wrong has no independent existence. Knowing this let man cease to arrogate to himself authorship and eschew untruth, violence and evil. Inscrutable Providence...the unique power of

the Lord...is ever at work. This in fact is avatar, incarnation. Strictly speaking there can be no birth for God.

9. He who knows the secret of this My divine birth and action is not born again, after leaving the body; he comes to Me, O Arjuna. For when a man is secure in the faith that Right always prevails, he never swerves therefrom, pursuing to the bitterest end and against serious odds, and as no part of the effort proceeds from his ego, but all is dedicated to Him, being ever one with Him, he is released from birth and death.

10. Freed from passion, fear and wrath, filled full with Me, relying on Me, and refined by the fiery ordeal of knowledge, many have become one with Me.

11. In whatever way men resort to Me, even so do I render to them. In every way, O Partha, the path men follow is Mine. That is, the whole world is under His ordinance. No one may break God's law with impunity. As we sow, so shall we reap. This law operates inexorably without fear or favour.

12. Those who desire their actions to bear fruit worship the gods here; for in this world of men the fruit of action is quickly obtainable. Gods, as indicated before, must not be taken to mean the heavenly beings of tradition, but whatever reflects the divine. In that sense man is also a god. Steam, electricity and the other great forces of Nature are all gods. Propitiation of these forces quickly bears fruit, as we well know, but it is short-lived. It fails to bring comfort to the soul and it certainly does not take one even a short step towards salvation.

13. The order of the four *varnas* was created by Me according to the different *gunas* and karma of each; yet know that though, therefore, author thereof being changeless I am not the author.

14. Actions do not affect Me, nor am I concerned with the fruits thereof. He who recognizes Me as such is not bound by actions. For man has thus before him the supreme example of One who though in action is not the Doer thereof. And when we are but instruments in His hands, where then is the room for arrogating responsibility for action?

15. Knowing this did men of old, desirous of Freedom, perform action; do thou, then just as they did - the men of old in days gone by.

16. 'What is action? What inaction?' - Here even the wise are perplexed. I will then expound to thee that action knowing which thou shalt be saved from evil.

17. For it is meet to know the meaning of action of forbidden action, as also of inaction. Impenetrable is the secret of action.[105]

18. Who sees inaction in action and action in inaction, he is enlightened among men, he is a yogi, he has done all he need do. The 'action' of him who, though ever active, does not claim to be the doer, is inaction, and the 'inaction', of him who, though outwardly avoiding action, is always building castles in his own mind, is action. The enlightened man who has grasped the secret of action knows that no action proceeds from him, all proceeds from God and hence he selflessly remains absorbed in action. He is the true yogi.

The man who acts self-fully misses the secret of action and cannot distinguish between Right and Wrong. The soul's natural progress is towards selflessness and purity and one might, therefore, say that the man who strays from the path of purity strays from selflessness. All actions of the selfless man are naturally pure.

19. He whose every undertaking is free from desire and selfish purpose and he who has burnt all his actions in the fire of knowledge - such a one the wise call a pundit.

20. He who has renounced attachment to the fruit of action, who is ever content, and free from all dependence - he, though immersed in action, yet acts not.

That is, action does not bind him.

21. Expecting naught, holding his mind and body in check, putting away every possession, and going through action only in the body, he incurs no stain. The purest act, if tainted by 'self', binds. But when it is done in a spirit of dedication, it ceases to bind. When 'self' has completely subsided, it is only the body that works. For instance, in the case of a man who is asleep his body alone is working. A prisoner doing his prison task has surrendered his body to the prison authorities and only his body, therefore, works. Similarly, he who has voluntarily made himself God's prisoner, does nothing himself. His body mechanically acts, the doer is God, not he. He has reduced himself to nothingness.

22. Content with whatever chance may bring, rid of the pairs of opposites, free from ill will, even minded in success and failure, he is not bound though he acts.

23. Of the free soul who has shed all attachment, whose mind is firmly grounded in knowledge, who acts only for sacrifice,

all karma is extinguished.

24. The offering of sacrifice is Brahman; the oblation is Brahman; it is offered by Brahman in the fire that is Brahman; thus he whose mind is fixed on acts dedicated to Brahman must needs pass on to Brahman.

25. Some yogis perform sacrifice in the form of worship of the gods, others offer sacrifice of sacrifice itself in the fire that is Brahman.

26. Some offer as sacrifice the sense of hearing and the other senses in the fires[106] of restraint; others sacrifice sound and the other objects of sense in the fires of the senses. The restraint of the senses...hearing and others...is one thing; and directing them only to legitimate objects, e.g., listening to hymns in the praise of God, is another, although ultimately both amount to the same things.

27. Others again sacrifice all the activities of the senses and of the vital energy in the yogic fire of self-control kindled by knowledge. That is to say, they lose themselves in the contemplation of the Supreme.

28. Some sacrifice with material gifts; with austerities; with yoga; some with the acquiring and some with the imparting of knowledge. All these are sacrifices of sters vows and serious endeavour.

29. Others absorbed in the practice of the control of the vital energy sacrifice the outward in the inward and the inward in the outward, or check the flow of both the inward and the outward vital airs. The reference here is to the three kinds of practices of the control of vital energy...*puraka*, *rechaka* and *kumbhaka*.[107]

30. Yet others, abstemious in food, sacrifice one form of vital energy in another. All these know what sacrifice is and purge themselves of all impurities by sacrifice.

31. Those who partake of the residue of sacrifice...call *amrita* (ambrosia)...attain to everlasting Brahman. Even this world is not for a nonsacrificer; how then the next, O Kurusattama?

32. Even so various sacrifices have been described in the Vedas; know them all to proceed from action; knowing this thou shalt be released. Action here means mental, physical and spiritual action. No sacrifice is possible without this triple action and no salvation without sacrifice. To know this and to put the knowledge into practice is to know the secret of sacrifice. In

fine, unless man uses all his physical, mental and spiritual gifts in the service of mankind, he is a thief, unfit for Freedom. He who uses his intellect only and spares his body is not a full sacrificer. Unless the mind and the body and the soul are made to work in unison, they cannot be adequately used for the service of mankind. Physical, mental and spritual purity is essential for their harmonious working. Therefore man should concentrate on developing, purifying, and turning to the best use all his faculties.

33. Knowledge-sacrifice is better, O Parantapa, than material sacrifice, for all action which does not bind finds its consummation in Knowledge (*jnana*). Who does not know that works of charity performed without knowledge often result in great harm? Unless every act, however noble its motive, is informed with knowledge, it lacks perfection. Hence the complete fulfilment of all action is in knowledge.

34. The masters of knowledge who have seen the truth will impart to thee this knowledge; learn it through humble homage and service and by repeated questioning. The three conditions of knowledge...homage, repeated questioningand service deserve to be carefully borne in mind in this age. Homage or obeisance means humility and service is a necessary accompaniment, else it would be mock homage. Repeated questioning is equally essential, for without a keen spirit of inquiry, there is no knowledge. All this presupposes devotion to and faith in the person approached. There can be no humility, much less service, without faith.

35. When thou hast gained this knowledge, O Pandava, thou shalt not again fall into such error; by virtue of it thou shalt see all beings without exception in thyself and thus in Me. The adage *'Yatha pinde tatha brahmande'* (...'as with the self so with the universe') means the same thing. He who has attained selfrealization sees no difference between himself and others.

36. Even though thou be the most sinful of sinners, thou shalt cross the ocean of sin by the boat of knowledge.

37. As a blazing fire turns its fuel to ashes, O Arjuna, even so the fire of Knowledge turns all actions to ashes.

38. There is nothing in this world so purifying as Knowledge. He who is perfected by yoga finds it in himself in the fulness of time.

39. It is the man of faith who gains knowledge...the man who is intent on it and who has mastery over his senses; having gained knowledge, he comes ere long to the supreme peace.

40. But the man of doubt, without knowledge and without faith, is lost; for him who is given to doubt there is neither this world nor that beyond, nor happiness.

41. He who has renounced all action by means of yog, who has severed all doubt by means of knowledge...him self-possessed, no actions bind, O Dhananjaya!

42. Therefore, with the sword of self-realization sever thou this doubt bred of ignorance, which has crept into thy heart! Betake thyself to yoga and arise, O Bhrata!

DISCOURSE V

This discourse is devoted to showing that renunciation of action as such is impossible without the discipline of selfless action and that both are ultimately one.

Arjuna said:

1. Thou laudest renunciation of actions, O Krishna, whilst at the same time thou laudest performance of action; tell me for a certainty which is the better.

The Lord said:

2. Renunciation and performance of action both lead to salvation; but of the two karmayoga (performance) is better than sannyasa (renunciation).

3. Him one should know as ever renouncing who has no dislikes and likes; for he who is free from the pairs of opposites is easily released from bondage. That is, not renunciation of action but of attachment to the pairs, determines true renuncation. A man who is always in action may be a good sannyasi (renouncer) and another who may be doing no work well be a hyprocite. See III. 6.

4. It is the ignorant who speak of samkhya and yoga as different, not so those who have knowledge. He who is rightly established even in one wins to the fruit of both. The yogi engorssed in samkhya (knowledge) lives even in thought for the good of the world and attains the fruit of karmayoga by the sheer power of his thought. The karmyogi ever engorssed in unattached action naturally enjoys the peace of the jnanayogi.

8. The yogi who has seen the Truth knows that it is not he that acts whilst seeing, hearing, touching, smelling, eating, walking, sleeping or breathing,

9. Talking, letting go, holding fast, opening or closing eyes...in the conviction that it is the senses that are moving in their respective spheres. So long as 'self' endures, this detachment cannot be achieved. A sensual man therefore may not shelter himself under the pretence that it is not he but his senses that are acting. Such a mischievous interpretation betrays a gross ignorance of the *Gita* and right conduct. The next *shloka* makes this clear.

10. He who dedicates his actions to Brahman and performs them without attachment is not smeared by sin, as the lotus-leaf by water.

13. Renouncing with the mind all actions, the dweller in the body, who is master of himself, rests happily in his city of nine gates, neither doing nor getting anything done. The principal gates of the body are the two eyes, the two nostrils, the two ears, the mouth, and the two organs of excretion...though really speaking the countless pores of the skin are no less gates. If the gate-keeper always remains on the alert and performs his task, letting in or out only the objects that deserve ingress or egress, then of him it can truly be said that he has no part in the ingress or egress but that he is a passive witness. He thus does nothing nor gets anything done.

14. The Lord creates neither agency nor action for the world; neither does He connect action with its fruit. It is nature that is at work. God is no doer. The inexorable law of karma prevails, and in the very fulfilment of the law...giving everyone his deserts, making everyone reap what he sows...lies God's abounding mercy and justice. In undiluted justice is mercy. Mercy which is inconsistent with justice is not mercy but its opposite. But man is not a judge knowing past, present and future. So for him the law is reversed and mercy or forgiveness is the purest justice. Being himself ever liable to be judged, he must accord to others what he would accord to himself, viz., forgiveness. Only by cultivating the spirit of forgiveness can he reach the state of a yogi, whom no actions bind, the man of evenmindedness, the man skilled in action.

15. The Lord does not take upon Himself anyone's vice or virtue; it is ignorance that veils knowledge and deludes all

creatures. The delusion lies in man arrogating to himself the authorship of action and then attributing to God the consequence thereof... punishment or reward as the case may be.

18. The men of self-realization look with an equal eye on a Brahmana possessed of learning and humility, a cow, an elephant, a dog and even a dogeater. That is to say, they serve every one of them alike, according to the needs of each. Treating a Brahmana and *shwapaka* (dog-eater) alike means that the wise man will suck the poison off a snake-bitten *shwapaka* with as much eagerness and readiness as he would from a snake-bitten Brahmana.

19. In this very body they have conquered the round of birth and death, whose mind is anchored in sameness; for perfect Brahman is same to all, therefore in Brahman they rest. As a man thinks, so he becomes, and therefore those whose minds are bent on being the same to all achieve that sameness and become one with Brahman.

20. He whose understanding is secure, who is undeluded, who knows Brahman and who rests in Brahman, will neither be glad to get what is pleasant, nor said to get what is unpleasant.

21. He who has detached himself from contacts without, finds bliss in *atman;* having achieved union with Brahman he enjoys eternal bliss. He who has weaned himself from outward objects to the inner *atman* is fitted for union with Brahman and the highest bliss. To withdraw oneself from contacts without and to bask in the sunshine of union with Brahman are two aspects of the same state, two sides of the same coin.

23. The man who is able even here on earth, ere he is released from the body, to hold out against the flood-tide of lust and wrath...he is a yogi, he is happy. As a corpse has no likes and dislikes, no sensibility to pleasure and pain, even so he who though alive is dead to these, he truly lives, he is truly happy.

27-28. That ascetic is ever free...who, having shut out the outward sensecontacts, sits with his gaze fixed between the brows, outward and inward breathing in the nostrils made equal; his senses, mind, and reason held in check, rid of longing, fear and wrath; and intent on Freedom.

These *shlokas* refer to some of the yogic practices laid down in the *Yoga-sutras*. A word of caution is necessary regarding these practices. They serve for the yogi the same purpose as athletics and gymnastics do for the *bhogi* (who pursues worldly pleasures). His physical exercises help the latter to keep his senses of enjoyment in full vigour. The yogic practices help the yogi to keep his body in condition and his senses in subjection. Men versed in these practices are rare in these days, and few of these turn them to good account. He who has achieved the preliminary stage on the path of self-discipline, he who has a passion for Freedom, and who having rid himself of the pairs of opposites has conquered fear, would do well to go in for these practices which will surely help him. It is such a disciplined man alone who can, through these practices, render his body a holy temple of God. Purity both of the mind and body is a *sine qua non,* without which these processes are likely, in the first instance, to lead a man astray and then drive him deeper into the slough of delusion. That this has been the result in some cases many know from actual experience.

That is why that prince of yogis, Patanjali, gave the first place to *yamas (cardinal vows)* and *niyamas* (casual vows) and held as eligible for yogic practices only those who have gone through the preliminary discipline.

The five cardinal vows are: non-violence, truth, non-stealing, celibacy, non-possession. The five casual vows are: bodily purity, contentment, the study of the scriptures, austerity, and meditation of God.

29. Knowing Me as the Acceptor of sacrifice and austerity, the great Lord of all the worlds, the Friend of all creation, the yogi attains to peace. This *shloka* may appear to be in conflict with *shlokas* 14 and 15 of this discourse and similar ones in other discourses. It is not really so. Almighty God is Doer and non-Doer, Enjoyer and non-Enjoyer, both. He is indescribable, beyond the power of human speech. Man somehow strives to have a glimpse of Him and in so doing invests Him with diverse and even contradictory attributes.[108]

DISCOURSE VI

This discourse deals with some of the means for the accomplishment of yoga or the discipline of the mind and its activities.

The Lord said:

1. He who performs all obligatory action, without depending

on the fruit thereof, is a sannyasi and a yogi... not the man who neglects the sacrificial fire nor he who neglects action. Fire here may be taken to mean all possible instruments of action. Fire was needed when sacrifices used to be performed with its help. Assuming that spinning were a means of universal service in this age, a man by neglecting the spinning-wheel would not become a sannyasi.

2. What is called sannyasa, know thou to be, yoga, O Pandava; for none can become a yogi who has not renounced selfish purpose.

3. For the man who seeks to scale the heights of yoga, action is said to be the means; for the same man, when he has scaled those heights, repose is said to be the means. He who has purged himself of all impurities and who has achieved even-mindedness will easily achieve self-realization. But this does not mean that he who has scaled the heights of yoga will disdain to work for the guidance of the world. On the contrary that work will be to him not only as the breath of his nostrils, but also as natural to him as breathing. He will do so by the sheer force of his will. See V.4

4. When a man is not attached either to the objects of sense or to actions and sheds all selfish purpose, then he is said to have scaled the heights of yoga.

5. By one's self should one raise oneself, and not allow oneself to fall; for *atman* (self) alone is the friend of self, and self alone is self's foe.

6. His Self alone is friend, who has conquered himself by his Self; but to him who has not conquered himself and is thus inimical to himself, even his Self behaves as foe.[109]

14. Tranquil in spirit, free from fear, steadfast in the vow of *brahmacharya,* holding his mind in control, the yogi should sit, with all his thoughts on Me, absorbed in Me. *Brahmacharya* (usually translated 'celibacy') means not only sexual continence but observance of all the cardinal vows for the attainment of Brahman.

15. The yogi, who ever thus, with mind controlled, unites himself to *atman,* wins the peace which culminates in *Nirvana,* the peace that is in Me.

29. The man equipped with yoga looks on all with an impartial eye, seeing *atman* in all beings and all beings in *atman.*

30. He who sees Me everywhere and everything in Me, never vanishes from Me nor I from him.

31. The yogi who, anchored in unity, worships Me abiding in all beings, lives and moves in Me, no matter how he live and move. So long as 'self' subsists, the Supreme Self is absent; when 'self' is extinguished, the Supreme Self is seen everywhere. Also see note on XIII. 23.

46. The yogi is deemed higher than the man of austerities; he is deemed also higher than the man of knowledge; higher is he than the man engrossed in ritual; therefore be though a yogi, O Arjuna! The man of austerities means the man practising them with an eye to fruit; the man of knowledge does not mean the *jnani* who has realized the truth, but a man of learning.

47. And among all yogis, he who worships Me with faith, his inmost self all rapt in Me, is deemed by Me to be the best yogi.

DISCOURSE VII

With this discourse begins an exposition of the nature of Reality and the secret of devotion.

The Lord said :

1. Hear, O Partha, how, with thy mind rivetted on Me, by practising yoga and making Me the sold refuge, thou shalt, without doubt, know Me fully.

4. Earth, Water, Fire, Air, Ether, Mind, Reason and Ego...thus eight fold is my *prakriti* divided. This eightfold *prakriti* is substantially the same as the field described in XIII.5 and the perishable Being in XV. 16.

5. This is My lower aspect; but know thou My other aspect, the higher...which is *jiwa* (the Vital Essence) by which,O Mahabahu, this world is sustained.

6. Know that these two compose the source from which all beings spring; I am the origin and end of the entire universe.

12. Know that all the manifestations of the three *gunas, sattva, rajas, and tamas,* proceed from none but Me; yet I am not in them, they are in Me. God is not dependent on them, they are dependent on Him. Without Him those various manifestations would be impossible.

13. Befogged by these manifestations of the three *gunas,* the

entire world fails to recognize Me, the Imperishable, as transcending them.

14. For this My divine delusive mysetry made up of the three *gunas* is hard to pierce; but those who make Me their sole refuge pierce the veil.

25. Veiled by the delusive mystery created by My unique power, I am not manifest to all; this bewildered world does not recognize Me, birthless and changeless. Having the power to create this world of sense and yet unaffected by it, He is described as having unique power.

29. Those who endeavour for freedom from age and death by taking refuge in Me, know in full that Brahman, *adhyatma* and all karma.

30. Those who know Me, including *adhibhuta, adhidaiva, adhiyajna,* possessed of even-mindedness, they know Me even at the time of passing away. The terms in italics are defined in the next discourse the subject of which is indicated in 29-30. The sense is that every nook and cranny of the universe is filled with Brahman, that He is the sole Agent of all action, and that the man who imbued with this knowledge and faith completely surrenders himself to Him, become one with Him at the time of passing hence. All his desires are extinguished in his vision of Him and he wins his freedom.

DISCOURSE VIII

The nature of the Supreme is further expounded in this discourse.

Arjuna said:

1. What is that Brahman? What is *adhyatma?* What karma, O Purushottama? What is called *adhibuta?* And what *adhidaiva?*

2. And who here in this body is *adhiyajna* and how? And how at the time of death art Thou to be known by the self-controlled?

The Lord said:

3. The Supreme, the Imperishable is Brahman; its manifestation is *adhyatma;* the creative process whereby all beings are created is called karma.

4. *Adhibhuta* is My perishable form; *adhidaiva* is the individual self in that form; and O best among the embodied, *adhiyajna* am I in this body, purified by sacrifice. That is, from the

Imperishable Unmanifest down to the perishable atom everything in the universe is the Supreme and an expression of the Supreme. Why then should mortal man arrogate to himself authorship of anything rather than do His bidding and dedicate all action to Him?[110]

5. And he who, at the last hour remembering Me only, departs leaving the body, enters into Me; of that there is no doubt.

6. Or whatever form a man continually contemplates, that same he remembers in the hour of death, and to that very form he goes, O Kaunteya.

7. Therefore at all times remember Me and fight on; thy mind and reason thus on Me fixed thou shalt surely come to Me.[111]

8. With thought steadied by constant practice, and wandering nowhere, he who meditates on the Supreme Celestial Being, O Partha, goes to Him.

17. Those men indeed know what is Day and what is Night, who know that Brahma's day lasts a thousand *yugas* and that his night too is a thousand *yugas* long. That is to say, our day and night of a dozen hours each are less than the infinitesimal fraction of a moment in that vast cycle of time. Pleasures pursued during these incalculably small moments are asillusory as a mirage. Rather than waste these brief moments, we should devote them to serving God through service of mankind. On the other hand, our time is such a small drop in the ocean of eternity that if we fail of our object here, viz., self-realization, we need not despair. We should bide our time.

18. At the coming of Day all the manifest spring forth from the Unmanifest, and at the coming of Night they are dissolved into that same Unmanifest. Knowing this too, man should understand that he has very little power over things. The round of birth and death is ceaseless.

23. Now I will tell thee, Bharatarshabha, the conditions which determine the exemption from return, as also the return, of yogis after they pass away hence.

24. Fire. Light, Day, the Bright Fortnight, the six months of the Northern Solstice…through these departing men knowing Brahman go to Brahman.

25. Smoke, Night, the Dark Fortnight, the six months of the Southern Solstice… therethrough the yogi attains to the lunar light and thence returns.

I do not understand the meaning of these two *shlokas*. They do not seem to me to be consistent with the teaching of the *Gita*. The *Gita* teaches that he whose heart is meek with devotion, who is devoted to unattached action and has seen the Truth must win salvation, no matter when he dies. These *shlokas* seem to run counter to this. They may perhaps be stretched to mean broadly that a man of sacrifice, a man of light, a man who has known Brahman finds release from birth if he retains that enlightenment at the time of death, and that on the contrary the man who has none of these attributes goes to the world of the moon...not at all lasting...and returns to birth. The moon, after all, shines with borrowed light!

26. These two paths...bright and dark...are deemed to be the eternal paths of the world; by the one a man goes to return not, by the other he returns again. The bright one may be taken to mean the path of knowledge and the dark one that of ignorance.

27. The yogi knowing these two paths falls not into delusion, O Partha; therefore, at all times, O Arjuna, remain steadfast in yoga. 'Will not fall into delusion' means that he who knows the two paths and has known the secret of even-mindedness will not take the path of ignorance.

28. Whatever fruit of good deeds is laid down as accruing from (a study of) the Vedas, from sacrifices, austerities, and acts of charity...all that the yogi transcends, on knowing this, and reaches the Supreme and Primal Abode. He who has achieved even-mindedness by dint of devotion, knowledge and service not only obtains the fruit of all his good actions, but also wins salvation.

DISCOURSE IX

This discourse reveals the glory of devotion.

4. By Me, unmanifest in form this whole world is pervaded; all beings are in Me, I am not in them.

5. And yet those beings are not in Me. That indeed is my unique power as Lord! Sustainer of all beings, I am not in them; My Self brings them into existence. The sovereign power of God lies in this mystery, this miracle, that all beings are in Him and yet not in Him, He is in them and yet not in them. This is the description of God in the language of mortal man. Indeed He

soothes man by revealing to him all His aspects by using all kinds of paradoxes. All beings are in Him inasmuch as all creation is His; but as He transcends it all as He really is not the author of it all, it may be said with equal truth that the beings are not in Him. He really is in all his true devotees, He is *not*, according to them, in those who deny Him. What is this if not a mystery, a miracle of God?

11. Not knowing My transcendent nature as the sovereign Lord of all beings, fools condemn Me incarnated as man. For they deny the existence of god and do not recognize the Director in the human body.

20. Followers of the three Vedas, who drink the *soma* juice and are purged of sin, worship Me with sacrifice and pray for going to heaven; they reach the holy world of the gods and enjoy in heaven the divine joys of the gods. The reference is to the sacrificial ceremonies and rites in vogue in the days of the *Gita*. We cannot definitely say what they were like nor what the *soma* juice exactly was.

21. They enjoy the vast world of heaven, and their merit spent, they enter the world of the mortals; thus those who, following the Vedic law, long for the fruit of their action earn but the round of birth and death.

22. As for those who worship Me, thinking on Me alone and nothing else, ever attached to Me, I bear the burden of getting them what they need. There are thus three unmistakable marks of a true yogi or *bhakta*...even-mindedness, skill in action, undivided devotion. These three must be completely harmonized in a yogi. Without devotion, there is no even-mindedness, without even-mindedness no devotion, and without skill in action devotion and even-mindedness might well be a pretence.

23. Even those who, devoted to other gods, worship them in full faith, even they, O Kaunteya, worship none but Me, though not according to the rule. "Not according to the rule" means not knowing Me as the Impersonal and the Absolute.

26. Any offering of leaf, flower, fruit or water, made to Me in devotion by earnest soul, I lovingly accept. That is to say, it is the Lord in every being whom we serve with devotion who accepts the service.

27. Whatever thou doest, whatever thou eatest, whatever thou offerest as sacrifice or gift, whatever austerity thou dost perform, O Kaunteya, dedicate all to Me.

28. So doing thou shalt be released from the bondage of action, yielding good and evil fruit; having accomplished both renunciation and performance, thou shalt be released (from birth and death) and come unto Me.

29. I am the same to all beings; with Me there is none disfavoured, none favoured; but those who worship Me with devotion are in Me and I in them.

30. A sinner, howsoever great, if he turns to Me with undivided devotion, must indeed be counted a saint; for he has a settled resolve. The undivided devotion subdues both his passions and his evil deeds.

31. For soon he becomes righteous and wins everlasting peace; know for a certainty, O Kaunteya, that My *bhakta* never perishes.

DISCOURSE X

For the benefit of His devotees, the Lord gives in this discourse a glimpse of His divine manifestations.

36. Of deceivers, I am the dice-play; of the splendid, the splendour; I am victory, I am resolution, I am the goodness of the good. The 'dice-play of deceivers' need not alarm one. For the good and evil nature of things is not the matter in question, it is the directing and immanent power of God that is being described. Let the deceivers also know that they are under God's rule and judgement and put away their pride and deceit.

39. Whatever is the seed of every being, O Arjuna, that am I; there is nothing whether moving or fixced, that can be without Me.

40. There is no end to my divine manifestations; what extent of them I have told thee now is only by way of illustration.

41. Whatever is glorious, beautiful and mighty, know thou that all such has issued from a fragment of My splendour.

DISCOURSE XI

In this discourse the Lord reveals to Arjuna's vision what Arjuna has heard with his ear...the Universal Form of the Lord. This *discourse is a favourite with the bhaktas. Here there is no argument,* there is pure poetry. Its solemn music[112] reverberates in one's ears and it is not possible to tire of reading it again and again.

53. Not by the Vedas, not by penance nor by gifts, nor yet by sacrifice, can any behold Me in the Form that thou has seen.

54. But by single-minded devotion, O Arjuna, I may in this Form be known and seen and truly entered into, O Parantapa!

DISCOURSE XII

Thus we see that vision of God is possible only through singleminded devotion. Contents of devotion must follow as a matter of course. This twelfth discourse should be learnt by heart even if all the discourses are not. It is one of the shortest. The marks of a devotee should be carefully noted.

Arjuna said:

1. Of the devotees who thus worship thee, incessantly attached, and those who worship the Imperishable Unmanifest, which are the better yogis?

The Lord said:

5. The greater is the travail of those whose mind is fixed on the Unmanifest; for it is hard for embodied mortals to gain the Unmanifest...Goal. Mortal man can only imagine the Unmanifest, the Impersonal, and as his language fails him he often negatively describes It as *'Neti'*. *'Neti'* (Not That, Not That). And so even iconoclasts are at bottom no better than idol-worshippers. To worship a book, to go to a church, or to pray with one's face in a particular direction...all these are forms of worshipping the Formless in an image or idol. And yet both the idol-breaker and the idol-worshipper cannot lose sight of the fact that there is something which is beyond all form, Unthinkable, Formless, Impersonal, Changeless. The highest goal of the devotee is to become one with the object of his devotion. The *bhakta* extinguishes himself and merges into, becomes, Bhagvan. This state can best be reached by devoting oneself to some form, and so it is said that the short cut to the Unmanifest is really the longest and the most difficult.

6. But those who casting all their actions on Me, making Me their all in all, worship Me with the meditation of undivided devotion,

7. Of such, whose thoughts are centred on Me, O Partha, I become ere long the Deliverer from the ocean of this world of death.

12. Better is knowledge than practice, better than knowledge is concentration, better than concentration is renunciation of the fruit of all action, from which directly issues peace. 'Practice' (*abhyasa*) is the practice of the yoga of meditation and control of psychic processes; 'knowledge' (*jnana)* is intellectual effort; 'concentration' (*dhyana*) is devoted worship. If as a result of all this there is no renunciation of the fruit of action, 'practice' is no 'practice', 'knowledge' is no 'knowledge', and 'concentration' is no 'concentration'.

DISCOURSE XIII

This discourse treats of the distinction between the body (not-Self) and atman (the Self).

1. This body, O Kaunteya, is called the Field; he who knows it is called the knower of the Field by those who know.

2. And understand Me to be, O Bharata, the knower of the Field in all the Fields; and the knowledge of the Field and the knower of the Field, I hold, is true knowledge.

3. What that Field is, what its nature, what is modifications, and whence is what, as also who He is, and what His power...hear this briefly from Me.

4. This subject has been sung by seers distinctly and in various ways, in different hymns as also in aphoristic texts about Brahman well reasoned and unequivocal.

5. The great elements, Individuation, Reason, the Unmanifest, the ten senses, and the one (Mind), and the five spheres of the senses;

6. Desire, dislike, pleasure, pain, association, consciousness, cohesion... this, in sum, is what is called the Field with its modifications. The great elements are Earth, Water, Fire, Air and Ether, 'Individuation' is the thought of I, or that the body is 'I', the 'Unmanifest' is *prakriti* or *maya*; the ten senses are the five senses of perception...smell, taste, sight, touch and hearing, and the five organs of action, viz., the hands; the feet, the tongue, and the two organs of excretion. The five spheres or objects of the senses are smell, savour, form, touch and sound. 'Association' is the property of the different organs to co-operate. *Dhriti* is not patience or constancy but cohesion, i.e., the property of all the atoms in the body to hold together; from 'individuation' springs this cohesion. Individuation is inherent in the unmanifest

prakriti. The undeluded man is he who can cast off this individuation or ego, and having done so the shock of an inevitable thing like death and the pairs of opposites caused by sense-contacts fail to affect him. The Field, subject to all its modifications, has to be abandoned in the end by the entlightended and the unenlightened alike.

11. Settled conviction of the nature of the *atman*, perception of the goal of the knowledge of Truth,... All this is declared to be knowledge and the reverse of it is ignorance.

12. I will (now) expound to thee that which is to be known and knowing which one enjoys immortality; it is the supreme Brahman which has no beginning, which is called neither Being nor non-Being. The Supreme can be described neither as Being nor as non- Being. It is beyond definition or description, above all attributes.

15. Without all beings; yet within; immovable yet moving; so subtle that it cannot be perceived; so far and yet so near It is. He who knows It is within It, close to It,; mobility and immobility, peace and restlessness, we owe to It, for It has motion and yet is motionless.

20. *Prakriti* is described as the cause in the creation of effects from causes; *Purusha* is described as the cause of the experiencing of pleasure and pain.

21. For the *purusha,* residing in *prakriti*, experiences the *gunas* born *of prakriti*; attachment to these *gunas* is the cause of his birth in good or evil wombs. *Prakriti* in common parlance is *maya*. *Purusha* is the *jiva*. *Jiva* acting in accordance with his nature experiences the fruit of actions arising out of the three gunas.

22. What is called in this body the Witness, the Assentor, the Sustainer, the Experiencer, the Great Lord and also the Supreme *Atman,* is the Supreme Being.

23. He who thus knows *purusha* and *prakriti* with its *gunas,* is not born again, no matter how he live and move.

Read in the light of discourses II, XI, and XII this *shloka* may not be taken to support any kind of libertinism. It shows the virtue of self-surrender and selfless devotion. All actions bind the self, but if all are dedicated to the Lord they do not bind, rather they release him. He who has thus extinguished the 'self' or the thought of 'I' has been extinguished, there is no sin. This *shloka* shows how to steer clear of all sin.

27. Who sees abiding in all beings the same Parameshvara, imperishable in the perishable, he sees indeed.

28. When he sees the same Ishvara abiding everywhere alike, he does not hurt himself by himself and hence he attains the highest goal. He who sees the same God everywhere merges in Him and sees naught else; he thus does not yield to passion, does not become his own foe and thus attains Freedom.

29. Who sees that it is *prakriti* that performs all actions and thus (knows) that *atman* performs them not, he sees indeed. Just as, in the case of a man who is asleep, his 'Self' is not the agent of sleep, but *prakriti*, even so the enlightened man will detach his 'Self' from all activities. To the pure everything is pure. *Prakriti* is not unchaste, it is when arrogant man takes her as wife those of these twain passion is born.

30. When he sees the diversity of beings as founded in unity and the whole expanse issuing thereform, then he attains to Brahman. To realize that everything rests in Brahman is to attain to the state of Brahman. Then *jiva* becomes Siva.

DISCOURSE XIV

The description of prakriti naturally leads on to that of its constituents, the gunas, which form the subject of this discourse. And that, in turn, leads on to a description of the marks of him who has passed beyond the three gunas. These are practically the same as those of the man of secure understanding (II. 54-72) as also those of the ideal bhakta (XII. 12-20).

19. When the seer perceives no agent other than the *gunas*, and knows Him who is above the *gunas*, he attains to My being. As soon as a man realizes that he is not the doer, but the *gunas* are the agent, the 'self' vanishes, and he goes through all his actions spontaneously, just to sustain the body. And as the body is meant to subserve the highest end, all his actions will ever reveal detachment and dispassion. Such a seer can easily have a glimpse of the One who is above the *gunas* and offer his devotion to Him.

20. When the embodied one transcends these three *gunas* which are born of his contact with the body, he is released from the pain of birth, death and age and attains deathlessness.

Arjuna said:

21. What, O Lord, are the marks of him who has transcended the three *gunas*? How does he conduct himself? How does he transcend the three *gunas*?

The Lord said:

22. He, O Pandava, who does not disdain light, activity, and delusion when they come into being, nor desires them when they vanish;

23. He who, seated as one indifferent, is not shaken by the *gunas,* and stays still and moves not, knowing it is *gunas* playing their parts;

24. He who holds pleasure and pain alike, who is sedate, who regards as same earth, stone and gold, who is wise and weighs in equal scale things pleasant and unpleasant, who is even-minded in praise and blame;

25. Who holds alike respect and disrespect, who is the same to friend and foe, who indulges in no undertakings...that man is called *gunatita. Shls.* 22-25 must be read and considered together. Light, activity and delusion, as we have seen in the foregoing *shlokas,* are the products or indications of *sattva, rajas* and *tamas,* respectively. The inner meaning of these verses is that he who has transcended the *gunas* will be unaffected by them. A stone does not desire light, nor does it disdain activity or inertness; it is still, without having the will to be so. If someone puts it into motion, it does not fret; if again it is allowed to lie still, it does not feel that inertness or delusion has seized it. The difference between a stone and a *gunatita* is that the latter has full consciousness and with full knowledge he shakes himself free from the bonds that bind an ordinary mortal. He has, as a result of his knowledge, achieved the repose of a stone. Like the stone he is witness, but not the doer, of the activities of the *gunas* or *prakriti.* Of such *jnani* one may say that he is sitting still, unshaken in the knowledge that it is the *gunas* playing their parts. We who are every moment of our lives acting as though we were the doers can only imagine the state, we can hardly experience it. But we can hitch our waggon to that star and work our way closer and closer towards it by gradually withdrawing the self from our actions. A gunatita has experience of his own condition but he cannot describe it, for he who can describe it ceases to be done. the moment he proceeds to do so, 'self' peeps in. the peace and light and bustle and inertness of our common experience are illusory. The *Gita* itself has made it clear in so

many words that the *sattvik* state is the one nearest that of a *gunatita*. Therefore everyone should strive to develop more and more *sattva* in himself, believing that some day he will reach the goal of the state of *gunatita*.

DISCOURSE XV

This discourse deals with the Supreme Form of the Lord, transcending *kshara* (perishable) and *akshara* (imperishable).

The Lord said:

1. With its root above and branches below the *ashvattha* tree, they say, is imperishable; it has Vedic hymns for its leaves; he who knows it knows the Vedas. *Shvah* means tomorrow, and *ashvattha* (*na shvopi sthata)* means that which will not last even until tomorrow, i.e., the world of sense which is every moment in a state of flux. But even though it is perpetually changing, as its root is Brahman or the Supreme, it is imperishable. It has for its protection and support the leaves of the Vedic hymns, i.e., dharma. He who knows the world of sense as such and who knows dharma is the real *jnani*, that man has really known the Vedas.

2. Above and below its branches spread, blossoming because of the *gunas*, having for their shoots the sense-objects; deep down in the world of men are ramified its roots, in the shape of the consequences of action.

This is the description of the tree of the world of sense as the unenlightened see it. They fail to discover its Root above in Brahman and so they are always attached to the objects of sense. They water the tree with the three *gunas* and remain bound to karma in the world of men.

3. Its form as such is not here perceived, neither is its end, nor beginning, nor basis. Let man first hew down this deep-rooted *asvattha* with the sure weapon of detachment;

4. Let him pray to win to that haven from which there is no return and seek to find refuge in the Primal Being from who has emanated this ancient world of action. *'Detachment'* in *shl.* 3 here means dispassion, aversion from the objects of the senses. Unless man is determined to cut himself off from the temptations of the world of sense he will go deeper into its mire every day. These verses show that one dare not play with the objects of the senses with impunity.

7. A part indeed of Myself which has been the eternal *jiva* in this world of life, attracts the mind and the five senses from their place in *prakriti*.

9. Having settled Himself in the senses...ear, eye, touch, taste, and smell as well as the mind, through them He frequents their objects. These objects are the natural objects of the senses. The frequenting or enjoyment of these would be tainted if there were the sense of 'I' about it; otherwise it is pure, even as a child's enjoyment of these objects is innocent.

11. Yogis who strive see Him seated in themsleves; the witless ones who have not cleansed themselves see Him not, even though they strive.

This does not conflict with the covenant that God has made even with the sinner in discourse 9. *Akritatman* who has not cleansed himself) means one who has no devotion in him, who has not made up his mind to purify himself. The most confirmed sinner, if he has humility enough to seek refuge in surrender to God, purifies himself and succeeds in finding Him. Those who do not care to observe the cardinal and the casual vows and expect to find God through bare intellectual exercise are witless, Godless; they will not find Him.

DISCOURSE XVI

This discourse treats of the divine and the devilish heritage.

23. He who forsakes the rule of Shastra and does but the bidding of his selfish desires, gains neither perfection, nor happiness, nor the highest state. Shastra does not mean the rites and formulae laid down in the so-called Dharmashastra, but the path of self-restraint laid down by the seers and the saints.

24. Therefore let Shastra be thy authority for determining what ought to be done and what ought not to be done; ascertain thou the rule of the Shastra and do thy task here (accordingly).

Shastra here too has the same meaning as in the preceding *shloka*. Let no one be a law unto himself, but take as his authority the law laid down by men who have known and lived religion.

DISCOURSE XVII

On being asked to consider Shastra (conduct of the worthy) as the authority, Arjuna is faced with a difficulty. What is the position of those who may not be able to accept the authority of Shastra but who may act in faith? An answer to the question is attempted in this discourse. Krishna rests content with pointing out the wocks and shoals on the path of one who forsakes the beaconlight of Shastra (conduct of the worthy). In doing so he deals with faith and sacrifice, austerity and charity performed with faith, and their divisions according to the spirit in which they are performed. He also sings the greatness of the mystic syllables AUM TAT SAT...a formula of dedication of all work to God.

23. AUM TAT SAT has been declared to be the threefold name of Brahman and by that name were created of old the *Brahmanas*, the Vedas and sacrifices.

24. Therefore, with AUM ever on their lips, are all the rites of sacrifice, charity and austerity, performed always according to the rule, by *Brahmavadins*.

25. With the utterance of TAT and without the desire for fruit are the several rites of sacrifice, austerity and charity performed by those seeking Freedom.

26. SAT is employed in the sense of 'real' and 'good'; O Partha, SAT is also applied to beautiful deeds.

27. Constancy in sacrifice, austerity and charity is called SAT; and all work for these purposes is also SAT. The substance of the last four *shlokas* is that every action should be done in a spirit of complete dedication of God. For AUM alone is the only Reality. That only which is dedicated to It counts.

DISCOURSE XVIII

This concluding discourse sums up the teaching of the Gita. It may be said to be summed up in the following: "Abandon all duties and come to Me, the only Refuge": (66). That is true renunciation. But abandonment of all duties does not mean abandonment of actions; it means the abandonment of the desire for fruit. Even the highest act of service must be dedicated to Him, without the desire. *That is tyaga (abandonment), that is sannyasa (renunciation).*

17. He who is free from all sense of 'I', whose motive is untainted, slays not nor is bound, even though he slay all these worlds. This *shloka* though seemingly somewhat baffling is not really so. The *Gita* on many occasions presents the ideal to attain

which the aspirant has to strive but which may not be possible completely to realize in the world. It is like definitions in geometry. A perfect straight line does not exist, but it is necessary to imagine it in order to prove the various propostions. Even so, it is necessary to hold up ideals of this nature as standards for imitation in matters of conduct. This then would seem to be the meaning of this *shloka*: He who has made ashes of 'self', whose motive is undtainted, may slay the whole world, if he will. But in reality he who has annilated 'self' has annihilated his flesh too, and he whose motive is untainted sees the past, present and future. Such a being can be one and only one...God. He acts and yet is no doer, slays and yet is no slayer. For mortal man the royal road ...the conduct of the worthy...is ever before him, viz., *ahimsa*...holding all life sacred.

36. Hear now from Me, O Bharatarshabha, the three kinds of pleasure which is enjoyed only by repeated practice, and which puts an end to pain,

37. Which, in its inception, is as poison, but in the end as nectar, born of the serene realization of the true nature of *atman*...that pleasure is said to be *sattvik*.

47. Better one's own duty, though uninviting, than another's which may be more easily performed; doing duty which accords with one's nature, one incurs no sin.

The central teaching of the *Gita* is detachment...abandonment of the fruit of action. And there would be no room for this abandonment if one were to perfer another's. It is the spirit in which duty is done that matters, and its unattached performance is its own reward.

68. He who will propound this supreme mystery to My devotees, shall, by that act of highest devotion to Me, surely come to Me.

69. Nor among men is there any who renders dearer service to Me than he; nor shall there be on earth any more beloved by Me than he. It is only he who has himself gained the knowledge and lived it in his life that can declare it to others. These two *shlokas* cannot possibly have any reference to him who, no matter how he conducts himself, can give a flawless reading and interpretation of the *Gita* while conducting himself anyhow.

Source: *The Gita According to Gandhi*

Notes

1. Literally, *'the* yoga of non-attachment'. The English translation by Mahadev Desai bore the title The *Gita According to Gandhi*. The English translation of the introduction to his Gujarati translation of the Gita was begun by Gandhiji on 16-12-1930, and was completed by him on 8-1-1931 in the Yeravda prison. The original manuscript in English (photostat: G.N. 7911), in addition to bearing the dates for each instalment of the translation, also mentions 24-6-1929 as the date on which introduction in Gujarati to the translation of the *Gita* was completed. However, in his letters to Mahadev Desai and Chhaganlal Joshi dated 28-6-1929 (*vide* pp. 133 & 135.), he mentions his having completed the *Gita* the previous day. The work therefore, is placed under June 27, 1929. The English translation appeared first in *Young India*, 26-8-1931, with this prefactory note and they were both reproduced in *The Gita According to Gandhi*.
2. On March 12, 1931 by Navajivan Publishing House, Ahmedabad
3. On January 26, 1931.
4. The original manuscript has "Even".
5. *Vide* "An Autobiography".
6. In the original manuscript the sentence reads: "We can appreciate your meaning of the message of the *Gita* only when you have translated the whole text with such notes as you may deem necessary and when we have gone through it all."
7. The original manuscript has "remark".
8. The original manuscript has "get".
9. In the original manuscript the sentence reads: "then I was imprisoned".
10. *Gita Rahasya*
11. The original manucript has "and asked me".
12. The original manucript has "I could not".
13. In the original manuscript the sentence reads: "This reading whetted my appetite for reading more about the Gita and I glanced through several works on it".
14. *Vide* "An Autobiography"
15. The original manuscript does not have the word "own".
16. In the original manuscript the sentence reads: "Then again my knowledge of Sanskrit is limited; my knowledge of Gujarati too is in no way of a higher type."
17. The origianl manuscript does not have the words "that of".

18. In the original manuscript the sentence reads : "It has become a spiritual reference book."
19. In the original manuscript the sentence reads : "The failure is due not to want of effort but in spite of it."
20. The original manuscript has "their".
21. The original manuscript has " In spite of my knowledge of Gujarati being limited".
22. The original manuscript has "In spite of my knowledge of Gujarati being limited".
23. In the original manuscript the sentence reads: "I do indeed wish that at a time when literary output of a questionable character is pouring in upon the Gujaratis they should have before them a readable rendering of a book that is regarded as unrivalled for its spiritual merit and so that they may be able to withstand the overwhelming flood of unclean literature".
24. The original manuscript has "any".
25. The original manuscript has "rendering".
26. The original manuscript has "thirty eight".
27. The original manuscript has "For this reason I do indeed harbour the wish that every Gujarati man or woman".
28. The original manuscript does not have the word "before".
29. The original manuscript does not have the word "merely".
30. The original manuscript has "attractive".
31. The original manuscript does net have the word "the".
32. The original manuscript has "teaches".
33. In the original manuscript the sentence reads: "In reading these verses I do not find a single characterstic of a perfected man that can correspond to physical warfare."
34. In the original manuscript the sentence reads: "The whole design of the Gita is inconsistent with the rules of conduct governing the relations between contending parties in domestic disputes."
35. The original manuscript has "perfect ".
36. The original manuscript does not have the words "In Hinduism".
37. In the original manuscript the sentence reads: "Future generations pay homage as an incarnation to one who, in his own generation, has been the most religious in his conduct."
38. The original manuscript has "more"
39. The original manuscript has "This incarnation habit".
40. In the original manuscript the sentence reads: "Man is not at peace with himself till he has become like unto God, he is not

happy without it."

41. In the original manuscript the sentence reads: "The endcavour to be that is the supreme, the only ambition worth having."
42. In the original manuscript the sentence reads: "This self-realization is the subject of all scriptures as it is of the Gita."
43. In the original manuscript the sentence reads: "But the object of the Gita appears to me to be to show the most excellent way of attaining self-realization."
44. In the original manuscript the sentence reads: "The Gita is woven round this as the centre."
45. In the original manuscript the sentence reads: "Devotion knowledge and the rest revolve like planets round this renunciation as the central sun."
46. The original manuscript does not have this sentence.
47. The original manuscript has "work".
48. The original manuscript has "exempt".
49. The original manuscript has "But every action".
50. The original manuscript has "little".
51. In the original manuscript the sentence reads: "And freedom is available only for those who become sinless".
52. The original manuscript has "Then".
53. The original manuscript has "activity".
54. The original manuscript has "do".
55. The original manuscript has "is necessary to attain".
56. The original manuscript has "but".
57. The original manuscript has "So".
58. In the original manuscript the sentence reads: "But this devotion is wrestling with death".
59. The original manuscript has "but they".
60. The original manuscript has "whom people do not fear".
61. The original manuscript has "them".
62. The original manuscript has "whose reason is disciplined".
63. In the original manuscript the sentence reads: "Such devotion is impossible in men or women with strong attachments".
64. In the original manuscript the sentence reads: "We thus see, that to know to be a real devotee is to realize oneself."
65. In the original manuscript the sentence reads: "Self-realization is not something apart from it."
66. In the original manuscript the sentence reads: "Just as one rupee

can purchase for us poison or nectar so may we not use knowledge or devotion for attaining either salvation or bondage."

67. In the original manuscript the sentence reads: "The salvation contemplated by Gita is perfect peace."
68. This sentence is not in the original manuscript.
69. In the original manuscript the sentence reads: "He will regard it as a bondage even to lift a little lota."
70. This sentence is not in the original manuscript.
71. In the original manuscript the sentence reads: "The popular notion of a bhakta is that he is a soft-hearted maniac, telling beads and disdaining to do even a loving service lest his telling of beads might be interrupted".
72. The original manuscript has "he".
73. The original manuscript has: "Both these have been clearly told by the Gita".
74. The original manuscript has "will".
75. The original manuscript has "But".
76. The original manuscript has "doing it".
77. In the original manuscript the sentence reads : "The manner in which the Gita has solved the problem, no other work has to my knowledge."
78. In the origianl manuscript the sentence reads: "This unmistakable and unmistakable teaching of the Gita" [sic].
79. The original manuscript has "fruit".
80. The original manuscript has "for". The original manuscript has "would".
81. The original manuscript has "doctrine".
82. The original manuscript has "would".
83. The original manuscript has "their".
84. In the Original manuscript the sentence reads: "It was accepted as primary duty even before the Gita age".
85. The original manuscript has "is".
86. In the original manuscript the sentence reads: "But in assessing the measure of renunciation of fruit, we are not required to probe the mind of the author of the Gita as to his limitation of ahimsa and the like".
87. The original manuscript has "he is able to reduce them in language".
88. In the original manuscript the sentence reads: "And in this lies

the greatness of the poem and the poet".

89. In the original manuscript the sentence reads: "The author of the Gita has himself extended the meanings of great current words".

90. In the original manuscript the sentence reads: "And this we are able to discover even on a superficial examination."

91. The original manuscript has "is impossible without perfect observance of truth and ahimsa".

92. The original manuscript has "the same thing has been said often".

93. The original manuscript adds "Therefore".

94. The original manuscript adds "Therefore".

95. The original manuscript has "learning".

96. In the original manuscript the sentence reads: "The author himself has said."

97. The original manuscript does not have the words "for this teaching".

98. The original manuscript has: "by the fact of this service of me will assuredly reach me."

99. The original manuscript has "will".

100. The original manuscript has "live".

101. The translation of the Gita verses not commented on or referred to by Gandhiji is not reproduced in this volume. The translation both of the verses and of Gandhiji's comments is from Mahadev Desai's The Gita According to Gandhi.

101. Son of Kunti.

102. Mahadev Desai in *The Gita according to Gandhi* explains: "For starves his senses', Gandhiji has 'facts'. I think there is no violence to the meaning of the verse in applying 'starvation' to all the senses, including that of hunger."

103. Mahadev Desai explains here: "The 'bondage of action' in Gandhiji's note is the bondage of sansara, the cycle of death and birth. All action will have its consequences the consequences in one case, as we shall see,.will be the bondage of sansara, in the other case it will be freedom from it."

104. Mahadev Desai explains: "Gandhiji's translation says: 'because of My Nature'. Prakriti is here Nature. God by His mysterious power...maya...assumes the garb of prakriti and looks as though He was born".

105. Mahadev Desai explains :

"Three classes of action are here mentioned:

(1) Karma, i.e., action which is capable of being performed

without attachment, but is not so performed and therefore binds; also including inaction or laziness which presupposes selfishness of attachment and therefore binds;

(2) Vikarma, forbidden action i.e., action which by its own nature is incapable of being performed without attachment, and hence necessarily binding e.g., murder, lying, adultery and so forth;

(3) Akarma, i.e. action, mental or physical, which is performed without attachment and therefore does not bind. Shri Vinoba has made a bold departure in his interpretation of the word 'vikarma'. It means, he says, specific action, i.e., when the mind co-operates with the body and helps to make a selfful action selfless. Mathematically he expresses it in this formula, Karma+vikarma=akarma.

106. Mahadev Desai explains: "Fires"...the plural is used to denote the different yogic processes of restraint...dharana (concentration), dhyana (meditation) and samadhi (absorption in the object of meditation)...all three constituting selfrestraint... sanyama.

107. Mahadev Desai explains: "Puraka practice consists in drawing the breath in and stopping all exhalation, i.e. in the language of shloka 29 'sacrificing the outward (called prana) in the inward (callled apana)'; rechaka practice consists in throwing the breath outward and stopping all inhalation, i.e. in the language of shloka 29, 'sacrificing the inward (apana) in the outward (prana)'; kumbhaka practice consists in checking the flow both ways and holding it in suspense either after an exhalation or inhalation."

108. Mahadev Desai explains: "We have had in the discourse a comparison of the jnanayogi or the philosophic mystic and the karmayogi or the active mystic. The shlokas v. 27-29 start a new comparison now...quite a parallel dichotomy as it evidences itself in the life of the devotee. Shloka 27-28 introduce to us the contemplative or meditative mystic...dhyanayogi...to be described in discourses VI, VII and VIII while shloka 29 describes the devotinal mystic, the bhaktiyogi who worships the Supreme in His one or many manifestations to be described in discourses XI-XII. To him God appears or reveals Himself as the Accepter of all sacrifices and the Friend of all creation."

109. Mahadev Desai explains: "I have in my translation distinguished 'atman', the higher self, from the lower self, though it is not quite clear whether Gandhiji does so in his trnaslation. Atman is, really speaking, neither friend nor foe, but the lower self makes Him friend or foe, according as it strives to lift itself up to Him or

drag itself down from Him. In order that the moral end of perfection may be fulfilled, the self has to look to Him as "the Goal, the Witness, the Refuge, the Friend" (XI. 18); but it often makes Him his enemy as mortal men know to their cost."

110. Mahadev Desai explains: "Gandhiji has summed up in his brief note the gist of this quatrain for those who will not bother about technical terms. A deeply spiritual friend has obliged me with an interpretation which lights up the apparent abracadabras with a deal of meaning: The shlokas describe the whole process in which the Absolute becomes conditioned and from the conditioned state becomes Absolute again. (1) We have form the Impersonal, Unmanifest, Unconditioned Absolute; (2) It chose to reveal one of Its aspects...that aspect was primordial unmanifest prakriti...here called adhyatma; (3) Prakriti next became active - this disturbance in the equilibrium of its gunas was karma work, action; (4) the next steps in the process were the countless manifestations of matter, with name and form...that is adhibhuta; (5) then the Absolute informed these with its Ego, i.e., became conditioned; that is adhidaiva; (6) but the conditioned had the potentiality to recover its pristine unconditioned state by means of giving of itself a pure sacrifice. The culmination of this self-sacrifice comes with the dissolution of the body and the merging or identification of the conditioned in the Unconditioned. In short, it is the cycle of sacrifice that is described. The Supreme Being sacrifices Himself in the first instance and ultimately the individual sacrifices himself to be merged in the original Essence. Cf. III 15, which describes the same cycle of sacrifice."

111. Mahadev Desai explains: "This shloka should make it abundantly clear that all through in his exhortation to Arjuna to fight, it was not only the actual warfare in front of them that was meant, but the fight...moral and spiritual...that is man's lot on earth. Cf. Jesus' words: 'Whosoever would come after me, let him renounce himself and take up his cross daily and follow me.' It is the taking up one's cross daily, at every moment, that is meant here. See also shloka 14. 'Life is a perpetual striving. There is always a tempest raging in us, and struggle against temptation is a perpetual duty. The Gita says this in several places.' "...*Harijan*, 8-7-'33.

112. Mahadev Desai explains: "The music, of course, of the original! In translation, 'the glory is gone'. For a very free rendering which brings out some at least of the haunting music of the original the reader must go to Sir Edwin Arnold's flowing stanzas."

PART THREE

LETTERS ON THE "GITA"[1]

CHAPTER I[2]

Tuesday Morning, November 11, 1930

The *Gita* is a small portion of the *Mahabharata*. The latter is generally looked upon as a historical work. To us, however, the *Mahabharata* and the *Ramayana* are not historical works but are treatises on religion. Or, if we call them histories, they narrate the history of the human soul; they do not tell of what happened thousands of years ago, but depict what takes place in the heart of every human being today. Both the works describe the eternal war between the God and the demon in man—between Rama and Ravana. The *Gita* does this in the form of a dialogue between Arjuna and Krishna. The dialogue is narrated to the blind Dhritarashtra by Sanjaya. Literally *Gita* means that which is sung. The adjective applies to the noun Upanishad, which is understood, and so the full meaning of the phrase is "the Upanishad which was sung". Upanishad means knowledge-teaching.

The word *'Gita?* therefore, means Shri Krishna's teaching to Arjuna. In reading the *Gita* we should feel that Shri Krishna--God—dwells in our hearts as the holy spirit within us, and that when, yearning for knowledge, like Arjuna, we take our spiritual difficulties to Him and seek His guidance, seek refuge in Him, He is ever ready to instruct us. We slumber, but the Lord within us is ever awake. He is only waiting for spiritual yearning to be awakened in us. We, however, do not know how to question Him, do not even feel the desire to do so. And so we read a work like the *Gita* every day and meditate over its teaching. By doing so, we wish to awaken spiritual yearning in us and learn what questions to put to the Lord. Whenever we are faced with spiritual difficulties, we turn to the *Gita* for their solution and obtain peace of mind through it. This is the spirit in which we should read the work. It is as it were our revered guru, our mother, and we should have faith that we shall be safe if we seek shelter in her lap. We can get all our spiritual difficulties solved through the *Gita*. Anyone who daily meditates over the teaching of the *Gita* in this manner will ever experience new joy in his study and find new meanings. There is no spiritual pro□blem which the *Gita* cannot solve, though it may be that owing to our imperfect faith we do not know how to read and under□stand the work. We read the *Gita* as daily spiritual practice so that our faith may increase from day to day and we may be□come vigilant. I give here, for the guidance of the inmates of the Ashram, the meaning of the *Gita* which my daily meditation over its teaching has revealed or reveals to me.

When the Pandavas and the Kauravas gathered together on the battle-field of Kurukshetra (the field of Kuru) with their armies, Duryodhana, the king of the Kauravas, approached Drona (his teacher in the science of war) and named the leading warriors on either side. As a signal for the battle to begin, conch-shell horns were sounded on both the sides and Shri Krishna who was Arjuna's charioteer drove his chariot into a place between the two armies. The scene which greeted Arjuna's eyes unnerved him, and he said to Shri Krishna: "How can I attack these in battle? I might readily enough if I had to fight with strangers, but these are my kinsmen. The Kauravas and the Pandavas are first cousins. We were brought up together. Drona is our teacher as well as the Kaunas'. Bhishma is a revered elder for both. How can I fight against him? It is true that the Kauravas are miscreants and doers of evil deeds. They have wronged the Pandavas and deprived them of their

lands. They have insulted the saintly Draupadi. But what shall I gain by killing them? They are fools indeed. But shall I also be equally foolish? I have some little knowledge. I can dis□criminate between right and wrong. I thus see that it is a sin to fight against relatives. Never mind if they have taken wrong□ful possession of the Pandavas[5] share in the kingdom. Never mind even if they kill us. But how dare we raise our hand against them? O Krishna, I will not fight against my kith and kin."

With these words, Arjuna sank down on the seat of the chariot, being overwhelmed by grief.

Here ends the first Chapter which is entitled "The Sorrow of Arjuna". All of us should feel pain even as Arjuna did. No acquisi□tion of knowledge is possible unless there is in us a sense of some□thing lacking and a desire to know the truth. If a man is not curious even to know what is wrong and what is right, what is the use of religion for him? The battle-field of Kurukshetra only provides the occasion for the dialogue between Arjuna and Krishna. The real Kurukshetra is the human heart, which is also a dharmakshetra (the field of righteousness) if we look upon it as the abode of God and invite Him to take hold of it. Some battle or other is fought on this battle-field from day to day. Most of these battles arise from the distinction between 'mine' and 'thine', between kinsmen and strangers. Therefore, as we shall find later on, the Lord tells Arjuna that attraction *(raga)* and repulsion *(dvesha)* lie at the root of sin, When I look upon a person or thing as 'mine', *raga* takes hold of my mind; and when I look upon him as a stranger, aversion or hatred enters the mind. Therefore we must forget the distinction between 'mine' and 'thine'. That is to say, we must give up our likes and dis□likes. This is the teaching of the *Gita* and all other scriptures. To say this is one thing; to practise it is quite another. The *Gita* is there to teach us how to practise We will try to understand the method it recommends.

Notes

1. Written during Gandhiji's incarceration in Yeravda Central Prison in 1930 and 1932, these were sent weekly along with letters to Narandas Gandhi for being read out at the Ashram prayer meetings. Gandhiji commenced the series with Chapter xsi; vide Vol. XLIV, p. 277. The following week Gandhiji sent Chapter I, with a general introductory note on the *Gita*.

   All the chapters are given here under February 19/21, 1932, the date of despatch of the letter to Narandas Gandhi, which carried the discourse on Chapter XVIII and concluded the series; vide the following item. The translation is reproduced from the *Discourses on the Gita* (Navajivan Publishing House, Ahmedabad-14, 1960) with slight changes to bring the text into conformity with the Gujarati original.

   The Translator's Preface in the *Discourses on the Gita* says: "Gandhiji's Gujarati translation of the Gita was published on March 12, 1930, the never-to-be-forgotten day on which he marched to Dandi from Sabarmati. A member of the Ashram who read it found it very difficult to understand and com□plained about it to Gandhiji who was then in Yeravda Prison. Thereupon, he wrote a series of letters to the Ashram in which he devoted one letter to each chapter on the Gita. ..."

For Gandhiji's discourses on the Gita at Ashram prayer meetings in 1926, vide Vol. XXXII, pp. 94-376, and for his Gujarati translation of the Gita with a commentary thereon written in 1929, vide vol. XLI, pp. 90-133.

2. This was sent along with "Letter to Narandas Gandhi" 11-11-1930; vide Vol. XLIV, pp. 293-95.

CHAPTER II[1]

Monday Morning, November 17, 1930

When Arjuna had picked himself up a little, the Lord rebuked him and said: "How is it that th s delusion has come to you? It is unworthy of a warrior like you." But even then Arjuna stuck to his first position, refused to fight and said: "If in order to get it, I have to slay elders and other relations, I do not want not only a kingdom on this earth but even the delights of paradise. My mind gropes in darkness. I do not know where my duty lies. I put myself into your hands. Please guide me."

Finding that Arjuna was bewildered and aspired after knowledge, Krishna had pity on him and proceeded to explain things to him: "Your sorrow is for nothing, and you utter words about wisdom without understanding. You have evidently forgotten the distinction between the body and the embodied soul. The soul never dies; but the body passes through childhood, youth and old age and perishes in the end. The body is born but the soul is birthless and unchanging. It ever was, is now and will be there for all time to come. For whom then do you grieve? Your grief arises from a delusion. You look upon these Kauravas as your own, but you are aware that their bodies will come to an end. And as for the souls which inhabit these bodies, no one can destroy them. The soul cannot be wounded by weapons, burned by fire, dried by the wind or drowned in water. Then again, consider this from the standpoint of your duty as a warrior with an army under his command. If you refuse to fight this righteous war, the consequences will be the very reverse of what you expect and you will become an object of ridicule. You have always enjoyed the reputation of being a brave man. But if now you withdraw from the battle, you will be supposed to have been driven from it by fear. If it were part of your duty to flee in the face of danger, disgrace would not matter, but if you retire from battle now, you will have failed to discharge your duty, and people will be justified in condemning your flight.

"Thus far, I have tried to reason out things, draw a distinction between the body and the soul and remind you of your duty as a warrior. But let me now explain karmayoga (the method of action). A practitioner of karmayoga never comes to harm. It has nothing to do with chopping logic. It is something to be translated into action and experience. An ounce of practice is more profitable than tons of argumentation. And this practice too must not be vitiated by speculation about its fruit. Lite-ralists perform Vedic rites directed to the acquisition of material rewards. If one rite does not yield the expected fruit, they have recourse to another, and being disappointed once more, they take up a third. And thus they suffer from utter mental confusion. As a matter of fact, it is up to us to do our duty without wasting a single thought on the fruits of our action. To fight is the duty you have to discharge at present. Gain or loss, defeat or victory, is not in your power. Why should you carry the needless burden of thinking about them and be like the dog who walks under a cart and imagines that it is being drawn by himself and not by the bullocks? Defeat and victory, heat and cold, pleasure and pain come to a man in turn and he must put up with them. Without worrying about the fruit of action, a man must devote himself to the performance of his duty with an evenness of temper. This is yoga, or skill in action. The success of an act lies in performing it, and not in its result, whatever it is. Therefore be calm and do your duty regardless of consequences."

On hearing all this Arjuna said: "The course of conduct you have mapped out for me seems to be beyond my capacity. Not to worry about defeat or victory, not to waste a thought on the result—how can one attain such evenness of temper and steadfastness in spirit? How does a man with such attainments behave, and how are we to recognize him?"

The Lord replied: "O King, one who renounces all the cravings which torment the heart and derives his contentment from within himself is said to be a *sthitaprajna* or *samadhistha* (one stable in spirit). He is unruffled in adversity, and he does not hanker after happiness. Pleasure and pain are felt through the fixe senses. Therefore this wise man draws his senses away from sense-objects even as a tortoise draws in his limbs. The tortoise withdraws into his shell when he apprehends danger. But in the case of human beings sense-objects are ready to attack the senses at all times; therefore their senses must always be drawn in, and they should be ever ready to fight against sense-objects. This is the real battle. Some people resort to self-mortification and fasting as weapons of defence against sense-objects. These measures have their limited use. The senses do not make for sense-objects so long as a man is fasting, but fasting alone does not destroy his relish for them. On the other hand that relish may be heightened when the fast is broken, and a man can get rid of it only with the grace of God. The senses are so powerful that they drag a man behind them by force if he is not on his guard. Therefore a man must always keep them under control. This end he can achieve only if he turns his eyes inward, realizes God who resides in his heart and is devoted to Him. One who thus looks upon Me as His goal and surrenders his all to Me, keeping his senses in control, is a yogi stable in spirit.

"On the other hand, if a man is not master of his senses, he is always musing on the objects of sense and conceives an attachment for them, so that he can hardly think of anything else. From this attachment arises desire; and when the desire is thwarted he gets angry. Anger drives him nearly mad. He cannot understand what he is about. He thus loses his memory, behaves in a disorderly manner and comes to an ignoble end. When a man's senses rove at will, he is like a rudderless ship which is at the mercy of the gale and is broken to pieces on the rocks. Men should therefore abandon all desires and restrain their senses, so that these do not indulge in undesirable activity. The eyes then will look straight and that too only at holy objects; the ears will listen to hymns in praise of God or to cries of distress; hands and feet will be engaged in service. Indeed all the organs of sense and of action will be employed in helping a man to do his duty and making him a fit recipient of the grace of God. And once the grace of God has descended upon him, all his sorrows are at an end. As snow melts in the sunshine, all pain vanishes when the grace of God shines upon him and he is said to be stable in spirit. "But if a man is not stable-minded, how can he think good thoughts? Without good thoughts there is no peace, and without peace there is no happiness. Where a stable-minded man sees things clear as daylight, the unstable man distracted by the turmoil of the world is as good as blind. On the other hand what is pure in the eyes of the worldly-wise looks unclean to and repels the stable-minded man. Rivers continuously flow into the sea, but the sea remains unmoved; in the same way all sense-objects come to the yogi, but he always remains calm like the sea. Thus one who abandons all desires, is free from pride and selfishness and behaves as one apart, finds peace. This is the condition of a perfect man of God, and he who is established therein even at the final hour attains the beatitude of Brahman."

Note

1. This was sent along with "Letter to Narandas Gandhi", 13/17-11-1930; *vide* Vol. XLIV, pp. 317-22.

CHAPTER III[1]

Monday Morning, November 24, 1930

When Krishna had thus set forth the marks of identification for a *sthitaprajna* person, Arjuna received the impression that one had only to sit quiet in order to attain such a state, as Krishna had not made the slightest reference to any need for action on his part. He therefore asked Krishna: "It seems as if you hold that knowledge is superior to action. If so, why are you urging me to this terrible deed and thus confusing my mind? Please tell me clearly where my welfare lies."

Krishna replied: "O sinless Arjuna, since the beginning of time seekers have taken one or the other of two different paths. In one of these the pride of place is given to knowledge and in the other it is given to action. But you will find that freedom from action cannot be attained without action, that wisdom never comes to a man simply on account of his having ceased to act. Man does not become perfect merely by renouncing everything. Don't you see that every one of us is doing something or other all the time? Our very nature impels us to action. Such being the law of nature, one who sits with folded hands but lets his mind dwell on the objects of sense is a fool and may even be called a hypocrite. Rather than indulge in such senseless inactivity, is it not better that a man should control the senses, overcome his likes and dislikes, and engage himself in some activity or other without fuss and in a spirit of detachment? Do your allotted duty, restraining the organs of sense, for that is better than inaction. An idler will only meet his end the sooner for his idleness. But while acting, remember that action leads to bondage unless it is performed in a spirit of sacrifice. Sacrifice *(yajna)* means exerting oneself for the benefit of others, in a word, service. And where service is rendered for service's sake, there is no room for attachment, likes and dislikes. Perform such a sacrifice; render such service. When Brahma created the universe, He created sacrifice along with it, as it were, and said to mankind: 'Go forth into the world; serve one another and prosper. Look upon all creatures as gods. Serve and propitiate those gods, so that being pleased they will be gracious to you and fulfil your wishes unasked.' Therefore understand that whoever enjoys the fruits of the earth, without serving the people and without having first given them their share, is a thief. And he who enjoys them after having given all creatures their share is entitled to such enjoyment and is thus freed from sin. On the other hand, those who labour only for themselves are sinners and eat the fruit of sin. It is a law of nature that creatures are sustained by food, food production depends on the rains, and the rains descend on the earth on account of *yajna,* that is to say, the labour of all creatures. There is no rain where there are no creatures, and it does rain where they are there. All live by labour; none can remain idle and live, and if this is true of the lower forms of life, it is still more applicable to man. Action takes its origin from Brahma and Brahma from the imperishable Brahman; therefore the imperishable Brahman is present in all kinds of sacrifice or service. And whoever breaks this chain of mutual service is a sinner and he lives in vain.

Tuesday Morning

"When a man enjoys peace of mind and contentment, it may be said that there is nothing left for him to do. He does not stand to gain by action or by inaction. He has no personal interests to serve; and yet he must not cease to offer sacrifice. Therefore do your duty from day to day without entertaining likes and dislikes and in a spirit of detachment. He who acts in such a spirit enjoys the beatific vision. Then again, if even a selfless king like Janaka reached perfection all the while working for the good of the people, how can you behave in a way different from his? Whatever a good and great man does, common people imitate. Take My own case for instance. I have nothing to gain by action, and yet ceaselessly do I pour myself out in action. Hence it is that people too go on working more or less. But what would happen if I ceased to work? The world would collapse if the sun, the moon and the stars ceased to move. And it is I who set them in motion and regulate their activity. But there is a difference between My attitude and the attitude of the common man. I act in the spirit of perfect detachment while he harbours attachment and works in his own interest. If a wise man like you ceased to act, others too would do the same and their minds would be unsettled. Therefore do your duty without attachment, so that others might not cease to work and might gradually learn to work without attachment. Man is bound to work in obedience, to and in conformity with his own nature. Only a fool thinks that he himself is the doer. To breathe is a part of man's nature; when an insect settles upon the eye, the eyelid moves of its own accord. And nobody says: 'I take in the air' or 'I move the eyelid'. In the same manner why should not all human actions be performed in accordance with the qualities of nature? Why should there be any egoism about it? In order that a man may be able thus to act naturally and without attachment, the best thing for him to do is to dedicate all his actions to Me and perform them without egoism as a mere instrument in My hands. When a man thus gets over selfishness, all his actions are natural and free from taint and he escapes many a trouble. Actions then have no binding force for him. Action being natural, it is sheer egoism to outrage nature and to claim to be inactive. The victim of such egoism will externally appear not to act, but his mind is always active in scheming. This is worse than external activity and has all the greater binding force.

"As a matter of fact the senses feel attraction and aversion for their respective objects. For instance the ears like to hear some things and do not like to hear other things. The nose likes to smell the rose, and does not like to smell dirt. This is also true of the other organs of sense. Therefore what man has to do is not to submit to these two robbers, namely, attraction and repulsion. If one wishes to escape their attentions, he must not go about in search of action. He must not hanker after this today, that tomorrow and the other thing the day after. But he should hold himself ready to render for the sake of God such service as falls to his share. Thus he will cultivate within himself the feeling that whatever he does is in fact an act of God and not his own, and his egoism will be a thing of the past. This is svadharma (one's own duty). One must stick to svadharma, for it is the best for oneself at any rate. Paradharma (another's duty) may appear to be better, but even so it should be looked upon as dangerous. Moksha (salvation) lies in embracing death while doing one's own duty."

When Krishna said that action performed by one who is free from likes and dislikes is sacrifice, Arjuna asked: "What is it that makes a man commit sin? Very often it seems as if he were driven to sin by some outsider against his own will."

Krishna replied: "The slave-drivers in this case are kama (desire) and krodha (anger). These are like blood brothers. If desire is not satisfied, anger is the inevitable consequence. One who is the slave of desire and anger is said to be inspired by rajoguna (the quality of passion), which is man's greatest enemy and against which he has to fight day in, day out. As dust hides a mirror, smoke suffocates a fire and the womb covers the embryo, even so anger deprives knowledge of its lustre and suffocates it. And desire is insatiable like fire, and taking possession of man's sense?, mind and intellect, knocks him down. Therefore first control your senses, and then conquer the mind. When you have done this, the intellect also will obey your orders. For, though among the senses, the mind and the intellect, the mind is greater than the senses and the intellect is greater than the mind, the soul is the greatest of all. Man has no idea of his own strength or soul-force, and tends to believe that the senses, the mind and the intellect are not amenable to his control. But when once he has gained confidence in soul-force, everything else becomes easy as a matter of course. And desire, anger and their countless hosts hold no terror for him who has mastered the senses, the mind and the intellect."

[Note.] I call this chapter the key to an understanding of the Gita, and the gist of it is that life is given us for service and not for enjoyment. We have therefore to impart a sacrificial character to our lives. Intellectual assent to this proposition is only the first step, but such assent and conduct in terms of that assent are bound to rid our heart of its impurities in course of time. But what is real service? In order to obtain the right answer to this question, restraint of the senses is essential, as it gives us a clearer and clearer vision of the God of truth. Service rendered with selfish motives ceases to be sacrifice. Hence the urgent need for the spirit of detachment. When this is understood, all manner of controversies lose their meaning for us. 'Did Krishna really ask Arjuna to kill his relatives? Could such killing ever be a part of one's duty?'

Questions like these are set at rest for ever. When detachment governs our actions, even the weapon raised in order to strike an enemy down falls out of our hand. But a mere pretence of detachment serves no useful purpose. If only we persevere in our effort, detachment may come to us perhaps the very first day, or maybe only after a thousand years. We must not worry over the time this takes, for the effort carries within itself the seeds of success. We must however be on our guard and make sure that it is a genuine effort, and that there is no self-deception. And this is certainly possible for us all.[2]

Notes

1. This was sent along with "Letter to Narandas Gandhi", 21/25-11-1930; *vide* Vol. XLIV, pp. 336-41.
2. This note has also appeared under the date of writing in Vol. XLIV, pp. 339-40.

CHAPTER IV[1]

Monday Morning [December 7, 1930]

The Lord says to Arjuna: "The yoga of selfless action which I commend to you is an ancient truth; I am not propounding any new doctrine. I have declared it to you, as you are my devoted friend, in order to heal the conflict in your mind. Whenever goodness weakens and evil grows from strength to strength, I incarnate Myself and protect the good and destroy the wicked. Those who are aware of this power *(maya)* of Mine are confident that evil is bound to go under. I am always by the good man's side. He never strays from the strait and narrow path and he comes to Me at last, for he meditates on Me and hides himself in Me and thus is delivered from passion and anger and is purified by austerity and wisdom. As a man sows, so he reaps. None can escape from the operation of the laws I have made. I established the four *varnas* (classes, not castes) by the different distribution of qualities and actions. However I am not their author, for I do not desire the fruits of action and have nothing to do with the merit or demerit arising therefrom. This divine *maya* (course of action) is worth knowing. All activities prevalent in the world are subject to divine laws, and yet God is not defiled by them. Therefore He is, and also is not, their author. And a man who does likewise and acts in a spirit of detachment without being defiled by actions and by the yearning for their fruit is sure to be saved. In action he sees inaction and he understands at once what is wrong action. Wrong actions are all those that are inspired by desire and cannot be performed in the absence of desire, such for instance as theft, adultery and the like. These simply cannot be done in a spirit of detachment. Therefore those who do the duty that lies nearest without desire and scheming for the fruit of the action may be said to have burnt up their actions in the fire of wisdom *(jnana)*. A man who has thus abandoned the attachment to the fruit of action is always contented, always independent. He has his mind under control. He gives up all his possessions. And his activity is natural like the bodily functions of a healthy individual. He is free from any pride or even consciousness that he is acting on his own. He has the realization that he is a mere instrument of the divine will. What does it matter whether he meets with success or with failure? He is neither elated by the one, nor unnerved by the other. All his work is done as a sacrifice *(yajna)*, that is to say, as service to the world. He meditates upon God in all his actions and in the end comes to Him.

"There are many forms of sacrifice, the root of which lies in purity and service, such as, for instance, control of the senses, charity and *pranayama* (breath-control) practised with a view to self-purification. Knowledge of these can be acquired from a wise teacher (guru) through humility, earnestness and service. If anybody indulges in various activities which he thinks are *yajna*, without any understanding of what *yajna* is, he will only do harm to himself and to the world. It is therefore necessary that all actions should be performed intelligently. This wisdom *(jnana)* is not mere book-learning. In it there is no room for doubt. It begins with faith and ends in experience. It enables a man to see all beings in himself and to see himself in God so that everything appears to him to be actually informed by God. Such wisdom effects the salvation of the worst of sinners. It releases the seeker from the bondage of action, so that he is not affected by its results. There is nothing else in the world so holy as this wisdom. Therefore try to obtain it with a heart full of faith in God and with the senses under control, so that you will enjoy perfect peace of mind."

[NOTE.] The third, the fourth and the following fifth chapter should be read together, as they explain to us what the yoga of selfless action *(anasakti)* is and what are the means of practising it. If these three chapters are properly understood, the reader will have less difficulty in tackling what follows. The remaining chapters deal in detail with the ways and means of achieving *anasakti*. We should study the *Gita* from this point of view, and if we pursue this study we shall find without much trouble a solution of the problems which confront us from day to day. This calls for daily practice. Let everybody try it. If for instance he is angry, let him remember the verse dealing with anger and subdue that enemy. Supposing we heartily dislike somebody, or are impatient or gluttonous or in doubt as to whether we should do or should not do something or other, all these difficulties can be solved with the help of Mother *Gita* if we have faith in it and give it constant study. Our daily recitation of the *Gita* as well as this series of letters is a means to this end.[2]

Notes

1. This was sent along with "Letter to Narandas Gandhi", November 27/December 3, 1930; *vide* Vol. XLIV, pp. 353-5.
2. This note has also appeared under the date of writing in Vol. XLIV, p. 355.

CHAPTER V[1]

December 9, 1930

Arjuna said: "You speak highly of knowledge, so that I am inclined to think that action is unnecessary. But then you also praise action, thus making me feel that unselfish performance of action is the thing to do. My mind will be at peace only if you tell me definitely which of the two is better."

The Lord replied: "Sannyasa means knowledge and karmayoga means selfless action. Both of them are good, but if I had to choose between the two, I should say that yoga or selfless action is better. The man who does not hate anyone or anything, does not long for anything and is free from the pairs of opposites such as heat and cold, pleasure and pain, is a sannyasi (wise man, literally, one who renounces the world), no matter whether he is or is not a performer of action. He easily casts off the chain that binds him. Only the ignorant speak of wisdom and action as different, not the learned. The fruit of both is the same; both lead to an identical goal. Therefore he who sees them as one sees truly. The man of pure wisdom achieves his object by merely willing it, and has no need to perform an outward act. When the city of Mithila was on fire, others were bound to rush to it and fight the fire. But King Janaka contributed to this fight by his mental determination only, for his servants were ready to obey his commands. If he had run about with a water-pot to quench the fire, he would only have done harm; others would have stared at him and failed to perform their own duty, or at the most would have rushed here and there with a view to the King's safety. But it is not given to every one of us to become a Janaka at once. It is indeed a very difficult task to reach a Janaka-like state. Only one in a million can reach it as the fruit of service extending over many lives^ and it is not a bed of roses either. As a man goes on performing selfless action, his thought grows from strength to strength and he resorts less and less to external action. But he is hardly conscious of this change, and he has not this change in view either. He is devoted only to service, with the result that his power of rendering service increases to such an extent that he hardly seems to rest from service. And finally his service is limited to thought alone, just as an object in extraordinary motion seems to be at rest. It is obviously improper to say that such a man does nothing. But this lofty state can, as a rule, be only imagined, and not experienced. Hence my preference for karmayoga. Millions derive the fruit of sannyasa (wisdom, literally, 'renunciation') from selfless action alone. They would fall between two stools if they tried their hand at sannyasa. If they take to sannyasa, it is very likely that they will become hypocrites, and as they have ceased to perform action, they are lost altogether. But a man who has purified himself by means of selfless action, who has his mind and his senses under control and who has identified himself with all beings, loving them as himself—such a man stands apart from action although he is acting all the time, and is not bound by it. He talks, he walks, he takes part in normal human activity, but his activity seems to be merely a function of his organs of sense, and he himself seems to be doing nothing. The bodily functions of a physically healthy person are natural and spontaneous. His stomach for instance functions independently of him; he has not to bother about its functioning. Similarly a spiritually healthy person, though acting through his body, is not tainted by it and may be said to be doing nothing. Therefore a man should dedicate all his actions to Brahma (God) and perform them on His behalf, so that in spite of his activity he does not earn either merit or demerit and is untouched by either, like a lotus leaf which is untouched by water.

Tuesday Morning

"Therefore a yogi (man of selfless action), performing action with the body, mind and understanding in a spirit of detachment and without egotism, purifies himself and enters into peace. The non-yogi, on the other hand, being attached to the fruit of action, is a prisoner bound by his own desires. The yogi lives blissfully in the city with nine gates, that is, his body, having renounced all actions by his mind, and realized that there is nothing at all that he himself is doing or getting done. The man with a purified soul does not commit sin, nor does he do any meritorious deed. He who acts in a spirit of detachment, having destroyed his egotism and renounced the fruit of action, becomes a mere machine moving at the will and pleasure of the Master Mechanic or an instrument in the hands of God. The question, therefore, of his earning merit or demerit does not arise. On the other hand, the ignorant man is always counting his merit and demerit, and sinking deeper and deeper into the pit, so that in the end the only thing he has earned is demerit. But as regards the man who destroys his own ignorance by knowledge from day to day, his spontaneous actions grow purer and purer, and appear perfect and meritorious in the world's eyes. He sees all things with an equal eye. He is equi-minded towards a learned and humble Brahma-knowing Brahmin, a cow, an elephant, a dog and a degraded human being who is worse than a beast. That is to say, he serves them all with equal devotion. He does not honour any one of them or treat another with contempt. The man of selfless action holds himself to be the world's debtor, and he repays what he owes to everyone else and does him full justice. Here on earth he takes the creation captive and is filled with the spirit of the Supreme. He is not elated if anybody does something pleasant; nor is he pained if foul abuse is poured upon him. The man attached to the world seeks happiness from outside himself. On the other hand, he who acts in a spirit of selfless detachment discovers the spring of eternal peace in himself, having withdrawn his mind from external objects. All sensual pleasures are a source of pain. One should resist the rush of desire, anger and the like. The selfless yogi is constantly engaged in doing good to all creatures. His mind is free from doubt. He is not of the world though he is in the world. He turns his eyes inward by means of *pranqyama* (control of breath), etc., and conquers desire, fear and anger. He knows Me alone to be the supreme Lord of all, the Friend, and the recipient of sacrificial offerings, and enters into My peace."

Note

1. This was sent along with "Letter to Narandas Gandhi", 4/9-12-1930; *vide* Vol. XLIV, pp. 371-4.

CHAPTER VI[1]

Tuesday Morning, December 16, 1930

The Lord said: "The man who does his duty without any sel□fish desire for fruit may be called a sannyasi as well as a yogi. But he who abstains from action altogether is only an idler. The root of the matter is that one should not allow his mind to flit from one object of desire to another and from that to a third. He who would practise yoga, i.e., evenness of temper (samatvam), cannot but perform action. The man who has achieved such evenness of temper will be serene, because his mere thoughts are charged with the strength of action. A yogi is one who is not attached to the objects of sense or to action and whose mind has ceased to roam restlessly.

"A man can be saved or ruined by himself alone. Therefore he becomes his own friend or his own enemy as the case may be. To one who has subdued his mind, his soul is a friend; while the soul is an enemy for him who has failed to achieve self-con□trol. The test for self-control is that heat and cold, pleasure and pain, honour and dishonour do not disturb one's inner serenity. He is a yogi who is a man of knowledge as well as experience, who is unwavering and master of his senses and to whom gold, stone and earth seem all alike. He regards with an equal eye friend and foe, sinner and saint. With a view to attaining this state a man should stabilize his mind, divest it of all sensual desires, and meditate in solitude on the Supreme Self. It is "not enough to practise yogic *asanas* (postures), etc. In order to achieve evenness of temper, one must scrupulously keep the major observances *{yra-tas)*, such as *brahmacharya* (chastity) and the like. A man who thus takes his place on a firm seat, keeps the observances and con□centrates his mind on God, enters into perfect peace.

"This equanimity is not for one who overeats or merely fasts, nor for one who is too much addicted to sleep or to vigils. Its seeker has to keep a sense of proportion in all his actions such as eating and drinking, sleeping and keeping awake. To overeat one day and fast the next day, to oversleep for a day and keep a vigil the next, to work hard for a day and pass the next in idleness is no characteristic of a yogi. The yogi is stable-minded at all times, and is without effort free from all desires. He is like an unflickering lamp burning in a windless place. He is not tossed to and fro by dramatic events on the world-stage or by his own brain waves. Such mental poise can be acquired by slow but steady effort. The mind is fickle and restless, but it should be gradually stabilized, for a man can have peace of mind only when he is firm of understanding. In order thus to stabilize the mind, he should constantly fix it on the soul. He will then see all beings in himself and himself in all beings, for he will see Me in all beings and all beings in Me. He who is absorbed in Me, and sees Me everywhere ceases to be himself, so that he is at all times attuned to Me irrespective of what he is doing, and is incapable of sin."

Yoga thus described seemed to Arjuna to be a tall order, and he exclaimed: "How is one to achieve such equanimity? The human mind is restless like a monkey, and as difficult to control as the wind. How is it to be curbed?"

The Lord replied: "You are right. But if a man earnestly sets about conquering attachment and aversion, yoga will not be difficult for him to practise. But it should be clear to you that it is not for one who cannot control his mind."

Then Arjuna posed another question: "Supposing a man has faith, but is lax in his effort and is thus unsuccessful in perfecting himself, what happens to him? Is he destroyed like a broken cloud in the sky?"

The Lord said: "Such a man of faith is never lost, for no one who takes the right path ever comes to an evil end. After death he lives for a time in some celestial world according to his merit and is then reborn on the earth into a holy family. But such a birth is difficult to obtain. He then regains the mental impressions developed in his former lives, and struggling harder for perfection, reaches the supreme goal. Thus making an assiduous effort some attain equanimity soon, while others do so after a number of lives in accordance with the measure of their faith and endeavour. This evenness of temper is superior to asceticism, to knowledge and to sacred rites, for these latter are after all only means to the end of equanimity. Do you therefore become even-minded and a yogi. And even among yogis hold him to be the best who dedicates his all to Me and worships Me alone in full faith."

[Note.] *Pranayama* (control of breath) and *asanas* (yogic postures) are referred to appreciatively in this chapter, but we should remember that at the same time the Lord has stressed the need for *brahmacharya*, i.e., keeping the observances calculated to take us nearer and nearer to God. It should be clearly understood that the mere practice of *asanas* and the like can never take us to the goal of evenmindedness. *Asanas* and *pranayama* may be of some slight help in steadying the mind and making it single-purposed, provided that they are practised to that end. Otherwise they are no better than other methods of physical training. They are very useful indeed as physical exercise and I believe that this type of exercise is good for the soul, and may be performed from a bodily standpoint. But I have observed that these practices do only harm when indulged in for the acquisition of supernormal powers *(siddhi)* and the performance of miracles. This chapter should be studied as a summary of the teaching in the preceding three chapters. It cheers us up in our spiritual struggle. We should never be down-hearted and give up the endeavour, to reach evenness of temper.[2]

Note

1. This was sent along with "Letter to Narandas Gandhi", 13/16-12-1930; vide Vol. XLV, pp. 1-3.
2. This note has also appeared under the date of writing in Vol. XLV, p. 2.

CHAPTER VII[1]

Tuesday Morning [December 23, 1930[1]]

The Lord said: "O King, I will tell you how a man who devotes his whole mind to Me, takes refuge in Me and practises karmayoga can have perfect knowledge of Me free from the shadow of a doubt. I will declare to you this knowledge based on experience, which having been known, nothing more here remains to be known. Hardly one from among thousands strives to acquire this knowledge, and perhaps one only of these strivers makes a success of it.

"Earth, water, fire, air, ether, mind, intellect and egoism—

this is the eightfold composition of My *prakriti* (nature). This is the lower nature; the other is higher nature, that is, life. This world is born of these two natures, that is to say, from the coming together of body and soul. Therefore I am the cause of the origin and destruction of all things. As pearls are strung on a thread, even so is the world held together by Me. Thus I am the taste in the waters, the light in the sun and the moon, the syllable 'Om[5] in the Vedas, the sound in ether, the spirit of enterprise .in men, the sweet smell in the earth the brightness in fire, the life in all that lives, the austerity of ascetics, the intelligence of the intelligent, the pure strength of the strong, and the craving of all beings which does not run counter to righteousness. In short you should understand that all that belongs to the states of *sattva*[2], *rajas*[3] and *tamas*[4] proceeds from Me, and depends upon Me alone. People deluded by these three qualities *(gunas)* do not recognize Me Who am imperishable. My *maya* made of these qualities is hard to overcome. But those who take refuge in Me pass beyond this *maya*, that is, the three *gunas*. Foolish evil-doers cannot think of coming to Me even in their dreams. Being steeped in illusion, they roam in darkness and do not acquire knowledge. But the doers of good deeds worship Me. Some of them do so in order to obtain relief in their distress; others seek for knowledge of Me. A third group are inspired by a desire to get something for themselves while others worship Me with understanding, thinking it to be their duty. Worship of Me means service of My creation. This service is rendered by some because of their misery, by others in order to gain some advantage, by a third group out of curiosity as regards the outcome of such activity and by a fourth group who know what they are about and for whom service of others is something that they cannot do without. These last are My wise devotees, dearer to Me than all the rest of them. Or rather they know Me best and are nearest to Me. Their wisdom is the fruit of a quest extending over a number of lives, and when they have acquired this wisdom, they see nothing in the world except Me, Vasudeva. But those who are smitten by a variety of desires resort to other deities. I alone, however, am the giver of rewards commensurate with the devotion of each. The achievement too of these devotees of limited understanding is limited, but they rest content with it. These men in their ignorance imagine that they know Me through the senses. They do not realize that My imperishable and supreme form is beyond the reach of the senses and cannot be grasped with the hands, the ears, the nose, the eyes. Thus the ignorant do not recognize Me though I am the Creator of all things. This is my *yogamaya* (creative power). Pleasure and pain are the necessary consequence of likes and dislikes and keep mankind under the influence of delusion. But those who have freed themselves from delusion and purified their thoughts and actions hold firmly to their vows and offer Me constant worship. They know Me in the form of perfect Brahman (the Absolute) as well as of individual selves embodied as various kinds of creatures *(adhyatma)*, and My creative action (karma). Those who thus know Me as the One who governs the material *(adhibhuta)* and the divine *(adhidaiva)* aspects and the sacrifices *(adhiyajna)* and have attained evenness of temper, are released from the bondage of birth and death after they have died. Because they have acquired the knowledge of reality their mind ceases to dwell on trivialities; they see the whole universe to be filled with the spirit of God and are absorbed in Him."

Notes

1. This was sent along with "Letter to Narandas Gandhi", 18/23-12-1930; *vide* Vol. XLV, pp. 19-25.

2, 3 & 4 Harmony, passion, sloth; or rhythm, activity, inertia.

CHATPER VIII[1]

Monday Morning, December 29, 1930

Arjuna asked: "You spoke of Brahman' (the Absolute), *'adhyatma,'* 'karma', *'adhibhuta'*, *'adhidaiva?* and *'adhiyajna'*, but I do not under□stand the meaning of all these words. Again you say that at the hour of death you are revealed to those who know you as *adhibhuta*, etc., and have attained evenness of temper. Please explain all this to me."

The Lord replied: "Brahman is the imperishable supreme aspect of God, and *adhyatma* is the individual soul living in the body of all beings as the doer and the enjoyer. Karma is the process through which all beings come into existence, or in other words, the process of creation. *Adhibhuta* is Myself as the perishable body, and *adhiyajna* is the individual soul purified through sacrifice. Thus whether as the body or as the foolish soul or as the purified soul or as Brahman, it is I who am everywhere. And never doubt this that he who meditates on Me in all these aspects at the hour of death, forgets himself, is careful of nothing and desirous of nothing will be united with Me. Whatever a man constantly dwells on in his mind and remembers at the time of death is realized by him. Therefore at all times you should remember Me and set your mind and heart upon Me and you will surely come to Me. You may say that it is hard thus to stabilize the mind. But you take it from Me that one can become single-minded by daily practice and constant endeavour, for as I told you just now, all embodied beings are in the essence Myself in various forms. For this he should prepare himself from the very first so that his mind does not go astray at the time of death, but is steeped in devotion, keeps the life force *(prana)* steady, and thinks only of Me as the Omniscient the Ancient, the Ruler, the subtle supporter of all and dispeller of ignorance like the sun which drives darkness away.

"This supreme state is known to the Vedas as *Akskara* (the Imperishable) Brahman and is reached by sages who have freed themselves from likes and dislikes! All who desire to reach it observe *brahmacharya,* i.e., keep body, mind and speech under control and give up all objects, of sense in these three ways. Men and women who die, having controlled the senses and uttering the sacred syllable Om' and remembering Me as they depart, reach the supreme state. Their mind is never distracted by other thoughts, and when they have thus come to Me, they are not reborn into this painful condition. To come to Me is the only means of breaking the vicious circle of birth and death.

"Men measure time by the human span of a hundred years, and during that period do thousands of questionable deeds. But time is infinite. A thousand *yugas* (ages) make up the day of Brahma; compared with it a human day or even a hundred years of human life are as nothing. What is the use of counting such infinitesimal measures of time? Human life is as only a moment in the in finite cycle of time. It is up to us therefore to think of God alone to the exclusion of all else. How can we afford to run after momentary pleasures? Creation and dissolution have gone on unceasingly during Brahma's day and night and will do so in future too.

"Brahma who creates and dissolves beings is only an aspect of Me. He is the unmanifested which cannot be perceived by the senses. Beyond this unmanifested there is yet another unmanifested aspect of Mine of which I have spoken to you. He who reaches it is not reborn, for there is no day or night so far as this is concerned. This is a calm and immovable aspect, which can be realized only by single-minded devotion. It supports and pervades the whole universe.

"It is said that one who dies in the bright half of the month during *Uttarayana* (the northward movement of the sun from January to July) comes to Me if he is mindful of Me at the last moment, and that he who dies in the dark half of the month during *Dakshinayana* (the southward movement from July to January) is reborn into the world. '*Uttarayana*' and the 'bright fortnight' here may be interpreted to mean the path of selfless service; and '*Dakshinayana*' and the 'dark half of month' to mean selfishness. The path of service is the path of knowledge, and the path of selfishness is the path of ignorance. He who treads the path of knowledge is released from the bondage of birth and death, while he who takes the path of ignorance becomes a bondslave. After having realized the difference between the two, who would be so foolish as to prefer to walk the way of ignorance? All men should learn to discriminate between the paths, renounce all fruits of merit, act in a spirit of detachment and discharge their duty with all their heart and soul, and thus endeavour to reach the supreme state described by Me."

Note

1. This was sent along with "Letter to Narandas Gandhi", 27/30-12-1930; vide Vol. XLV, pp. 37-9.

CHAPTER IX[1]

Monday Morning [January 5, 1931]

Having described the lofty state of a yogi in the last verse of the preceding chapter, the Lord now naturally proceeds to sing the glory of *bhakti* (devotion). For the yogi in terms of the *Gita* is neither a dry-as-dust man of knowledge, nor a devotee carried away by his own enthusiasm, but a selfless performer of action imbued with the spirit of wisdom as well as devotion.

So the Lord said: "As you are free from hatred, I shall now tell you the secret of wisdom, a knowledge of which will contribute to your welfare. This is the holy knowledge above all other and is easy to translate into action. Those who have no faith in it fail to find Me. Men cannot perceive My unmanifested form by their senses; yet it pervades the universe. It supports the universe; the universe does not support it. Again in a sense it may be said that all these beings are not in Me, and I am not in them. Although I am the source of all beings and their sustainer, they are not in Me and I am not in them; for in ignorance they do not know Me and are not devoted to Me. Know this to be My divine mystery.

"But though it seems as if I am not in these beings, I am like the air moving everywhere. All creatures pass into My nature at the end of a cycle and are reborn at the beginning of creation. These acts are Mine, but they do not bind Me, for I act in a spirit of detachment and am indifferent as to the fruit they bear. These events happen as such is My nature. But people do not recognize Me in such a guise and deny My existence altogether. They entertain vain aspirations, perform vain actions and are full of ignorance, so that they can be said to partake of the nature of demons. But those who abide in the divine nature know and worship Me as the imperishable Creator. They are firm in their determination. They are always striving for virtue, praising Me, and meditating on Me. Others again believe Me to be one or to be many. There are countless attributes of Me; therefore those who believe Me to be many think of different attributes as so many different faces of Mine. But one and all, they are My devotees.

"I am the intention to offer a sacrifice, I the sacrifice itself, I the offering made to the spirits of the fathers, I the herb, I the sacred verse *(mantra)*, I the oblation, I the fire to which it is offered. I am the Father of this world, I the Mother, the supporter and the Grandsire, the object of knowledge, the syllable 'Om', *Rig-Veda, Sam-Veda* and *Yajur-Veda*. I am the end of the pilgrim's path, the sustainer, the Lord, the Witness. I am the shelter, the lover, the origin, the dissolution, heat and cold, being and non-being. Those who perform the rites mentioned in the Vedas do so in order to gain their fruit. They may thus attain the world of heaven, but they have to return to the world of mortals and to die. But if a man meditates upon Me with an undis-tracted mind and worships Me alone, I bear all his burdens, supply all his needs and protect his possessions. Some others who worship other deities with faith in their hearts are victims of ignorance, but they are really worshipping Me for I am the Lord of all sacrifices. However, they do not know Me in My comprehensive nature and therefore are unable to reach the supreme state. Worshippers of the gods go to the world of the gods, the ancestor-worshippers to the world of the fathers and those who worship the spirits go to the spirits, while those who worship Me with the right approach come to Me. I accept the offering of love made by seekers, even if it be only a leaf or a flower. Therefore whatever you do, do it only as an offering to Me, so that your responsibility for the good and evil results will cease altogether. As you will have renounced all the fruits of action, there will be no more births and deaths for you. I am the same to all beings; none is hateful or dear to Me. But those who worship Me with devotion are in Me, and I am in them. This is not partiality but only the natural consequence of their devotion. Devotion indeed works wonders. He who worships Me in utter devotion becomes a saint even if he has been a sinner. As darkness vanishes before the sun, a man abandons his evil ways as soon as he comes to Me. Therefore know for certain that My devotee shall not perish. He becomes a man of religion and enters into My peace. Those who are born in the so-called lower castes and illiterate women, Vaishyas and Sudras who take refuge in Me come to Me. It goes without saying that so do Brahmins and Kshatriyas who lead a holy life. Every devotee enjoys the fruit of his devotion. Therefore you who have been born in this unsubstantial world should worship Me and work out your salvation. Fix your mind on Me, be devoted to Me, offer your sacrifices for My sake, prostrate yourself before Me. And if you are intent on Me and reduce yourself to zero by attuning yourself to Me, you are sure to come to Me.

Tuesday Morning, [January 6, 1931]

NOTE. We learn from this Chapter that devotion *(bhakti)* means attachment *(asakti)* to God. This is the royal road to the cultivation of a selfless spirit. Therefore we are told at the very beginning that devotion is the sovereign yoga and is easy to practise. It is easy to practise if it takes hold of our heart, but hard going if it does not. Hence it has been described as something for which we have to offer our life itself as the price. But he who has plunged into it enjoys perfect bliss though it scares the mere spectator. Sudhanva[2] was laughing as he lay in the boiling oil while the bystanders were seized with terror and anxiety. The 'untouchable' Nanda is said to have danced as he was tried by the ordeal of fire.[3] We need not bother whether or not these are true stories. But the fact is that a man reaches such a state of calmness and imperturbability when he is absorbed in something or other. He forgets himself. But who would set his heart on anything except God? 'Do not prefer the bitter *neem* to sugarcane or the glow-worm to the sun and the moon.' The ninth chapter thus shows that renunciation of the fruit of action is impossible without devotion *(bhakti)*. Its last verse sums up the whole chapter and in a word means, "Seeking nothing, give yourself utterly to Me."

Notes

1. This was sent along with "Letter to Narandas Gandhi", 1/6-1-1931; vide Vol. XLV, pp. 64-7.
2. Son of King Hansadhwaj of Champavati in the *Mahabharata*. He was thrown into boiling oil for disobeying his father who was an atheist; but he came out unscathed because of his devotion to God.
3. Nanda was not subjected to any ordeal. The legend is that he went up in flames as he entered the shrine.

CHAPTER X[1]

Monday Morning, January 12, 1931

The Lord said: "Hear once more what I say with a view to the welfare of devotees. Even gods and great sages do not know my beginning, for the very simple reason that I am without beginning myself and am the origin of the universe including gods and sages. The wise man who knows Me to be unborn and without beginning is liberated from all sins, for when he realizes Me as such and himself as My child or as part and parcel of Me, he overcomes the human liability to sin. Ignorance of one's real nature is the root of sin.

"As all beings derive from Me, so do the various natures distributed to them, such as for instance forgiveness, truth, joy and sorrow, birth and death, fear and fearlessness. Those who know all these to be My glorious manifestations easily become even-minded, as they cease to be egotistic. Their heart is fixed on Me. They dedicate their all to Me. I am the only subject of their conversation. They glorify Me and live in happiness and contentment. To these loving worshippers always aware of Me I grant the power of understanding, by means of which they come to Me." Arjuna then praised the Lord: "You are the Supreme Brahman, the highest Abode, and the Lord. You yourself say that sages worship you as the First of the Gods, the Birthless, the All-pervading.

O Lord, O Father, no one knows- your real nature; it is known to you alone. Now please tell me your glorious manifestations, and explain to me how I may recognize you by meditation."

The Lord replied: "There is no end to My divine manifestations, but I shall name the chief of these only. I am the *atman* (soul) dwelling in the heart of all beings. I am the beginning, the middle and the end of them all. Of the Adityas I am Vishnu. Among the lights I am the light-giving sun. Of the Maruts (wind-gods) I am Marichi. Among the stars I am the moon. Of the Vedas I am the *Sama-Veda*. Of the gods I am Indra. Of the sense-organs I am the mind. Of beings I am consciousness. Of the Rudras I am Shankara (Siva). Of the Yakshas and Rakshasas I am Kubera. Of the Daityas (demons) I am Prahlada. Of beasts I am the lion. Of birds I am the eagle. Indeed I am even the gambling of the cheats. Whatever, good or evil, happens in this world happens only by My permission. Realizing this, men should give up their pride and steer clear of evil, for I am the dispenser of the fruits of their good and bad deeds. You should realize that only a single fraction of Mine sustains the entire universe."

Note

1. This was sent along with "Letter to Narandas Gandhi", 12-1-1931; *vide* Vol. XLV, pp. 85-6.

CHAPTER XI[1]

Monday Morning and Afternoon [January 19, 1931]

Arjuna, asking the Lord for a favour, said: "O Supreme Lord, by teaching me the truth about the soul, you have dispelled my ignorance. You are All, the Creator and the Destroyer, being Imperishable yourself. If possible, please let me have a vision of your divine Form."

The Lord said: "There are thousands of my divine forms in various colours. The Adityas[2], the Vasus[3] and the Rudras[4]—all are unified in My body, as well as all things, animate and inanimate. But you cannot see this My form with those fleshly eyes. Therefore I give you divine sight with which to see Me."

Sanjaya said to Dhritarashtra: "O king, speaking thus to Arjuna, the Lord revealed to him His marvellous form which defies description. We see a single sun in the sky every day, but supposing a thousand suns were blazing in the sky, the glory of what Arjuna saw was more dazzling than their accumulated light. The ornaments and the weapons of that form were similarly divine. Arjuna's hair then stood erect. And he spoke, shaking all over."

Arjuna said: "O God, I see everything and everybody within your body. Brahma and Siva are there, and so are the sages and the holy serpents. I see you with countless arms and f^ces, and find no beginning, middle or end. You shine like a mass of insufferable light, and blaze like fire. You are the ultimate foundation of the universe, the Ancient of Days, and the guardian of eternal law. Wherever I look, I see parts of your body. The sun and the moon are your eyes as it were. You pervade heaven and earth. Your splendour burns up the universe. This world is seized with awe. The gods, the sages, and the *siddhas*—all are standing with clasped hands and sing your praise. On seeing this stupendous form and brilliance I lose my nerve. My patience and peace are gone. O God, have mercy on me. I see these people rush into your mouth frightful with tusks as moths fly into a flame and you crush them to powder. Who are you with such an awful form? I cannot understand your ways."

The Lord said: "I am Time, the destroyer of worlds. You may or may not fight, but the warriors on both the sides are bound to perish. You are only an instrument of the divine will."

Arjuna said: "O God, home of all the worlds, you are the Imperishable, Being and non-Being and what is beyond either of them. You are the First of the Gods, the Ancient of Days; you are the refuge of the world. You are the one thing which is to be known. You are Vayu (wind), Yama (the God of Death and Judgment), Agni (fire) and Prajapati (the Creator). Hail to you a thousand times. Now please show me your original form again."

The Lord then said: "I showed My world-wide Form to you, because I love you. You have seen today something the vision of which cannot be won by Vedic or any other studies, rituals, alms or austerities. Do not be bewildered because you have seen it. Cast away fear, be calm and see my familiar form. That shape of Mine which you have seen is hard to see even for the gods and can be seen only by pure devotion. Whoever works for Me, makes Me his supreme good, becomes my devotee, frees himself from attachment and loves all beings, comes to me."

NOTE. This chapter, like the tenth, I have deliberately cut short. This one is full of poetry and therefore should be read frequently either in the original or in translation, so that we may be imbued with the spirit of devotion. Whether we are or not thus imbued can be found by applying the acid test mentioned in the last verse. Devotion is impossible in the absence of total self-surrender and all-embracing love. Self-surrender and a sense of solidarity with all living beings become easy of attainment if we meditate on God as world-destroying time into whose gaping mouths the universe rushes to its doom. This fate is bound to overtake us too all of a sudden, whether we wish for it or not. Thus all distinctions of small and big, high and low, man and woman, men and the lower animals, disappear. Seeing that we are all a mere morsel in the mouth of God as the Destroyer, we should become humble and reduce ourselves to zero and cultivate friendship with everyone else. If we do this, we. shall cease to be afraid of this terrible Form of God. On the other hand it will give us peace of mind.

Notes

1. This was sent along with "Letter to Narandas Gandhi", 14/19-1-1931; *vide* Vol. XLV, pp. 102-5.

2,3&4 Various classes of gods.

CHAPTER XII[1]

Tuesday Morning, November 4, 1930

Arjuna asks the Lord: "Some devotees adore a personal *(sakara)* God while others worship the Absolute *(nirakara)*. Which of these two courses is better?"

The Lord replies: "Those who fix their minds on Me (as the One Life in all) with perfect faith and are absorbed in Me are My devotees indeed. But those who worship the Absolute and restrain and subdue their senses are equiminded towards all living beings and serve them without looking on some as of a superior and others as of an inferior grade—they also will come to Me. Neither of these two classes of devotees is superior to the other. But a full realization of the Absolute is almost impossible for an embodied being. The Absolute is devoid of all attributes and thus difficult for men even to imagine. Therefore they are all worshippers of a personal God, whether they are aware of it or not. Do you therefore place your mind in Me (the personal God in the universal form) and offer Me your all. If this is not possible, try to restrain the aberrations of the mind; that is to say, by observing the *yamas* and *niyamas,* and with the help of *pranayama* and yogic exercises, obtain control over the mind. If even this is beyond your capacity, perform all actions for My sake, so that your delusion will be destroyed, and you will be imbued with the spirit of detachment and devotion. If you cannot do even this, renounce the fruits of action, that is, cease to have a desire for the fruits of action, and do the task which is allotte4 to you. A man can never have any say as regards the fruit of his action, as the nature of the fruit is determined by a number of in□dependent factors. Be you therefore a mere instrument in My hands. I have thus described four methods, none of which is superior to the others. You may adopt any one of the four you like. It may seem as if the path of knowledge (hearing the doc□trine, pondering over it, etc.) is easier to take than that of *yamas, niyamas, pranayama, asanas,* etc. Meditation in worship is easier still and the renunciation of the fruit the easiest of all. But the same method is not equally well suited for all. And some seekers have to adopt all the four methods, which are inter-connected. You must become a devotee one way or other; you may take any path that leads to this destination.

"Let me tell you what the true devotee is like. He does not hate or bear ill will to any living creature. He looks on all with love and compassion. He is free from the delusion of I and 'mine'. He reduces himself to zero. Pleasure and pain are equally acceptable to him. He forgives the wrong-doer even as he expects to be forgiven himself. He is always contented with his lot, and is unshakable in his resolve. He dedicates his intellect and mind and all to Me. He never molests his fellow-creatures; these are therefore never afraid of him. He does not allow himself to become perturbed by the world. He is free from exul□tation, sorrow, anger, fear and the like. He seeks nothing for himself. He is pure and skilful in action. He renounces every undertaking.[2] Although he is firm in his resolve, he is indifferent as regards the success or failure of his action; that is to say, he is not anxious about its" result. He is alike to friend and foe. Honour and insult are the same to him. He is silent and content with what comes. He moves freely as if he were alone. He has a steady mind at all times and places. A devotee who behaves like this in faith is dear to Me."[3]

Notes

1. This letter, the first in this series, was sent along with "Letter to Narandas Gandhi", October 30/November 4, 1930; vide Vol. XLIV, pp. 274-7.
2. In his "Letter to Narandas Gandhi", 13/17-11-1930 {vide Vol. XLIV, pp. 317-8), Gandhiji had explained: "The devotee 'renounces all undertakings'. This means the devotee will not draw up schemes of future expansion. For example, if a merchant who deals in cloth now has any plans of selling fire-wood as well in the future, or if he, having one shop only, thinks of opening five more shops, that would be arambha (undertaking) on his part, and the devotee will have none of it. This principle is applicable to service of the nation as well. For instance, a worker in the khadi department today will not take up cow-keeping tomorrow, agriculture the day after and medical aid on the fourth day. He will do his best in whatever has come to him. When I am free from egoism, no thing remains for me to do.

   "The Lord has bound me with a cotton thread; I am His, no matter where He leads me. I have been stabbed with the dagger of love.' A devotee's every activity is planned by God. It comes to him as in the natural course of things. He therefore rests content with, 'this, that or anything else'. (येन केन चित्) This is the meaning of 'renouncing all undertakings'. The devotee does not cease to work; indeed he is nothing if not a worker. He only ceases to think needless thoughts about his work. It is these that he has to renounce."
3. The chapters which follow are from M.M.U./II.

CHAPTER XIII

Monday Morning [January 25, 1932]

The Lord said: "*Ksketra* (the Field) is another name for the human body and *kshetrajna* means one who knows the Field. Understand Me as the knower of the Field in all bodies. Real knowledge means discrimination between the Field and the knower of the Field.

"The five great elements, namely, earth, water, fire, air and ether, individuality *(ahamkara)*, intellect, the unmanifest, the ten senses[1], mind, the five sense-objects, desire and hatred, pleasure and pain, *sanghata* (the power of combination inherent in the constituents of the body), consciousness and cohesion,—these constitute the Field with its modifications. Knowledge of these is essential, as they have to be renounced. Wisdom is the foundation on which such renunciation can be based. Wisdom here means and includes humility, unpretentiousness, non-violence, forgiveness, rectitude, service of the teacher, purity, steadfastness, self-restraint, indifference to sense-objects, absence of egoism, insight into the evil of birth, death, old age, disease and pain, detachment from wife and children, hearth and home, friends and relations, equimindedness to good and bad fortune, whole-hearted devotion to God, love of solitude, dislike for the enjoyment of sensual pleasures in company with others, thirst for knowledge of the soul, and at last the beatific vision. And the reverse of this is ignorance.

"Now let me tell you something about that which has to be known with a view to salvation. That is beginningless supreme Brahman. Brahman is beginningless because it is unborn and was there when there was nothing. It is neither *sat* (existent) nor *asat* (non-existent) but beyond them both. But from another standpoint it can be called *sat,* because it is eternal. Human beings cannot recognize it as such; therefore it is said to be beyond even *sat*. It pervades the whole universe. It may be said to have a thousand hands and feet, and though it seems to have hands and feet, it is devoid of the organs of sense for it does not need these organs. Sense organs are transitory while Brahman is eternal. And although being all-pervasive and all-sustaining, it may be said to be enjoying the qualities *(gunas)*, it is free from them. Where there are *gunas,* there is change *(vikara)*, but Brahman is changeless. It may be said to be outside all beings, because it is out for those who do not know it. And it is within all beings as it is all-pervading. Similarly it is both moving and unmoving. It is subtle and hence imperceptible. It is distant as well as near. It is undivided in the sense that it is imperishable though name *(nama)* and form *(rupa)* perish, but it also seems to be divided as we say that it is within all creatures. It creates, preserves and destroys. It is the light of lights beyond darkness, and the end of all knowledge. Brahman which is planted in every heart is *jneya,* the one thing worth knowing. All knowledge is a means to the end of being united with it.

"God and his *mqya* (nature) are both without beginning. Modifications *(vikaras)* are born of *mqya* and these give rise to various kinds of action *(karma).* On account of *mqya,* the soul experiences pleasure and pain and the fruit of merit *(punya)* and demerit *(papa).* He who, having realized this, does his duty in a spirit of detachment is not born again in spite of his activity, for he beholds the face of God in all faces, and seeing that not a leaf moves but by the divine will, he is free from egotism, understands that he is separate from the body and that the soul, though living in the body, remains by means of knowledge unaffected like the omnipresent ether."

Finished at about 2 p.m.

Not revised.

Note

1. The five organs of perception, viz., ears, skin, eyes, palate and nose, and the five organs of action, viz., tongue, feet, hands and the organs of evacuation and reproduction.

CHAPTER XIV[1]

Silence Day, January 25, 1932

The Lord said: "Once more I will teach you that supreme wisdom which enabled sages to reach the highest perfection. People who find that wisdom and do their duty accordingly are delivered from the cycle of births and deaths. O Arjuna, know Me to be the Father and Mother of all beings. The three *gunas* born of nature, viz., *sattva* (goodness), *rajas* (passion) and *tamas* (ignorance) bind the soul down. They may be described respectively as the highest, the middling and the lowest. Of these sattva is pure and unsullied and gives light; it is therefore the source of happiness. *Rajas* arises from attachment and craving and makes a man indulge in all manner of activities. Tamas is rooted in ignorance and delusion and makes one negligent and indolent. In short, sattva makes for happiness, *rajas* for restlessness and *tamas* for sloth. Sometimes *sattva* prevails, overpowering rajas and tamas; at other times *rajas* prevails, overpowering *sattva* and *tamas;* at still other times tamas prevails, overpowering sattva and rajas. When the light of wisdom shines through all the activities of the body it may be known that sattva is increasing. Where greed, bustle, unrest and competition are observed, rajas is the ruler. And the predominance of tamas is characterized by ignorance, sloth and delusion. If sattva prevails in a man's life, he is born in the sinless worlds of the great sages after death. If rajas dominates his life, he is born among those who are attached to action. And if tamas is the ruling principle, he returns to the womb of the senseless. The fruit of sattvik action is purity, while the fruit of rajas is pain and the fruit of tamas is ignorance. A sattvik man rises to the higher regions; a rajasik person remains in this world, while a tamasik individual sinks to the underworld. When a man per« ceives no doer of action other than these qualities and knows Me who am beyond them he enters into My nature. When the dweller in the body has overcome the three qualities from which all bodies arise, he is freed from birth and death, old age and pain and drinks the nectar of eternal life."

On hearing that one who transcends the qualities makes such great progress on the pilgrim's path, Arjuna asked: "What are the marks of such perfection? How does such a perfect being conduct himself? And how does he cross over the qualities?"

The Lord replied: "A man is said to have risen above the qualities when he is not angry if the light and knowledge of sattva or the activity and bustle of rajas or the delusion and ignorance of tamas are there and is not wishful if they are not. He sits like one who is unconcerned and is not disturbed by the qualities. He stands apart unmoved, being aware that they are the doers of all actions. He is even-minded to pleasure and pain as well as to a lump of earth, a stone and gold. The pleasant and the unpleasant are alike to him. He is unaffected by either praise or blame. He is the same in honour and evil fame. He is alike to friend and foe. And he has abandoned all undertakings. Do not think that this is a goal you can never reach and that therefore you need not exert yourself. What I have described is the state of a perfect man. The way to it is to serve Me with single-minded devotion.

"From the third chapter onwards I have pointed out that a man cannot so much as even breathe without action (karma), from which no human being can ever hope to escape. He who would transcend the qualities should dedicate all his actions to Me, and cease to desire their fruits. If he does this, his actions will not be an impediment to his progress, for I am Brahman, moksha, the eternal dharma and joy for ever.

"When a man reduces himself to zero, he sees Me alone everywhere. Htisguna-atita (one who has transcended the qualities)."

Note

1. This was sent along with "Letter to Narandas Gandhi", 23/25-1-1932; vide pp. 31-3.

CHAPTER XV[1]

Night, January 31, 1932[2]

The Lord said: "This world is like an *ashvattha* (sacred fig) tree with roots above and branches below and with the Vedic hymns as its leaves. And he who knows it knows the Vedas. The branches of this cosmic tree nourished by the qualities shoot to heaven and sink to earth. Sense-objects are its sprouts. It is these things of the senses which bind the soul with the bonds of karma in the world of men. The real nature of this tree cannot be known here, nor its beginning, nor end, nor foundation.

"This strongly rooted cosmic tree should be cut down with the weapon of non-co-operation, so that the soul may rise to a higher world from which there is no return [to the world of mortals]. With this end in view a man should engage himself in the constant worship of the Ancient of Days, from whom all this acti□vity (the cosmic process) seems to flow. The wise man who is free from pride and delusion, victorious over the vice of attachment and devoted to the Supreme Soul, who is free from cravings and to whom pleasure and pain are alike—that wise man reaches the state which is beyond all change, and which does not need to be illumined by the sun, the moon or fire. That is my Supreme abode.

"An eternal part of Myself tansformed into the individual soul in this world draws to itself the senses including the mind which reside in matter. When the soul enters the body or leaves it, it takes these senses with it even as the wind carries fragrance from its places. It enjoys sense-objects with the help df the ear, the eye, the senses of touch and taste, the nose and the mind. The ignorant cannot recognize it as it goes or stays or enjoys itself under the influence of the qualities, but the sages see it [with the eye of wisdom]. Striving yogis see it living in their own bodies, but those who have not achieved evenness of temper cannot see it even if they try.

"The light of the sun that illumines all the world, that which is in the moon and in fire—know that all that light is Mine. Permeating the soil[3] I sustain all living beings. I become the sap-producing moon and feed the plants. Becoming the fire of life in the bodies of all living creatures and being united with the life-breaths, I digest the four kinds of food. I abide in all hearts. From Me are memory and wisdom as well as their absence. I am that which is to be known by all the Vedas. So also I am the Author of Vedanta and the Knower of the Vedas.

"There may be said to be two kinds of personalities in this world, namely, kshara (the perishable) and akshara (the imperishable). The perishable is all beings; and the imperishable is I who am the same for ever. But beyond either is the highest spirit who is called the Supreme Soul, and who, pervading all, sustains the three worlds. This too is I. I therefore transcend the perishable and even the imperishable, and am known in the world as well as in the Vedas as the Supreme Reality. The wise man who recognizes Me as such knows all that need be known, and serves Me with his whole being.

"O sinless Arjuna, I have told you this most secret teaching. By knowing this a man becomes truly wise and reaches the shores of salvation."

•

Notes

1. This was sent along with "Letter to Narandas Gandhi", January 28/ Fabruary 1, 1932; vide pp. 56-8.
2. The source has "1931".
3. Literally, 'having entered their bodies'.

CHAPTER XVI[1]

February 7, 1932

The Lord said: "I will now point out the distinction between the divine and the demoniacal natures. I have earlier described at length what is meant by divine nature but I will repeat its distinctive features. Among the signs of the divine are fearlessness, purity of heart, wisdom, evenness of temper, self-control, alms-giving, sacrifice, study of the scriptures, austerity, straightforwardness, non-violence, truth, freedom from anger, renunciation, peacefulness, not speaking evil of others, compassion to all living beings, absence of greed, gentleness, modesty, absence of fickleness, vigour, forgiveness, fortitude, purity, internal as well as external, freedom from malice and pride.

"Among the signs of the demoniacal are hypocrisy, arrogance, conceit, anger, cruelty and ignorance.

"The divine nature leads to liberation while the demoniacal leads to bondage. O Arjuna, you are born with endowments of the divine nature.

"I will say something more about the demoniacal nature, so that people may easily give it up.

"Men of such a nature do not know what to do and what to refrain from doing. There is no purity or truth in them, so that they do not observe the rules of good conduct.

"They hold that the world is unreal, without basis or rule. For them sex is all the world so that they think of nothing except enjoyment of the objects of sense.

"They do horrible deeds. They are dull-witted. They hold fast to their wicked thoughts and all their activity is directed only to the destruction of the world. Their desires are insatiable. They are full of hypocrisy, pride and arrogance. They a^e thus plagued by innumer□able cares. They want fresh sensual pleasures every day. They are 'ensnared in nooses of a hundred idle hopes', and by unlawful means amass wealth in order to gratify their desires.

" 'I got this today; I will get that tomorrow. I killed this one enemy today; I will also kill others. I am a man of might. I have great possessions. Who is my equal? With a view to fame I will sacrifice to the gods, give alms and make merry.[5] They say this to themselves with a chuckle, and being caught in the net of delusion, go to hell at last.

"Men with such a nature, given over to pride, speak ill of others and thus hate God who dwells in all hearts. They are therefore frequently born in the wombs of degraded parents.

"There are three gates to hell, leading to the ruin of the soul: lust, anger and greed. Therefore we should renounce them all.

Turning aside from them, men go by the strait and narrow path and reach the highest state.

"He who disregards the scriptures composed of eternal principles and gives himself up to pleasure cannot attain happiness or peace characteristic of the right way.

"Therefore in deciding what you must do and what you must not do, you should acquire the knowledge of fundamental and immutable principles from wise men and think and act accordingly."

Note

1. This was sent along with "Letter to Narandas Gandhi", 3/8-2-1932; *vide, pp. 74-7.*

CHAPTER XVII[1]

February 14, 1932

Arjuna asked: "What happens to those who serve in faith, neglecting the prevailing code of conduct?"

The Lord replied: "There are three kinds of faith, characterized by *sattva, rajas* or *tamas* as the case may be. As is a man's faith, so is he.

"*Sattvik* men worship the gods; *rajasik* men worship demigods and demons; and *tamasik* men worship the spirits of the dead.

"The nature of a man's faith cannot be ascertained offhand. In order to assess it correctly, one must know the precise nature of his food, austerity, sacrifice and alms-giving.

"Foods which make for long life and increase the vital force, energy, strength and health are said to be *sattvik. Rajasik* foods are violently bitter, sour, hot or pungent and give rise to disease and aches and pains. And cooked food which is stale or gives out a bad smell and the leavings of others are said to be *tamasik.*

"The sacrifice which is offered as a matter of duty without expecting a reward and with mental concentration is said to be *sattvik.* A *rajasik* sacrifice is that in which a reward is desired and which is offered for outward show. And a *tamasik* sacrifice is one in which scriptural rules are disobeyed, no eatables or alms are given away and no hymns are chanted.

"Honouring the saintly purity, *brahmacharya* and non-violence constitute austerity of the body. Truthful, pleasant and beneficial speech as well as a study of the scriptures is austerity of speech. And cheerfulness, gentleness, silence, self-control and purity of motive—these are called austerity of the mind. Such austerity of the mind, body and speech as is practised without desire of fruit by men with an evenness of temper is said to be *sattvik*. Austerity practised for ostentation and with a view to gaining honour is said to be *rajasik*. And austerity done by obstinate fools with self-torture or with the object of hurting others is said to be *tamasik*.

"A gift 'made in due place, due time and to a fit recipient' without expecting a reward and with a feeling that it is right for a man to give is said to be *sattvik*. A gift made grudgingly with a view to getting something in return is regarded as *rajasik*. And the gift which is given in a contemptuous spirit, and without honour done to the recipient and without considering the proper time and place for it is said to be *tamasik*.

"Brahman is designated in the Vedas as *Om tat sat*. Therefore men of faith pronounce the sacred syllable 'Om' when they commence any rite of sacrifice, alms-giving or austerity. This single syllable stands for Brahman. *Tat* means *that*. And *sat* means *satya*, beneficient. That is to say, God is one, He alone is, He alone is truth and the benefactor of the world. He who offers a sacrifice, makes gifts or practises austerity with a realization of this truth and in a spirit of dedication is a man of *sattvik* faith. And he is free from blame if he knowingly or unknowingly does something different from the correct procedure in the spirit of dedication. But acts undertaken in the absence of such a spirit are said to be performed without faith and therefore are *asat* (unreal)."

Notes

1. This was sent along with "Letter to Narandas Gandhi", 11/15-2-1932; vide pp. 95-6.

CHAPTER XVIII[1]

February 21, 1932

Even after he had pondered over the teaching in all the previous Chapters, there was still a doubt in Arjuna's mind. So he said: "The sannyasa of the *Gita* seems to be different from renunciation as currently understood. Are sannyasa and *tyaga* really different?"

While resolving Arjuna's doubt in answer to this question, the Lord summarized the *Gita* doctrine in a concise manner: "Some actions are motivated by desire. Various activities are indulged in by men with a view to fulfilling various desires. These are called *kamya* actions. Then again there are certain necessary and natural actions such as breathing, eating, drinking, lying down, sitting, etc., with a view to keep the body-[a fit instrument of service]. And thirdly there are actions done with a view to serving others. Giving up *kamya* actions is sannyasa, and renunciation of fruits of all actions is *tyaga* as recommended to you all along.

"Some people maintain that there is evil, no matter how little, in all actions whatever. Even so, a man must not give up actions done with a view to *yajna* (sacrifice), that is to say, the service of others. Alms-giving and austerity are included in *yajna*. But even while serving others, a man should act in a spirit of detachment. Otherwise his activity is likely to be mixed up with evil.

"Renunciation owing to ignorance of duties that must be done is said to be inspired by *tamas*. Giving up any action merely because it involves physical suffering is said to be *rajasik*. But service rendered to others because of a feeling that it must be done and without the desire for the fruits is real *sattvik tyaga*. In this *tyaga* therefore there is no giving up of all actions; but only of the fruit of duties that must be done, and of course of other, that is, *kamya* actions. When a [wise] man acts in such a selfless spirit, all his doubts are dispelled, his motives are pure and he has no thought of personal comfort and discomfort.

"He who does not abandon the fruits of action must enjoy or put up with the natural consequences of his own acts, and is thus a bondslave for ever. But he who gives up the fruits of action achieves freedom.

"And why should a man feel attachment for action? It is idle for anybody to imagine that he himself is a doer. There are five causes for the accomplishment of all actions, namely, this body, the doer, the various instruments, efforts, and last but by no means the least, providence.

"Realizing this, a man should give up pride. He who does something without egoism may be said to be not doing it in spite of his doing it, for he is not bound by his action. Of a humble man who has reduced himself to zero it may be said that he does not kill though he kills. This does not mean that the man in spite of his humility may kill and yet be unaffected by the killing. For no occasion can arise for such a man to indulge in violence.

on: knowledge, the object of knowledge and the knower. And there are three constituents of action: the organ, the deed and the doer. The thing to be done is the object of knowledge; the method of doing it is knowledge and he who knows it is the knower. After he has thus received an impulse to action, he performs an action in which the senses serve as instruments. Thought is thus translated into action.

"That by which a man is able 'To see one changeless Life in all the lives' and to realize the essential unity that underlies all diversities is *sattvik* knowledge. In *rajasik* knowledge one holds that there are different souls in different creatures, while in *tamasik* knowledge a man does not know a thing and imagines that everything is mixed up without rhyme or reason.

"Similarly there are three kinds of action. Action in which there are no likes and dislikes and no desire for personal gains is *sattvik*. That in which there are desires for enjoyment, egoism and restlessness is *rajasik* action. And *tamasik* action is one in which no thought at all is given to personal capacity and consequential injury or violence and which is undertaken through delusion.

"So also there are three classes of doers. Of course having understood the action it could not be difficult to know the doer. A *sattvik* doer is free from attachment and egoism and yet firm and enterprising and is neither elated by success nor worried by failure. A *rajasik* doer is impassioned, greedy and violent, 'slave by turns of sorrow and of joy' and of course desires to obtain the fruit of his actions. And a *tamasik* doer is unsystematic, procrastinating, obstinate, malicious and indolent; in short without an iota of self-culture.

"Intellect, firmness and happiness also are said to be of three kinds.

"The *sattvik* intellect is able properly to distinguish between action and non-action,

What must be done, and what must not be done,

What should be feared, and what should not be feared,
What binds and what emancipates the soul.

The *rajasik* intellect tries to draw these distinctions but generally fails to do so correctly, while the *tamasik* intellect 'looks upon wrong as right and sees all things contrariwise of truth.'

"Firmness is the power of taking up some thing and sticking to it through thick and thin. It is more or less inherent in all things; otherwise the world could not subsist for a single moment. Firmness is *sattvik* when there is a constantly maintained balance between the activities of the mind, the vital airs *(pranas)* and the senses. The firmness by which a man holds fast to duty, pleasure and wealth from attachment and with a view to perso.nal advantage is *rajasik.* And firmness is *tamasik,*

wherewith the fool
Cleaves to his sloth, his sorrow and his fears,
His vanity and despair.

"*Sattvik* happiness is the
pleasure that endures,
Banishing pain for aye, bitter at first
As poison to the soul, but afterwards
Sweet as the taste of amrit.

It arises from true self-knowledge.

"*Rajasik* happiness arises from sensual enjoyment.
Sweet
As amrit is its first taste, but its last
Bitter as poison.

"And tamasik happiness is that
which springs
From sloth and sleep and foolishness.

—Edwin Arnold

"This threefold classification is thus applicable to all things. The duties of the four varnas are fixed by reason of the dominance or recession of the qualities planted in each.

"A Brahmin's conduct is characterized by calmness, self-discipline, austerity, purity, forgiveness, uprightness, wisdom, experience and faith in God. The characteristics of a Kshatriya are valour, splendour, firmness, resourcefulness, not flying from battle, open-handedness and leadership. A Vaishya's task is 'to till the ground, tend cattle, venture trade', and service is the Sudra's work. This is not to say that a member of any one of these classes may not be endowed with qualities characteristic of other classes or is not entitled to cultivate them in himself. But qualities and work as mentioned above serve as signs for the recognition of a man's varna. If the qualities and tasks of each varna are recognized, there is no undesirable competition or feeling of hatred among them. There is no question here of high and low. But if each does his duty selflessly according to his nature, he will reach perfection. Therefore one's own duty, though it appears to be valueless, is better than the duty of another which seems to be easy. A man may remain free from sin when he performs the task naturally allotted to him, as he is then free from selfish desires; the very wish to do something else arises from selfishness. For the rest, all actions are clouded by defects as fire by smoke. But the natural duty is done without desire for its fruit, and thus loses its binding force.

"The calm yogi who has been sanctified by thus performing his own duty, who has his mind under control, who has given up the five sense-objects, who has overcome likes and dislikes, who lives in solitude, i.e., whose eyes are turned inward, who achieves mastery of his mind, body and speech by abstemiousness, who is ever conscious of the living presence of God, and who has given up pride, desire, anger, acquisitiveness and the like—that yogi is fit to be united with Brahman. He is equi-minded towards all men. He neither rejoices nor indulges in grief. Such a devotee has true knowledge of God and is absorbed in Him. Thus taking refuge in Me, he gains the eternal place.

"Therefore dedicate your all to Me, regard Me as the supreme object of your love, and with discrimination, fix your mind on Me. As you do this, you will overcome all difficulties. But if out of egoism you do not listen to Me, you will persh. The one thing needful is that, abandoning all conflicting views, you should come to Me alone for shelter, and thus be freed from sin.

"Do not tell this truth to anyone who is not a devotee, austere in life, and hating Me, does not wish to listen. But one who communicates this great secret to My devotees will surely come to Me in virtue of his devotion."

After having thus reported to Dhritarashtra the dialogue between Arjuna and Krishna, Sanjaya said:

"Where there is Krishna, the prince of yoga, and Arjuna with his bow and arrows, there are prosperity, victory, happiness and fundamental morality."

[NOTE.] Krishna to whom the epithet 'prince of yoga' has here been applied means pure knowledge based on spiritual experience, and by referring to Arjuna as an archer it is suggested that where there is action in accordance with such knowledge, the doer obtains every wish that is not contrary to lofty morals.

Notes

1. This was sent along with "Letter to Narandas Gandhi", 19/21-2-1932; *vide* pp. 150-1.

From microfilms of the Gujarati: M.M.U./I. & II